EYESHIELD 21
Vol. 26: Rough-n-Tumble
The SHONEN JUMP ADVANCED Manga Edition

STORY BY RIICHIRO INAGAKI
ART BY YUSUKE MURATA

English Adaptation & Translation/HC Language Solutions, Inc.
Touch-up Art & Lettering/James Gaubatz
Cover and Graphic Design/Sean Lee
Editor/Kit Fox

Editor in Chief, Books/Alvin Lu
Editor in Chief, Magazines/Marc Weidenbaum
VP, Publishing Licensing/Rika Inouye
VP, Sales & Product Marketing/Gonzalo Ferreyra
VP, Creative/Linda Espinosa
Publisher/Hyoe Narita

Printed in Canada

Published by VIZ Media, LLC
P.O. Box 77010
San Francisco, CA 94107

SHONEN JUMP ADVANCED Manga Edition
10 9 8 7 6 5 4 3 2 1
First printing, June 2009

www.viz.com

PARENTAL ADVISORY
EYESHIELD 21 is rated T+ for Older Teen
and is recommended for ages 16 and up.
It contains graphic fantasy violence and
crude humor.
ratings.viz.com

THE WORLD'S MOST
CUTTING-EDGE MANGA
SHONEN JUMP ADVANCED
www.shonenjump.com

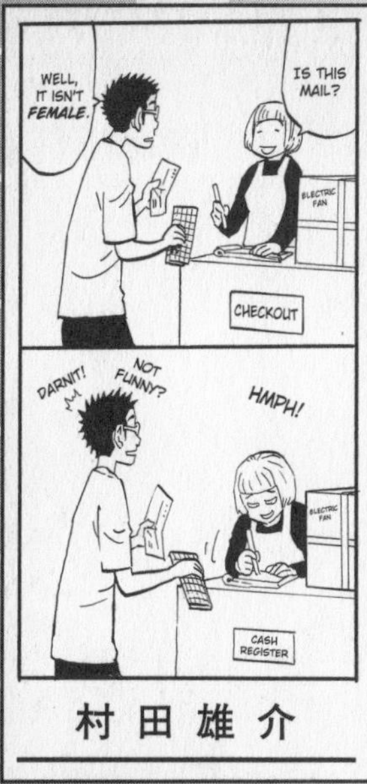
IS THIS MAIL?
WELL, IT ISN'T *FEMALE*.
ELECTRIC FAN
CHECKOUT
HMPH!
NOT FUNNY?
DARNIT!
ELECTRIC FAN
CASH REGISTER
村田雄介

Yusuke Murata

Don't you hate it when people won't laugh at your bad jokes?

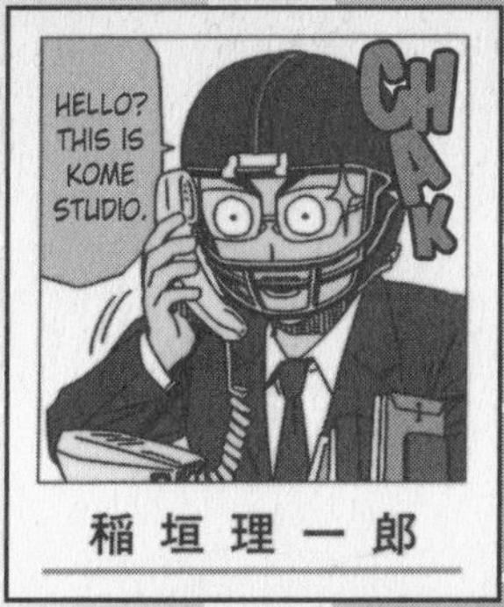
CHAK
HELLO? THIS IS KOME STUDIO.
稲垣理一郎

Riichiro Inagaki

I moved out of my home office just so I'll feel like I have a real job. I even purchased a business phone line! Now I can have business-like phone conversations like in the (imaginary) picture above! I've been waiting with great anticipation for the phone to ring, but so far I haven't received even one single call! Of course not. My work contacts would call me on my cell. Someone... anyone...please...call me!!

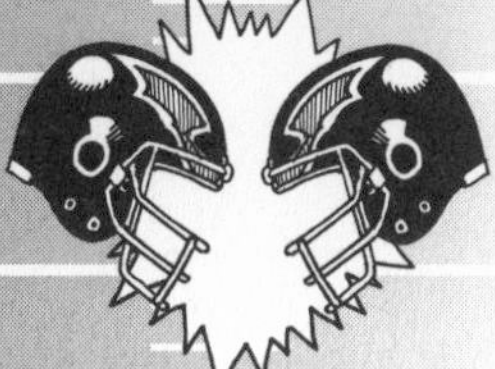

Eyeshield 21 is the most exciting football manga to hit the scene. A collaborative effort between writer Riichiro Inagaki and artist Yusuke Murata, ***Eyeshield 21*** was originally serialized in Japan's ***Weekly Shonen Jump***. An OAV created for Shueisha's Anime Tour is available in Japan, and the ***Eyeshield 21*** hit animated TV series debuted in spring 2005!

EYESHIELD 21

Rawlings
PRO5
official

Vol. 26:
Rough-n-Tumble

STORY BY **RIICHIRO INAGAKI** ART BY **YUSUKE MURATA**

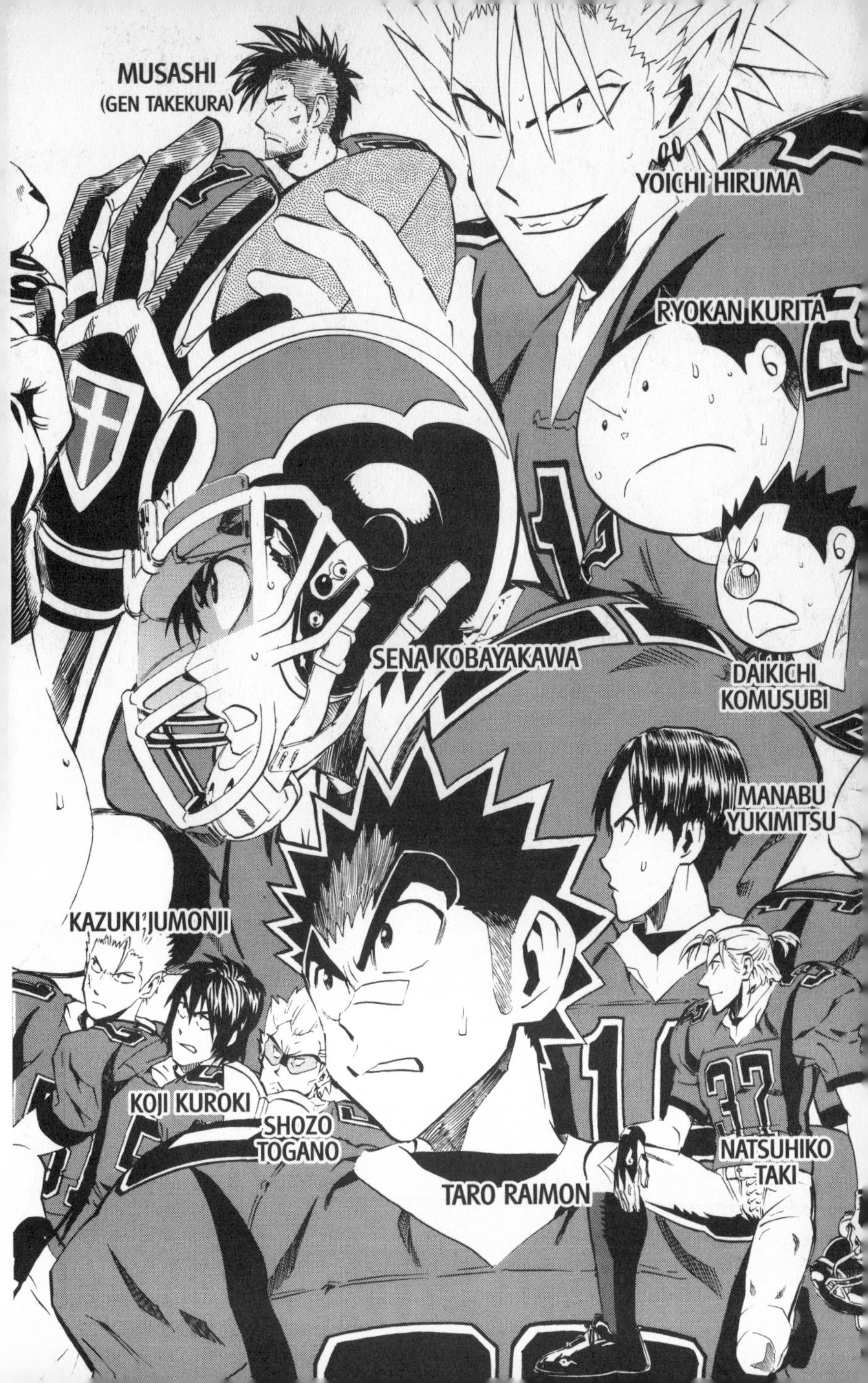
MUSASHI
(GEN TAKEKURA)
YOICHI HIRUMA
RYOKAN KURITA
SENA KOBAYAKAWA
DAIKICHI
KOMUSUBI
MANABU
YUKIMITSU
KAZUKI JUMONJI
KOJI KUROKI
SHOZO
TOGANO
NATSUHIKO
TAKI
TARO RAIMON

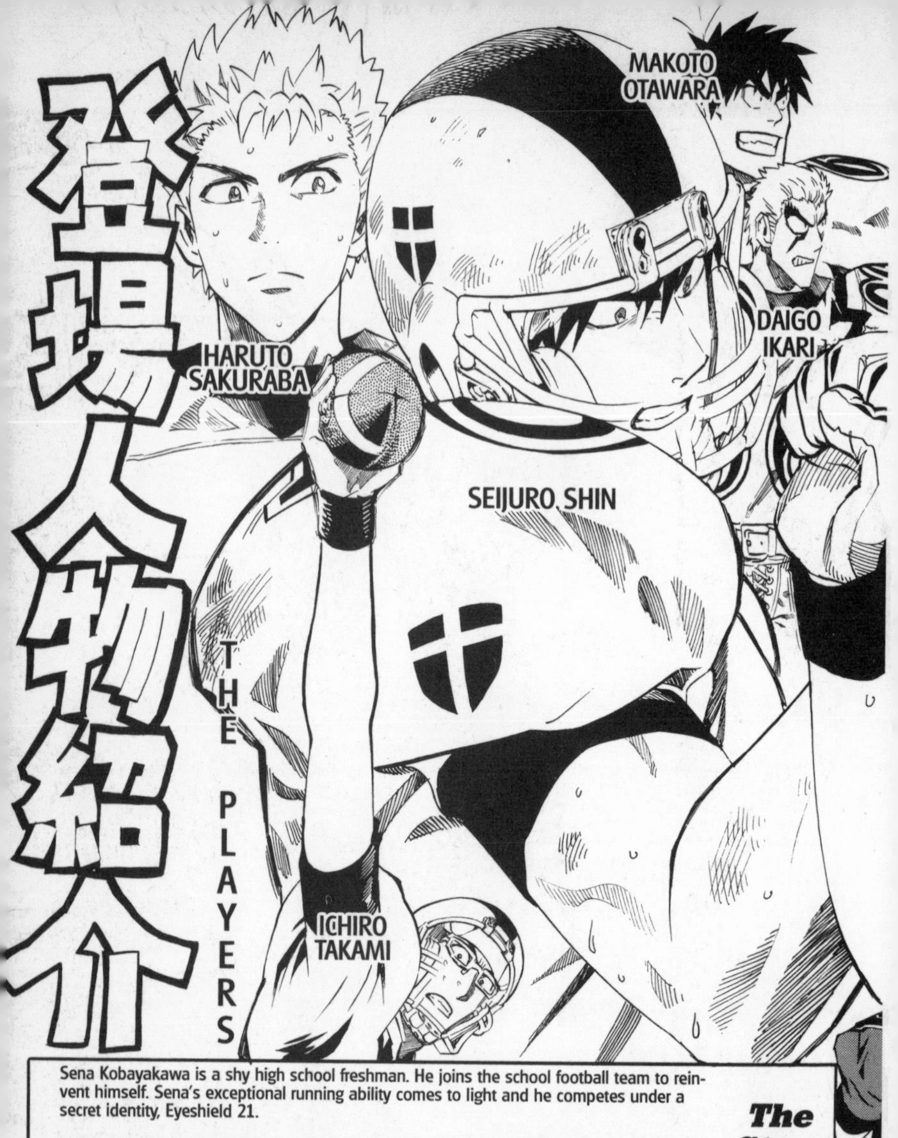
登場人物紹介
THE PLAYERS
MAKOTO OTAWARA
HARUTO SAKURABA
DAIGO IKARI
SEIJURO SHIN
ICHIRO TAKAMI

The Story So Far

Sena Kobayakawa is a shy high school freshman. He joins the school football team to reinvent himself. Sena's exceptional running ability comes to light and he competes under a secret identity, Eyeshield 21.

The goal is the Christmas Bowl! United under the same ambition, Deimon moves on to the Kanto Tournament and, in their first match, they manage to beat the nine-time consecutive champion, Shinryuji.

For the semi-final game, fate brings Deimon and their archrivals, Ojo, to a face-off! Ojo's biggest strength comes from their new offensive formation, the Ballista, which adds their core defensive player, Shin, to offense!

Sena's super-fast running is stopped cold, and Deimon trails 6 to 13. In the second half, Hiruma orders Sena to get in close to Shin and dispose of him using sheer strength! Once again, Sena must face his greatest opponent!!

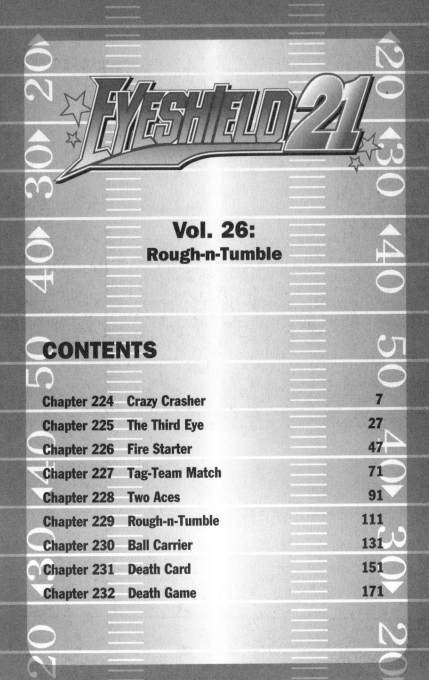

EYESHIELD 21

Vol. 26:
Rough-n-Tumble

CONTENTS

Chapter 224	Crazy Crasher	7
Chapter 225	The Third Eye	27
Chapter 226	Fire Starter	47
Chapter 227	Tag-Team Match	71
Chapter 228	Two Aces	91
Chapter 229	Rough-n-Tumble	111
Chapter 230	Ball Carrier	131
Chapter 231	Death Card	151
Chapter 232	Death Game	171

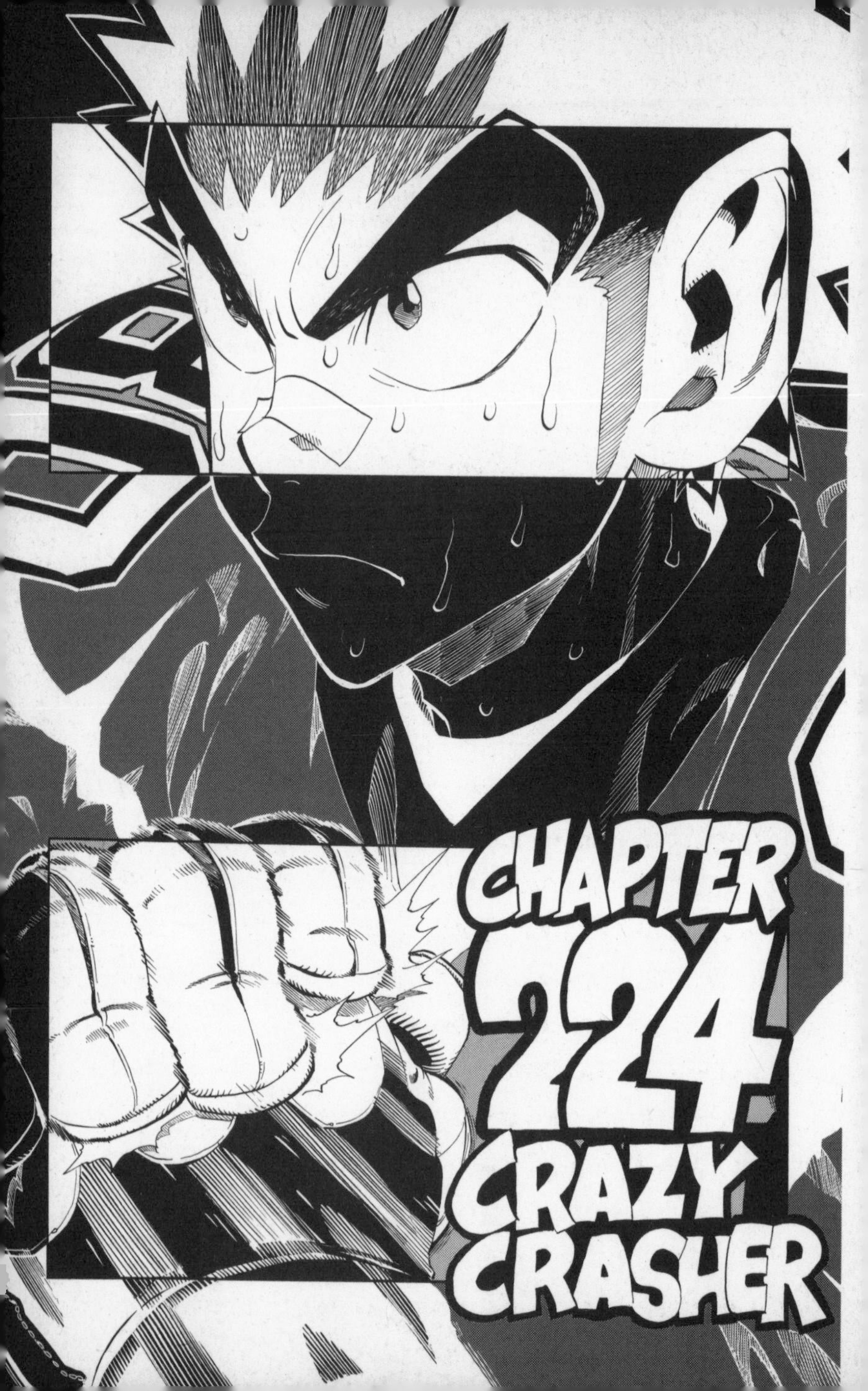
CHAPTER 224
CRAZY CRASHER

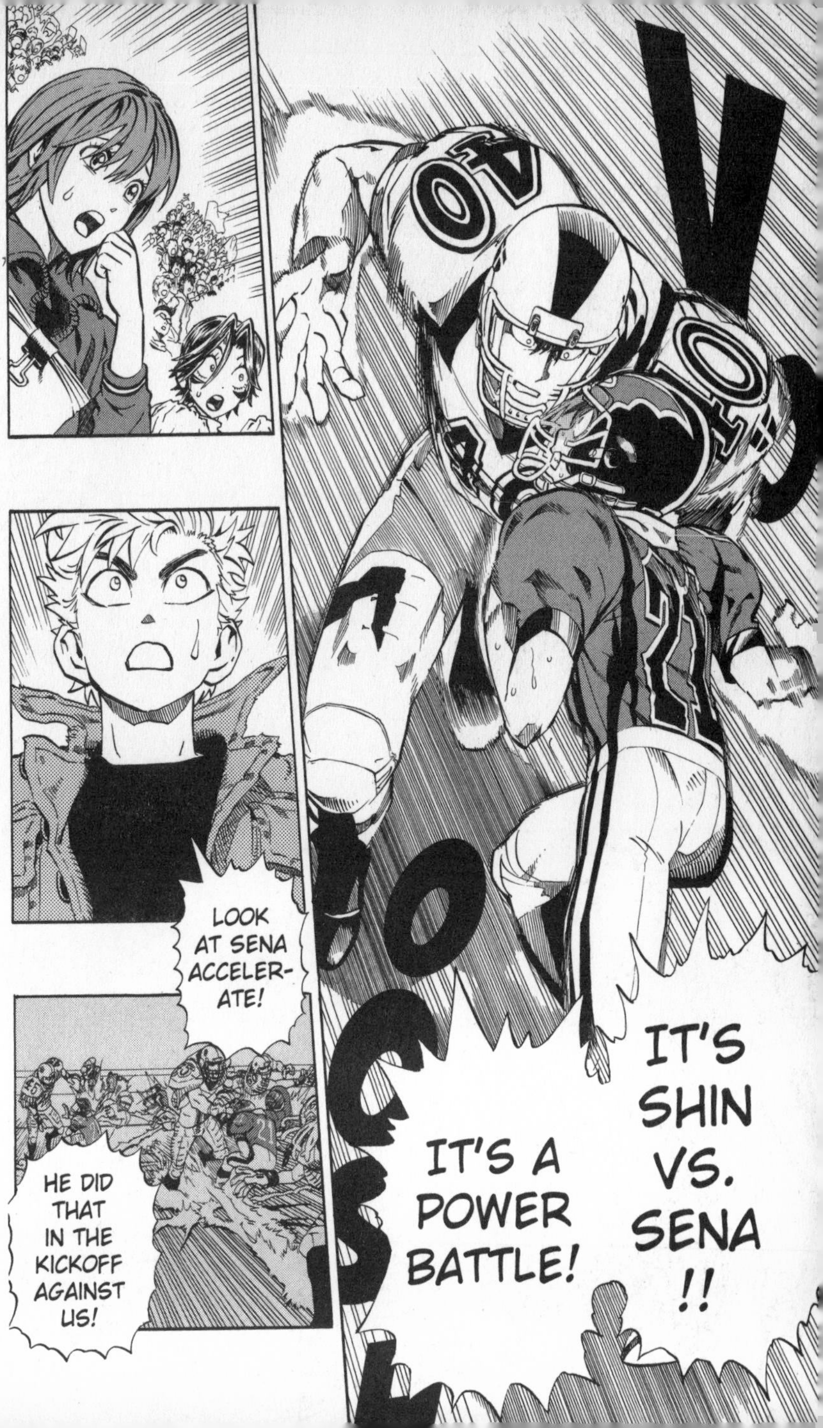
IT'S SHIN VS. SENA !!
IT'S A POWER BATTLE!
LOOK AT SENA ACCELER-ATE!
HE DID THAT IN THE KICKOFF AGAINST US!

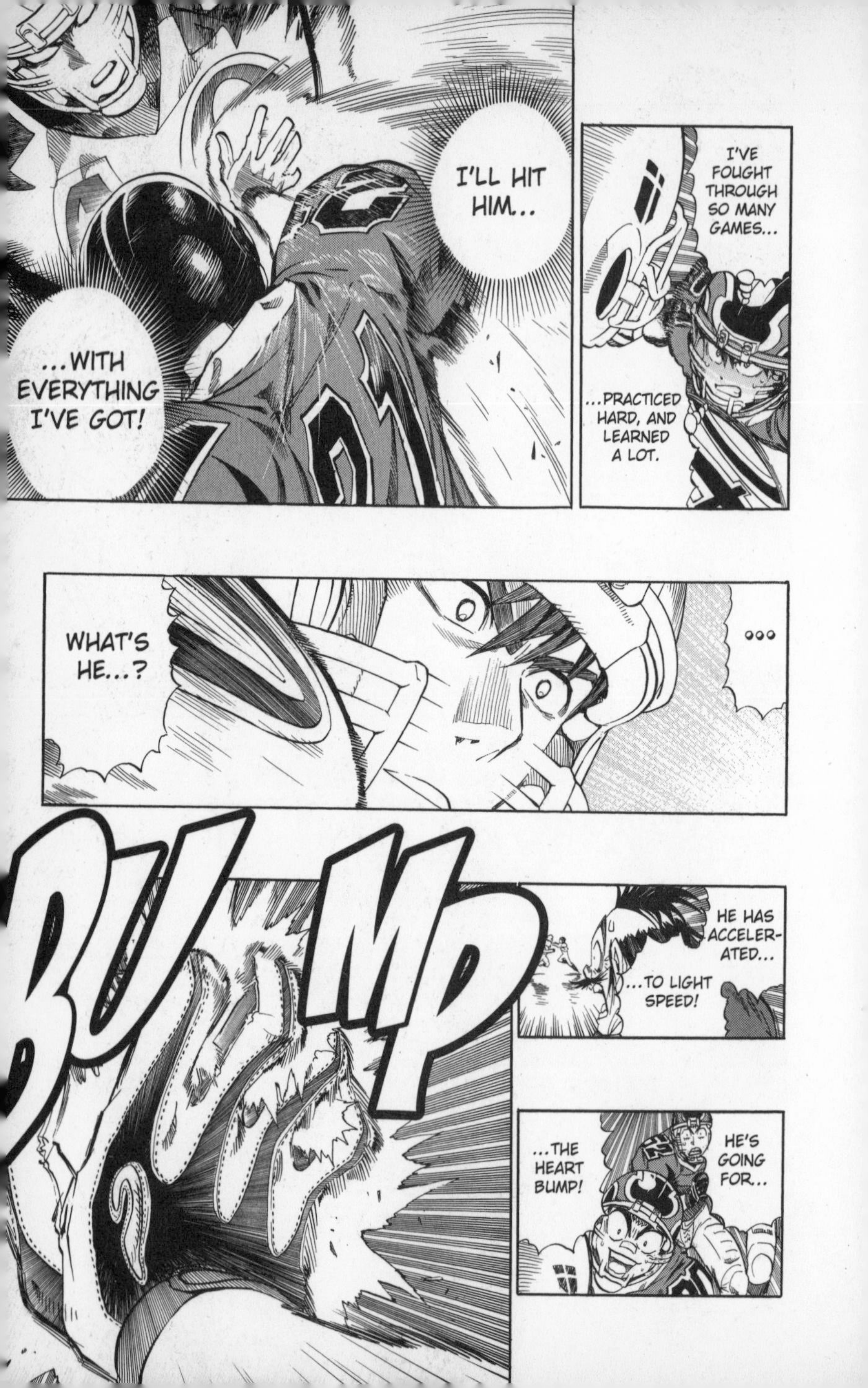
I'VE FOUGHT THROUGH SO MANY GAMES...
...PRACTICED HARD, AND LEARNED A LOT.
I'LL HIT HIM...
...WITH EVERYTHING I'VE GOT!
WHAT'S HE...?
HE HAS ACCELER-ATED...
...TO LIGHT SPEED!
HE'S GOING FOR...
...THE HEART BUMP!
BUMP

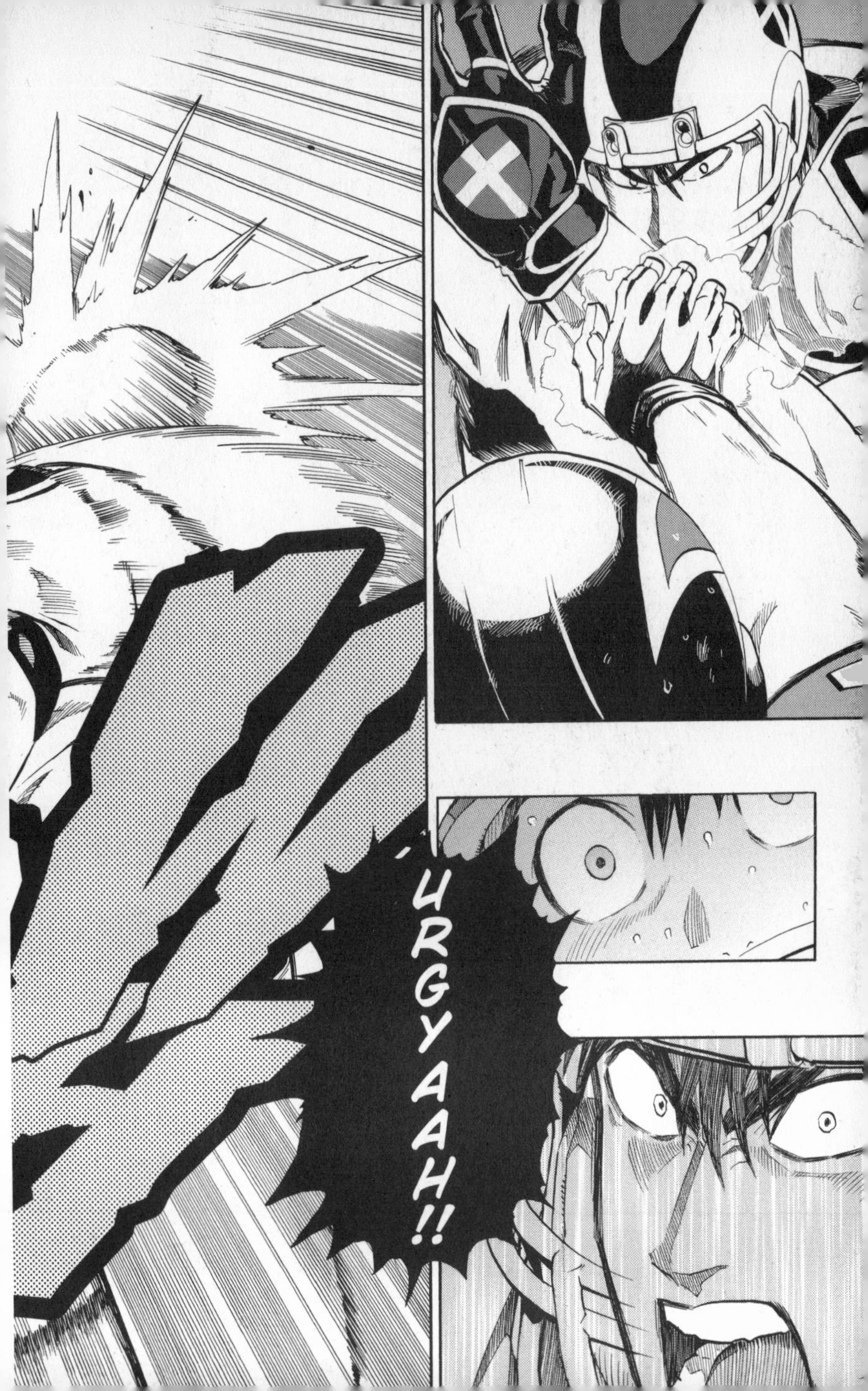
URGYAAAH!!

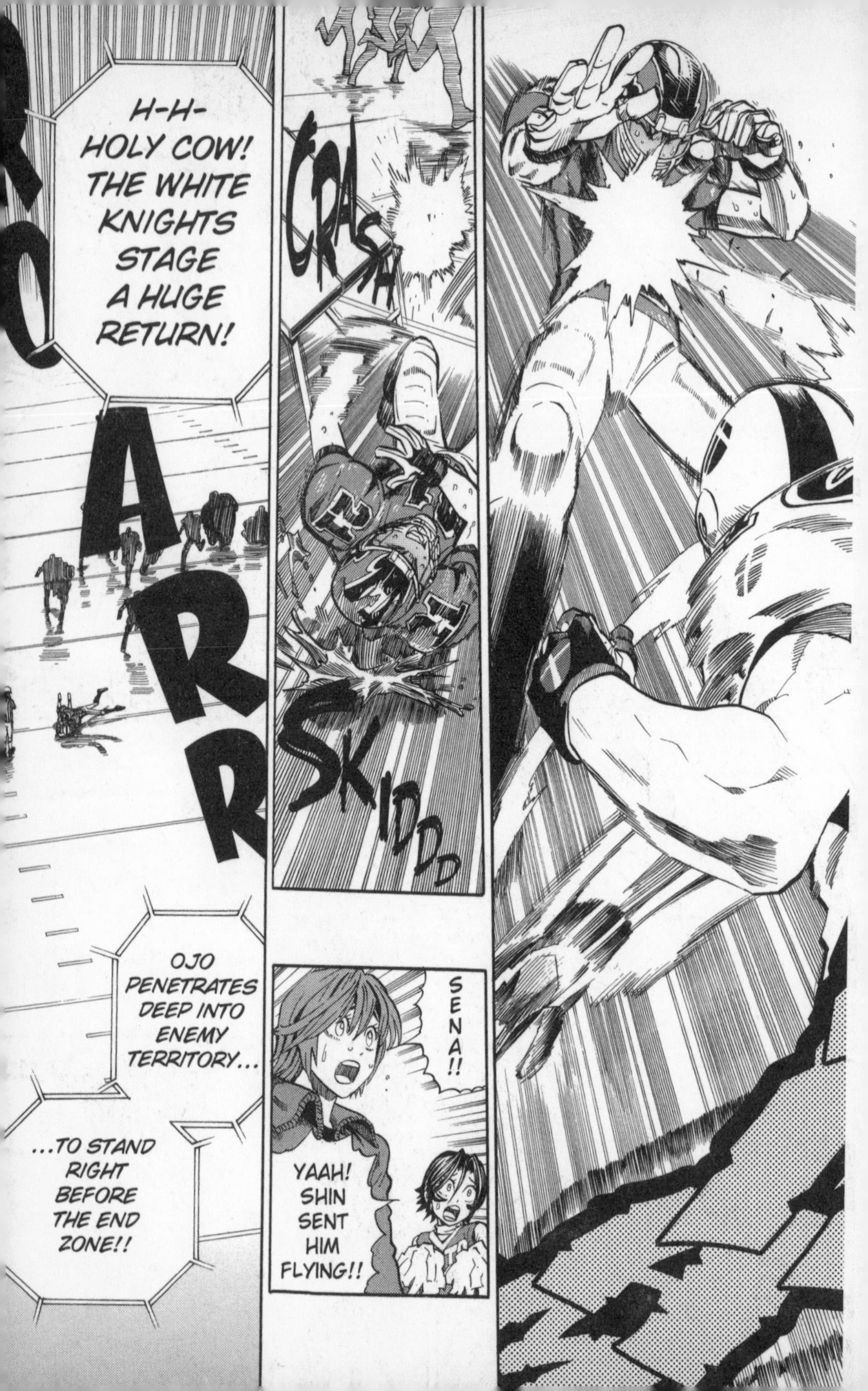
CRASH
SKIDDD
SENA!!
YAAH! SHIN SENT HIM FLYING!!
ROARR
H-H-HOLY COW! THE WHITE KNIGHTS STAGE A HUGE RETURN!
OJO PENETRATES DEEP INTO ENEMY TERRITORY...
...TO STAND RIGHT BEFORE THE END ZONE!!

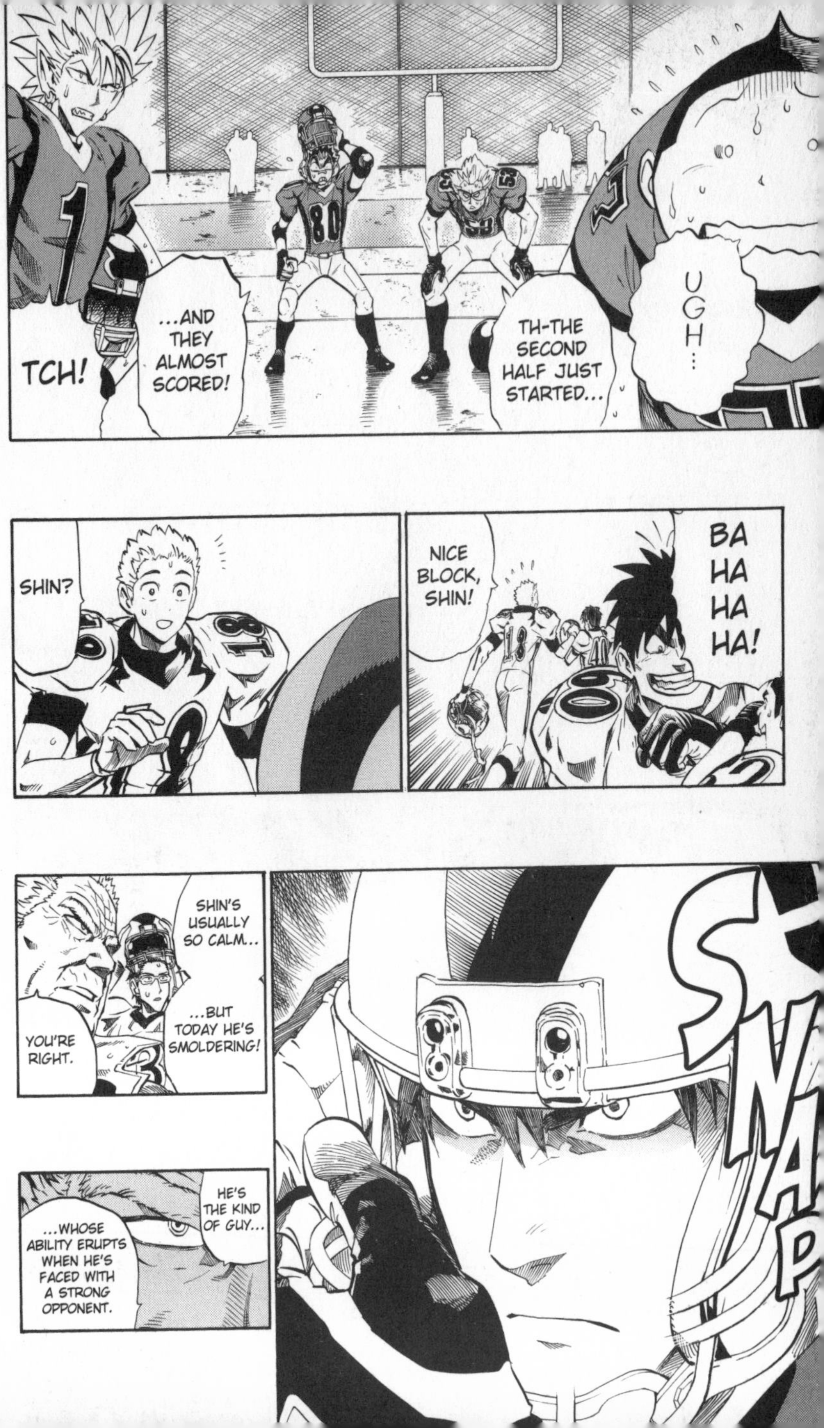
UGH...
TH-THE SECOND HALF JUST STARTED...
...AND THEY ALMOST SCORED!
TCH!
BA HA HA HA!
NICE BLOCK, SHIN!
SHIN?
SNAP
SHIN'S USUALLY SO CALM...
...BUT TODAY HE'S SMOLDERING!
YOU'RE RIGHT.
HE'S THE KIND OF GUY...
...WHOSE ABILITY ERUPTS WHEN HE'S FACED WITH A STRONG OPPONENT.

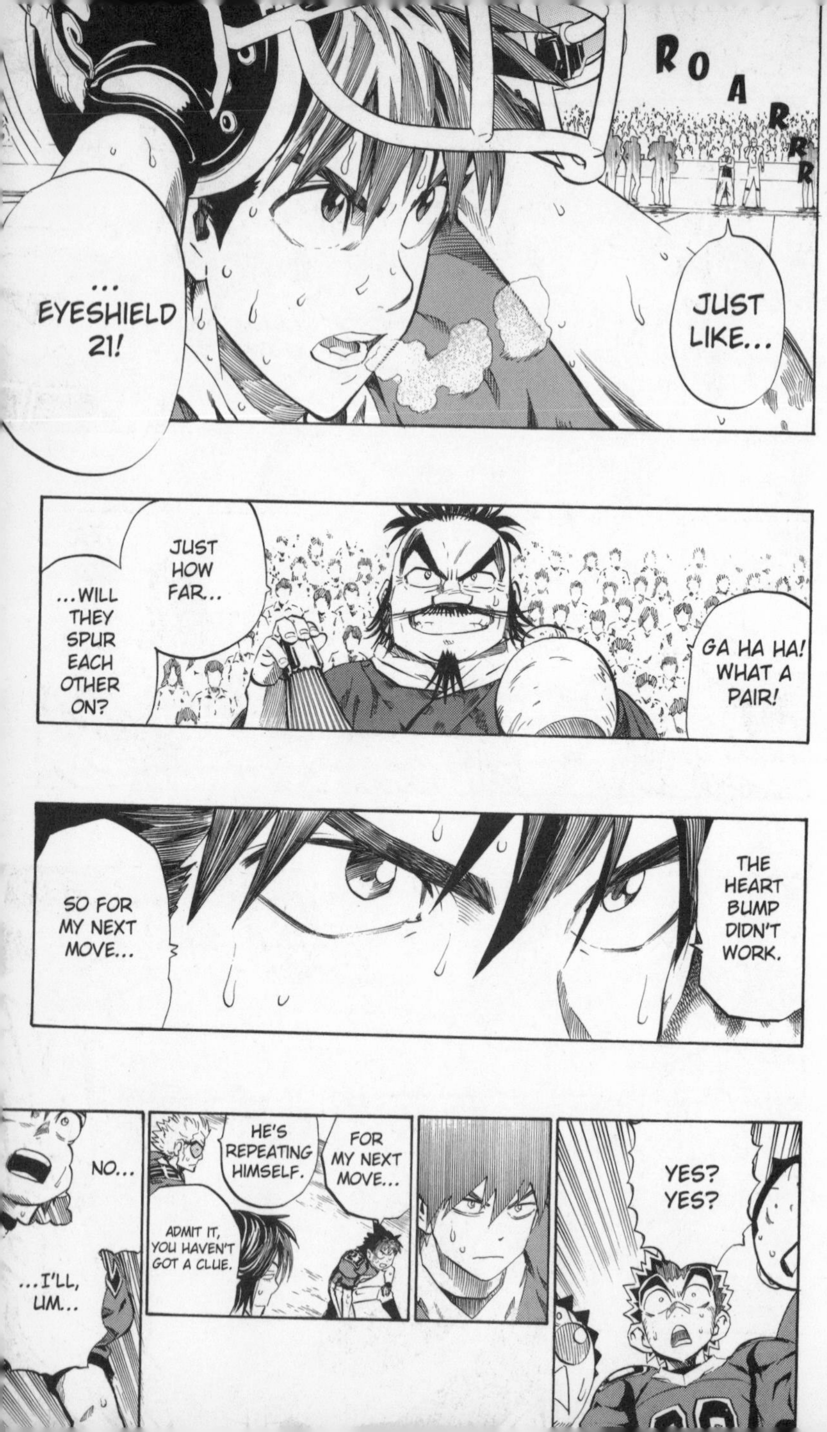
ROARRR
JUST LIKE...
... EYESHIELD 21!
GA HA HA! WHAT A PAIR!
JUST HOW FAR...
...WILL THEY SPUR EACH OTHER ON?
THE HEART BUMP DIDN'T WORK.
SO FOR MY NEXT MOVE...
YES? YES?
FOR MY NEXT MOVE...
HE'S REPEATING HIMSELF.
ADMIT IT, YOU HAVEN'T GOT A CLUE.
NO...
...I'LL, UM...

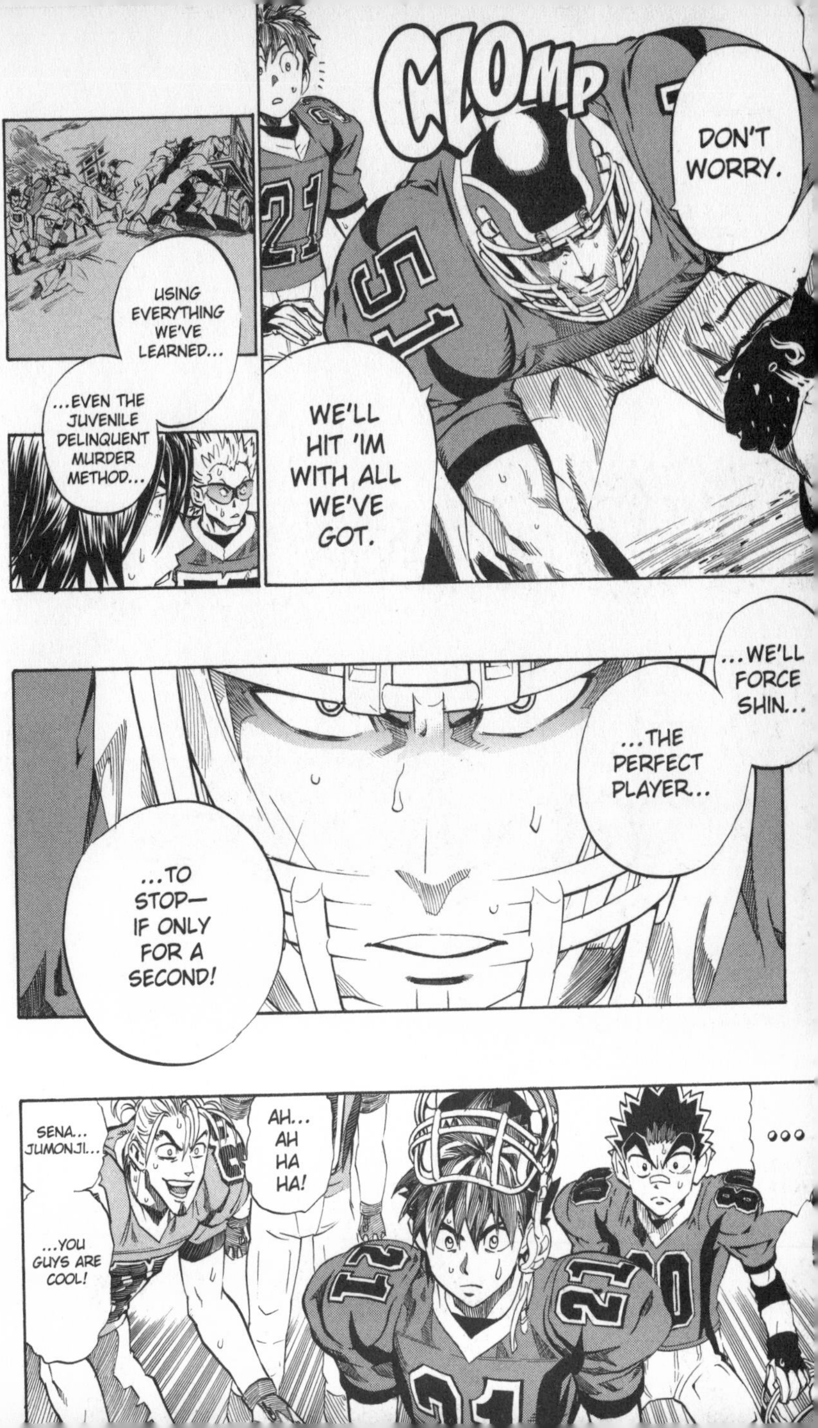
CLOMP
DON'T WORRY.
WE'LL HIT 'IM WITH ALL WE'VE GOT.
USING EVERYTHING WE'VE LEARNED...
...EVEN THE JUVENILE DELINQUENT MURDER METHOD...
...WE'LL FORCE SHIN...
...THE PERFECT PLAYER...
...TO STOP— IF ONLY FOR A SECOND!
...
AH... AH HA HA!
SENA... JUMONJI...
...YOU GUYS ARE COOL!

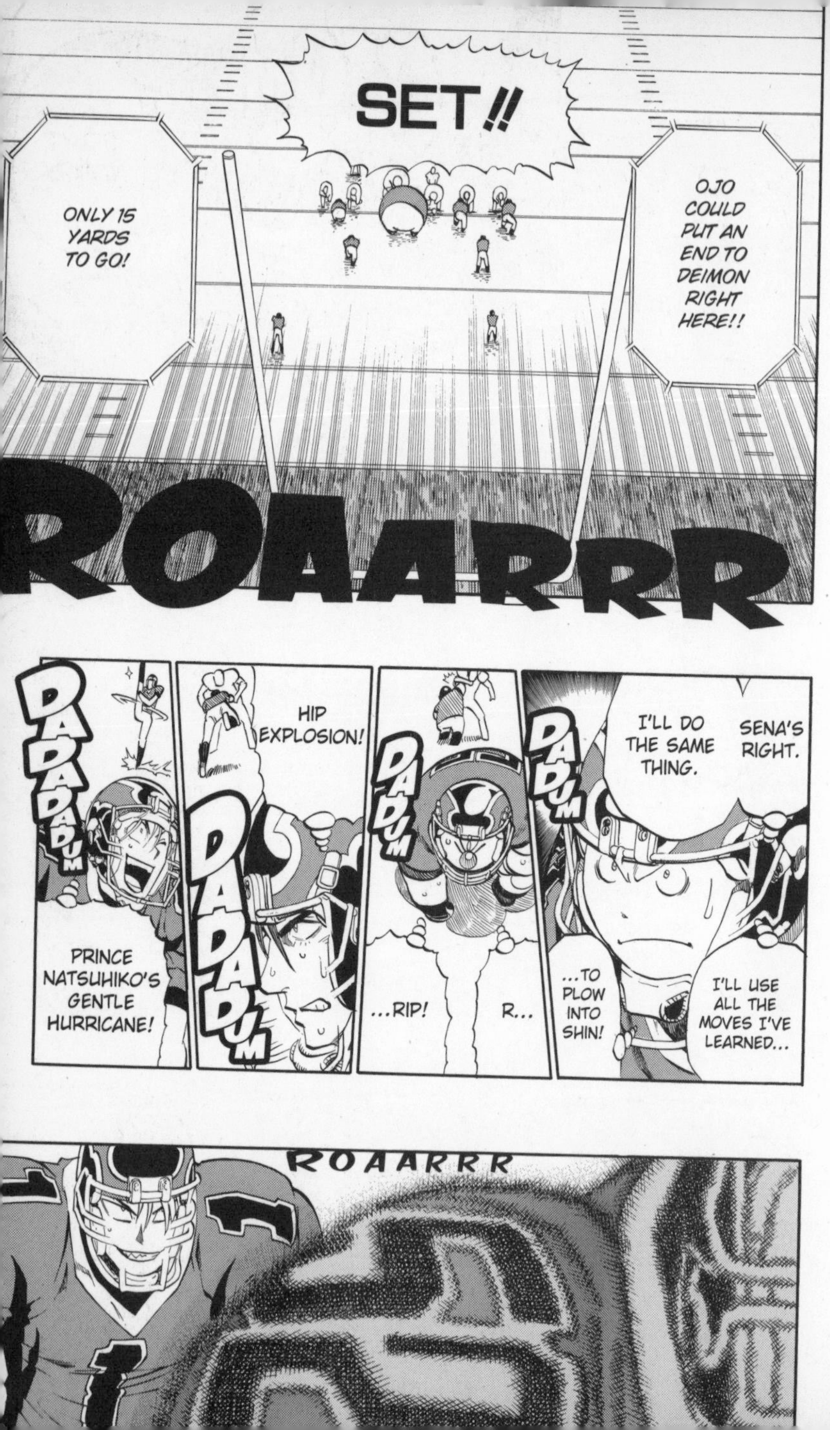
SET!!
OJO COULD PUT AN END TO DEIMON RIGHT HERE!!
ONLY 15 YARDS TO GO!
ROAARRR
SENA'S RIGHT.
I'LL DO THE SAME THING.
DADUM
I'LL USE ALL THE MOVES I'VE LEARNED...
...TO PLOW INTO SHIN!
DADUM
R...
...RIP!
HIP EXPLOSION!
DADADUM
DADADADUM
PRINCE NATSUHIKO'S GENTLE HURRICANE!
ROAARRR

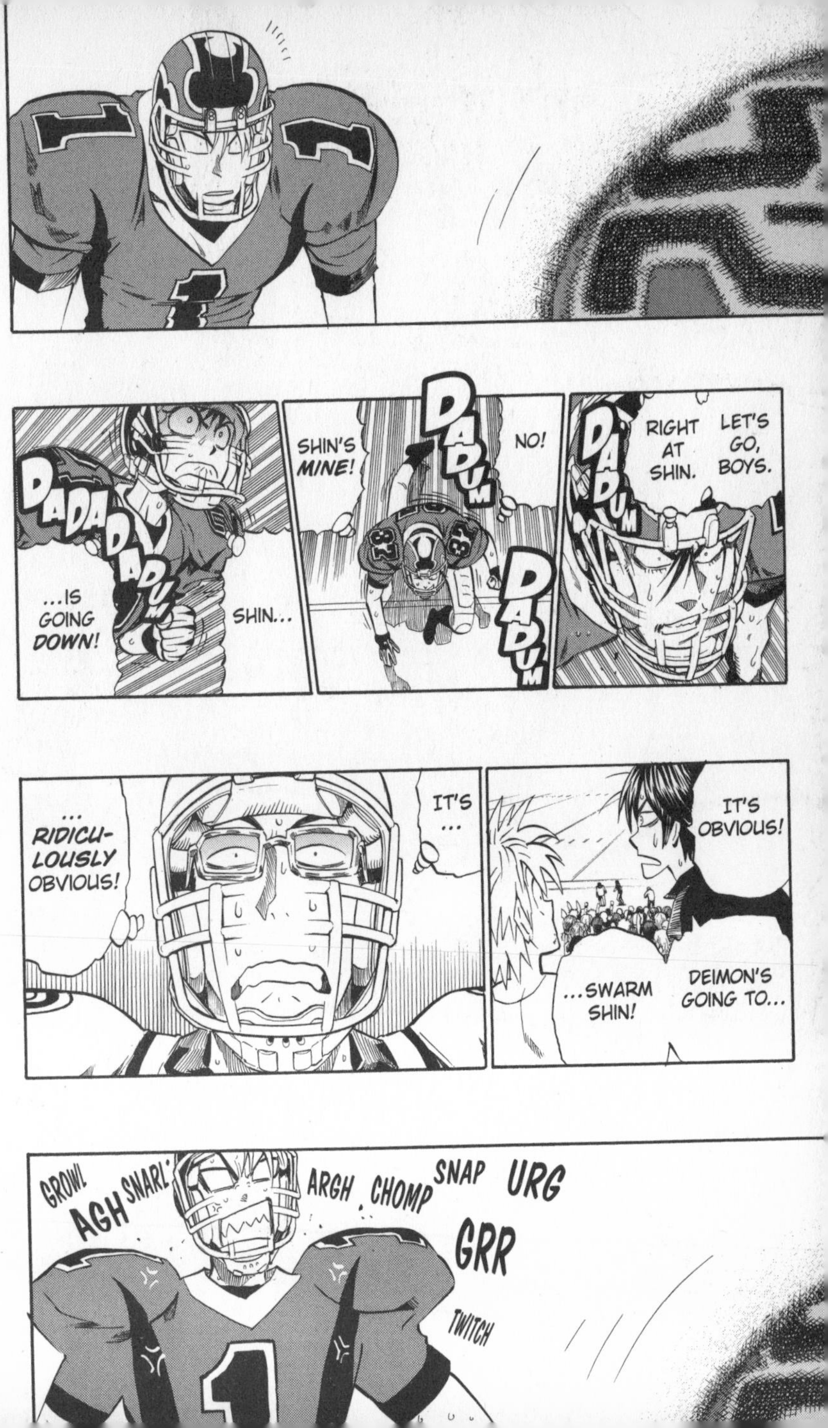
LET'S GO, BOYS.
RIGHT AT SHIN.
DADUM
NO!
SHIN'S MINE!
DADUM
DADUM
SHIN...
...IS GOING DOWN!
DADADADUM
IT'S OBVIOUS!
DEIMON'S GOING TO...
...SWARM SHIN!
IT'S ...
... RIDICU-LOUSLY OBVIOUS!
URG
SNAP
CHOMP
ARGH
SNARL
AGH
GROWL
GRR
TWITCH

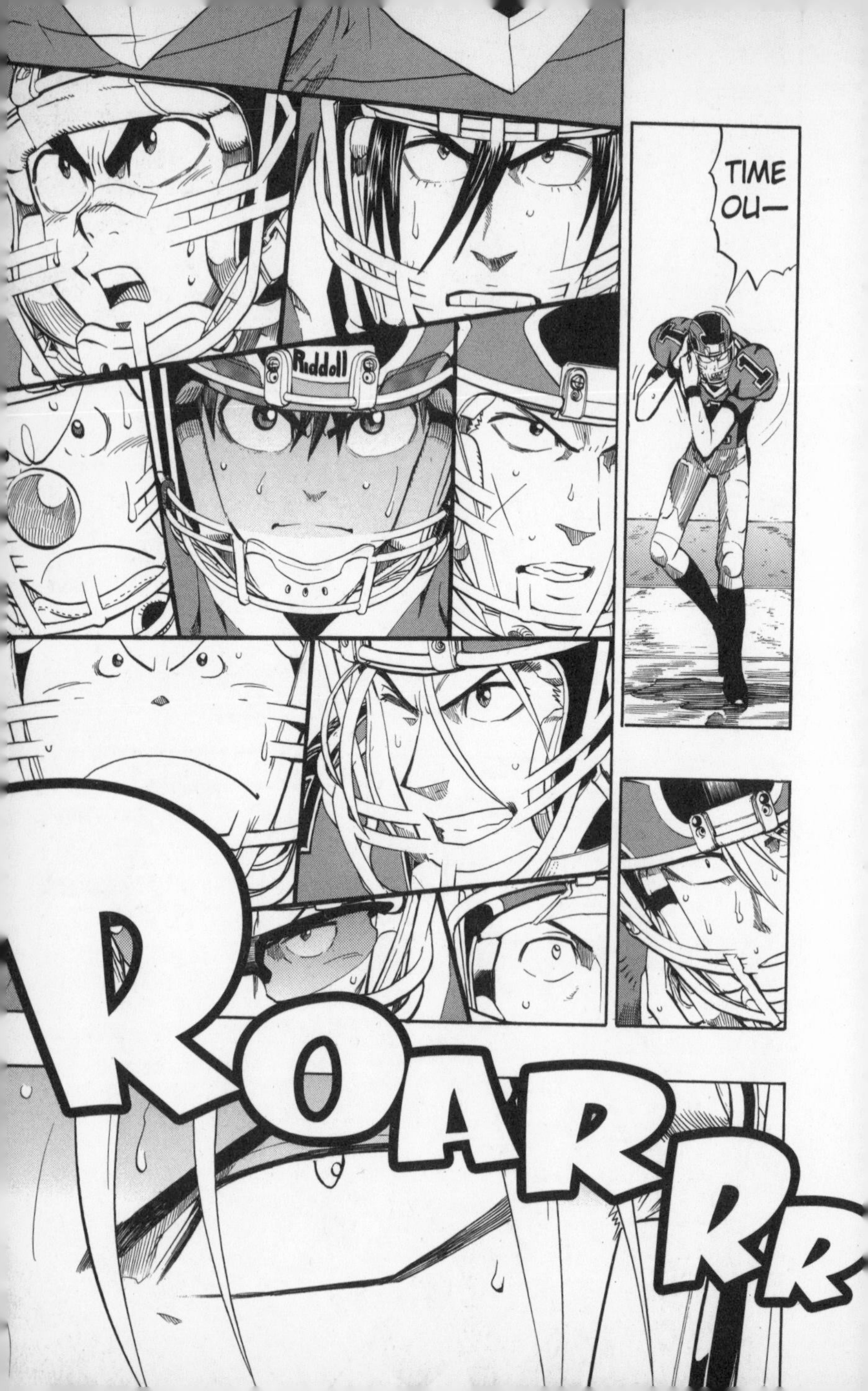
TIME OU—
Riddoll
ROARRR

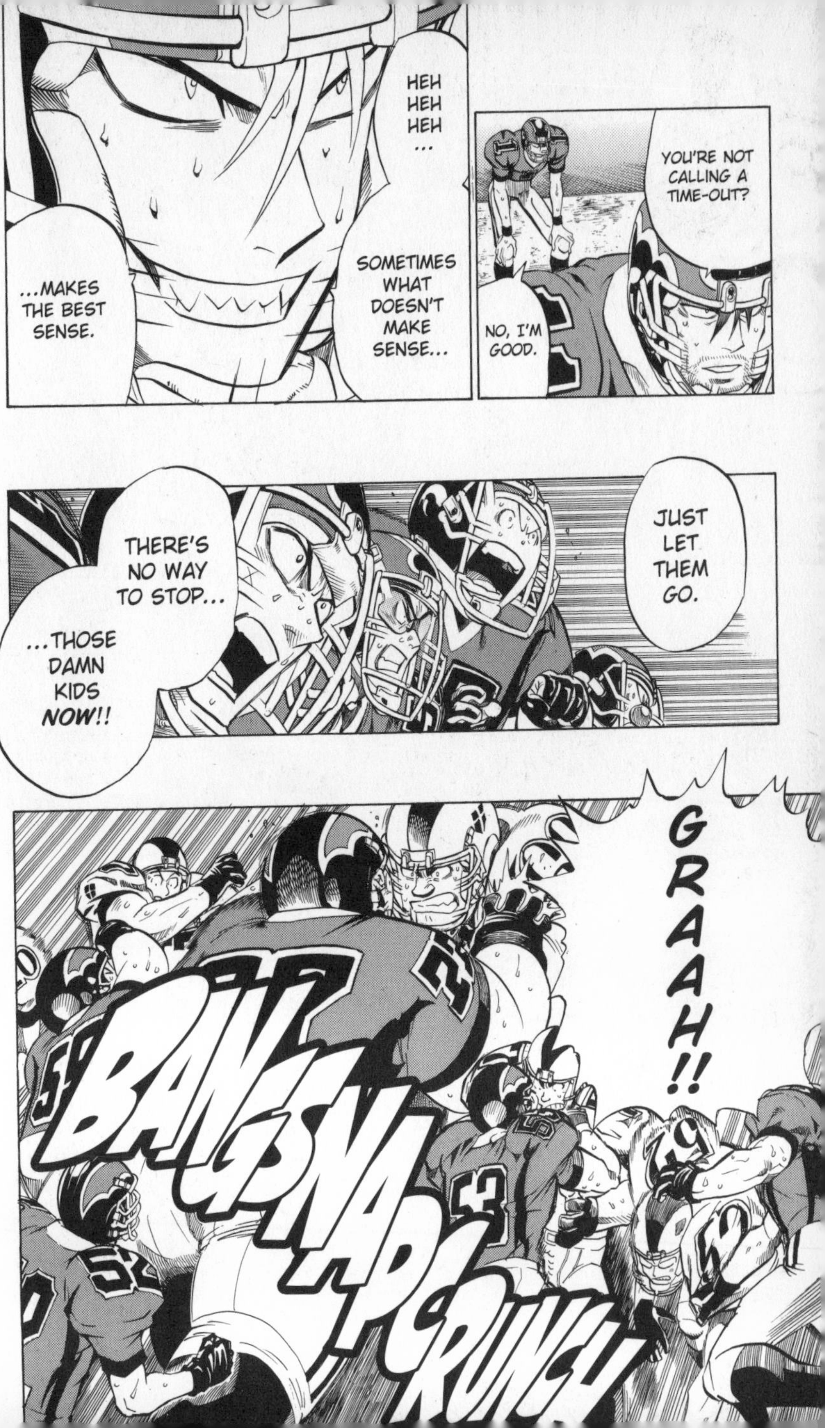
YOU'RE NOT CALLING A TIME-OUT?
NO, I'M GOOD.
HEH HEH HEH ...
SOMETIMES WHAT DOESN'T MAKE SENSE...
...MAKES THE BEST SENSE.
JUST LET THEM GO.
THERE'S NO WAY TO STOP...
...THOSE DAMN KIDS NOW!!
GRAAAH!!
BANG SNAP CRUNCH!!

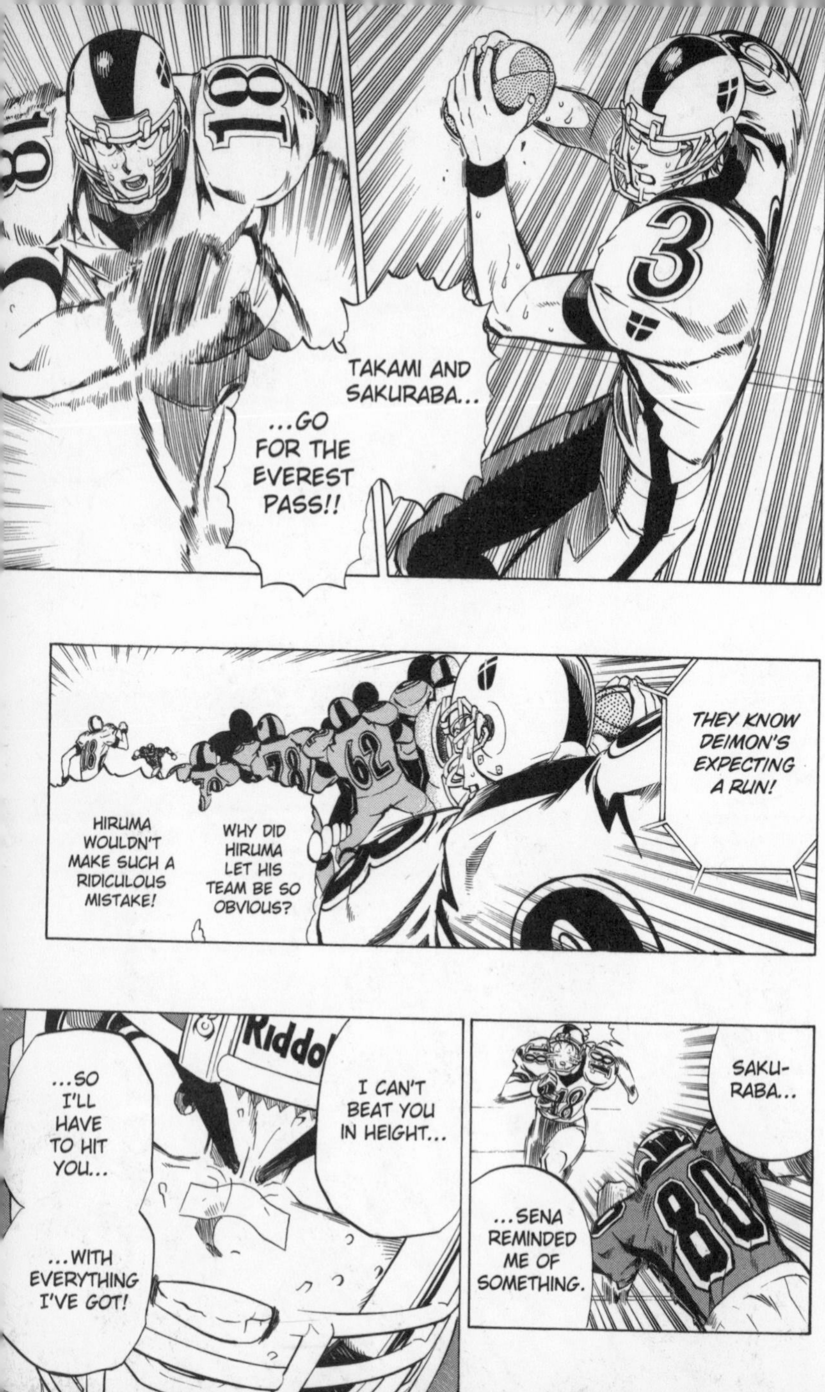
TAKAMI AND SAKURABA...
...GO FOR THE EVEREST PASS!!
THEY KNOW DEIMON'S EXPECTING A RUN!
WHY DID HIRUMA LET HIS TEAM BE SO OBVIOUS?
HIRUMA WOULDN'T MAKE SUCH A RIDICULOUS MISTAKE!
SAKU-RABA...
...SENA REMINDED ME OF SOMETHING.
I CAN'T BEAT YOU IN HEIGHT...
...SO I'LL HAVE TO HIT YOU...
...WITH EVERYTHING I'VE GOT!

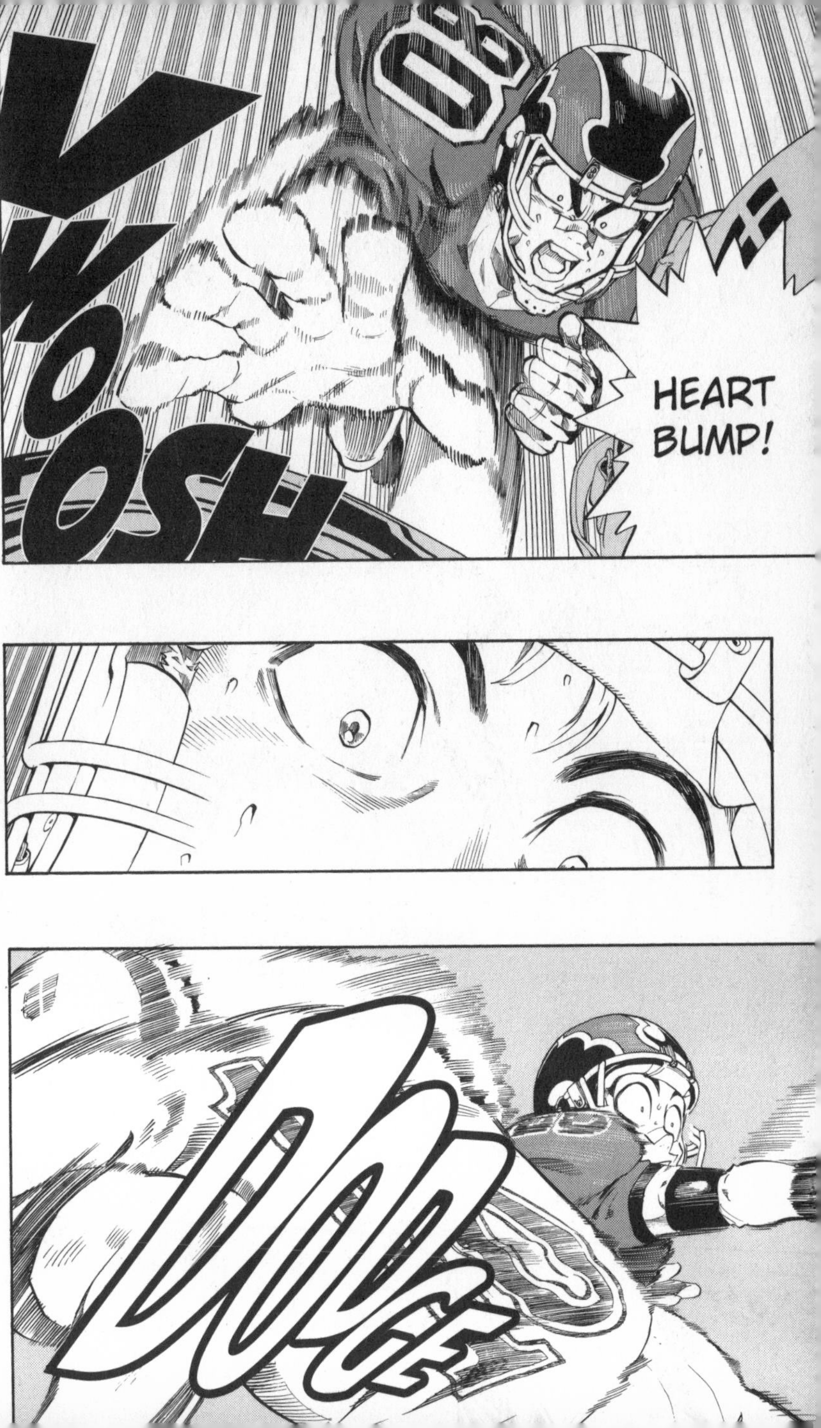
HEART BUMP!

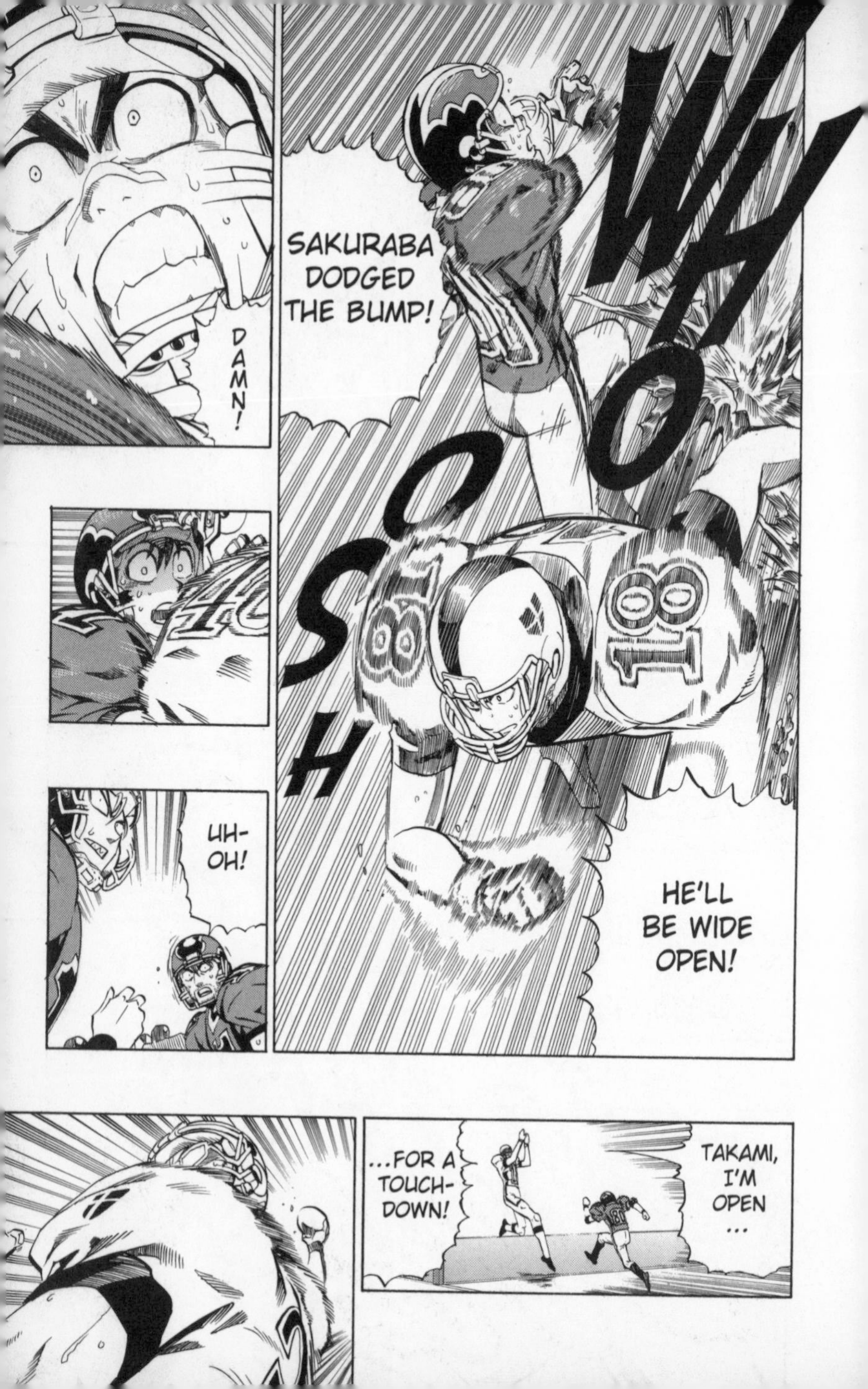
WHOOOSH
SAKURABA DODGED THE BUMP!
HE'LL BE WIDE OPEN!
DAMN!
UH-OH!
TAKAMI, I'M OPEN ...
...FOR A TOUCH-DOWN!

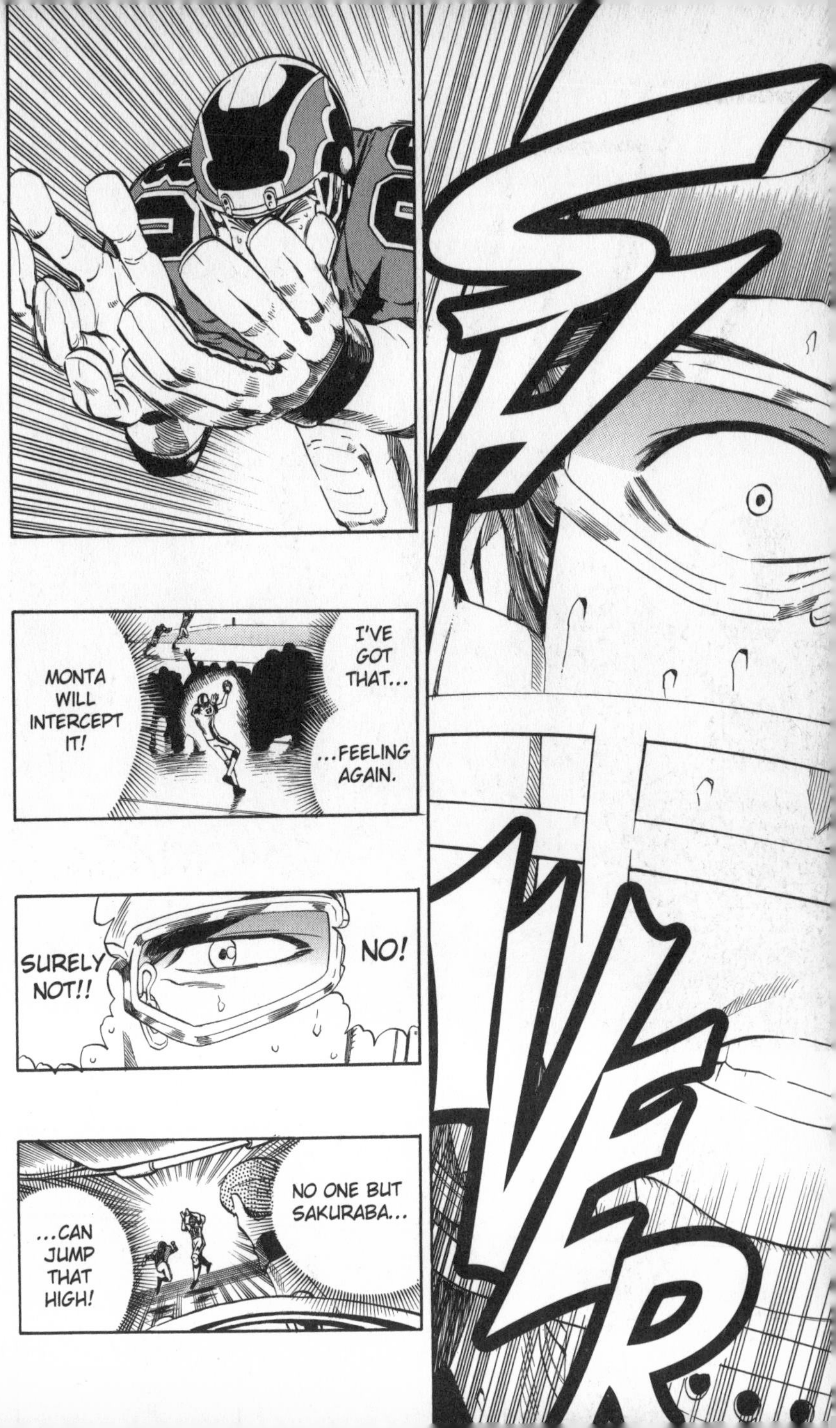
I'VE GOT THAT...
...FEELING AGAIN.
MONTA WILL INTERCEPT IT!
NO!
SURELY NOT!!
NO ONE BUT SAKURABA...
...CAN JUMP THAT HIGH!

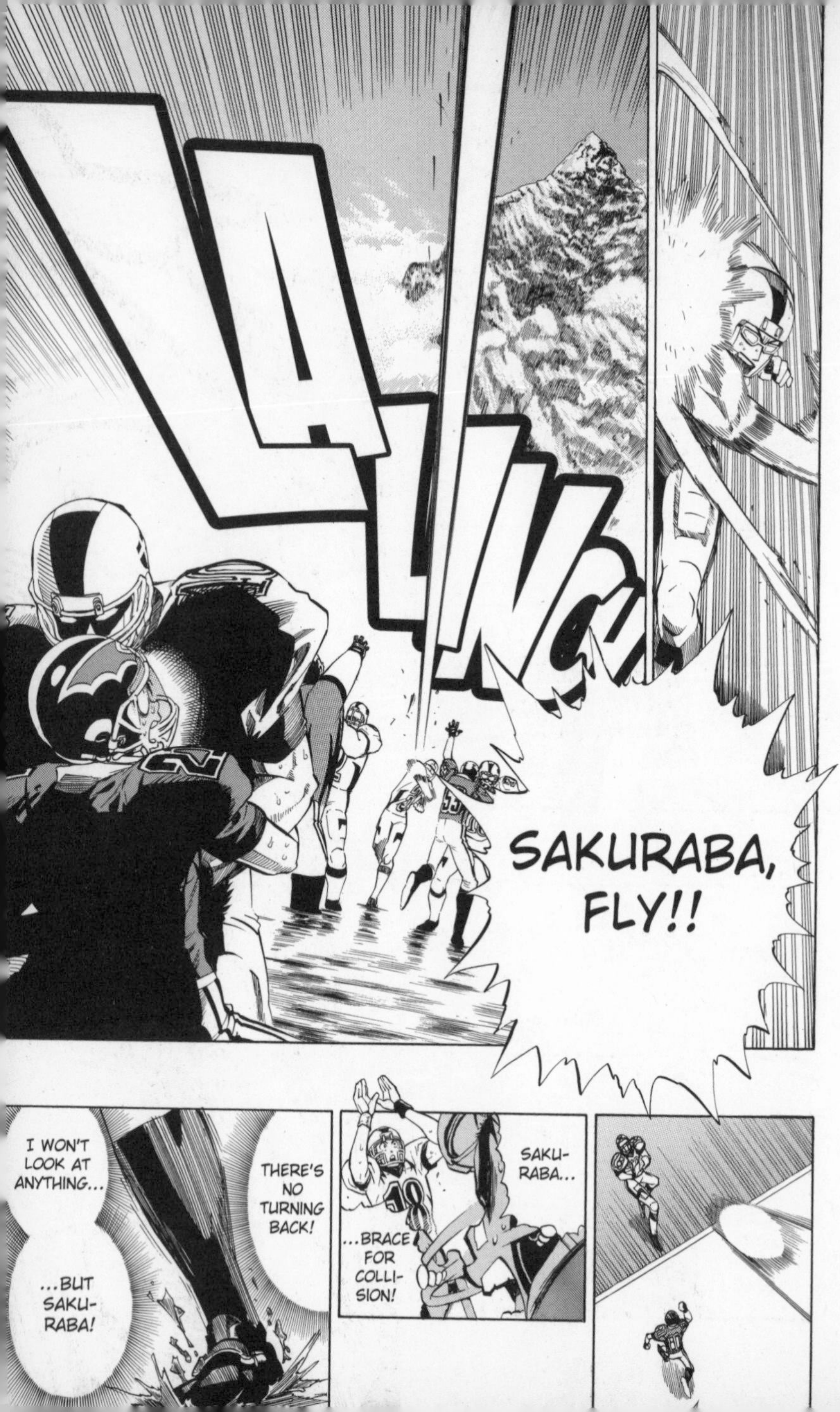
SAKURABA, FLY!!
SAKURABA...
...BRACE FOR COLLISION!
THERE'S NO TURNING BACK!
I WON'T LOOK AT ANYTHING...
...BUT SAKURABA!

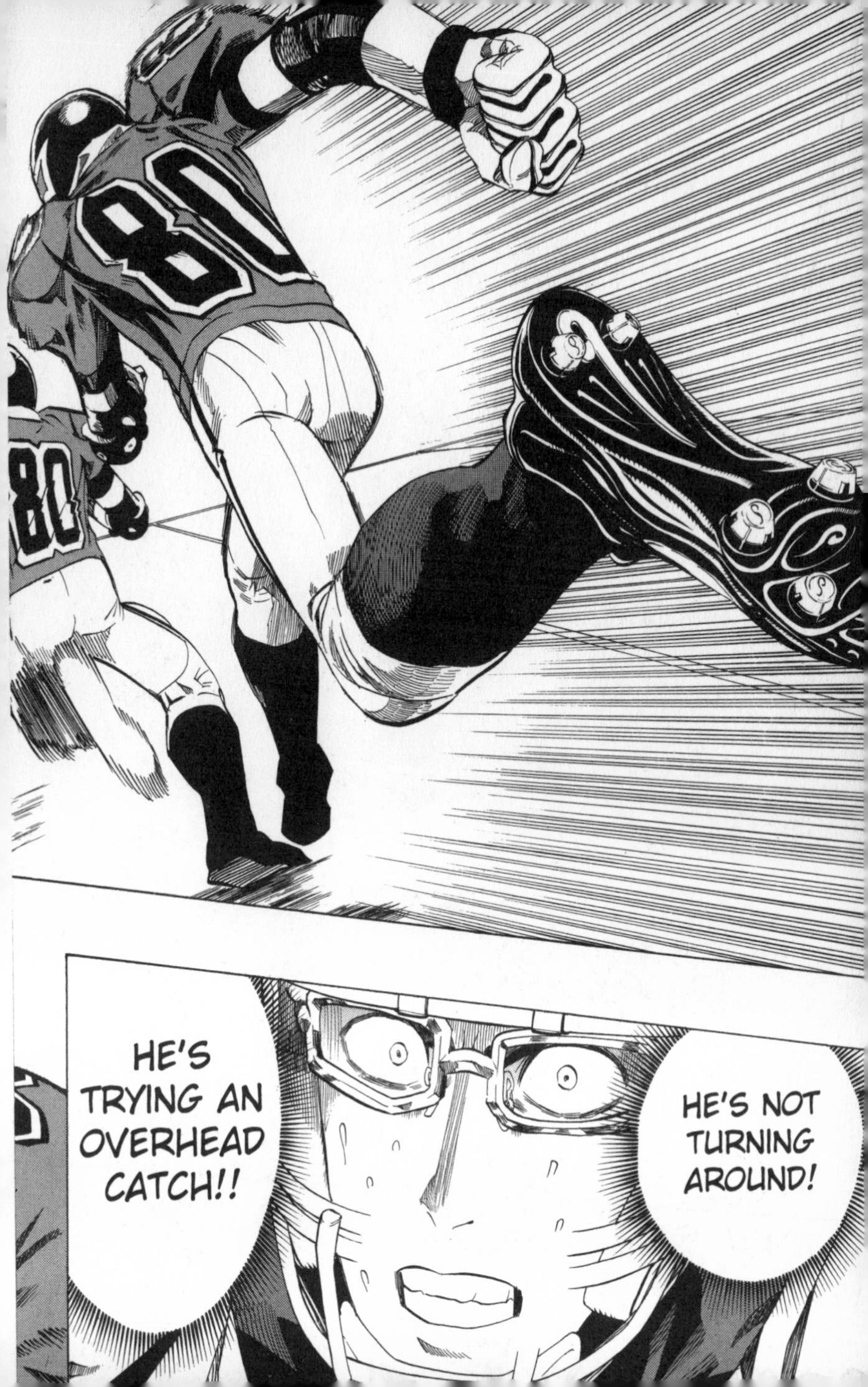
HE'S NOT TURNING AROUND!
HE'S TRYING AN OVERHEAD CATCH!!

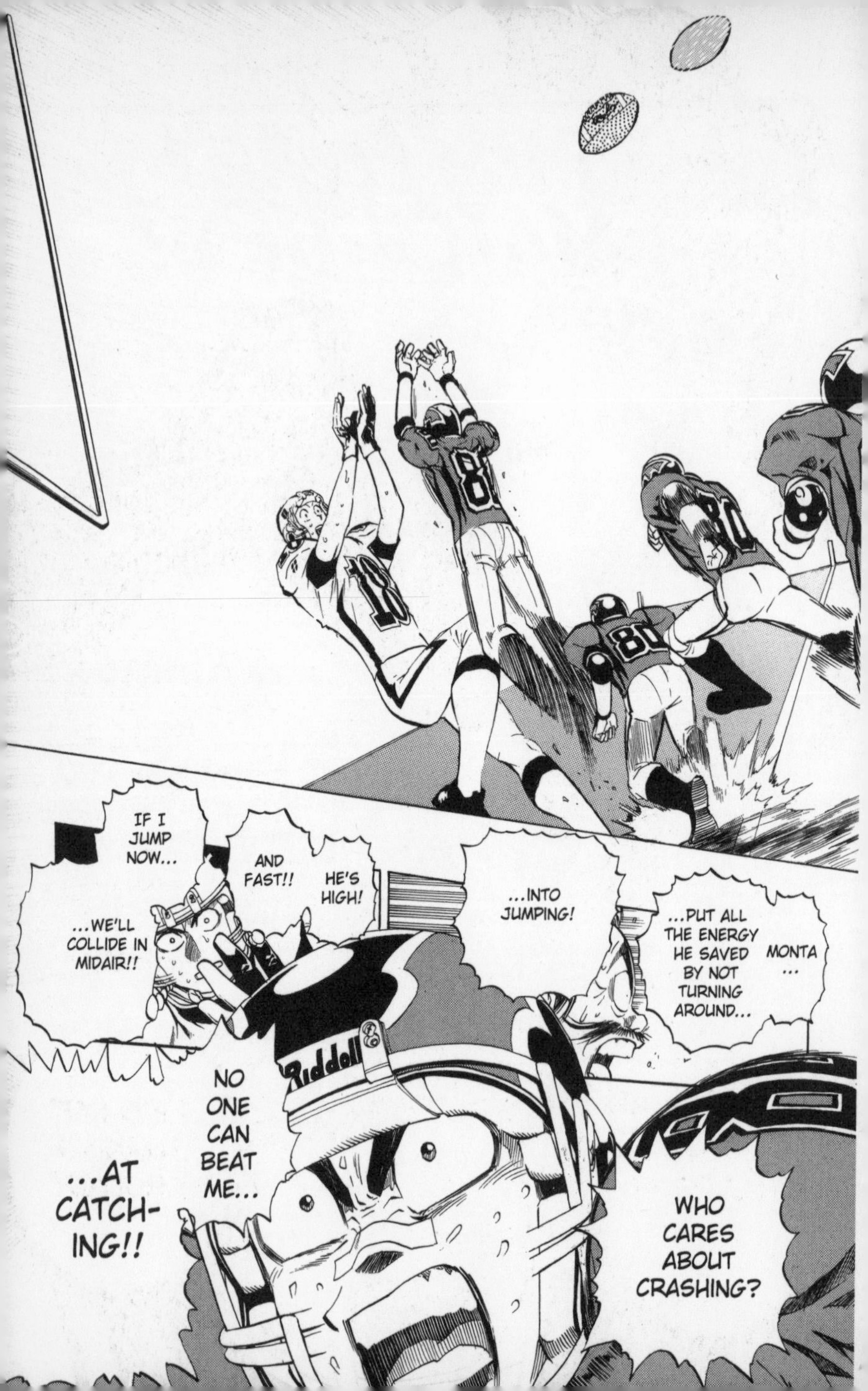

MONTA...
...PUT ALL THE ENERGY HE SAVED BY NOT TURNING AROUND...
...INTO JUMPING!
HE'S HIGH!
AND FAST!!
IF I JUMP NOW...
...WE'LL COLLIDE IN MIDAIR!!
WHO CARES ABOUT CRASHING?
Riddell
NO ONE CAN BEAT ME...
...AT CATCHING!!

RIVAL BATTLE ★ DEIMON VS. OJO

SUPER MISCELLANY MATCH-UPS!!

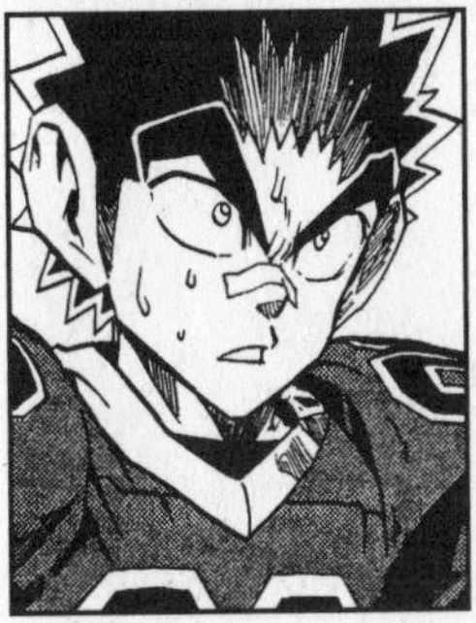

VS.

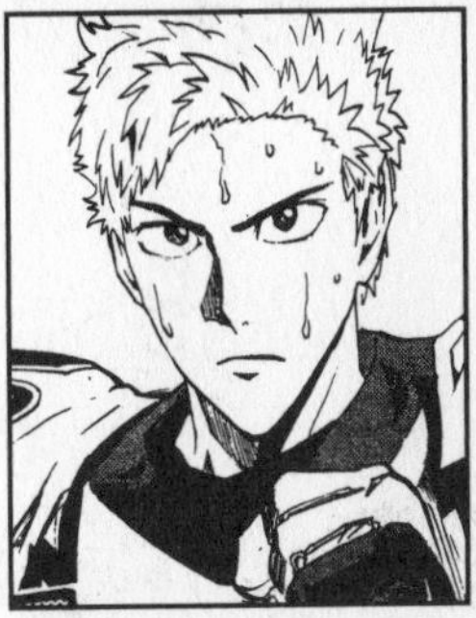

MONTA

SAKURABA

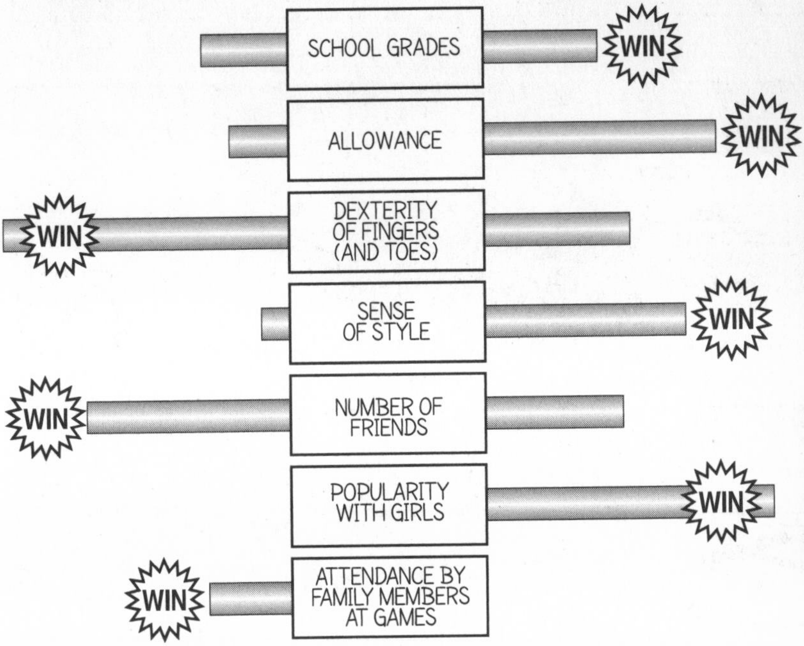
SCHOOL GRADES
WIN
ALLOWANCE
WIN
WIN
DEXTERITY OF FINGERS (AND TOES)
SENSE OF STYLE
WIN
WIN
NUMBER OF FRIENDS
POPULARITY WITH GIRLS
WIN
WIN
ATTENDANCE BY FAMILY MEMBERS AT GAMES

Chapter 225 The Third Eye

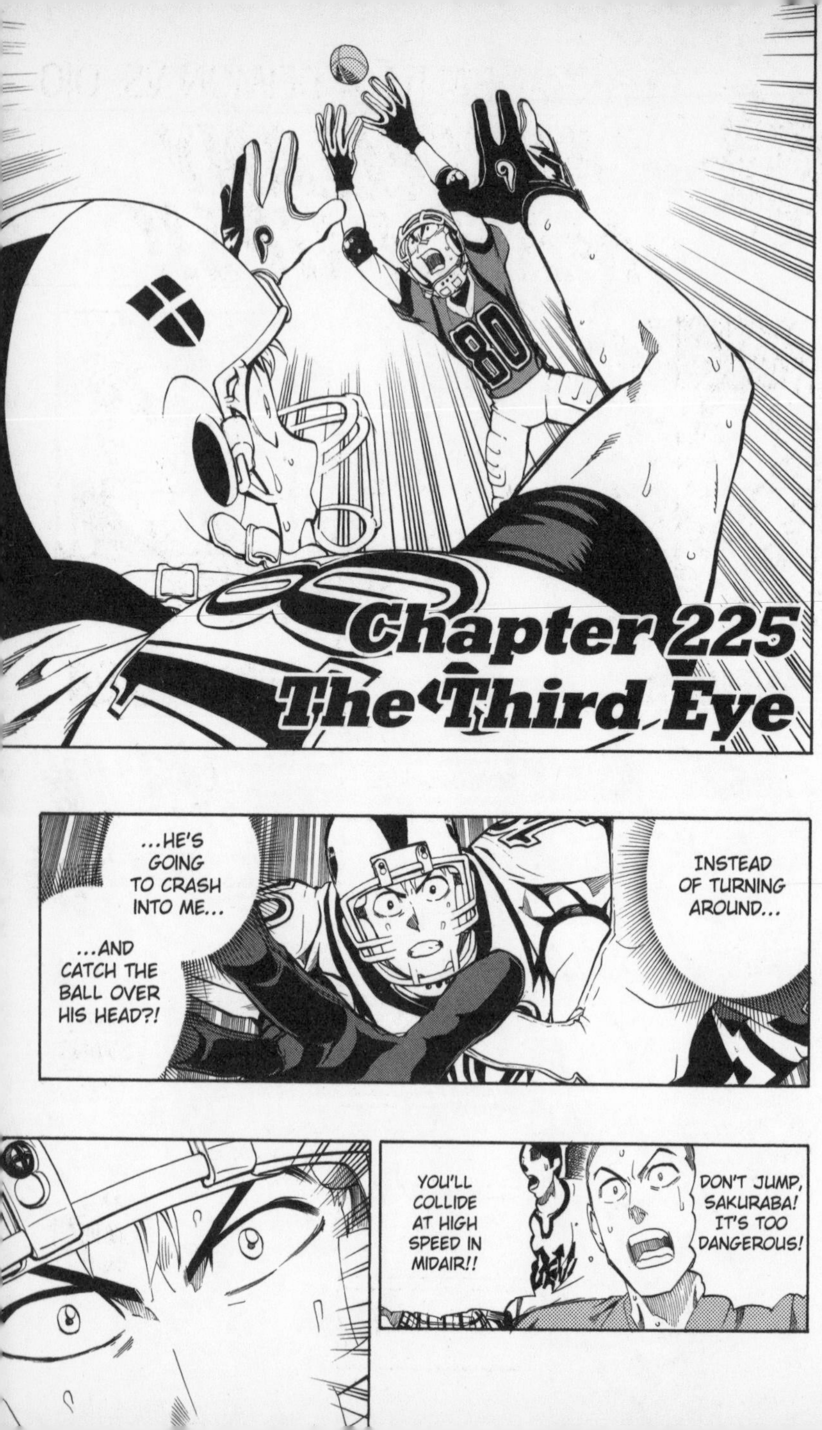
INSTEAD OF TURNING AROUND...
...HE'S GOING TO CRASH INTO ME...
...AND CATCH THE BALL OVER HIS HEAD?!
DON'T JUMP, SAKURABA! IT'S TOO DANGEROUS!
YOU'LL COLLIDE AT HIGH SPEED IN MIDAIR!!

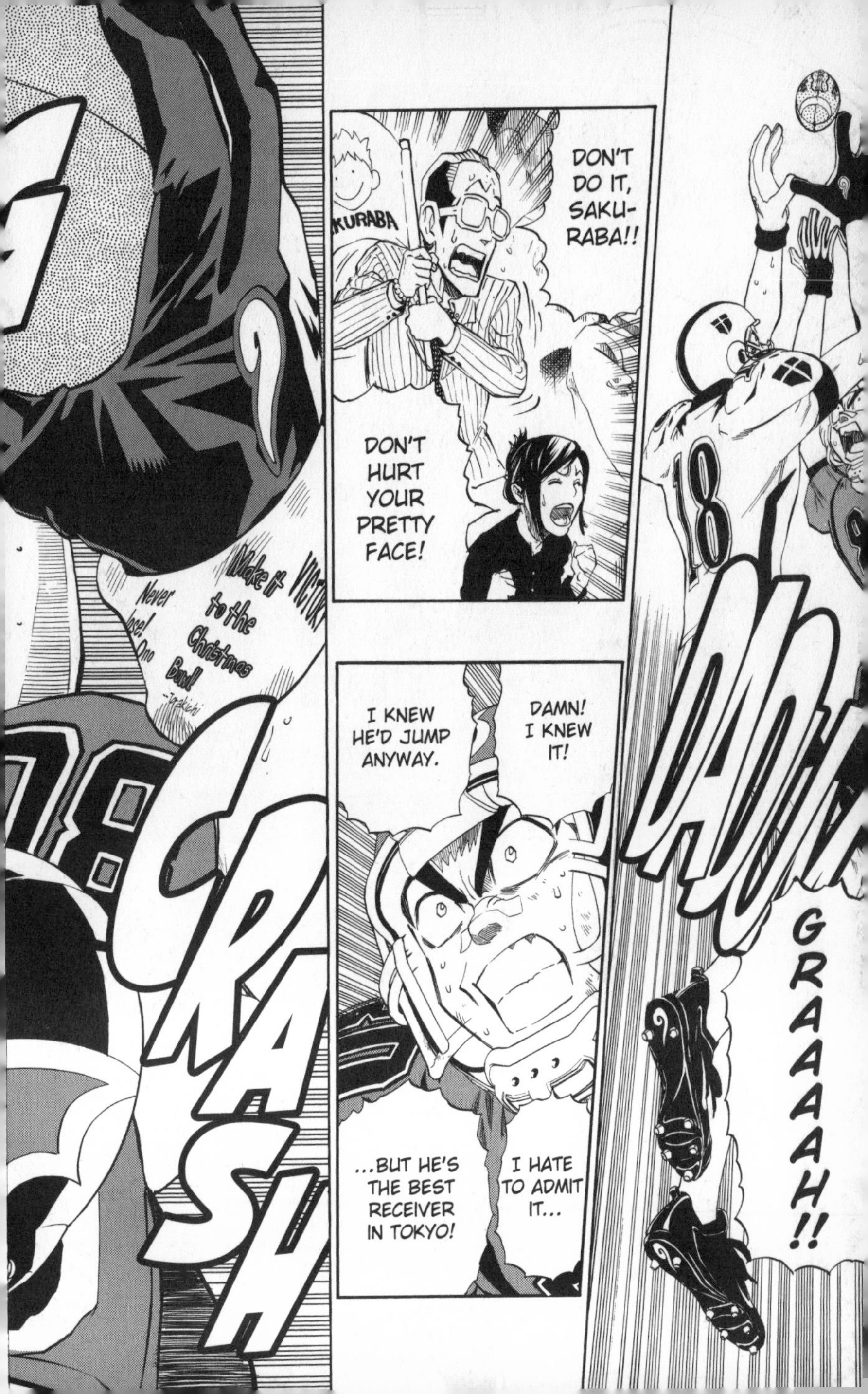
GRAAAAAH!!
DON'T DO IT, SAKU-RABA!!
DON'T HURT YOUR PRETTY FACE!
DAMN! I KNEW IT!
I KNEW HE'D JUMP ANYWAY.
I HATE TO ADMIT IT...
...BUT HE'S THE BEST RECEIVER IN TOKYO!
Make it to the Christmas Bowl!
Never lose! Ono
CRASH

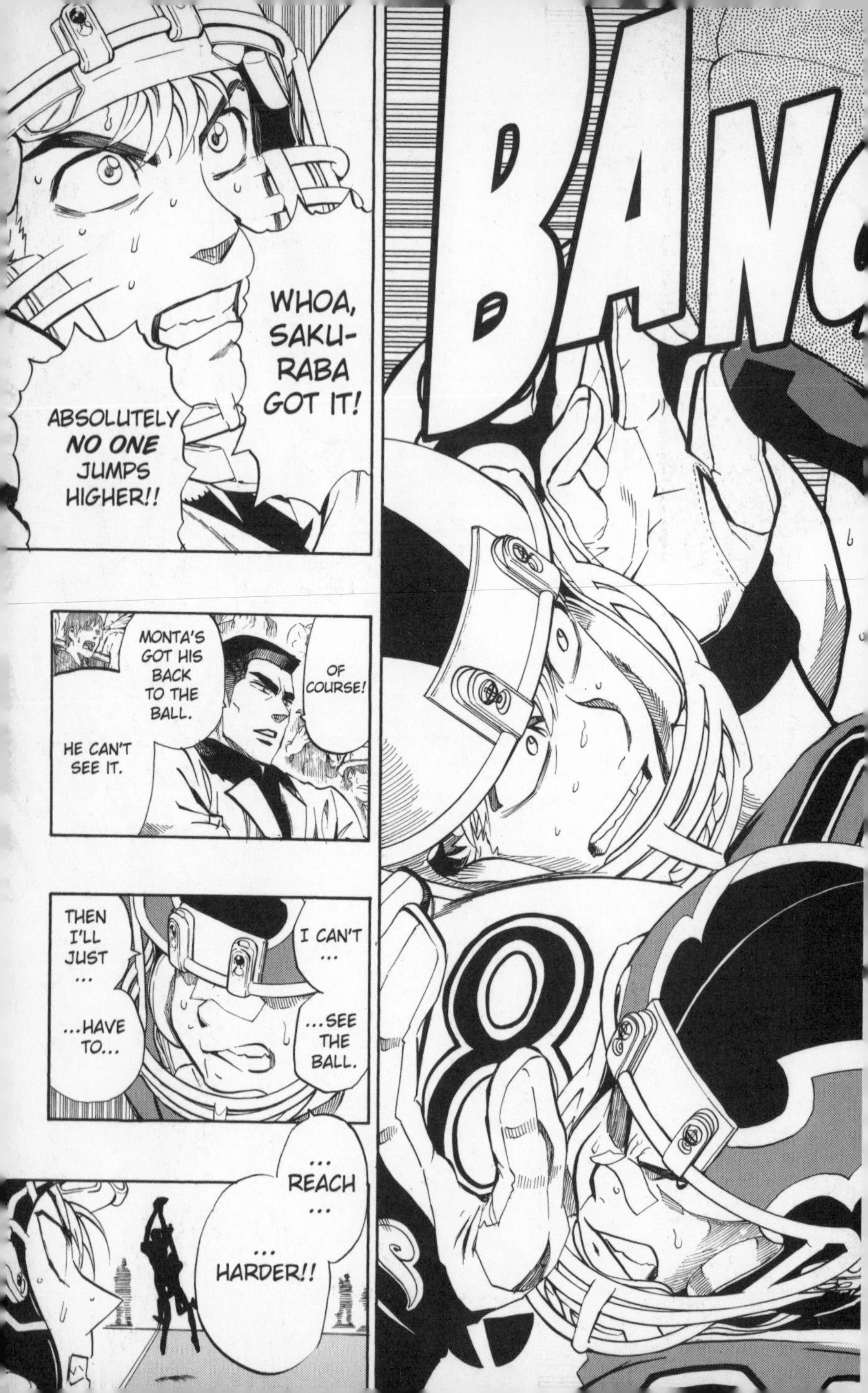
BANG
WHOA, SAKU-RABA GOT IT!
ABSOLUTELY **NO ONE** JUMPS HIGHER!!
OF COURSE!
MONTA'S GOT HIS BACK TO THE BALL.
HE CAN'T SEE IT.
I CAN'T ...
...SEE THE BALL.
THEN I'LL JUST ...
...HAVE TO...
... REACH ...
... HARDER!!

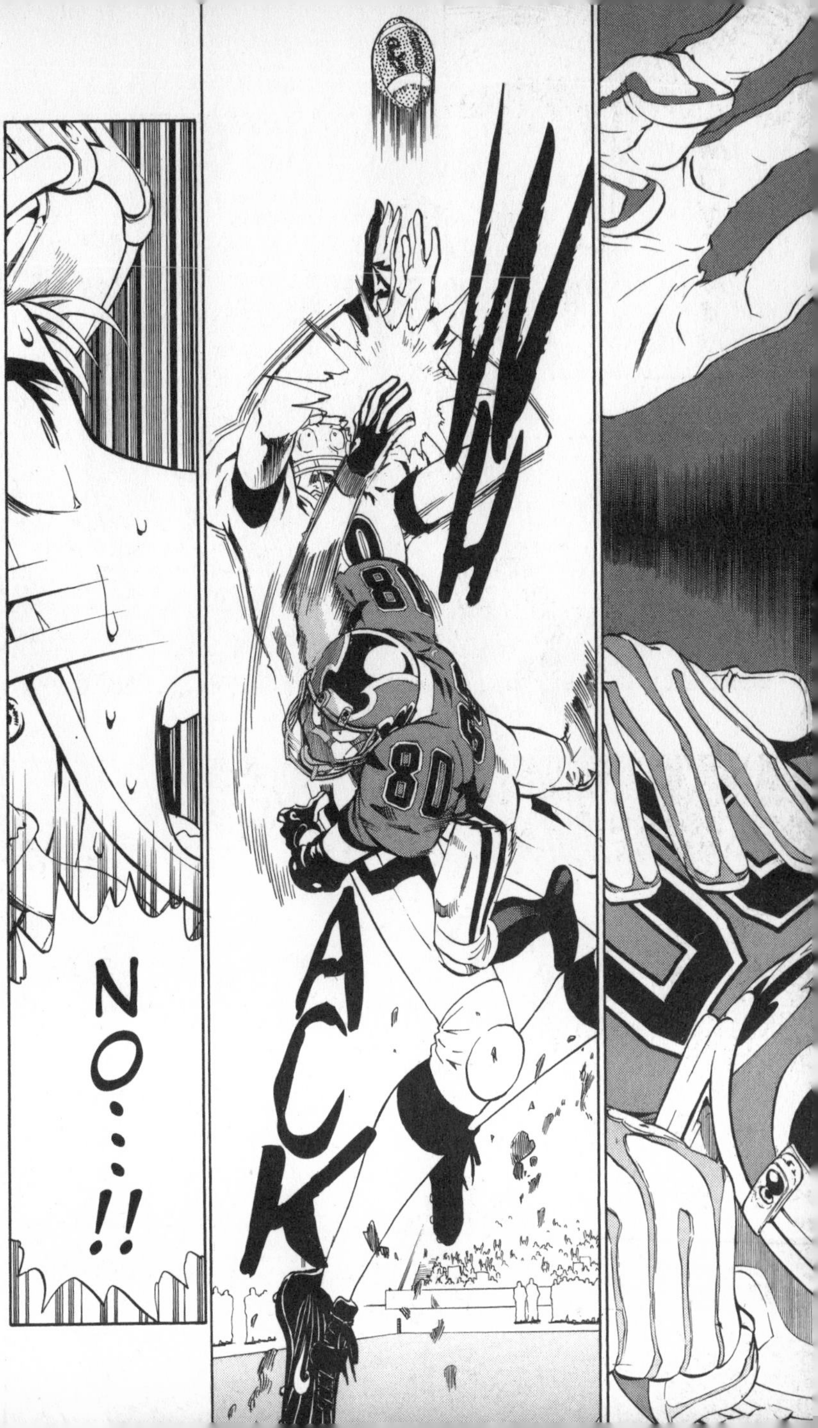
WHACK
NO...!!

MONTAA!!

HE KNOCKED THE BALL...

...BACK INTO THE AIR!!

SKIDDDDD

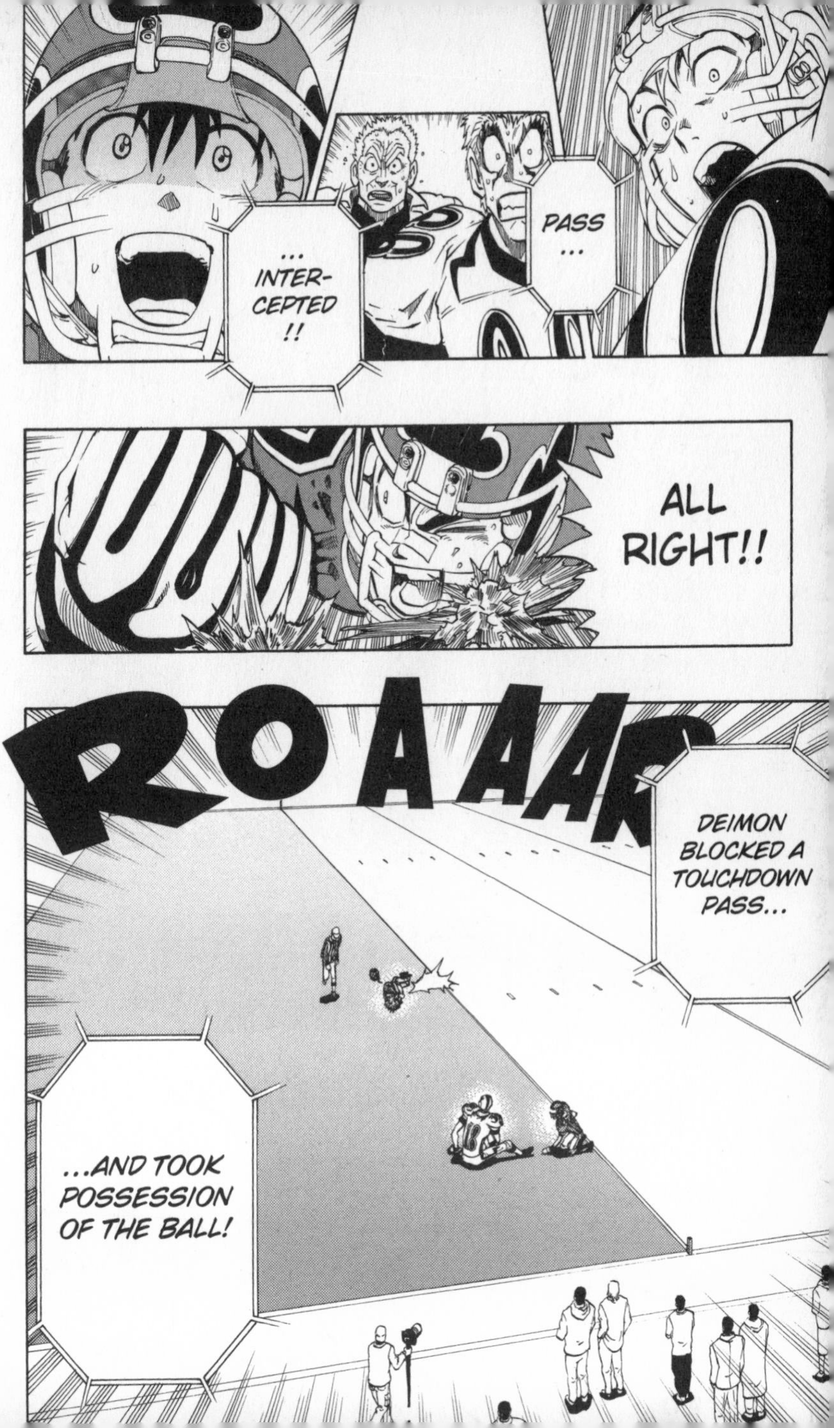
PASS ...
... INTER-CEPTED !!
ALL RIGHT!!
ROAAAR
DEIMON BLOCKED A TOUCHDOWN PASS...
...AND TOOK POSSESSION OF THE BALL!

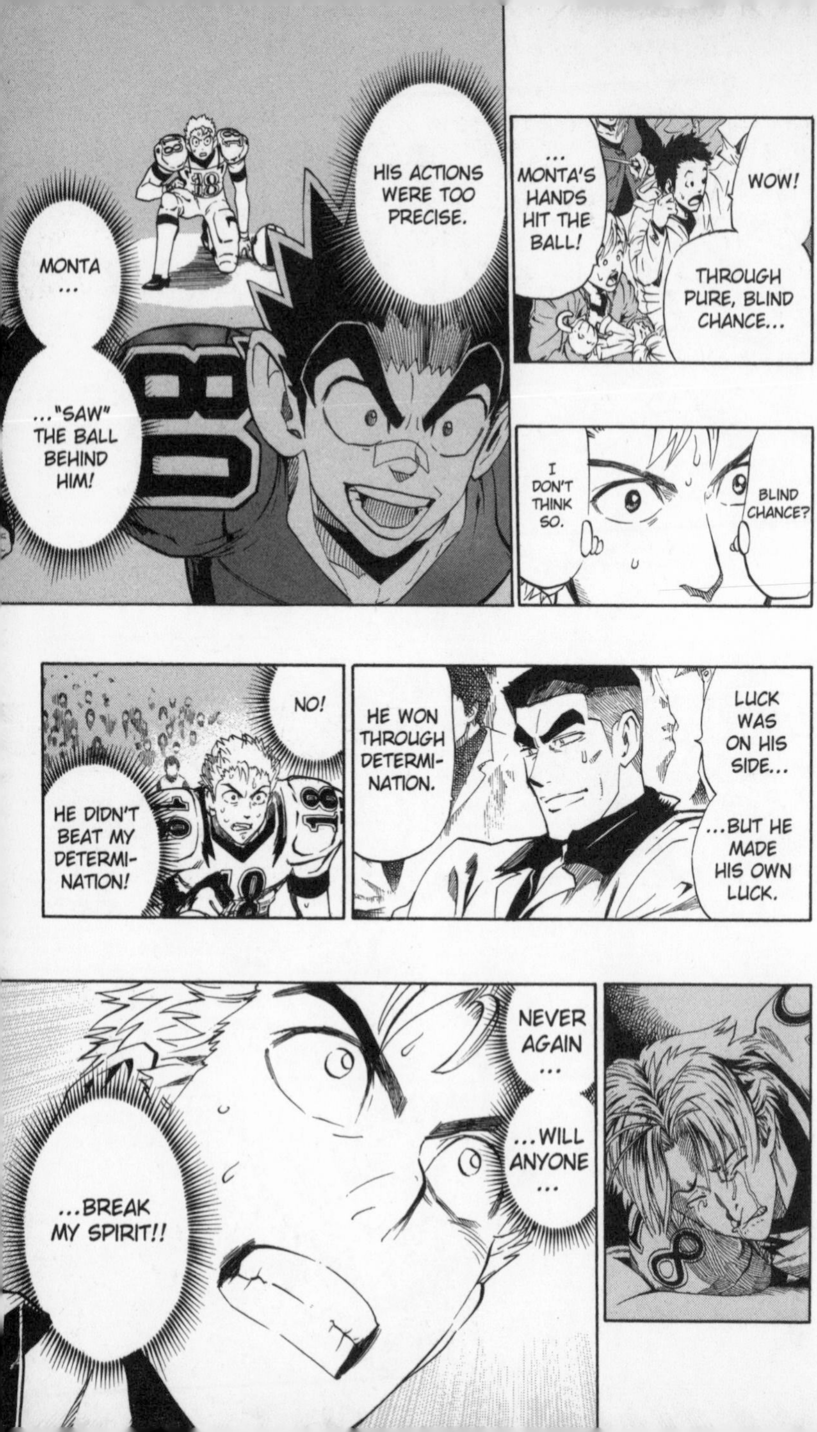
WOW!
...MONTA'S HANDS HIT THE BALL!
THROUGH PURE, BLIND CHANCE...
BLIND CHANCE?
I DON'T THINK SO.
HIS ACTIONS WERE TOO PRECISE.
MONTA...
..."SAW" THE BALL BEHIND HIM!
LUCK WAS ON HIS SIDE...
...BUT HE MADE HIS OWN LUCK.
HE WON THROUGH DETERMINATION.
NO!
HE DIDN'T BEAT MY DETERMINATION!
NEVER AGAIN...
...WILL ANYONE...
...BREAK MY SPIRIT!!

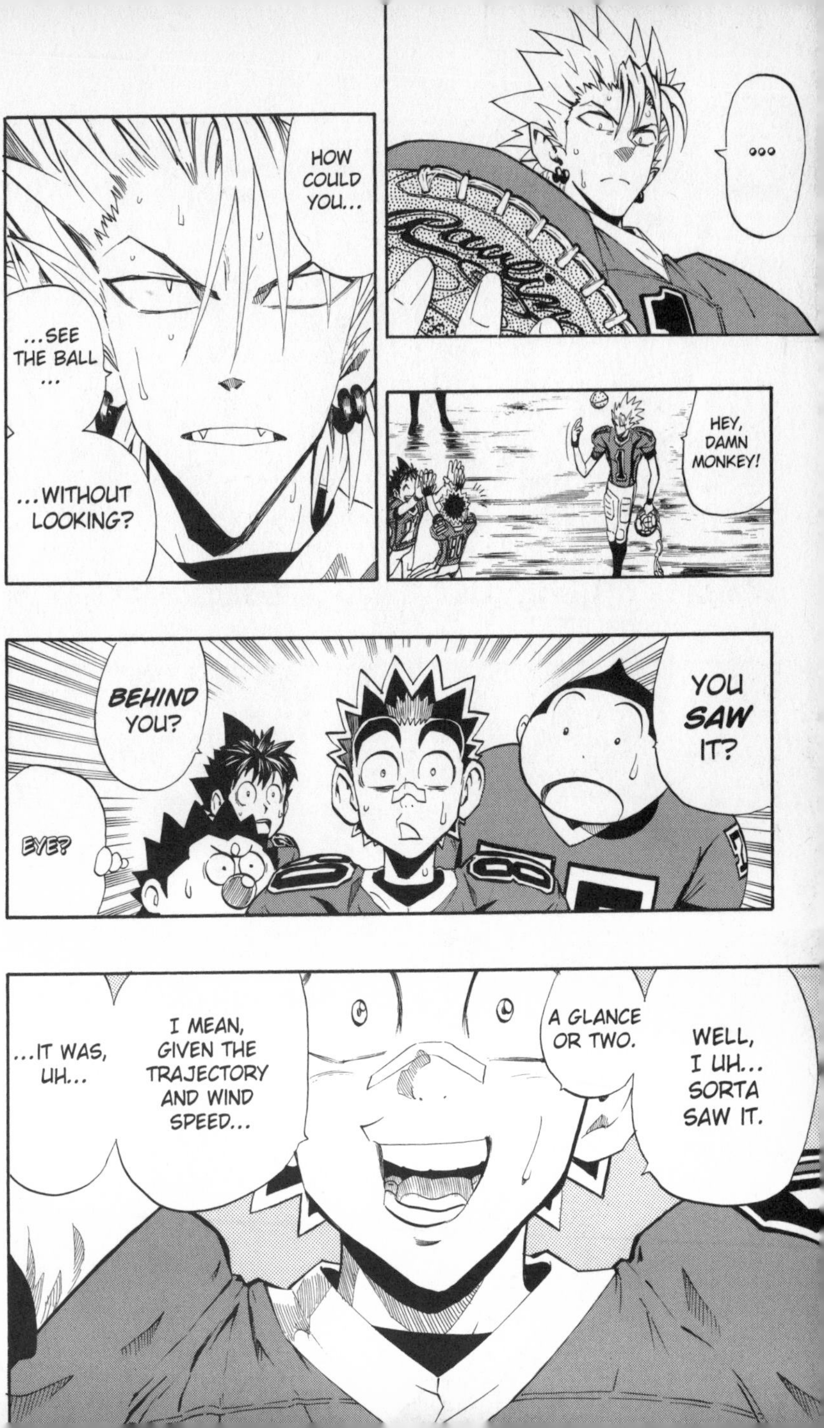
...
HEY, DAMN MONKEY!
HOW COULD YOU...
...SEE THE BALL...
...WITHOUT LOOKING?
YOU SAW IT?
BEHIND YOU?
EYE?
WELL, I UH... SORTA SAW IT.
A GLANCE OR TWO.
I MEAN, GIVEN THE TRAJECTORY AND WIND SPEED...
...IT WAS, UH...

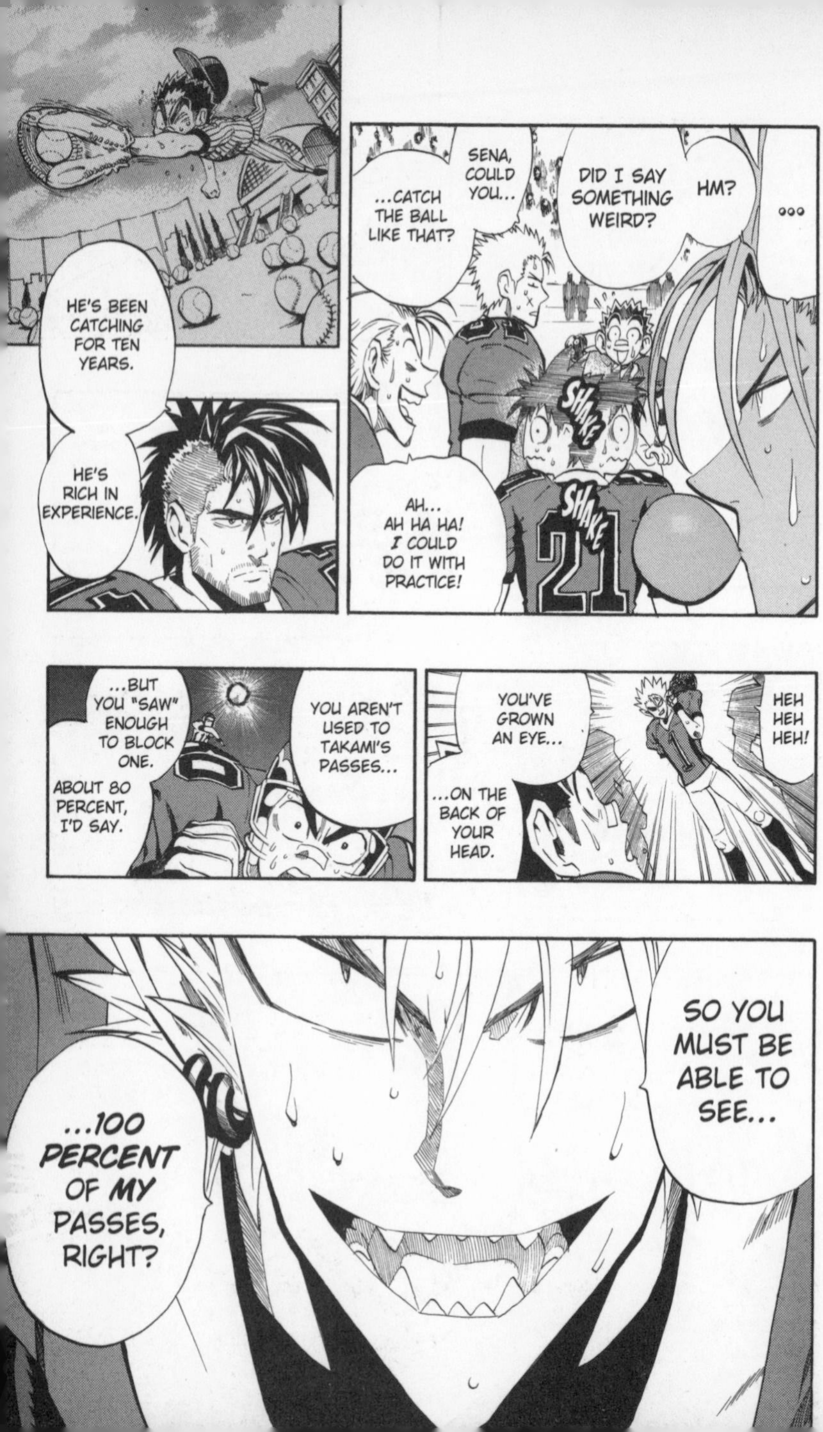

...
HM?
DID I SAY SOMETHING WEIRD?
SENA, COULD YOU...
...CATCH THE BALL LIKE THAT?
SHAKE
SHAKE
AH... AH HA HA! I COULD DO IT WITH PRACTICE!
HE'S BEEN CATCHING FOR TEN YEARS.
HE'S RICH IN EXPERIENCE.
HEH HEH HEH!
YOU'VE GROWN AN EYE...
...ON THE BACK OF YOUR HEAD.
YOU AREN'T USED TO TAKAMI'S PASSES...
...BUT YOU "SAW" ENOUGH TO BLOCK ONE.
ABOUT 80 PERCENT, I'D SAY.
SO YOU MUST BE ABLE TO SEE...
...100 PERCENT OF MY PASSES, RIGHT?

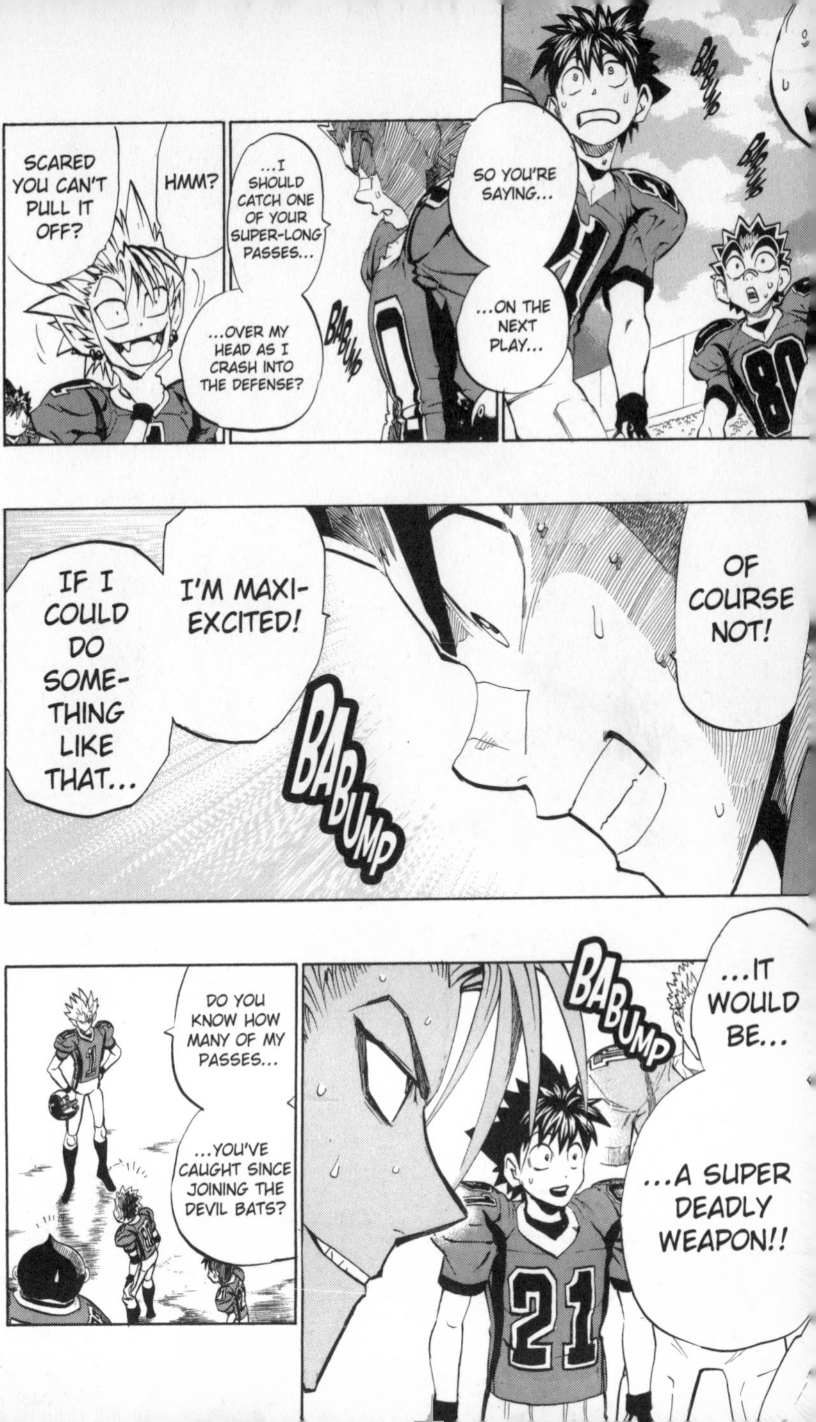
BABUMP
BABUMP
SO YOU'RE SAYING...
...ON THE NEXT PLAY...
...I SHOULD CATCH ONE OF YOUR SUPER-LONG PASSES...
...OVER MY HEAD AS I CRASH INTO THE DEFENSE?
BABUMP
HMM?
SCARED YOU CAN'T PULL IT OFF?
OF COURSE NOT!
I'M MAXI-EXCITED!
IF I COULD DO SOME-THING LIKE THAT...
BABUMP
...IT WOULD BE...
BABUMP
...A SUPER DEADLY WEAPON!!
DO YOU KNOW HOW MANY OF MY PASSES...
...YOU'VE CAUGHT SINCE JOINING THE DEVIL BATS?

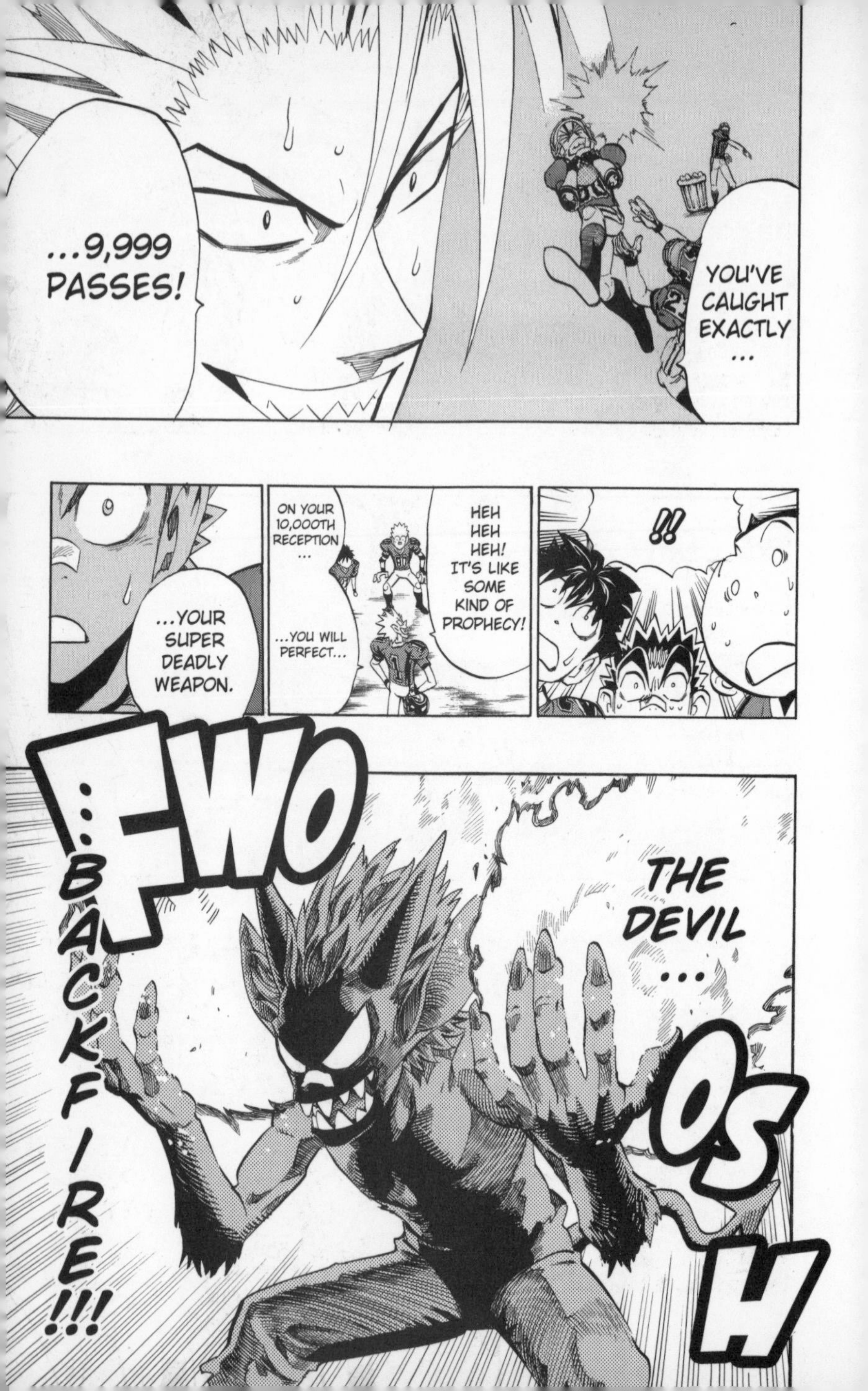
YOU'VE CAUGHT EXACTLY ...
...9,999 PASSES!
!!
HEH HEH HEH! IT'S LIKE SOME KIND OF PROPHECY!
ON YOUR 10,000TH RECEPTION ...
...YOU WILL PERFECT...
...YOUR SUPER DEADLY WEAPON.
THE DEVIL ...
FWOOSH
...BACKFIRE!!!

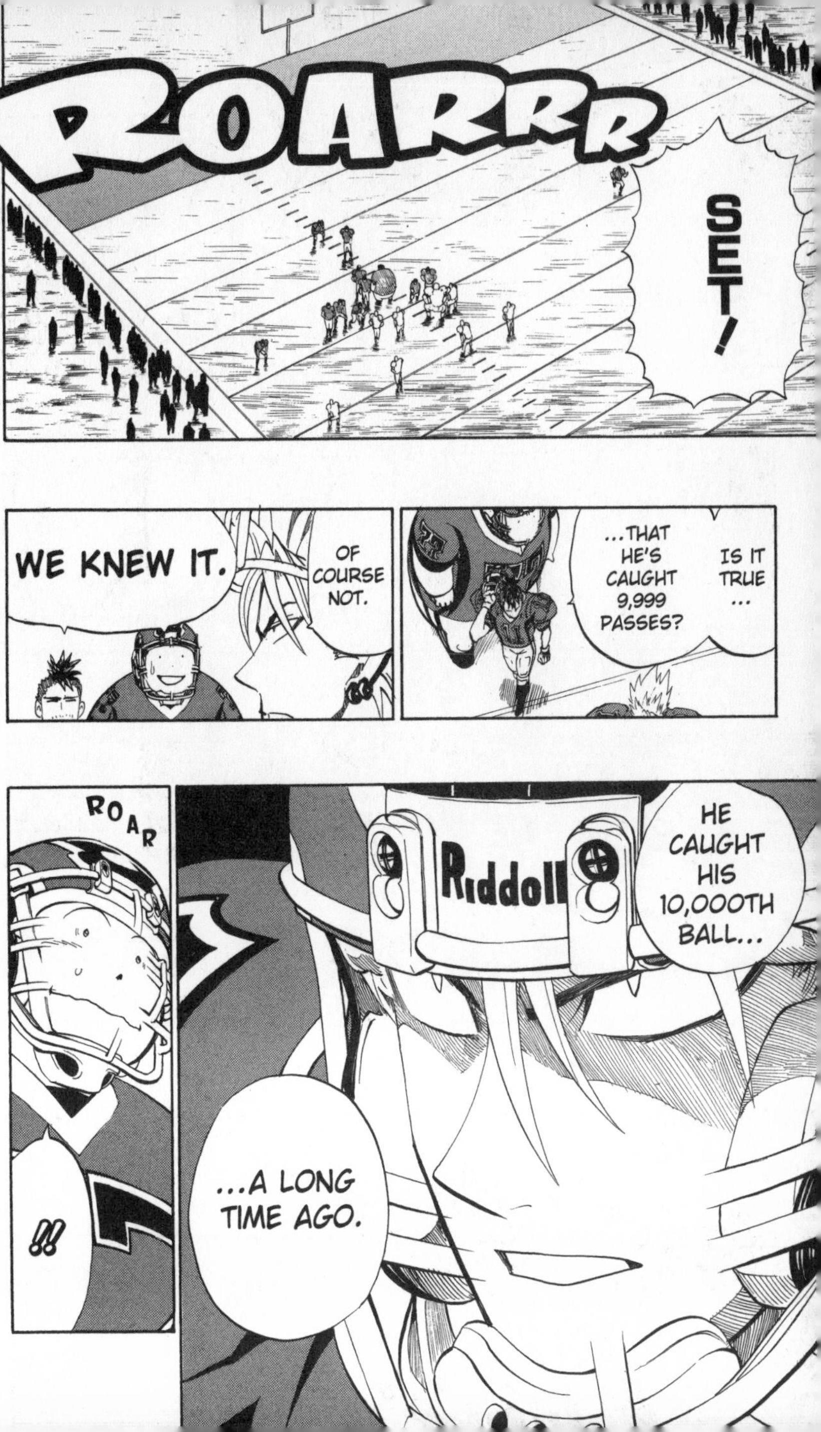
ROARRR
SET!
IS IT TRUE ...
...THAT HE'S CAUGHT 9,999 PASSES?
OF COURSE NOT.
WE KNEW IT.
Riddoll
HE CAUGHT HIS 10,000TH BALL...
...A LONG TIME AGO.
ROAR
!!

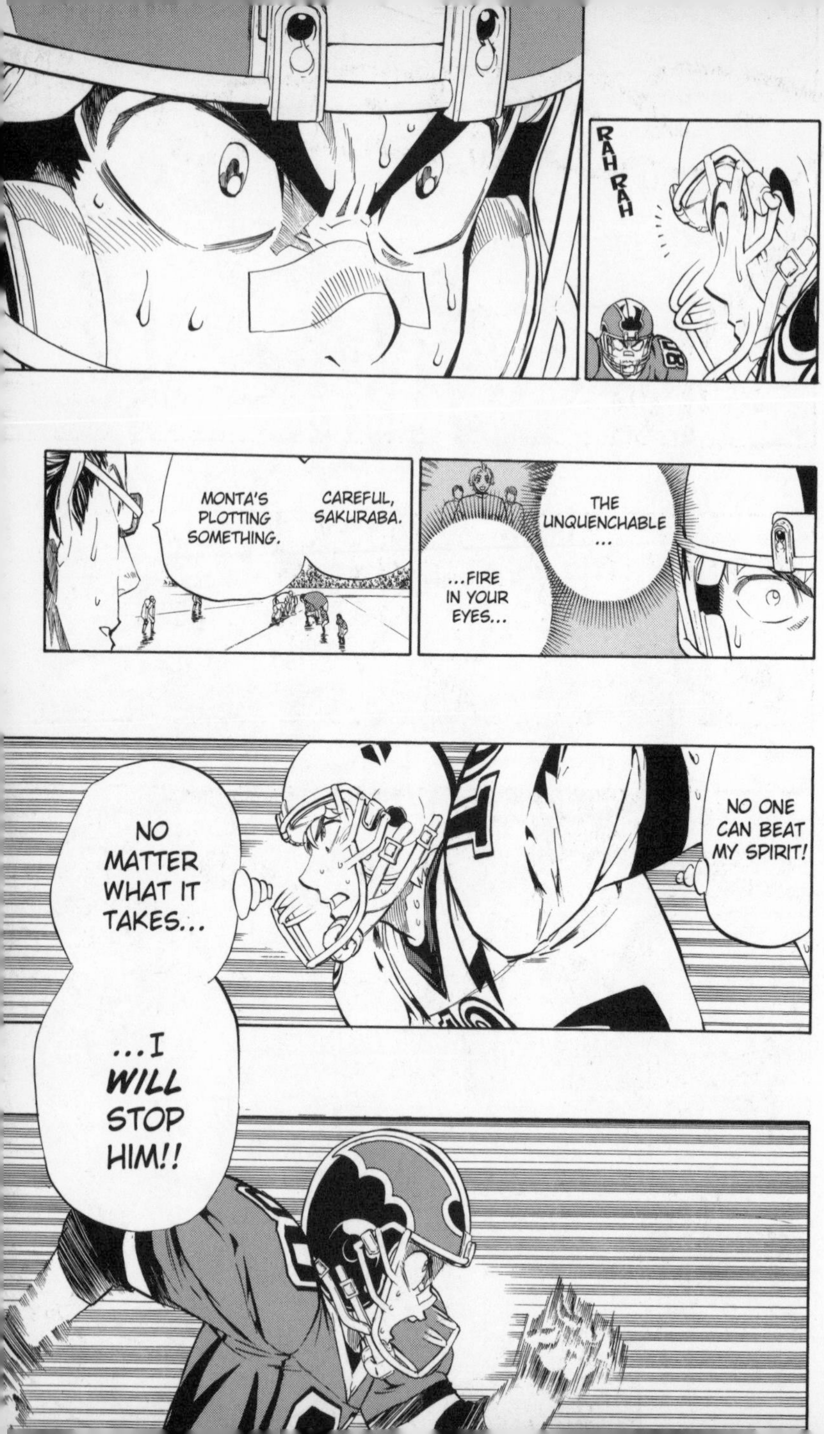
RAH RAH
THE UNQUENCHABLE...
...FIRE IN YOUR EYES...
CAREFUL, SAKURABA.
MONTA'S PLOTTING SOMETHING.
NO ONE CAN BEAT MY SPIRIT!
NO MATTER WHAT IT TAKES...
...I WILL STOP HIM!!

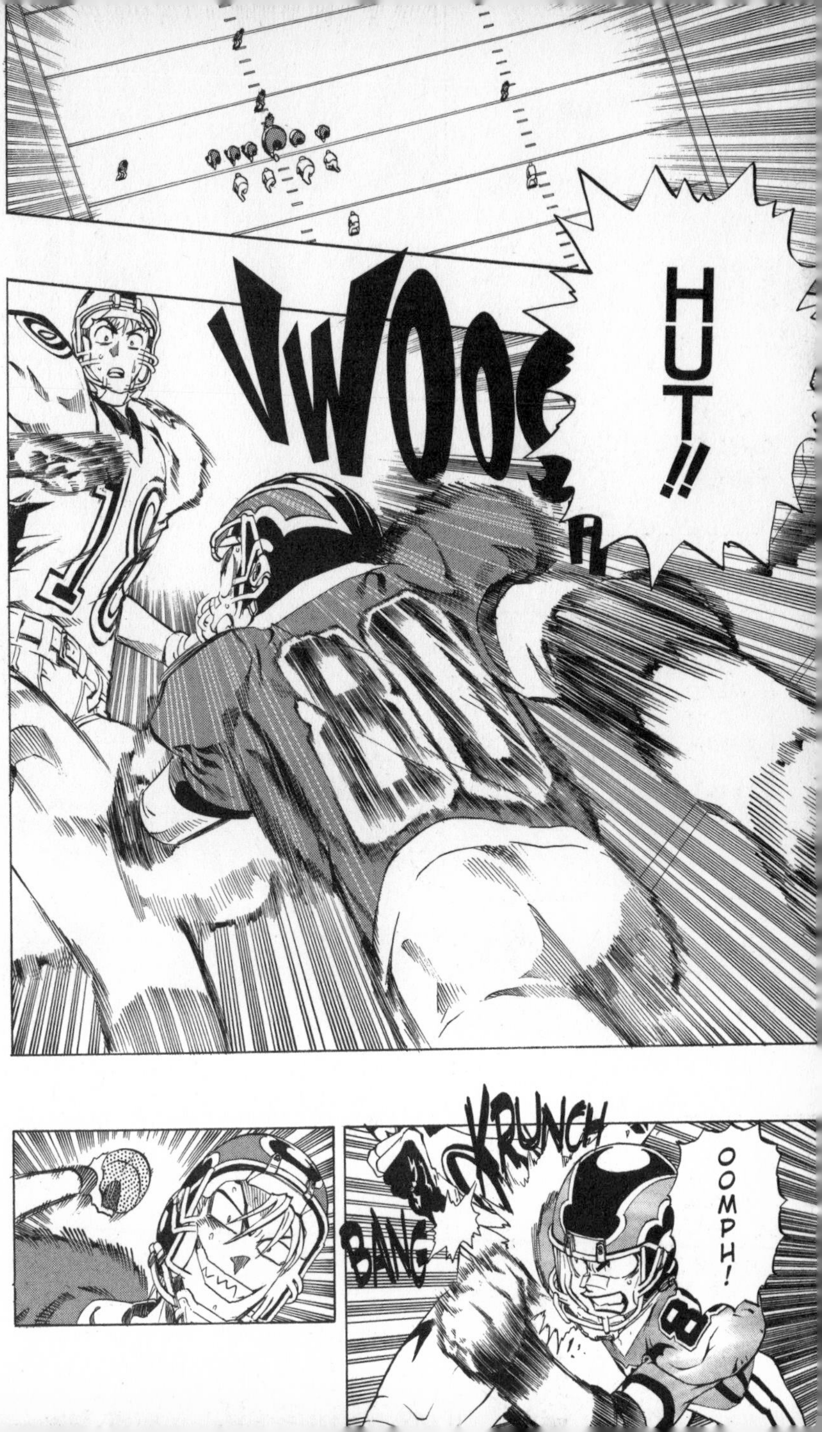
HUT!!
VWOOSH
KRUNCH
OOMPH!
BANG

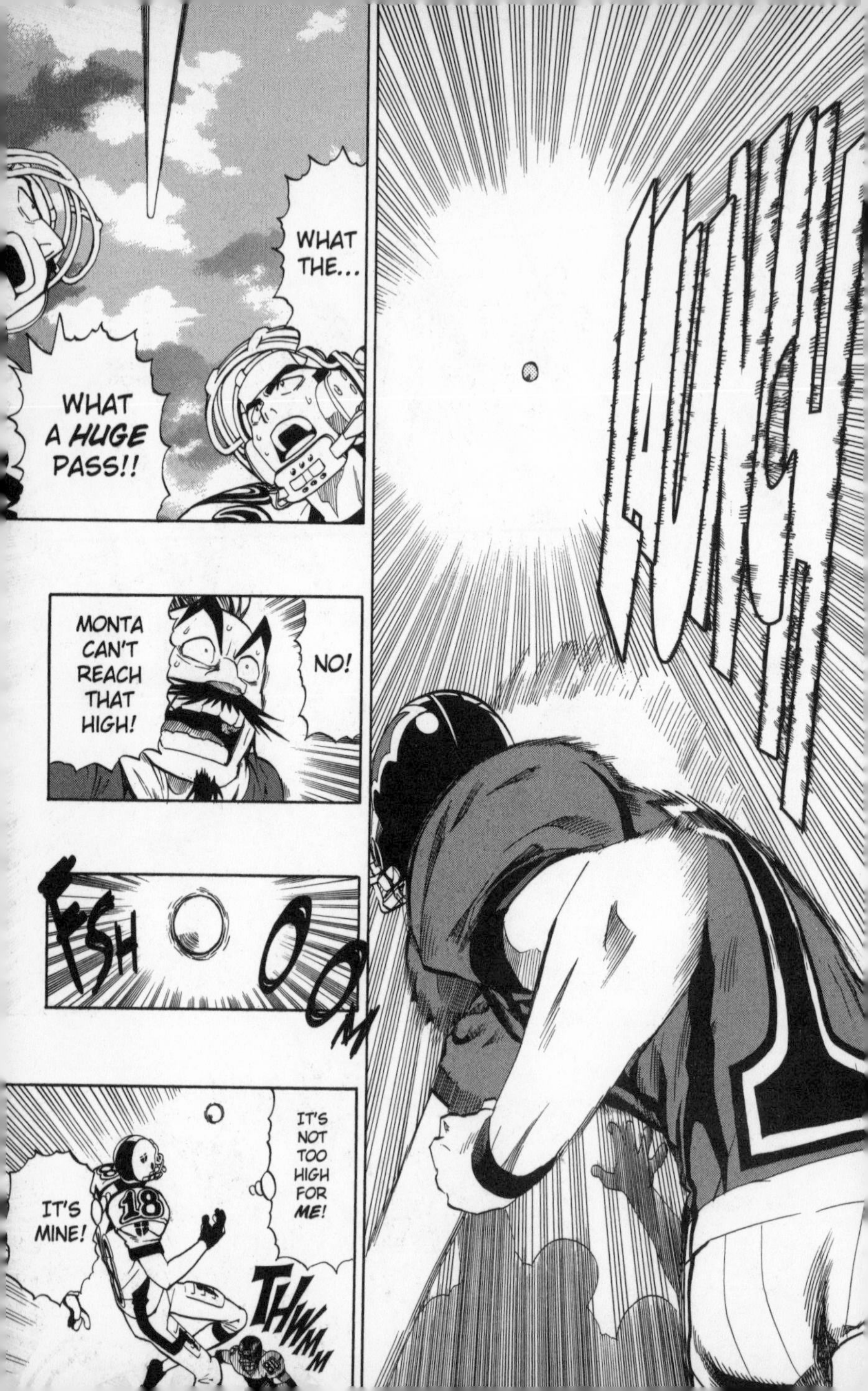
WHAT THE...
WHAT A HUGE PASS!!
NO!
MONTA CAN'T REACH THAT HIGH!
FSH OOOM
IT'S NOT TOO HIGH FOR ME!
IT'S MINE!
THWMM

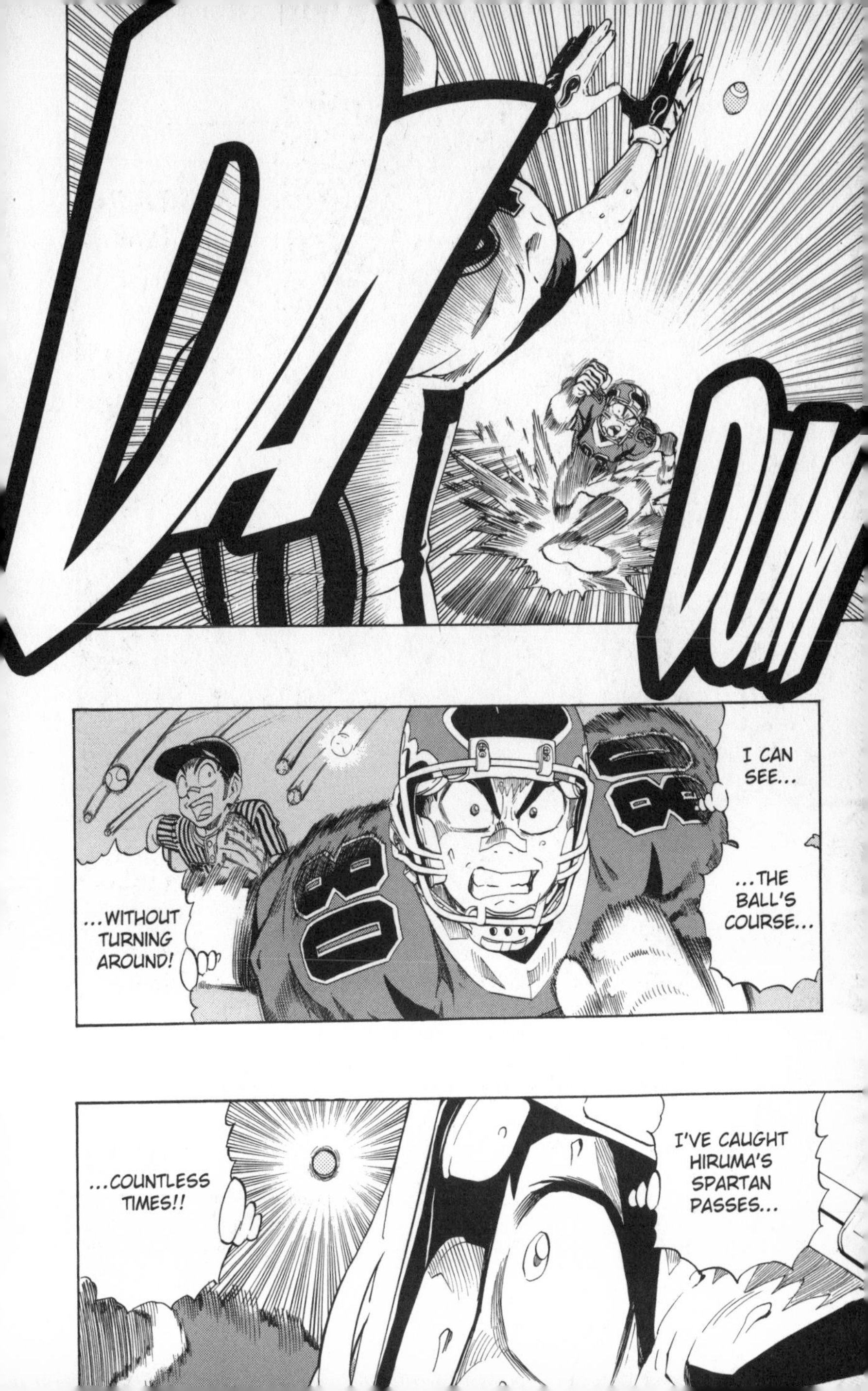
I CAN SEE...
...THE BALL'S COURSE...
...WITHOUT TURNING AROUND!
I'VE CAUGHT HIRUMA'S SPARTAN PASSES...
...COUNTLESS TIMES!!

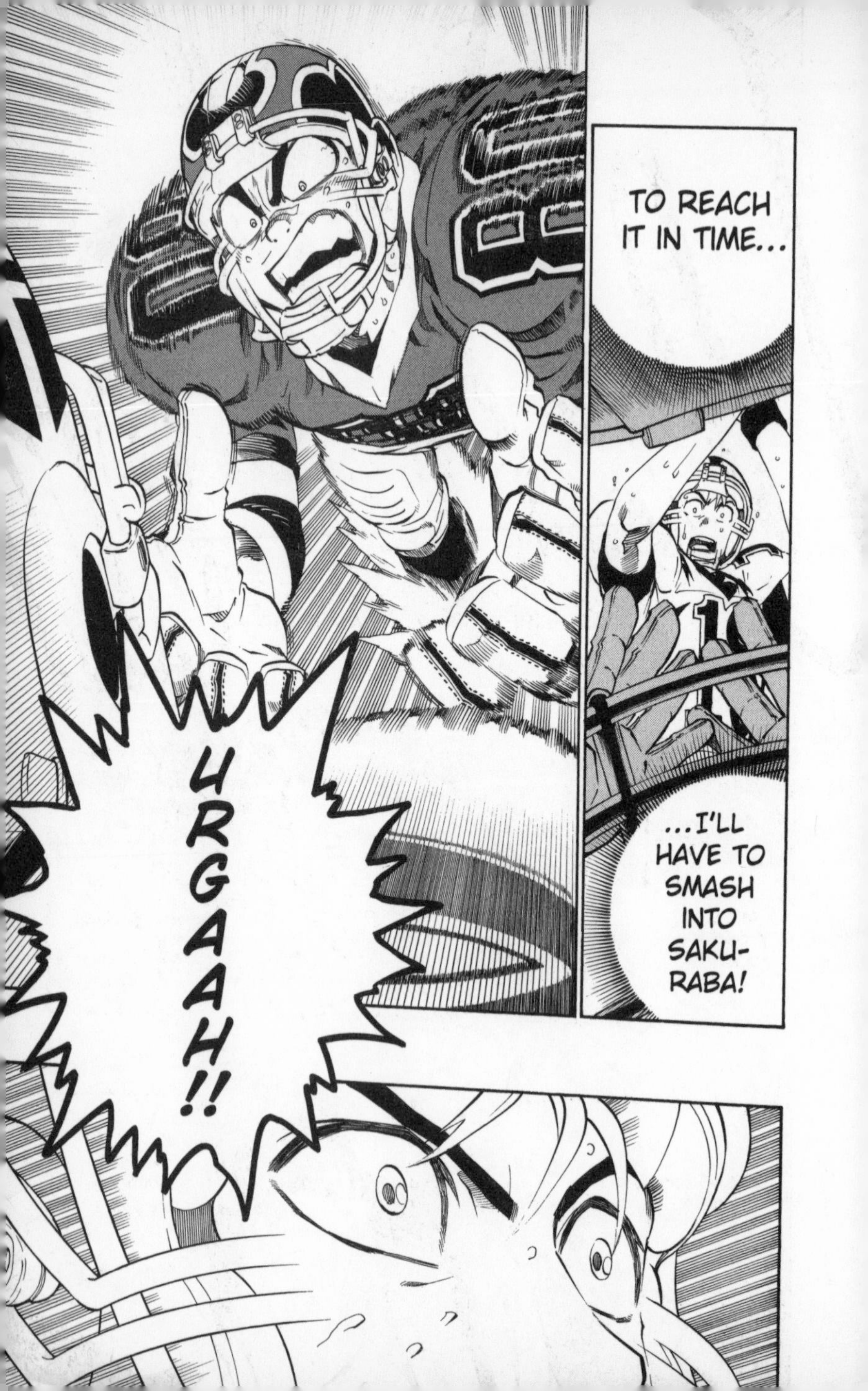
TO REACH IT IN TIME...
...I'LL HAVE TO SMASH INTO SAKU-RABA!
URGAAAH!!

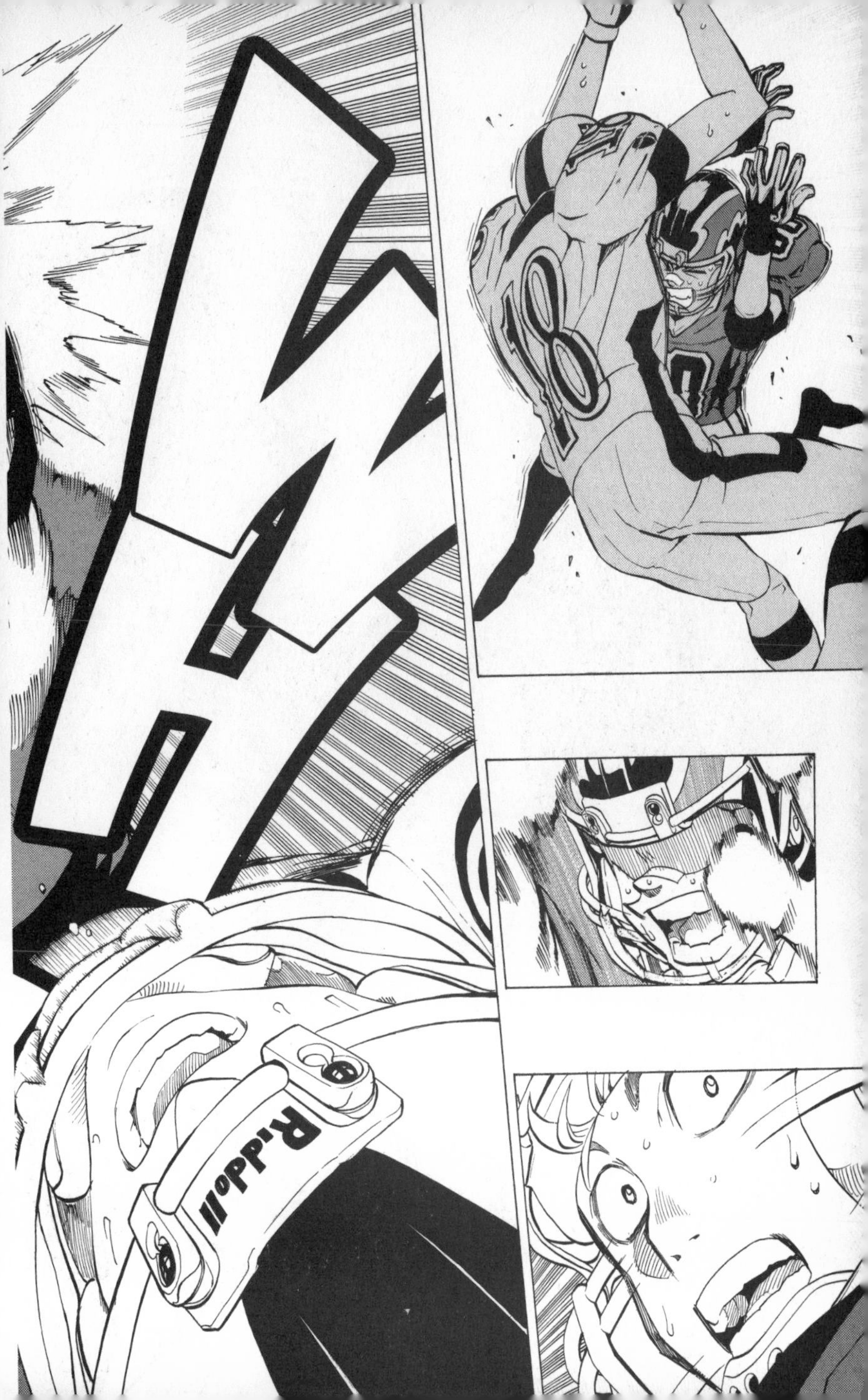
Riddell

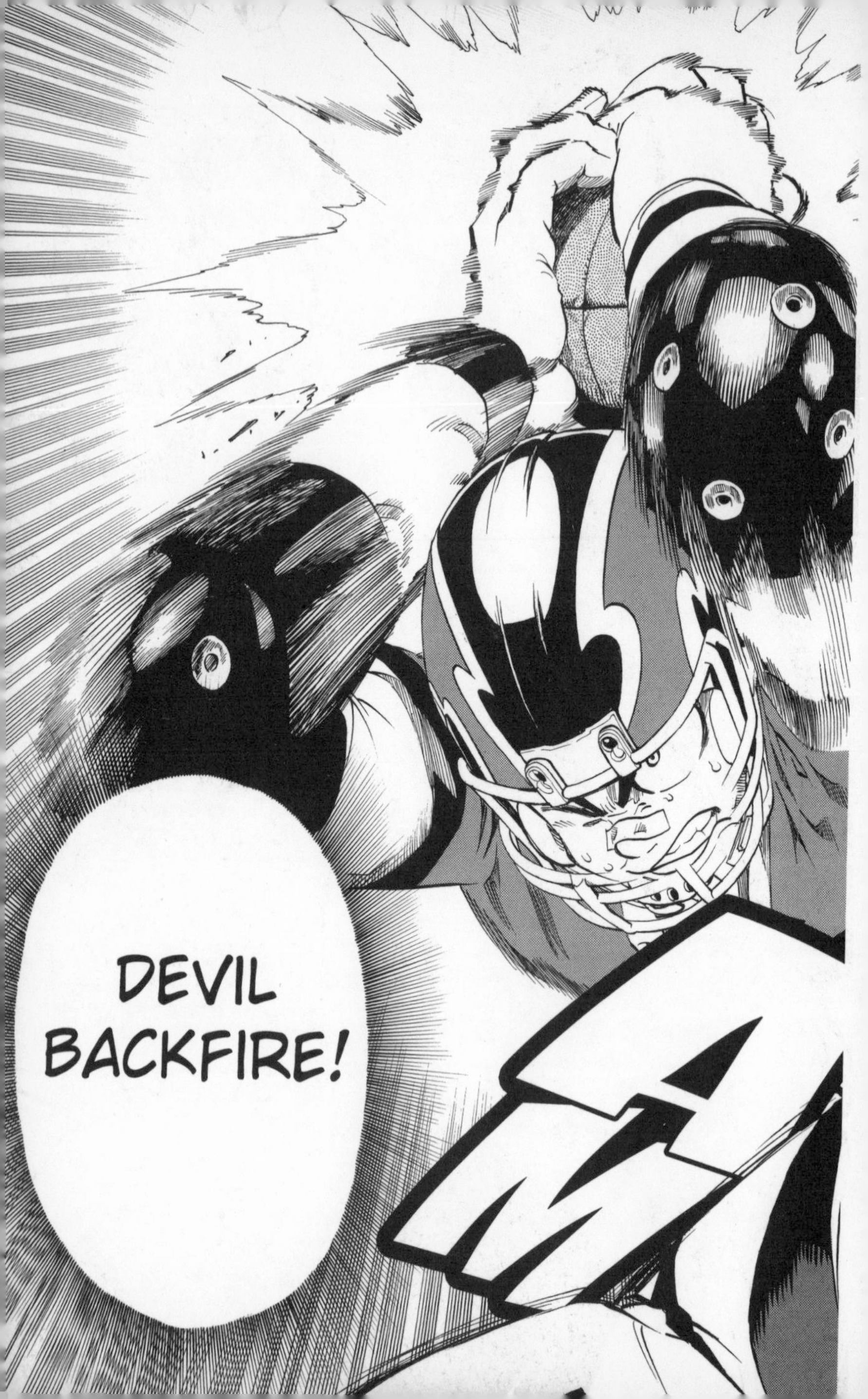
DEVIL BACKFIRE!

RIVAL BATTLE ★ DEIMON VS. OJO

SUPER MISCELLANY MATCH-UPS!!

SENA

VS.

SHIN

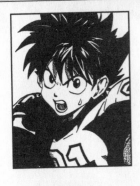

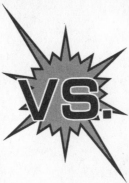

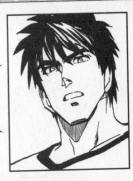

SENA		SHIN
	SCHOOL GRADES	WIN
	COOKING SKILL	WIN
WIN	CONVERSATIONAL SKILL	
	WAKING UP EARLY/ GOING TO BED EARLY	WIN
WIN	NUMBER OF MANGA OWNED	
WIN	REPEATED LATERAL JUMP	
	NEITHER ONE FIGHTS, BUT IF THEY DID, WHO WOULD WIN?	WIN

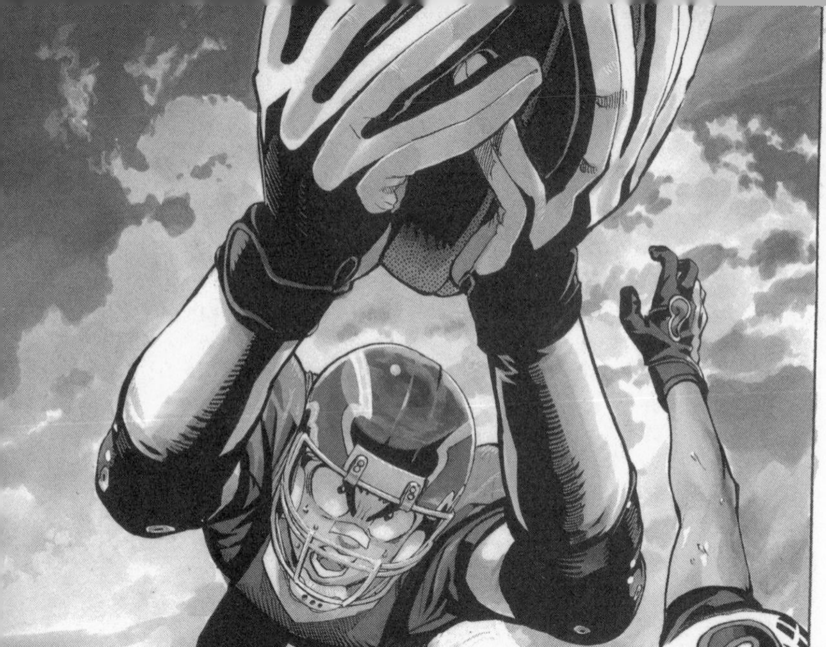

Chapter 226 Fire Starter

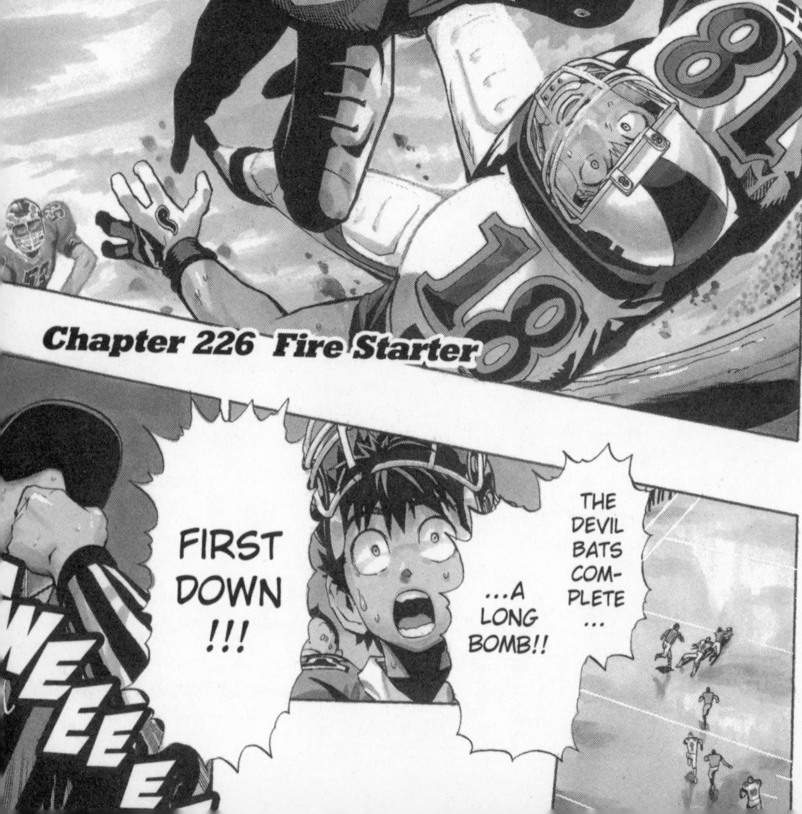
THE DEVIL BATS COMPLETE...
...A LONG BOMB!!
FIRST DOWN!!!
WEEEEE

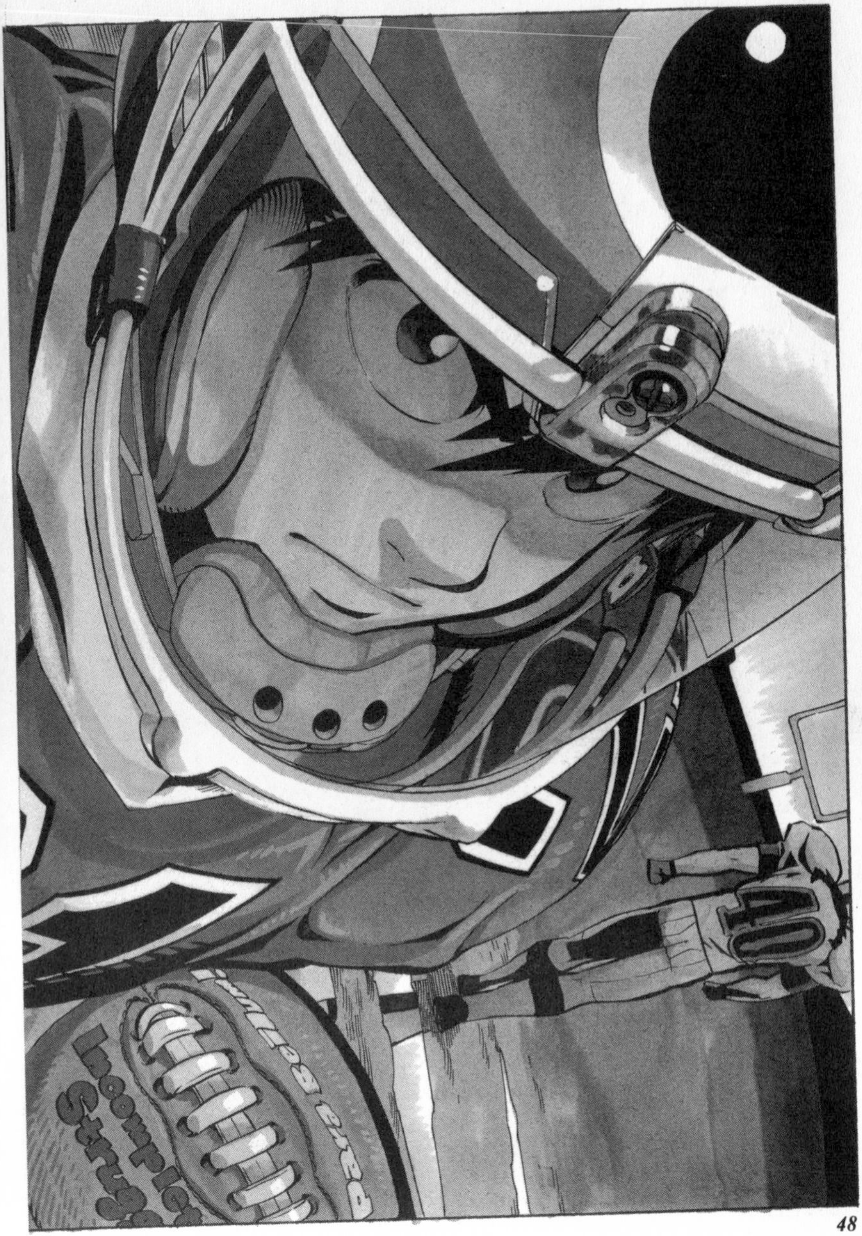

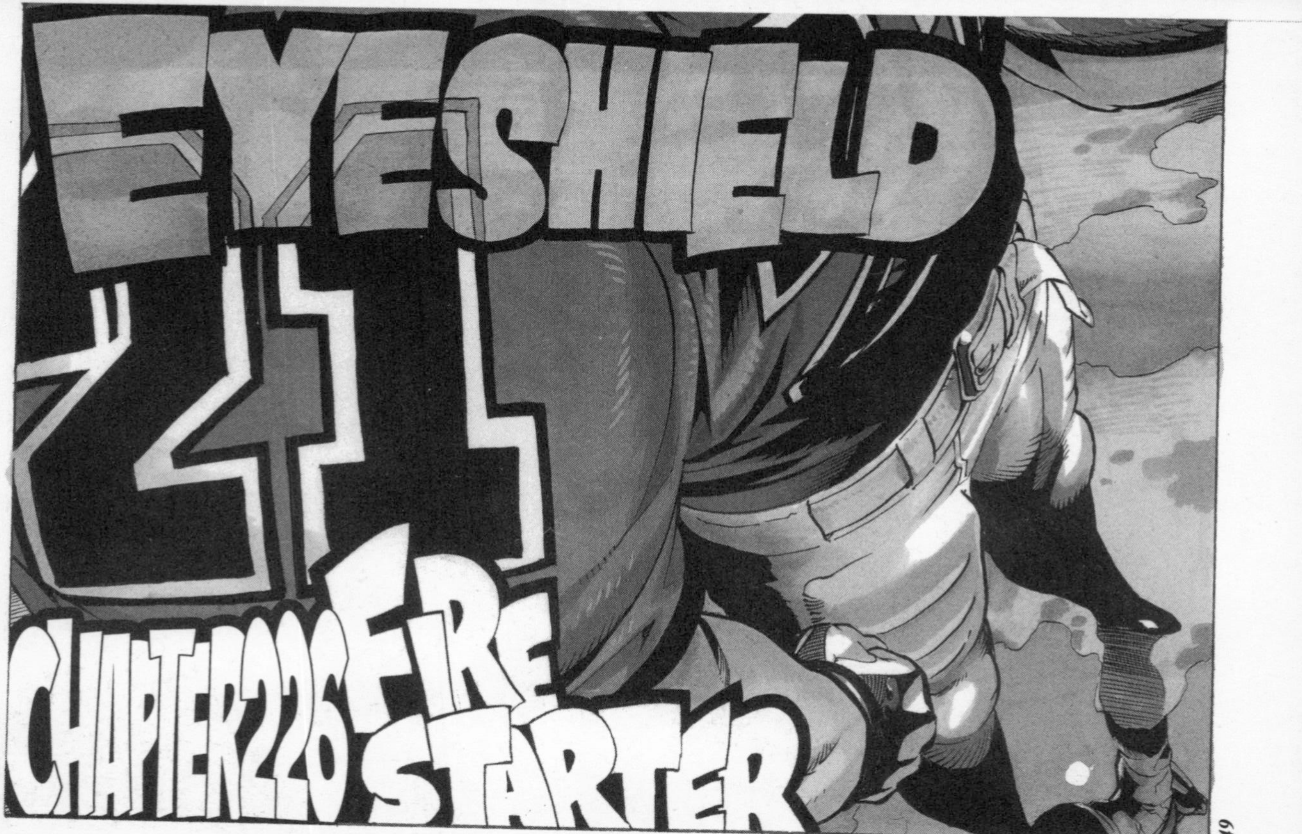
EYESHIELD 21
CHAPTER 226 FIRE STARTER

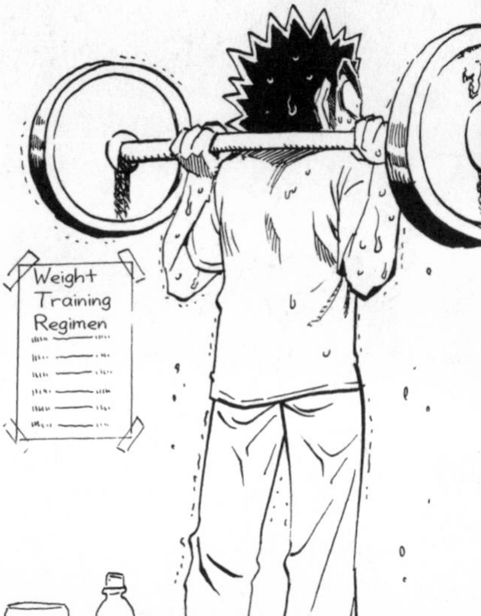
Weight Training Regimen

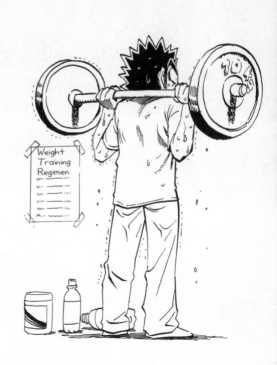

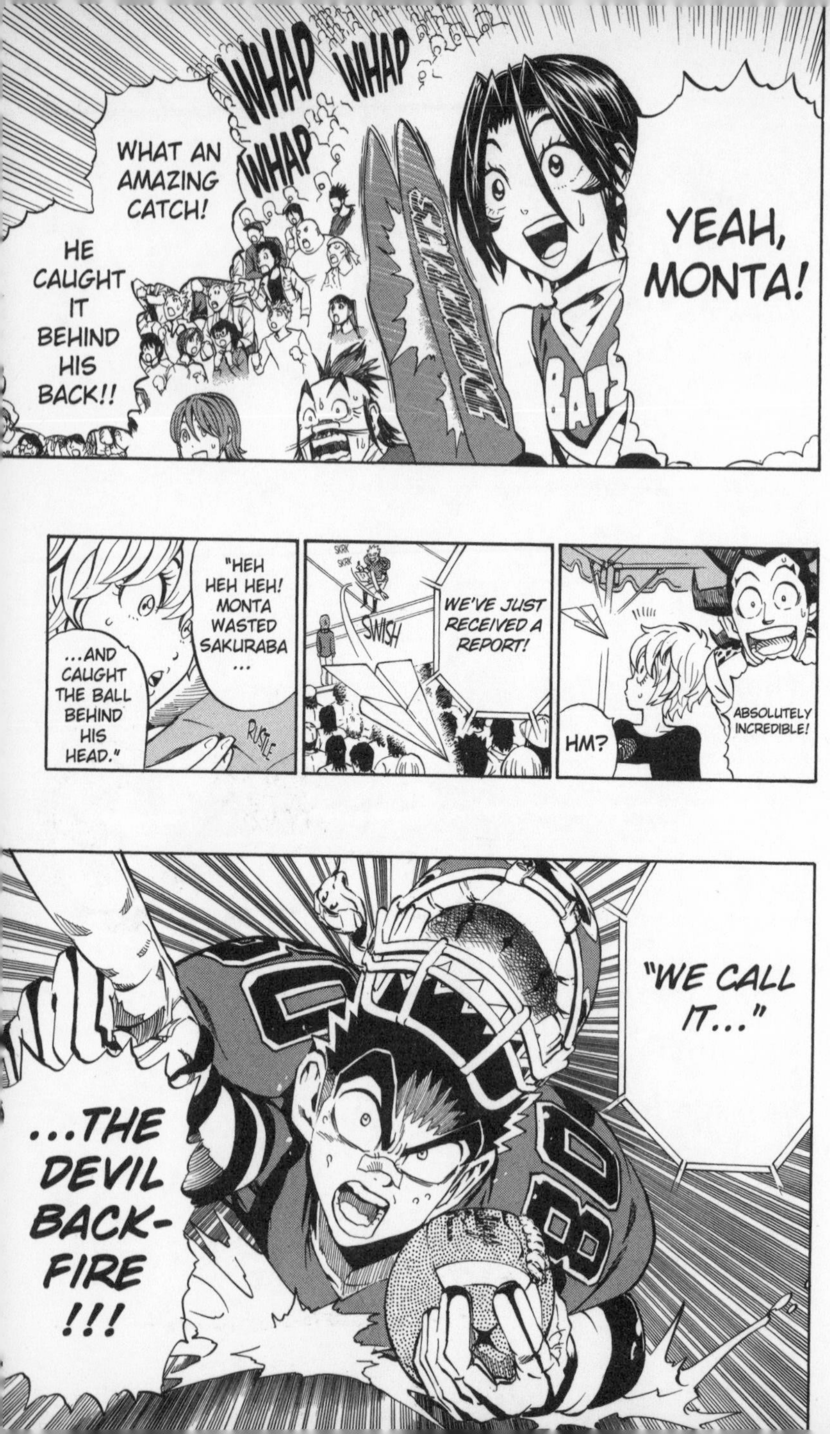
YEAH, MONTA!
WHAP WHAP
WHAP WHAP
WHAT AN AMAZING CATCH!
HE CAUGHT IT BEHIND HIS BACK!!
ABSOLUTELY INCREDIBLE!
HM?
SKRK SKRK
WE'VE JUST RECEIVED A REPORT!
SWISH
"HEH HEH HEH! MONTA WASTED SAKURABA ...
...AND CAUGHT THE BALL BEHIND HIS HEAD."
RUSTLE
"WE CALL IT..."
...THE DEVIL BACK-FIRE!!!

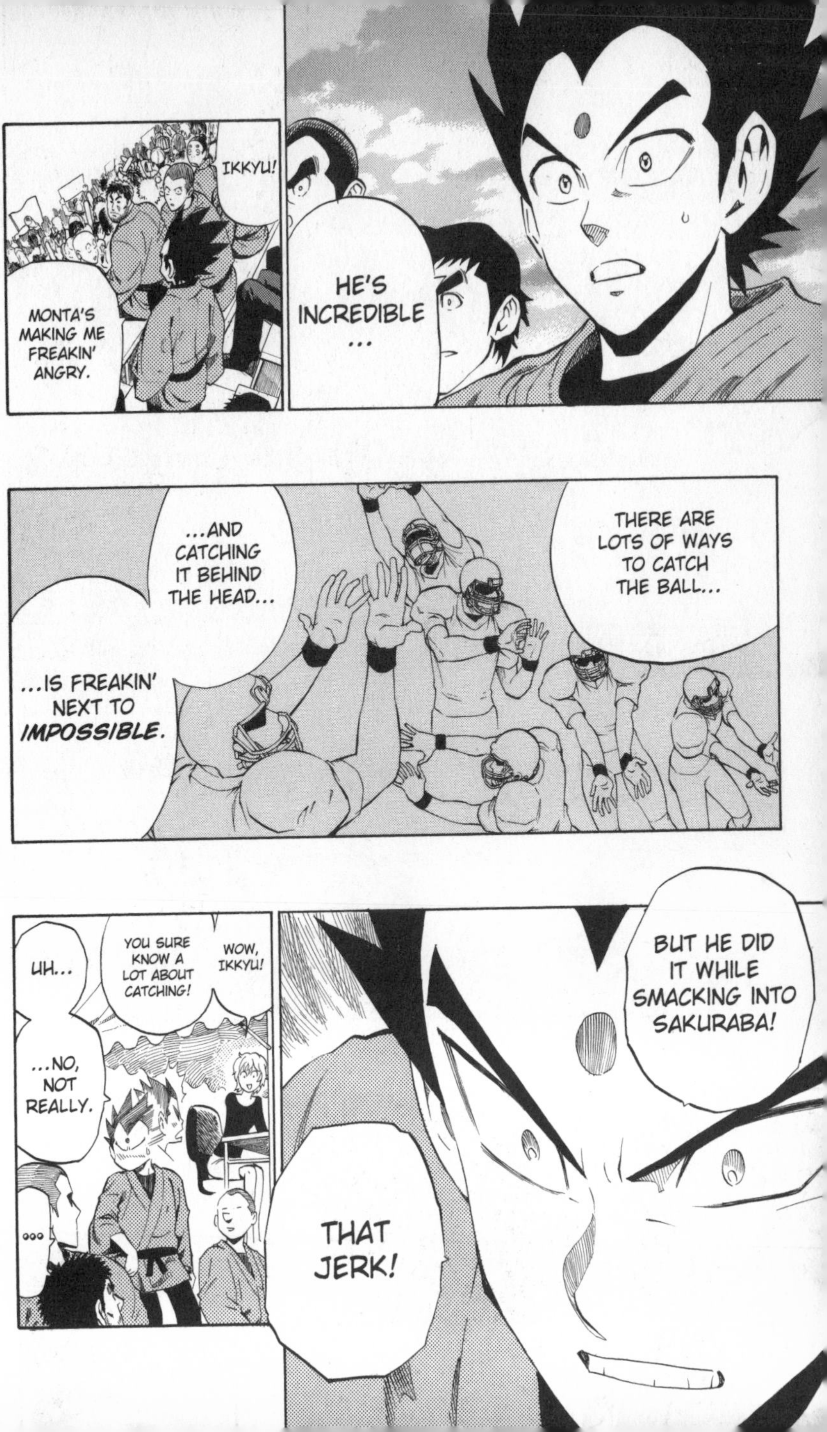
HE'S INCREDIBLE ...
IKKYU!
MONTA'S MAKING ME FREAKIN' ANGRY.
THERE ARE LOTS OF WAYS TO CATCH THE BALL...
...AND CATCHING IT BEHIND THE HEAD...
...IS FREAKIN' NEXT TO *IMPOSSIBLE*.
BUT HE DID IT WHILE SMACKING INTO SAKURABA!
THAT JERK!
WOW, IKKYU!
YOU SURE KNOW A LOT ABOUT CATCHING!
UH...
...NO, NOT REALLY.

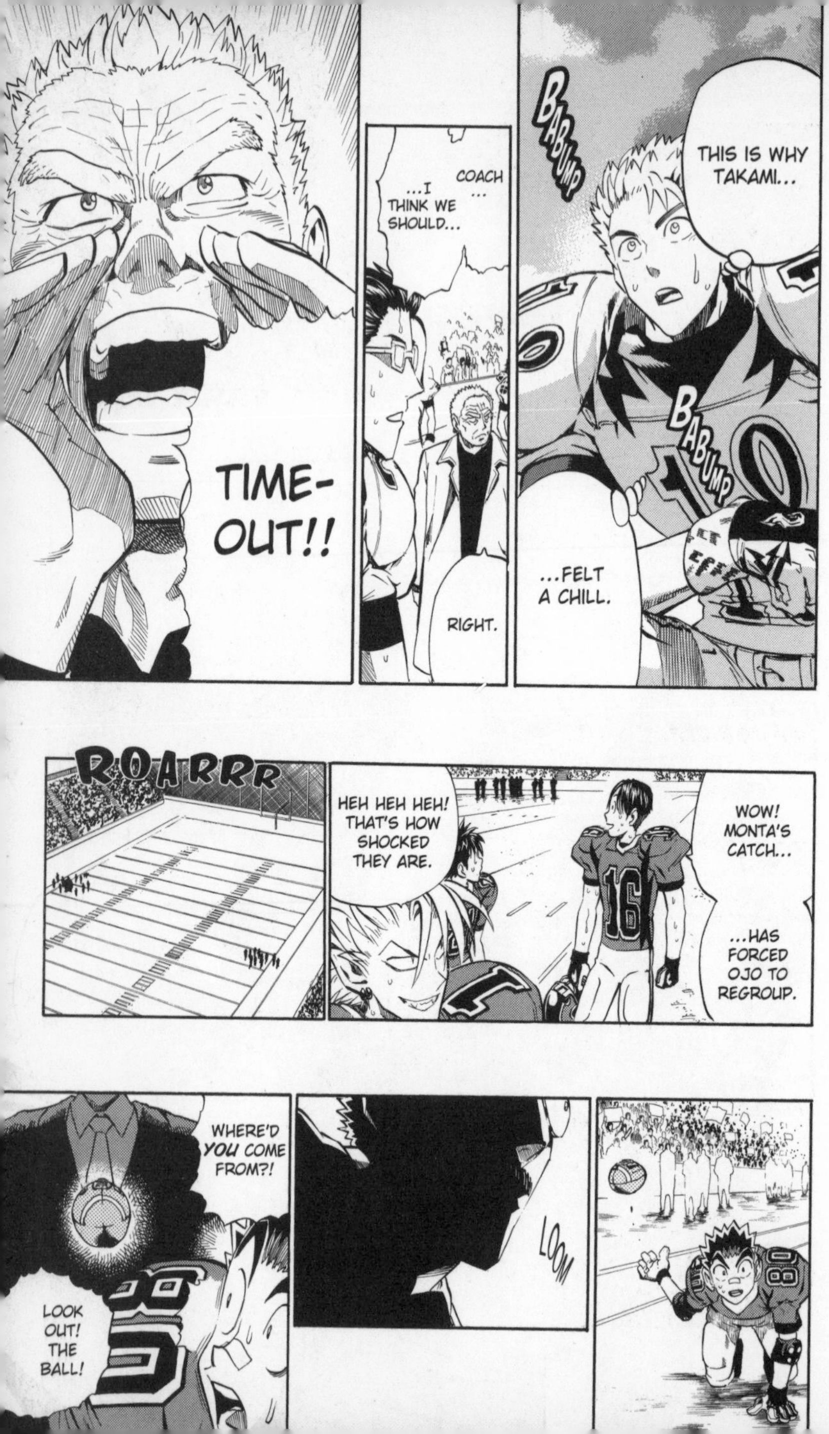
THIS IS WHY TAKAMI...
BABUMP
BABUMP
...FELT A CHILL.
COACH...
...I THINK WE SHOULD...
RIGHT.
TIME-OUT!!
WOW! MONTA'S CATCH...
...HAS FORCED OJO TO REGROUP.
HEH HEH HEH! THAT'S HOW SHOCKED THEY ARE.
ROARRR
LOOM
WHERE'D *YOU* COME FROM?!
LOOK OUT! THE BALL!

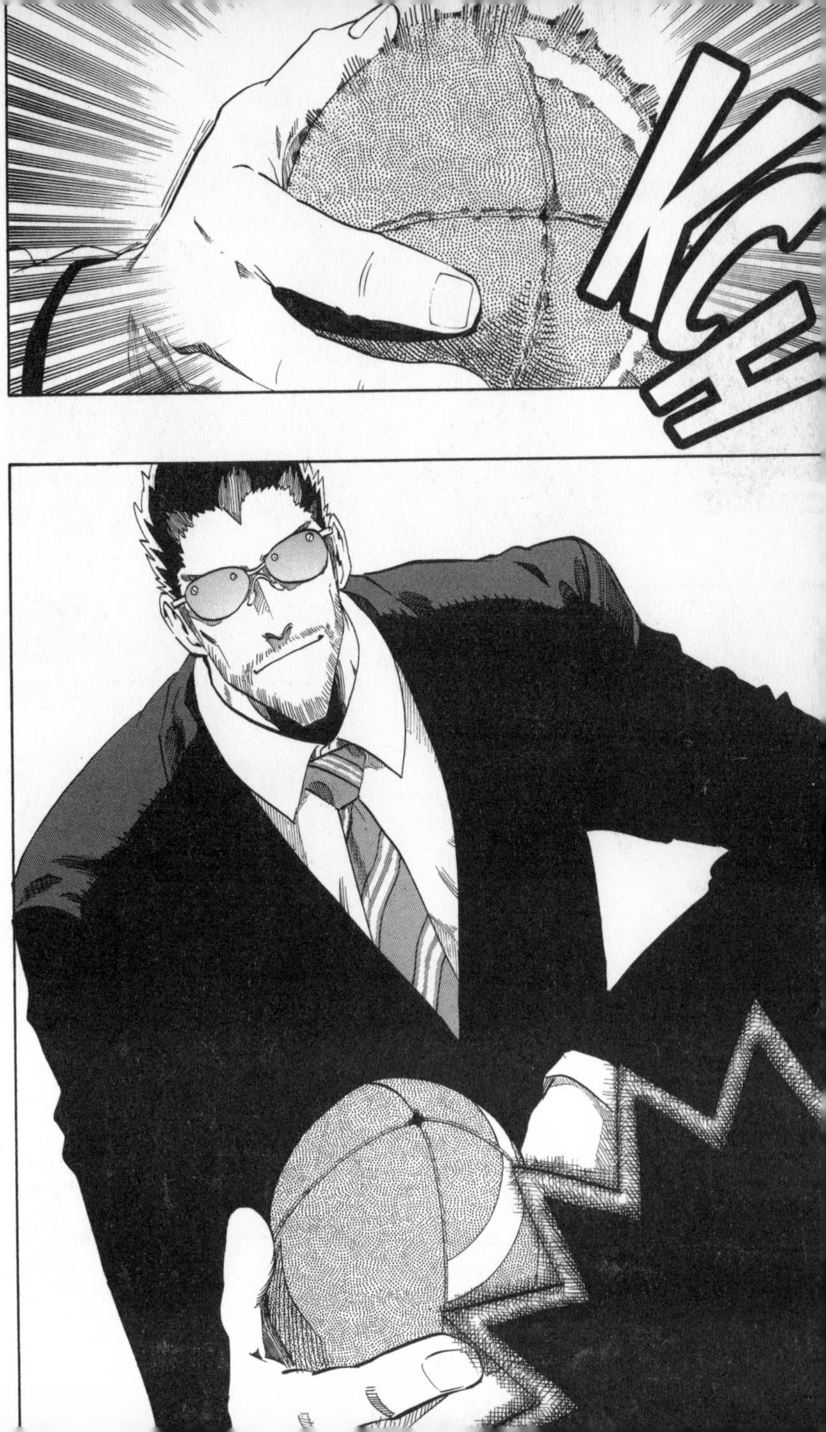
KCH!

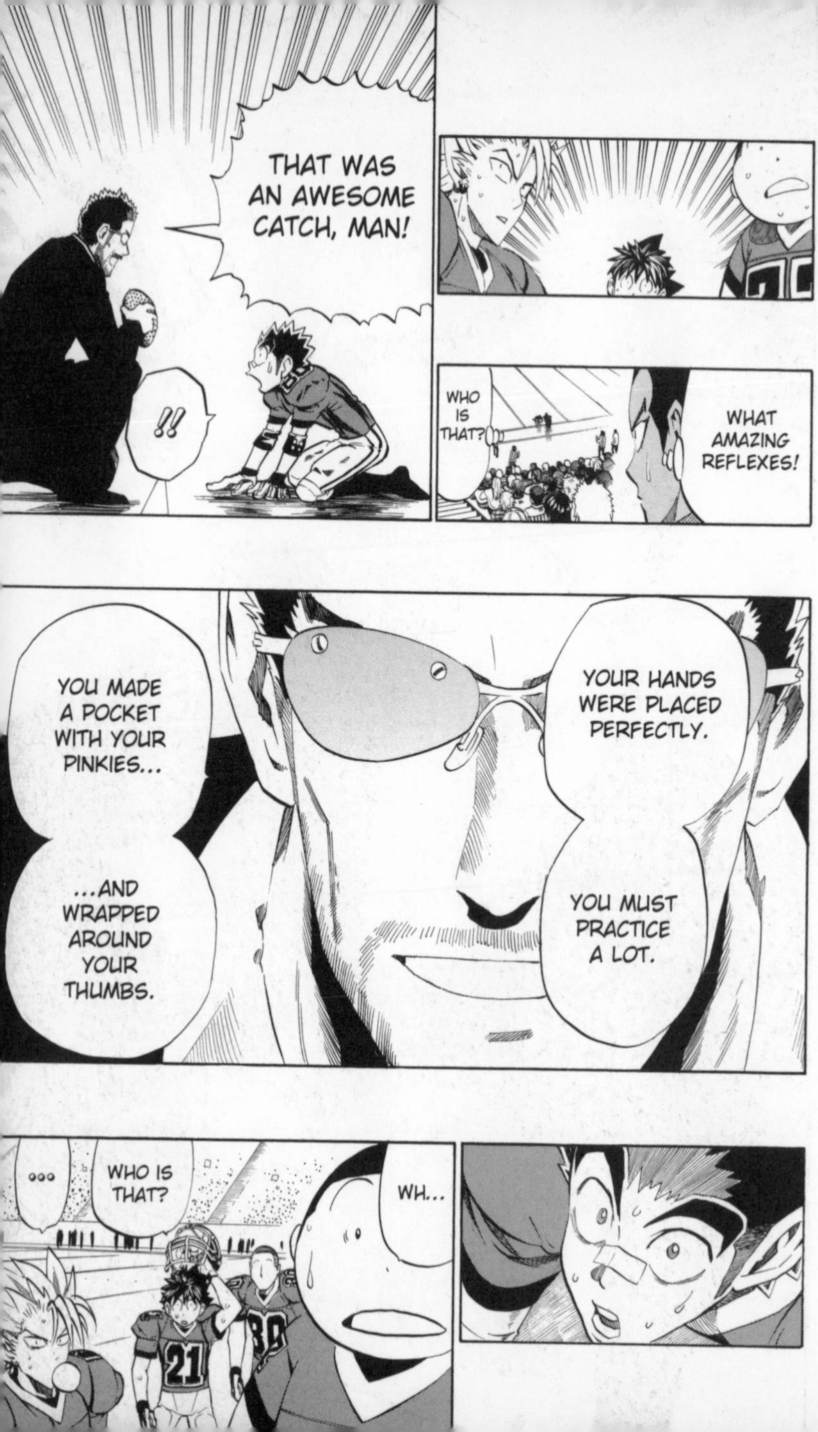
WHAT AMAZING REFLEXES!
WHO IS THAT?
THAT WAS AN AWESOME CATCH, MAN!
!!
YOUR HANDS WERE PLACED PERFECTLY.
YOU MUST PRACTICE A LOT.
YOU MADE A POCKET WITH YOUR PINKIES...
...AND WRAPPED AROUND YOUR THUMBS.
WH...
WHO IS THAT?
...

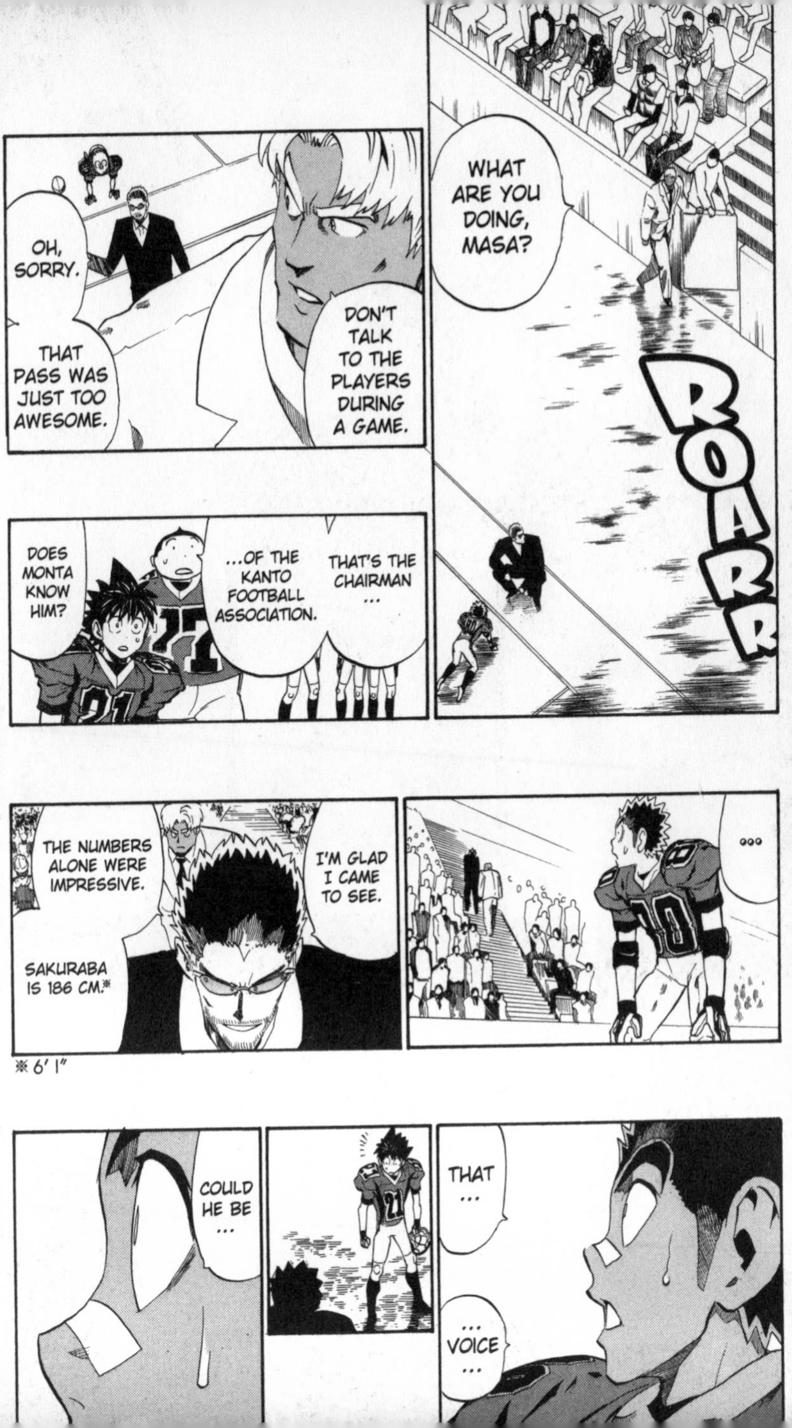
WHAT ARE YOU DOING, MASA?
ROARR
DON'T TALK TO THE PLAYERS DURING A GAME.
OH, SORRY.
THAT PASS WAS JUST TOO AWESOME.
THAT'S THE CHAIRMAN ...
...OF THE KANTO FOOTBALL ASSOCIATION.
DOES MONTA KNOW HIM?
...
I'M GLAD I CAME TO SEE.
THE NUMBERS ALONE WERE IMPRESSIVE.
SAKURABA IS 186 CM.※
※6' 1"
THAT ...
... VOICE ...
COULD HE BE ...

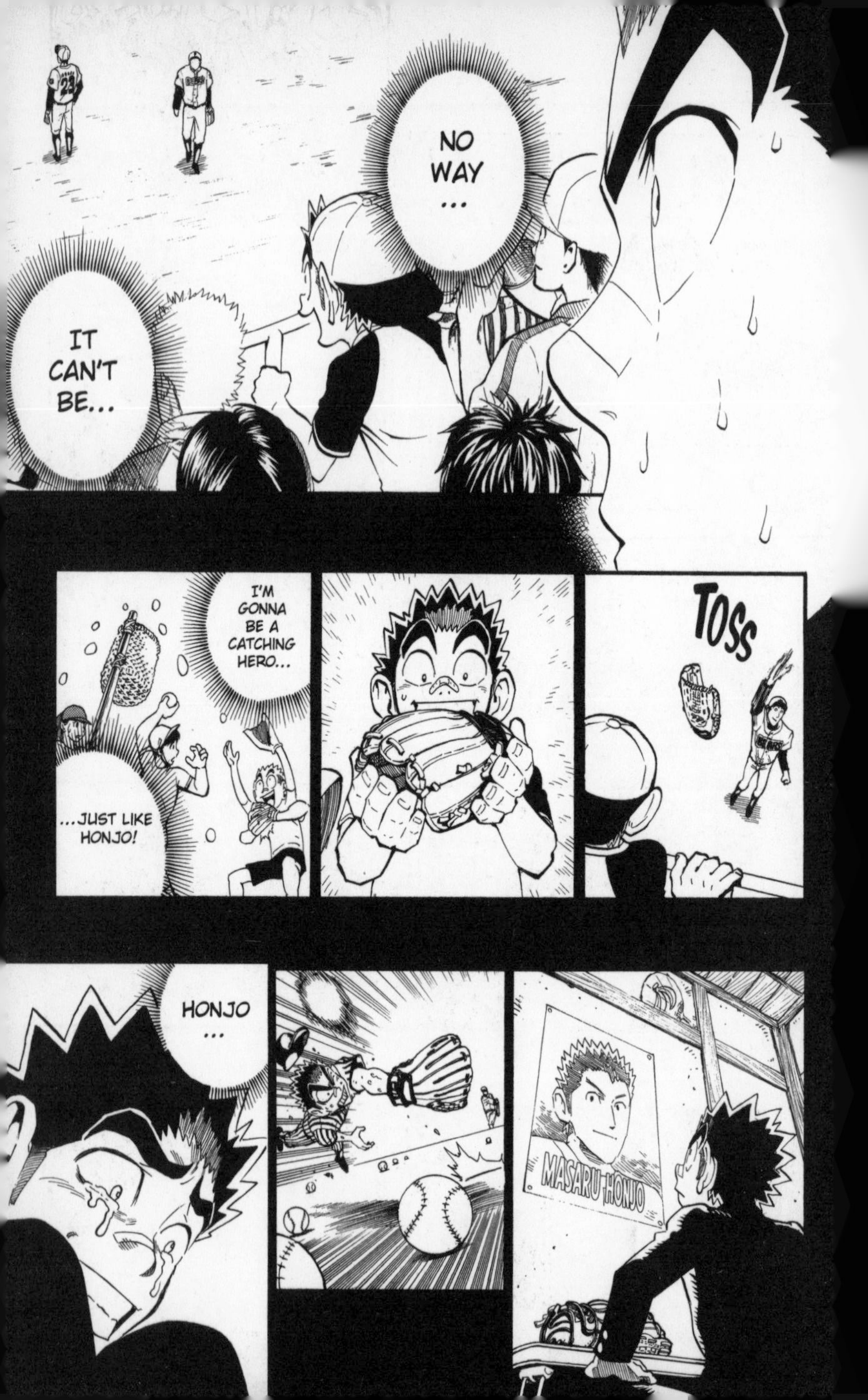
NO WAY...
IT CAN'T BE...
TOSS
I'M GONNA BE A CATCHING HERO...
...JUST LIKE HONJO!
MASARU HONJO
HONJO...

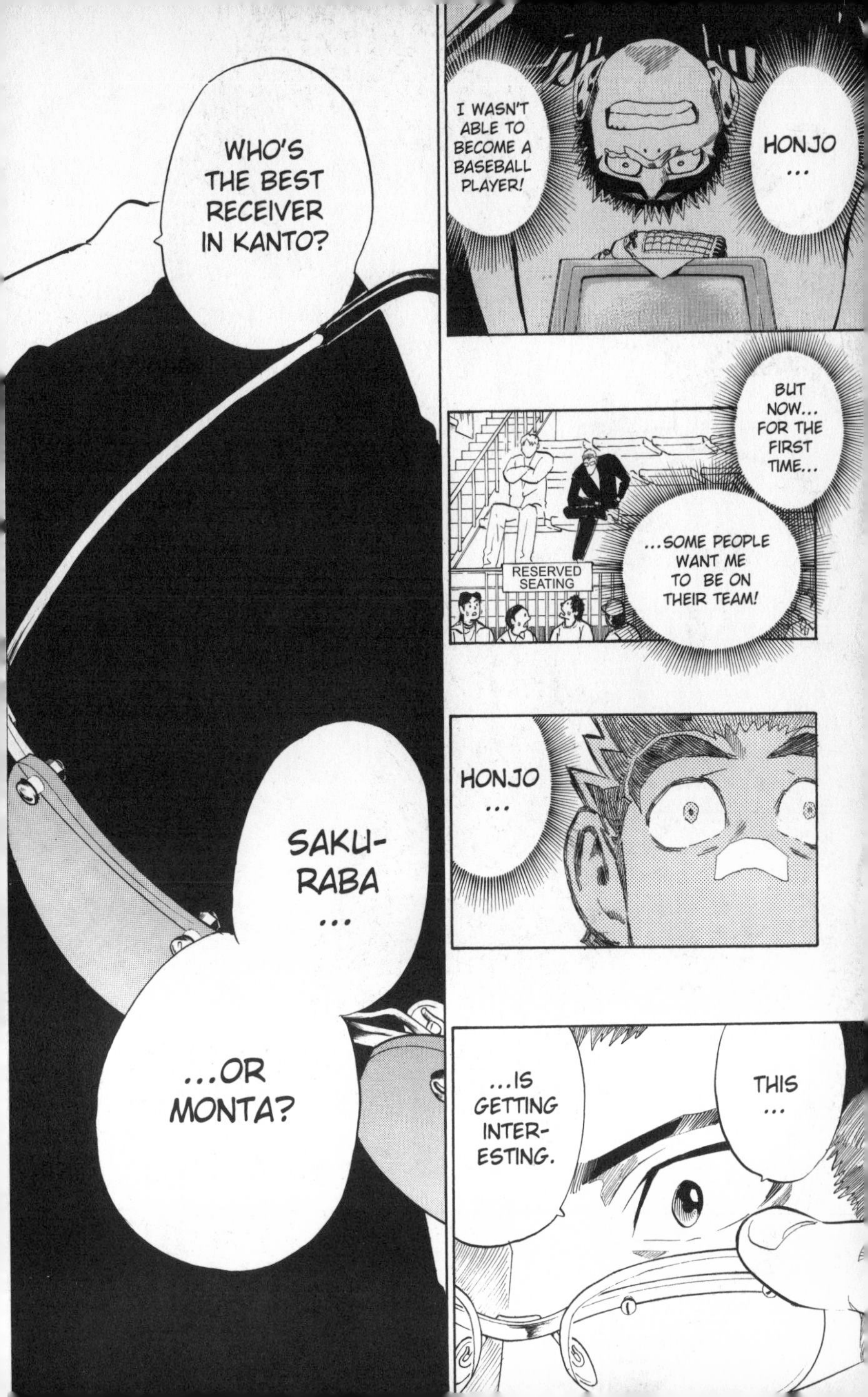
HONJO ...
I WASN'T ABLE TO BECOME A BASEBALL PLAYER!
BUT NOW... FOR THE FIRST TIME...
...SOME PEOPLE WANT ME TO BE ON THEIR TEAM!
RESERVED SEATING
HONJO ...
THIS ...
...IS GETTING INTER-ESTING.
WHO'S THE BEST RECEIVER IN KANTO?
SAKU-RABA ...
...OR MONTA?

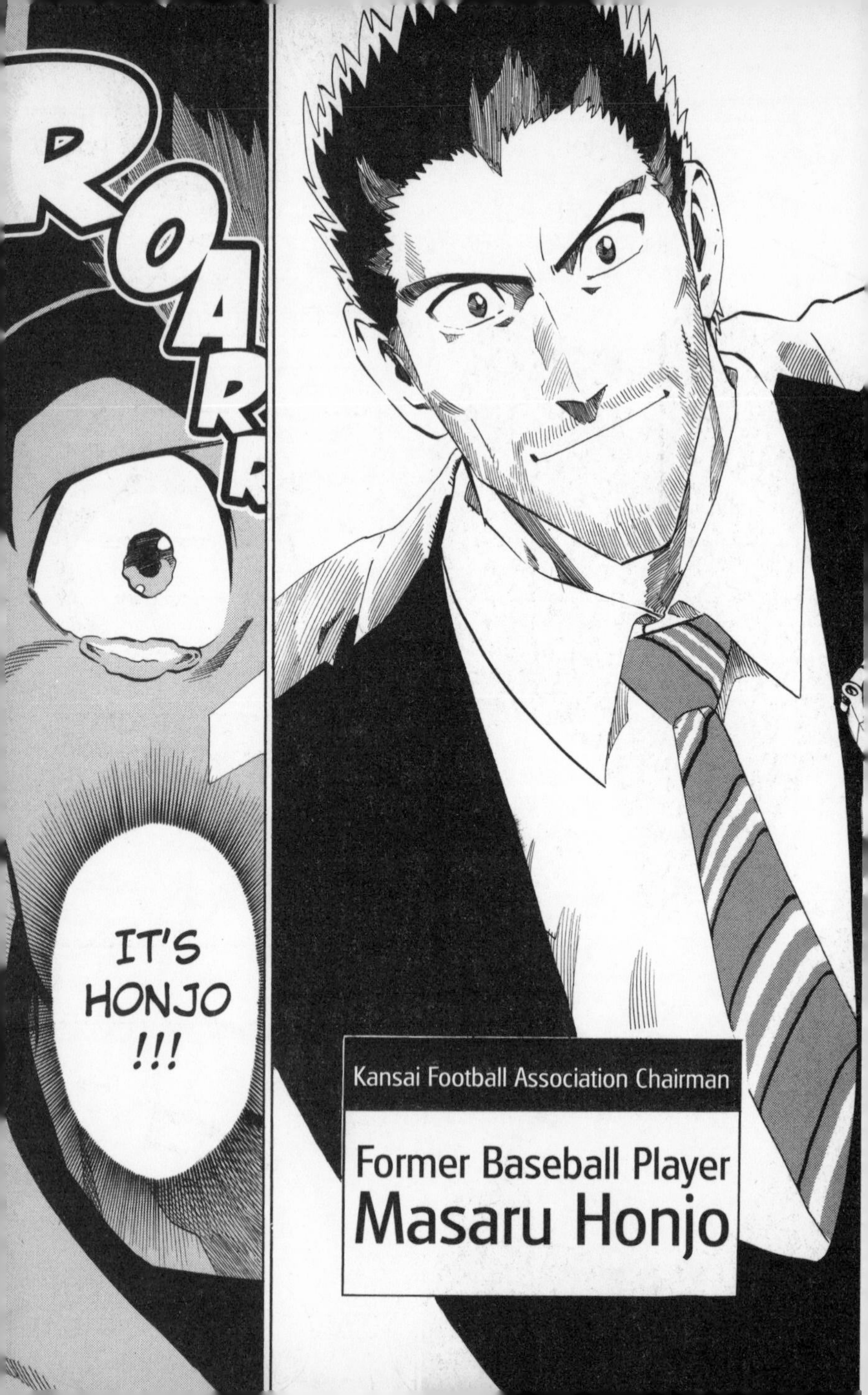
Kansai Football Association Chairman
Former Baseball Player
Masaru Honjo
ROARR
IT'S HONJO !!!

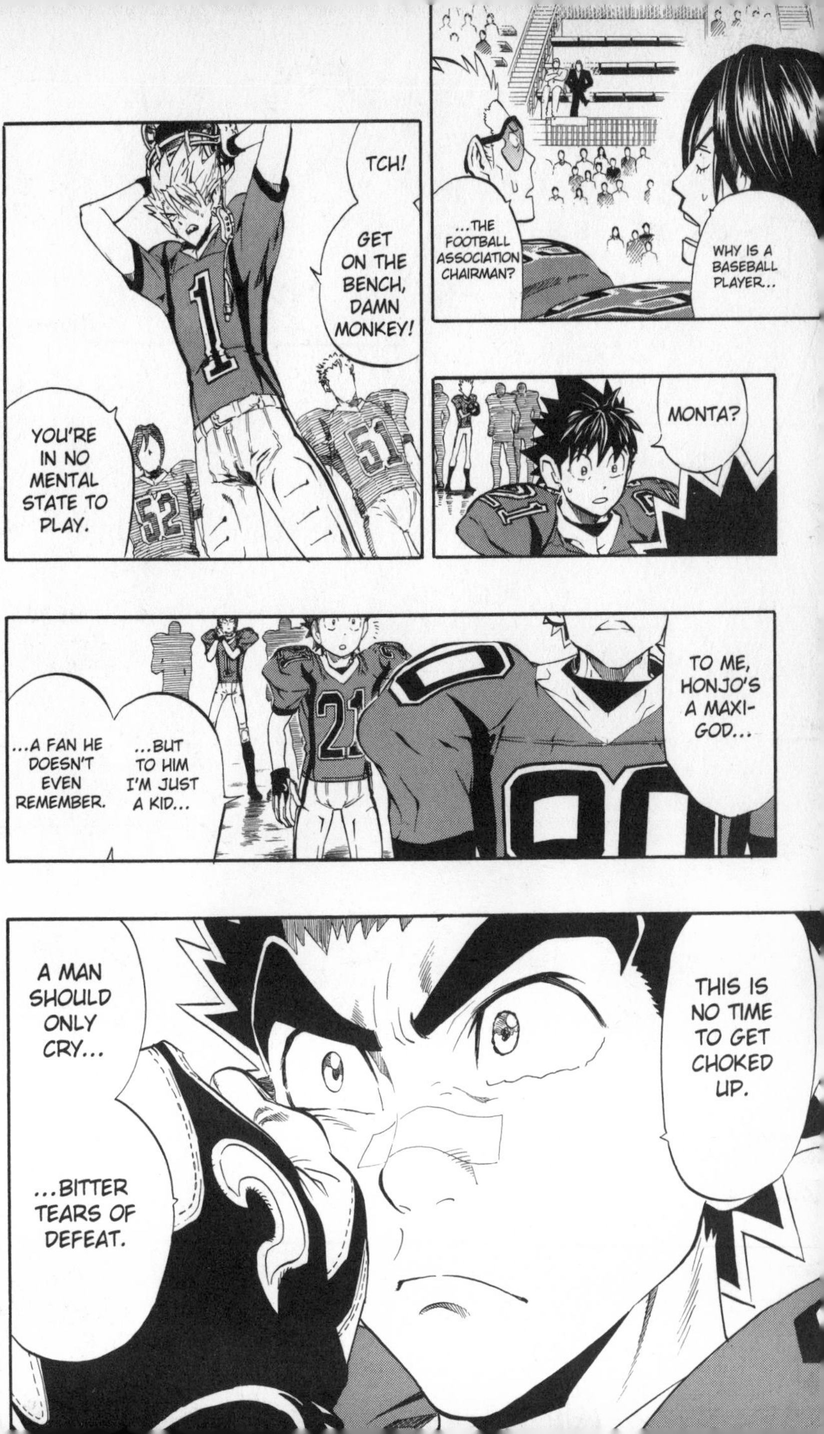
WHY IS A BASEBALL PLAYER...
...THE FOOTBALL ASSOCIATION CHAIRMAN?
MONTA?
TCH!
GET ON THE BENCH, DAMN MONKEY!
YOU'RE IN NO MENTAL STATE TO PLAY.
TO ME, HONJO'S A MAXI-GOD...
...BUT TO HIM I'M JUST A KID...
...A FAN HE DOESN'T EVEN REMEMBER.
THIS IS NO TIME TO GET CHOKED UP.
A MAN SHOULD ONLY CRY...
...BITTER TEARS OF DEFEAT.

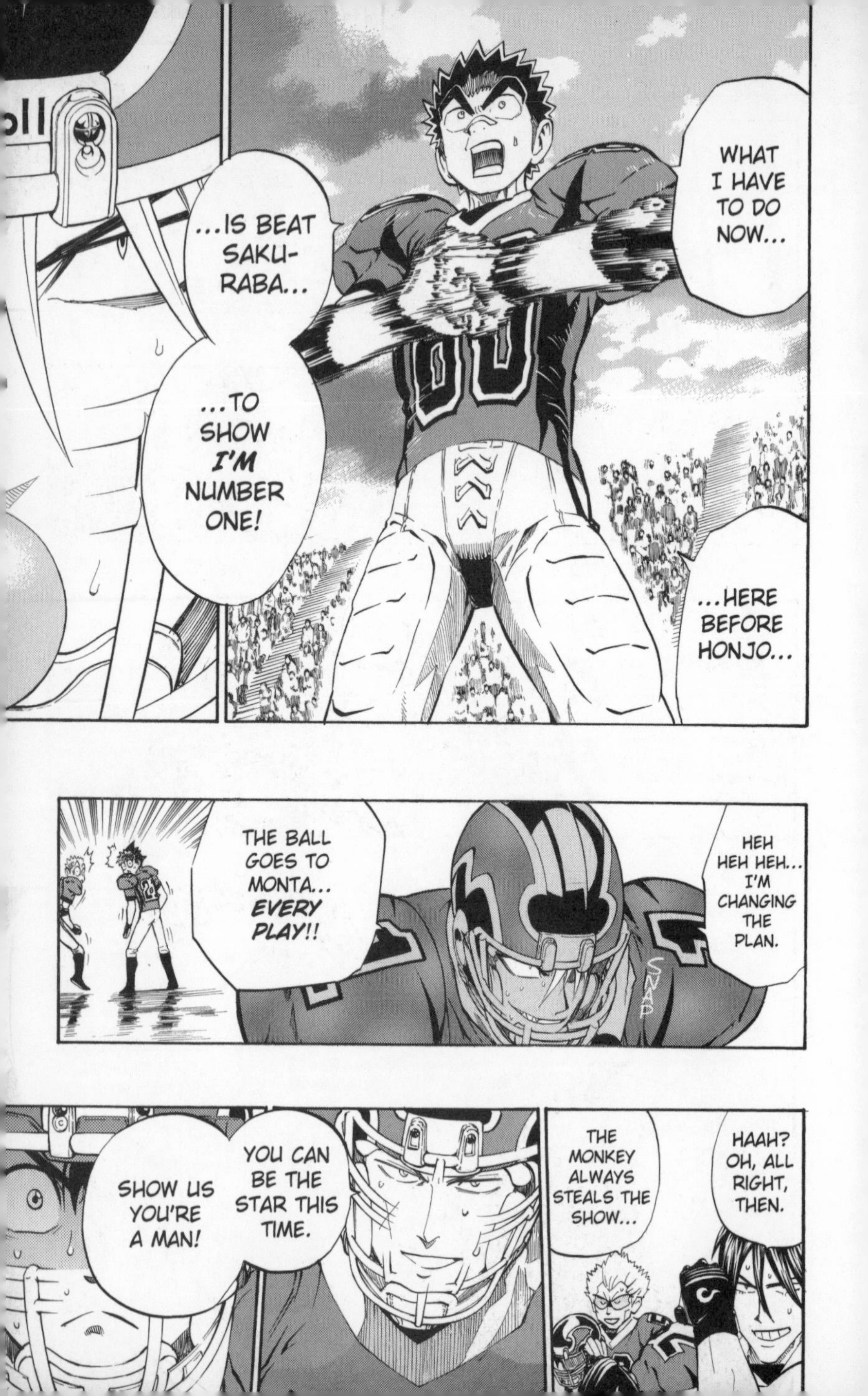
WHAT I HAVE TO DO NOW...
...IS BEAT SAKU-RABA...
...HERE BEFORE HONJO...
...TO SHOW I'M NUMBER ONE!
HEH HEH HEH... I'M CHANGING THE PLAN.
SNAP
THE BALL GOES TO MONTA... EVERY PLAY!!
HAAH? OH, ALL RIGHT, THEN.
THE MONKEY ALWAYS STEALS THE SHOW...
YOU CAN BE THE STAR THIS TIME.
SHOW US YOU'RE A MAN!

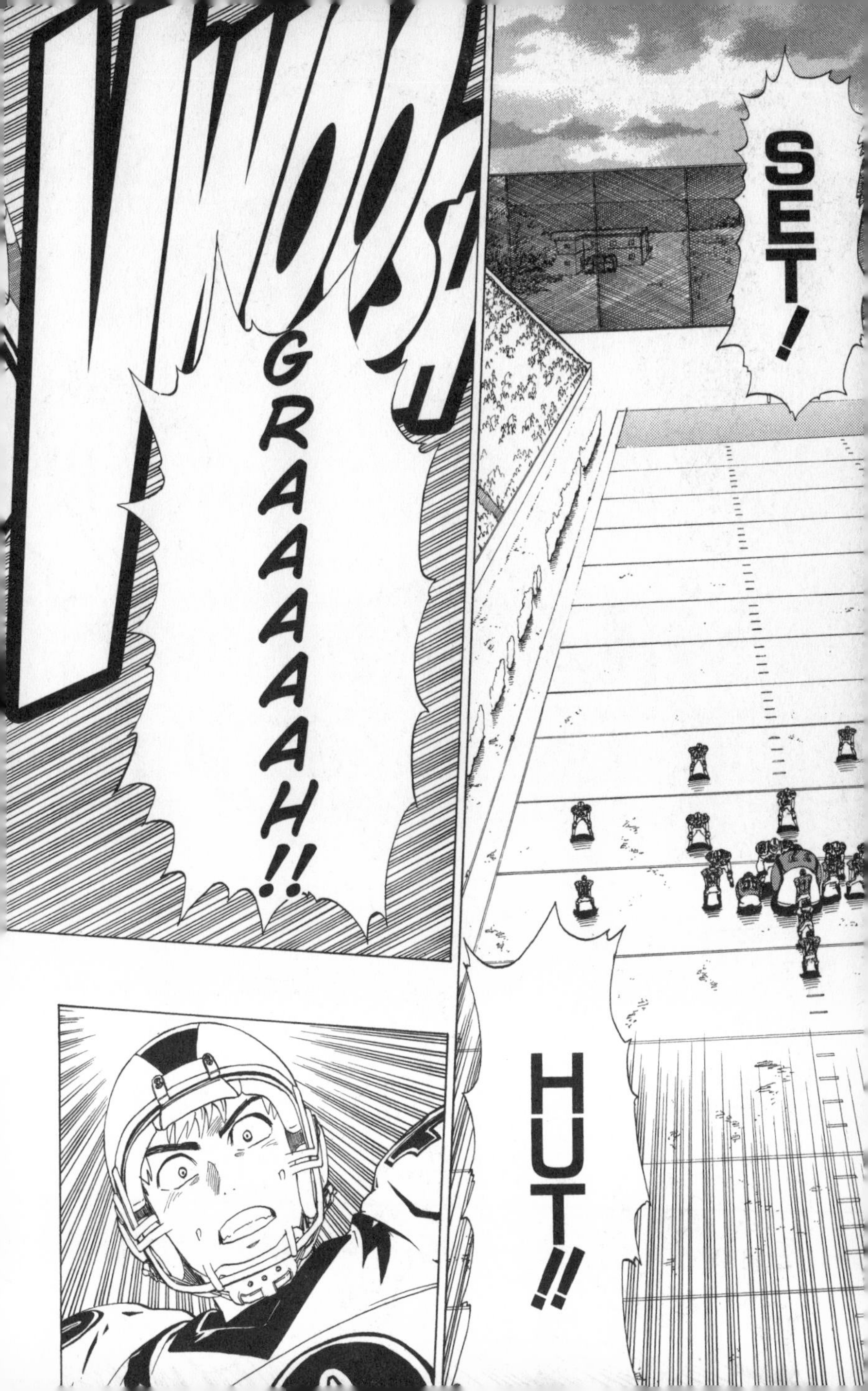
SET!
HUT!!
GRAAAAAH!!

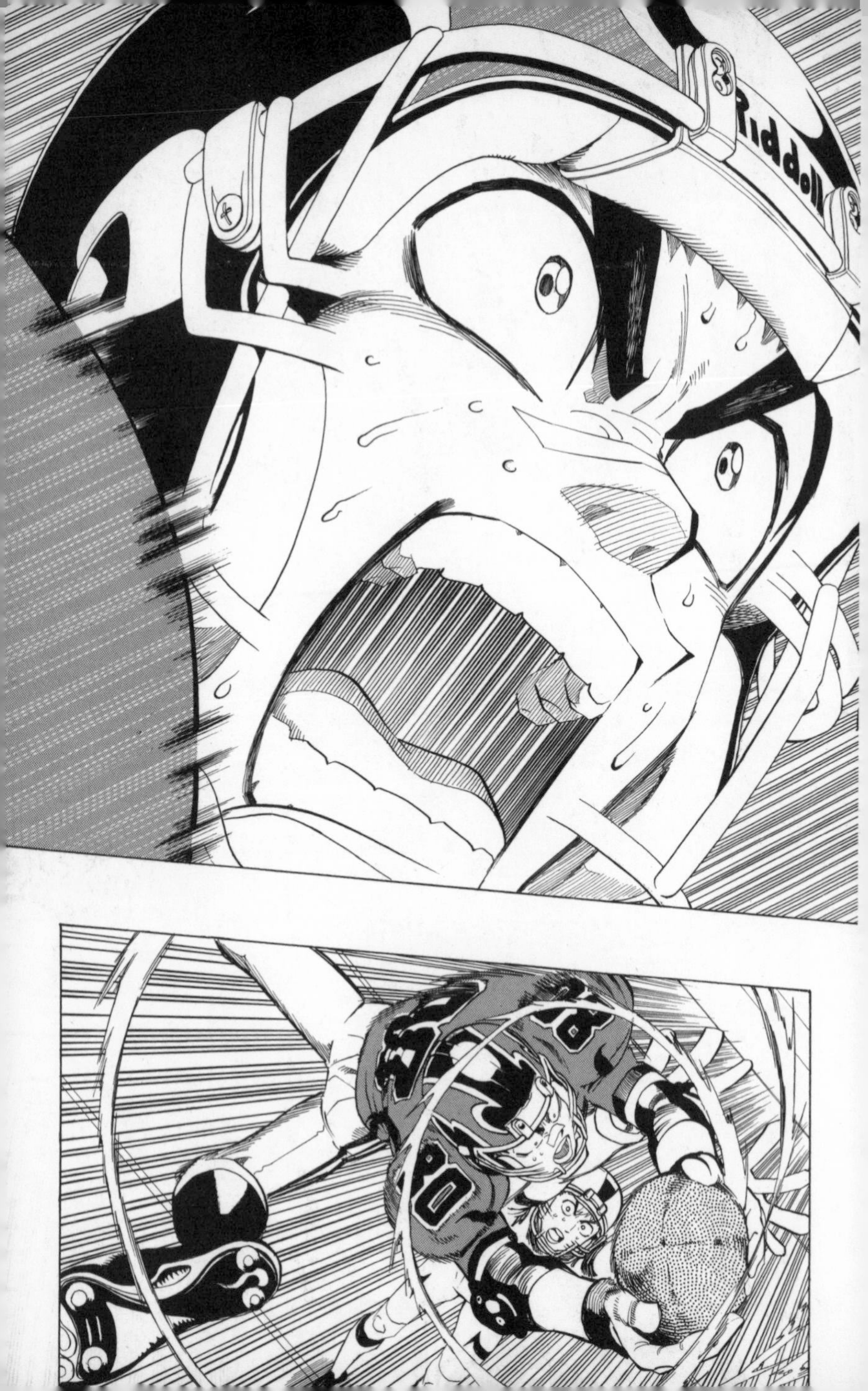

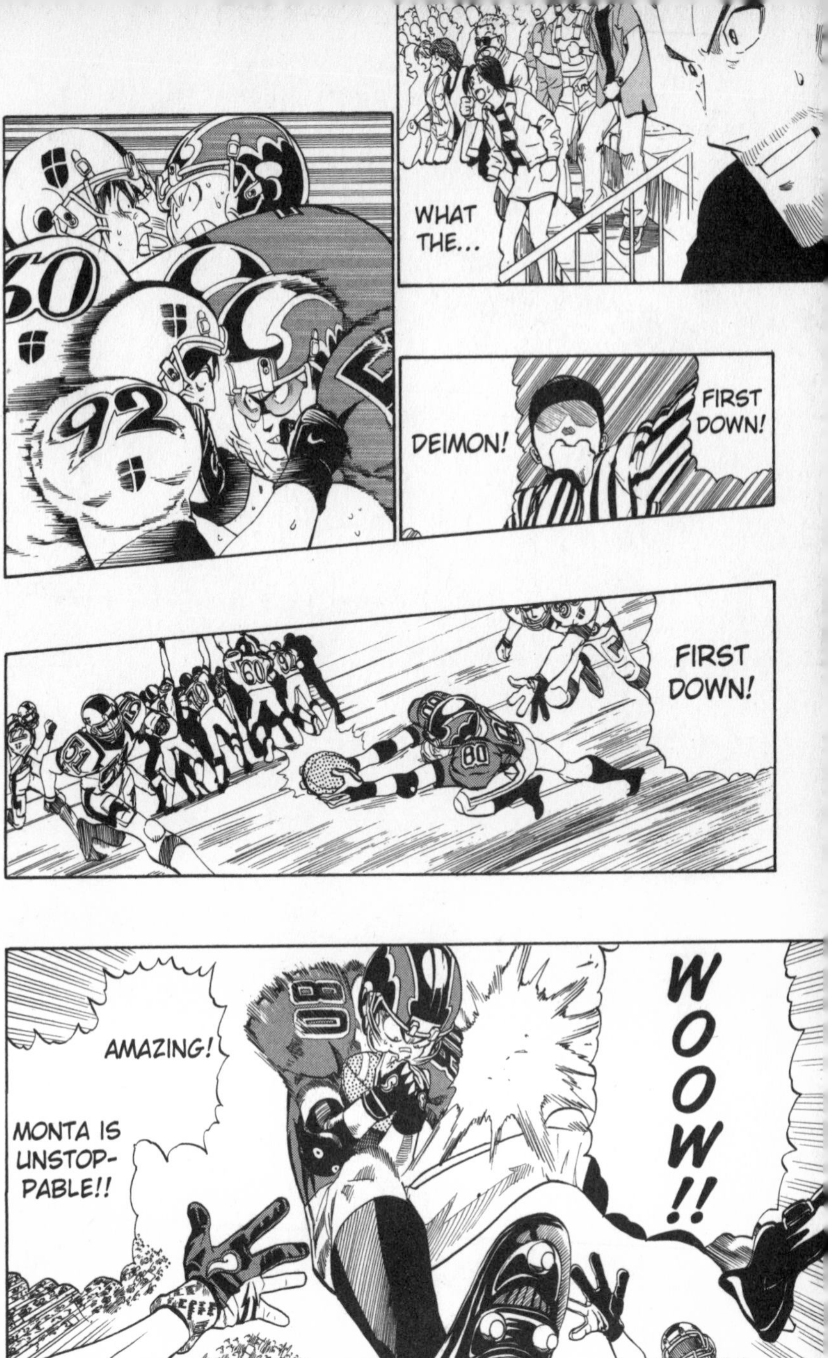
WHAT THE...
FIRST DOWN!
DEIMON!
FIRST DOWN!
WOOOW!!
AMAZING!
MONTA IS UNSTOP-PABLE!!

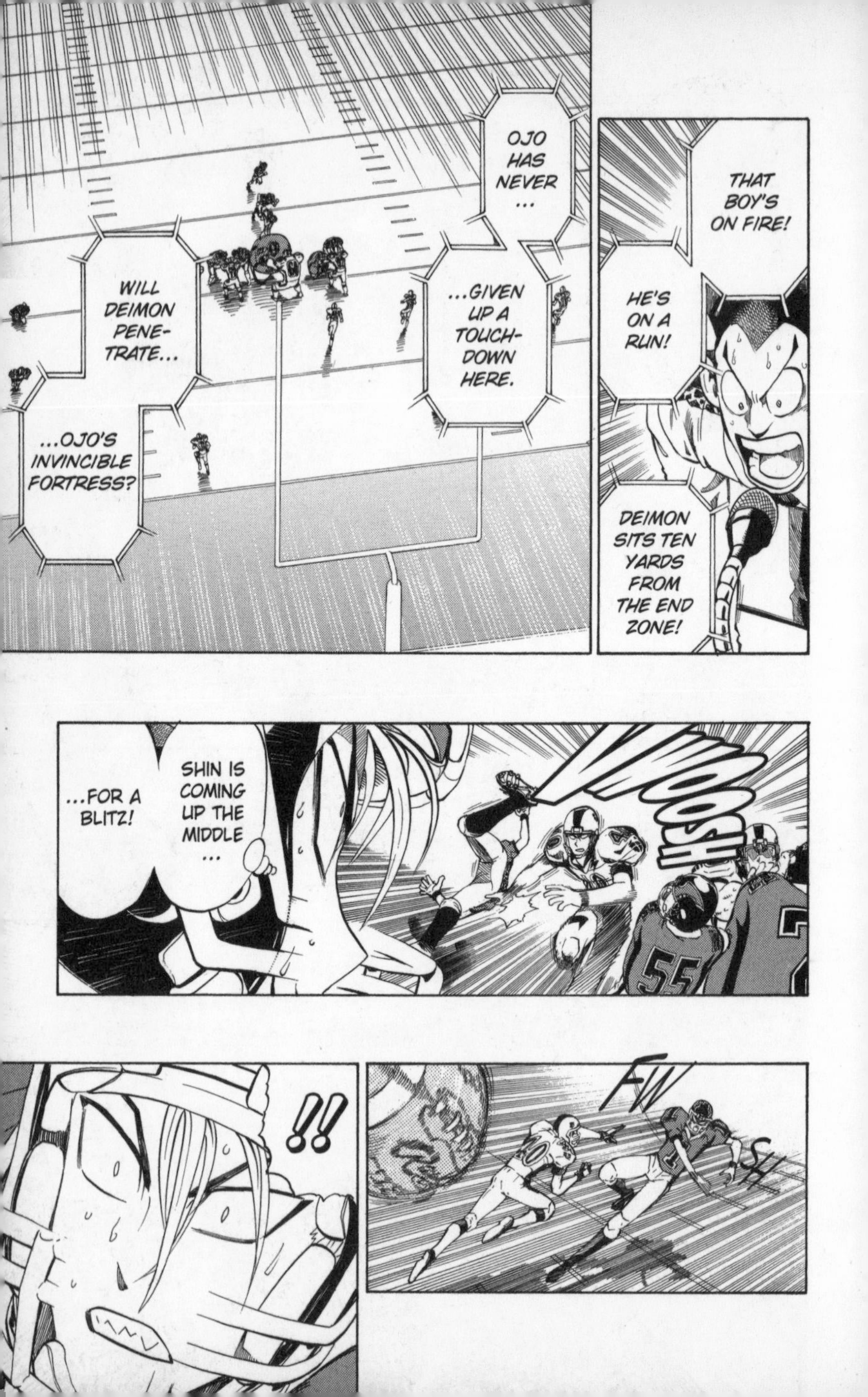
THAT BOY'S ON FIRE!
HE'S ON A RUN!
DEIMON SITS TEN YARDS FROM THE END ZONE!
OJO HAS NEVER...
...GIVEN UP A TOUCHDOWN HERE.
WILL DEIMON PENETRATE...
...OJO'S INVINCIBLE FORTRESS?
WHOOSH
SHIN IS COMING UP THE MIDDLE...
...FOR A BLITZ!
FW
SH
!!

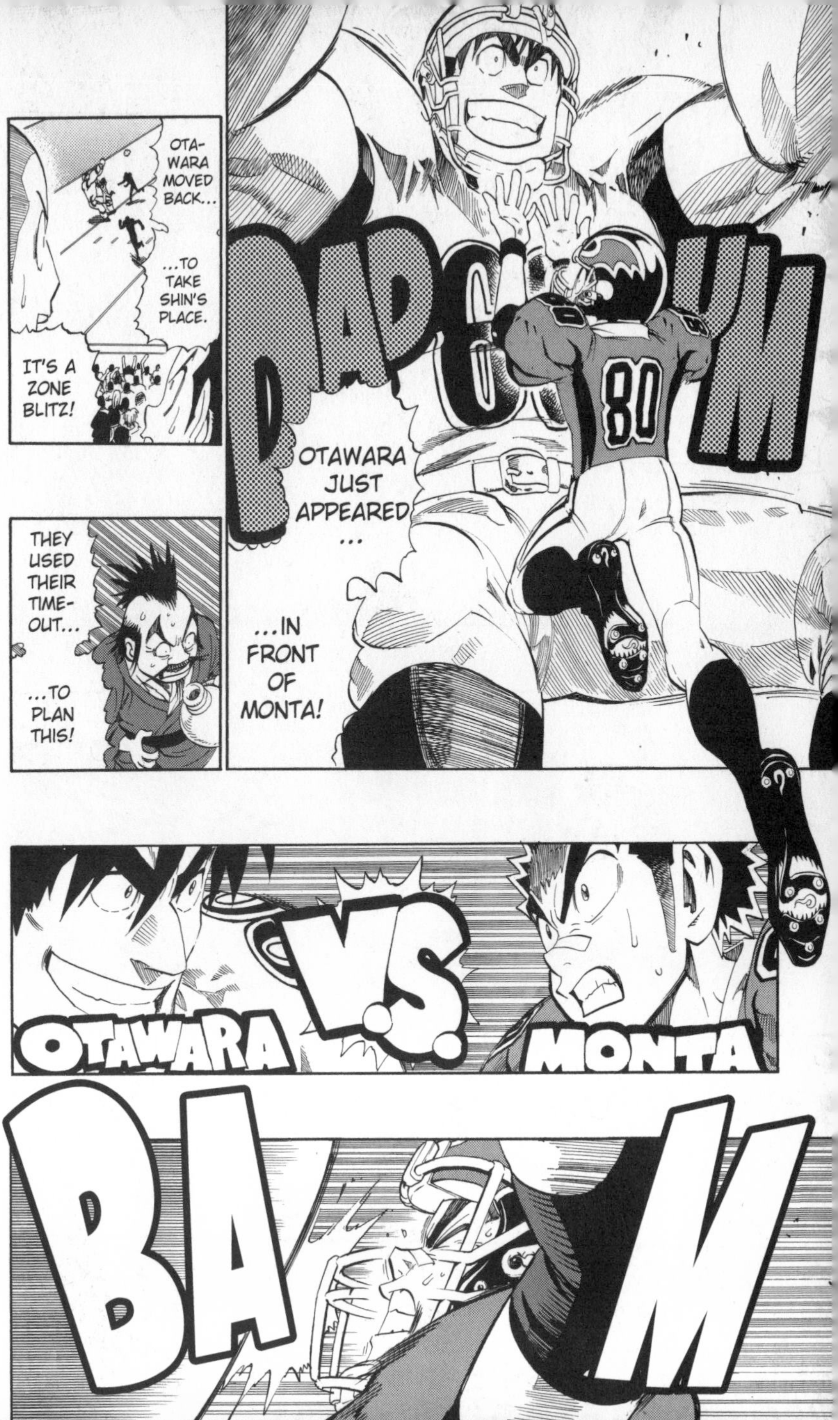
OTAWARA JUST APPEARED ...
...IN FRONT OF MONTA!
OTA-WARA MOVED BACK...
...TO TAKE SHIN'S PLACE.
IT'S A ZONE BLITZ!
THEY USED THEIR TIME-OUT...
...TO PLAN THIS!
OTAWARA V.S. MONTA

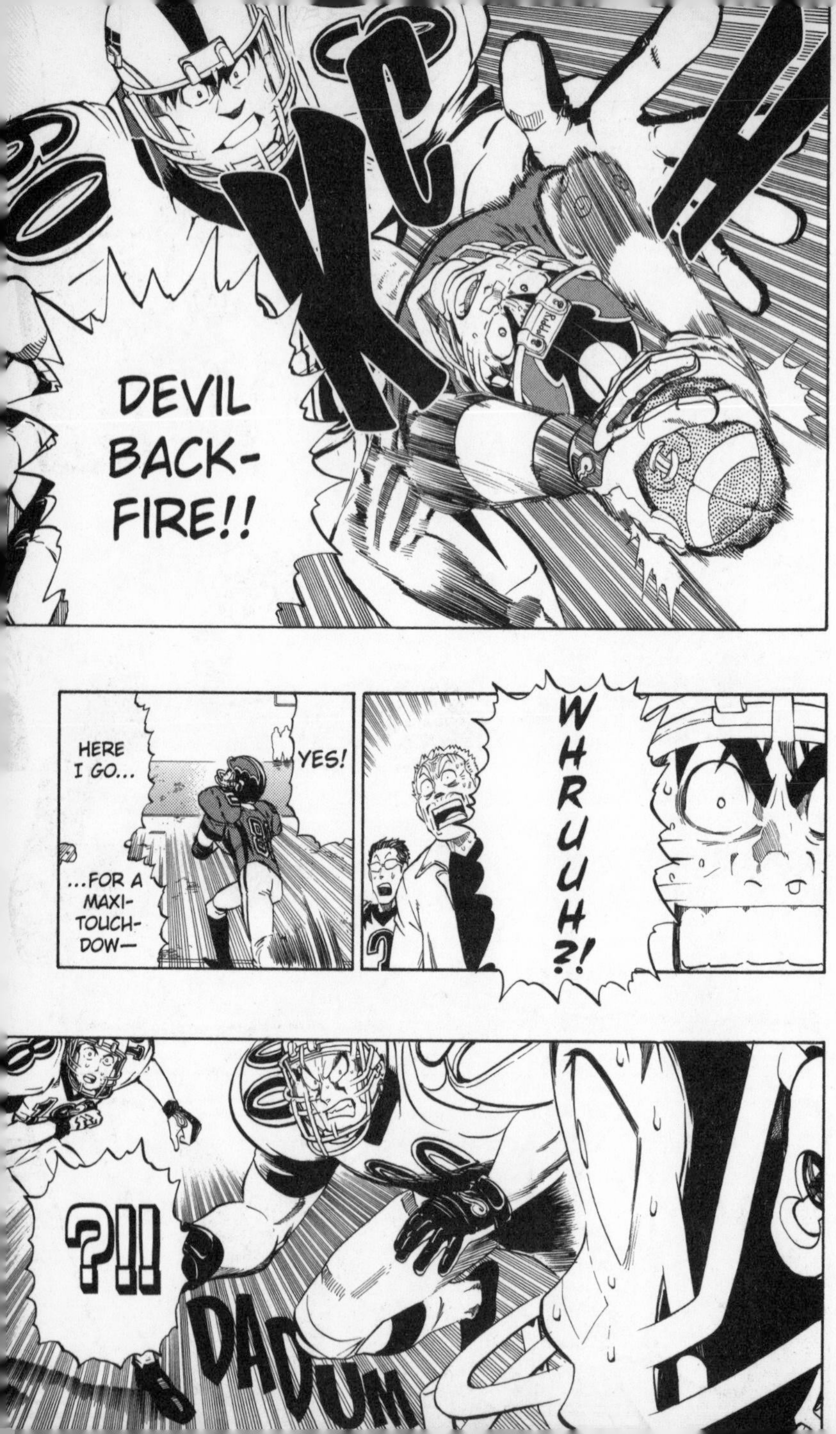
DEVIL BACK-FIRE!!
WHRUUH?!
YES!
HERE I GO...
...FOR A MAXI-TOUCH-DOW—
?!!
DADUM

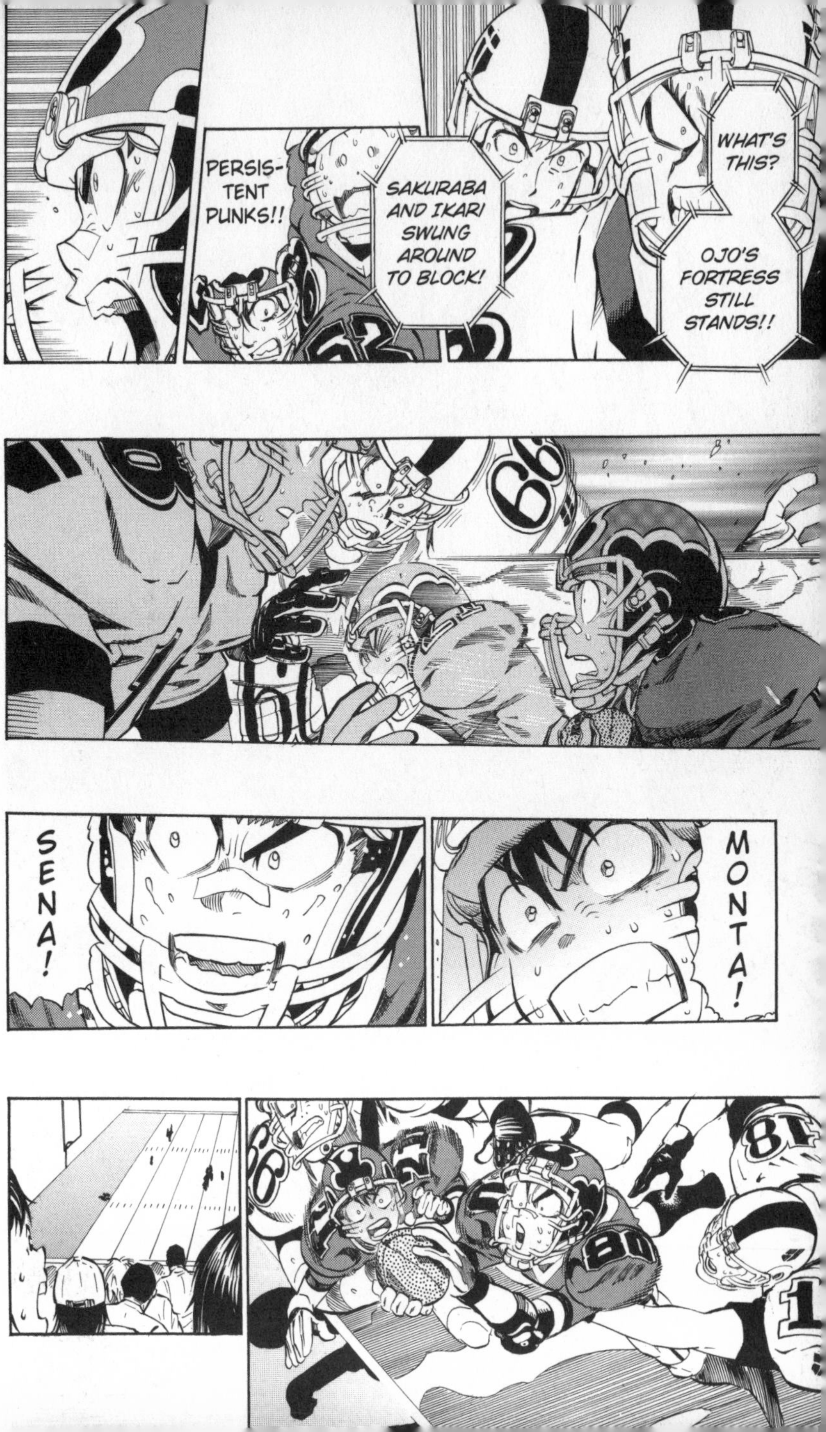
WHAT'S THIS?
OJO'S FORTRESS STILL STANDS!!
SAKURABA AND IKARI SWUNG AROUND TO BLOCK!
PERSIS-TENT PUNKS!!
MONTA!
SENA!

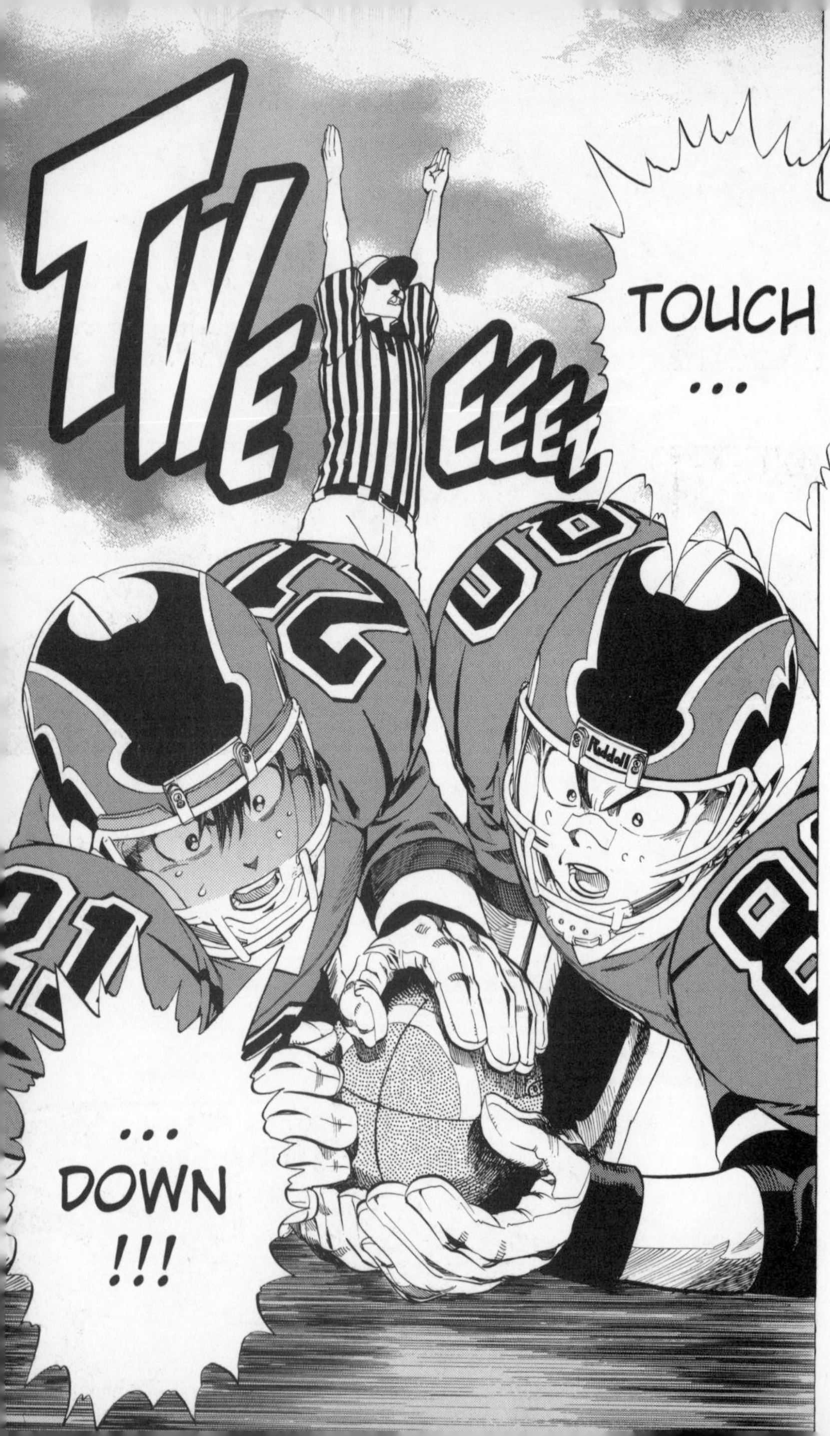
TOUCH ...
TWEEET
... DOWN !!!

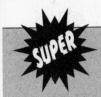

RIVAL BATTLE ★ DEIMON VS. OJO

SUPER MISCELLANY MATCH-UPS!!

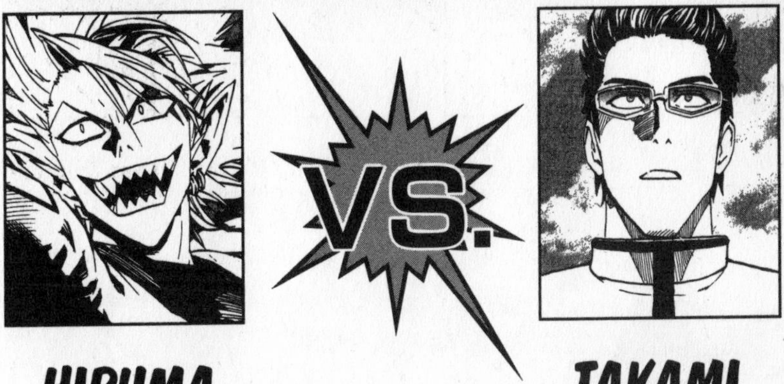
VS.

HIRUMA **TAKAMI**

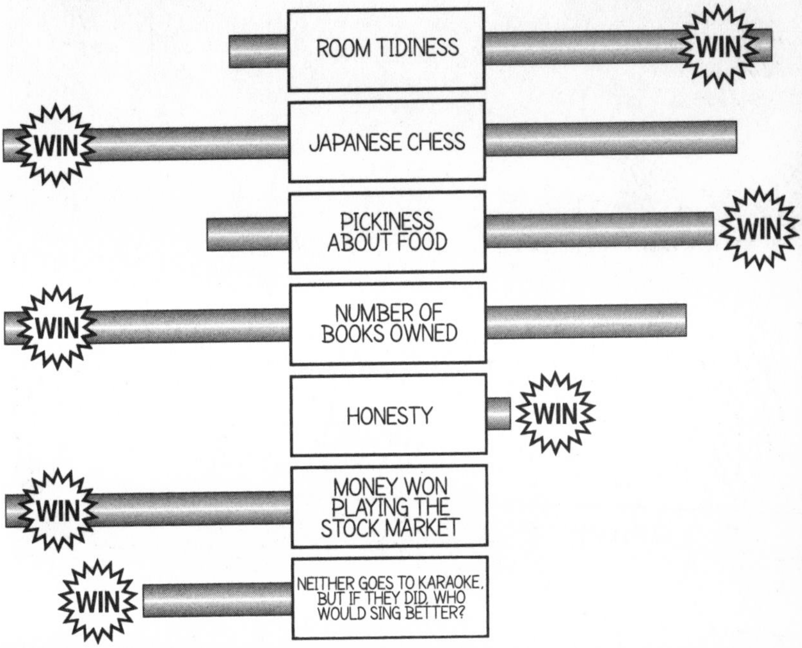
ROOM TIDINESS
WIN
JAPANESE CHESS
WIN
PICKINESS ABOUT FOOD
WIN
NUMBER OF BOOKS OWNED
WIN
HONESTY
WIN
MONEY WON PLAYING THE STOCK MARKET
WIN
NEITHER GOES TO KARAOKE, BUT IF THEY DID, WHO WOULD SING BETTER?
WIN

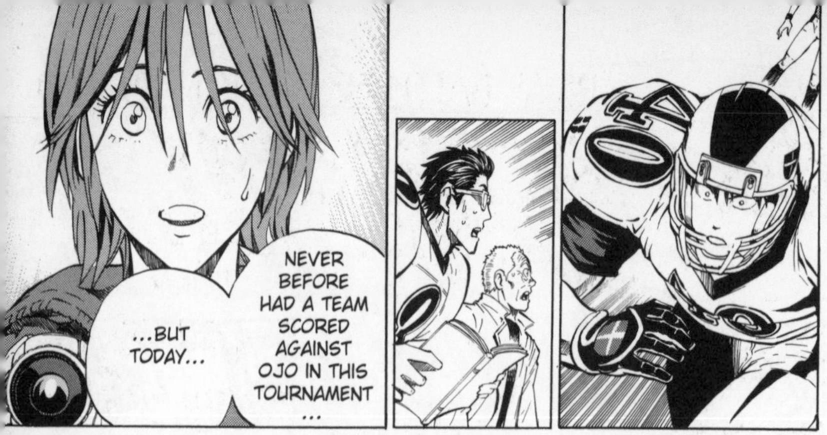
NEVER BEFORE HAD A TEAM SCORED AGAINST OJO IN THIS TOURNAMENT...
...BUT TODAY...

Chapter 227 Tag-Team Match

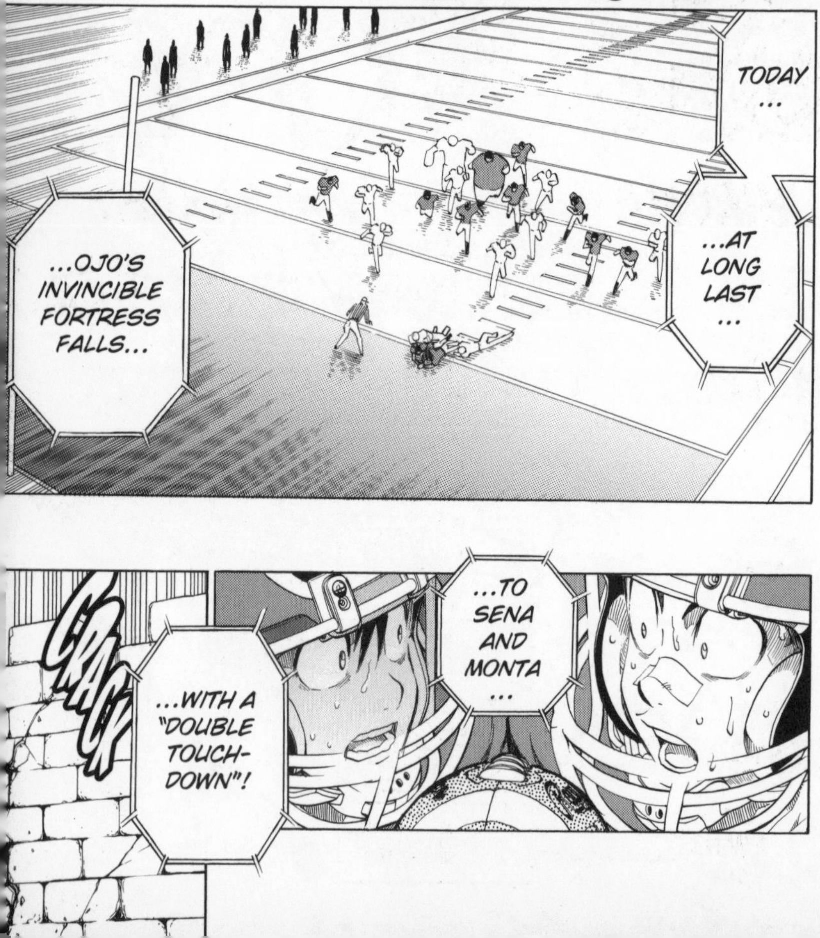
TODAY...
...AT LONG LAST...
...OJO'S INVINCIBLE FORTRESS FALLS...
...TO SENA AND MONTA...
...WITH A "DOUBLE TOUCH-DOWN"!
CRACK

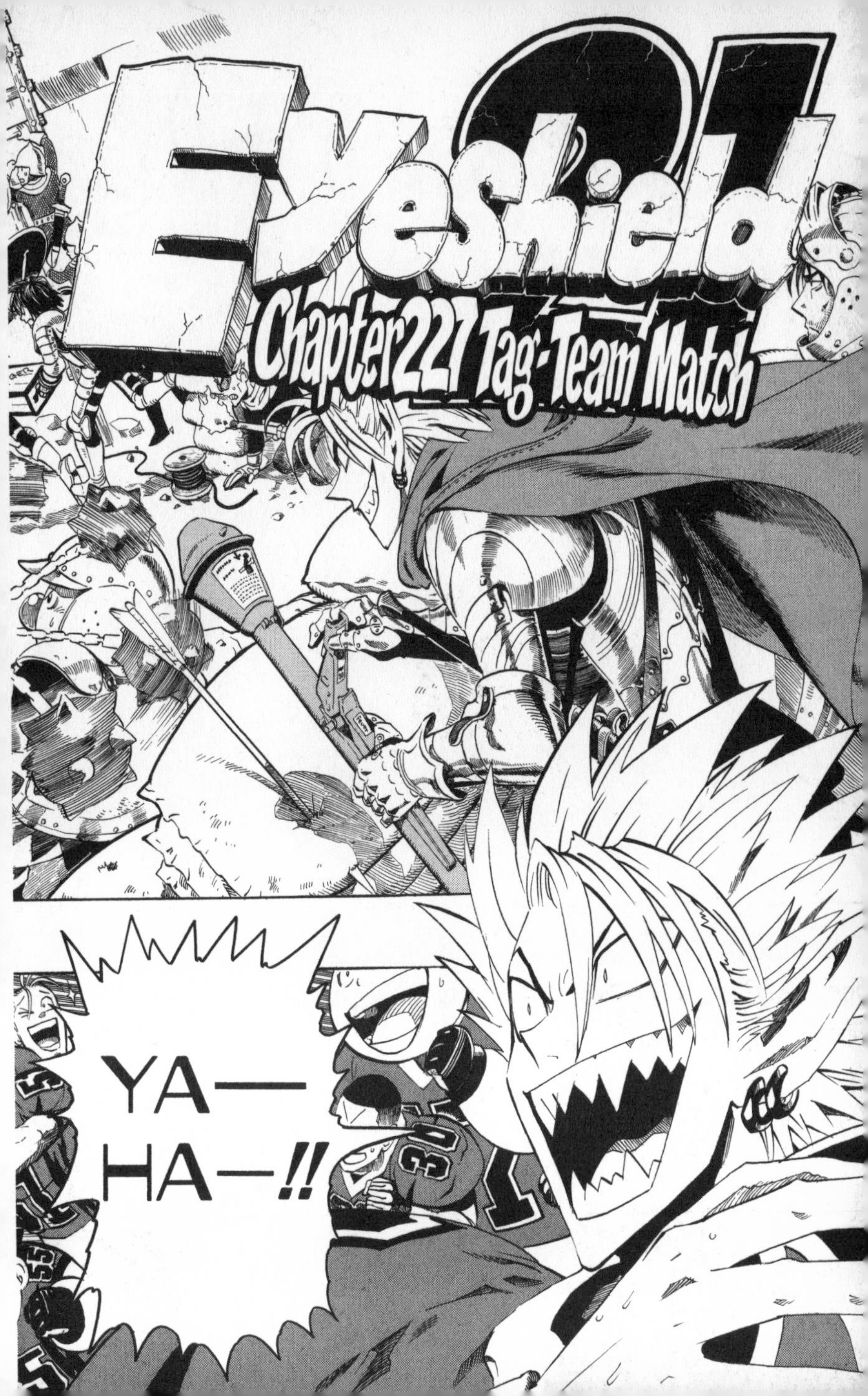
Eyeshield 21
Chapter 227 Tag-Team Match
YA—
HA—!!

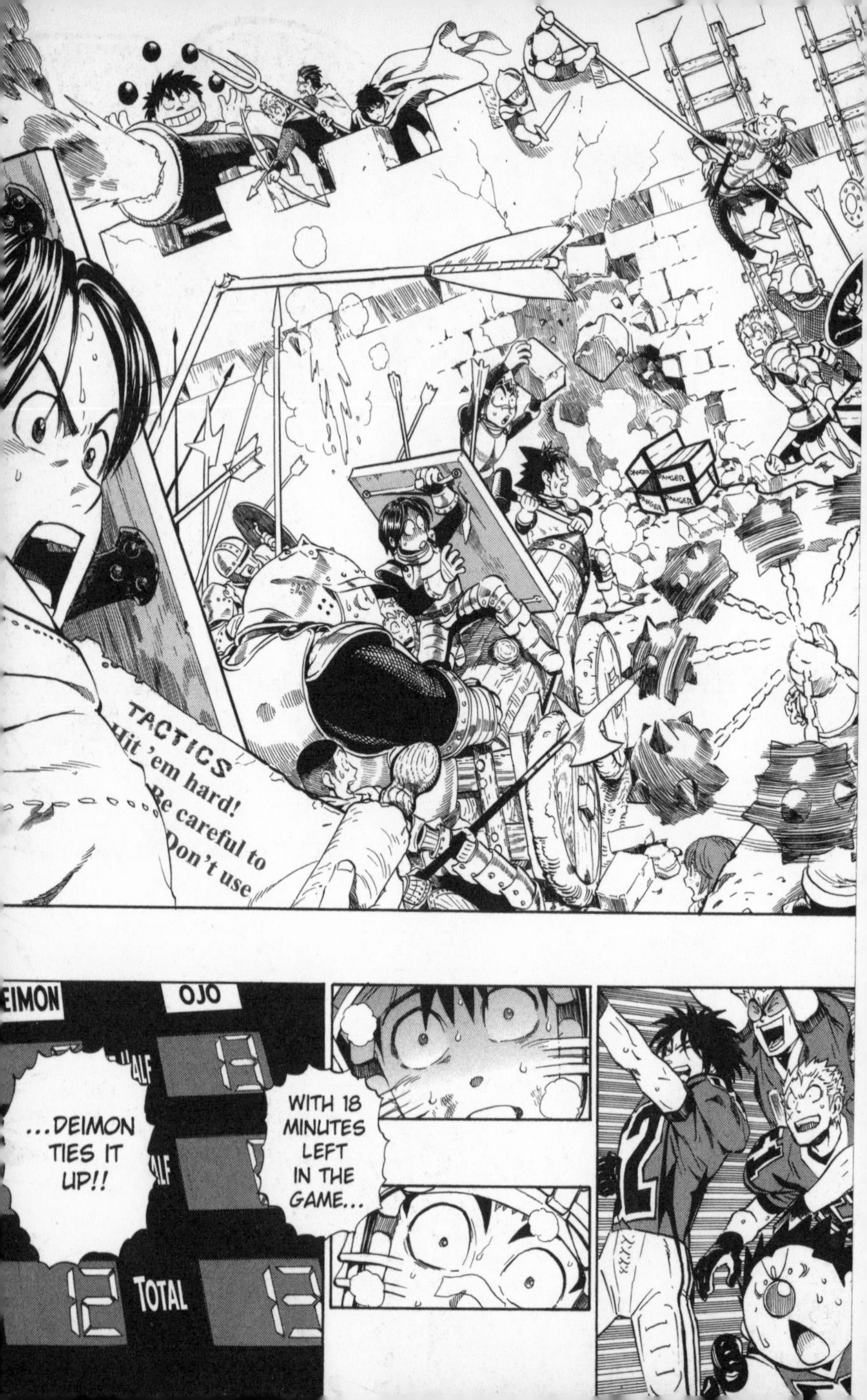
DANGER
TACTICS
Hit 'em hard!
Be careful to
Don't use
WITH 18 MINUTES LEFT IN THE GAME...
DEIMON
OJO
...DEIMON TIES IT UP!!
TOTAL

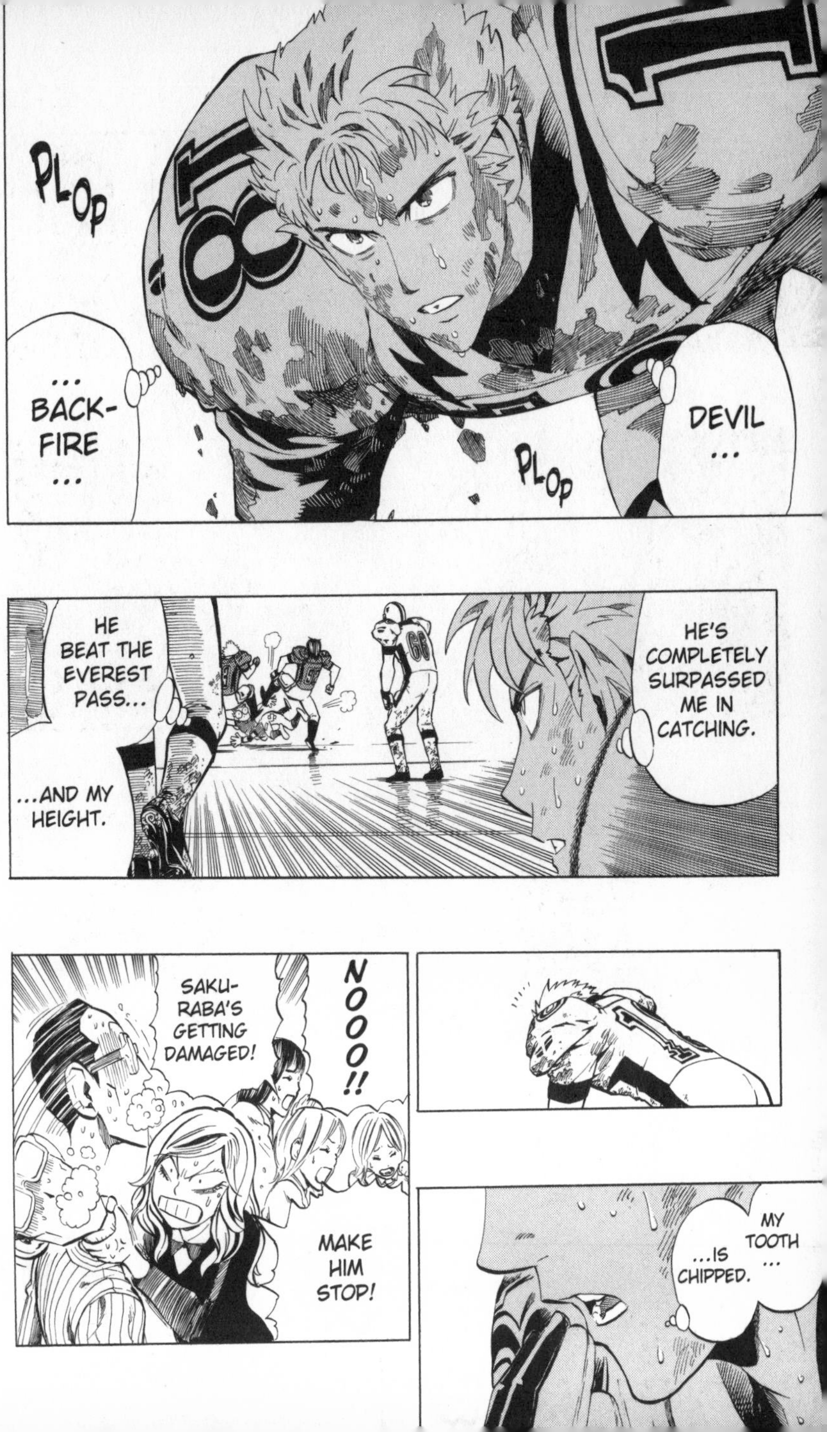
DEVIL ...
PLOP
PLOP
... BACK-FIRE ...
HE'S COMPLETELY SURPASSED ME IN CATCHING.
HE BEAT THE EVEREST PASS...
...AND MY HEIGHT.
MY TOOTH ...
...IS CHIPPED.
NOOOO!!
SAKU-RABA'S GETTING DAMAGED!
MAKE HIM STOP!

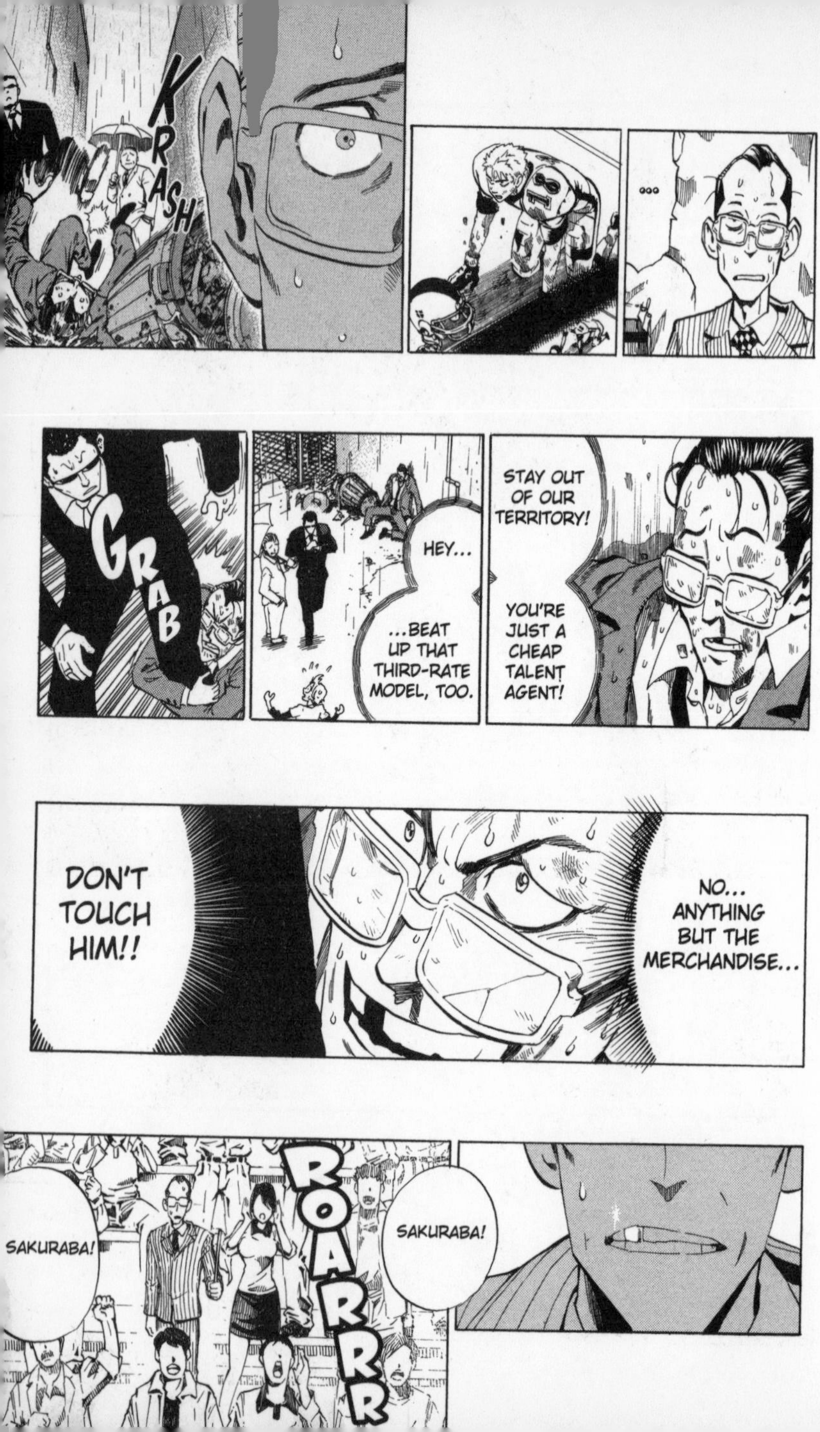
...
KRASH
STAY OUT OF OUR TERRITORY!
YOU'RE JUST A CHEAP TALENT AGENT!
HEY...
...BEAT UP THAT THIRD-RATE MODEL, TOO.
GRAB
NO... ANYTHING BUT THE MERCHANDISE...
DON'T TOUCH HIM!!
SAKURABA!
ROARRR
SAKURABA!

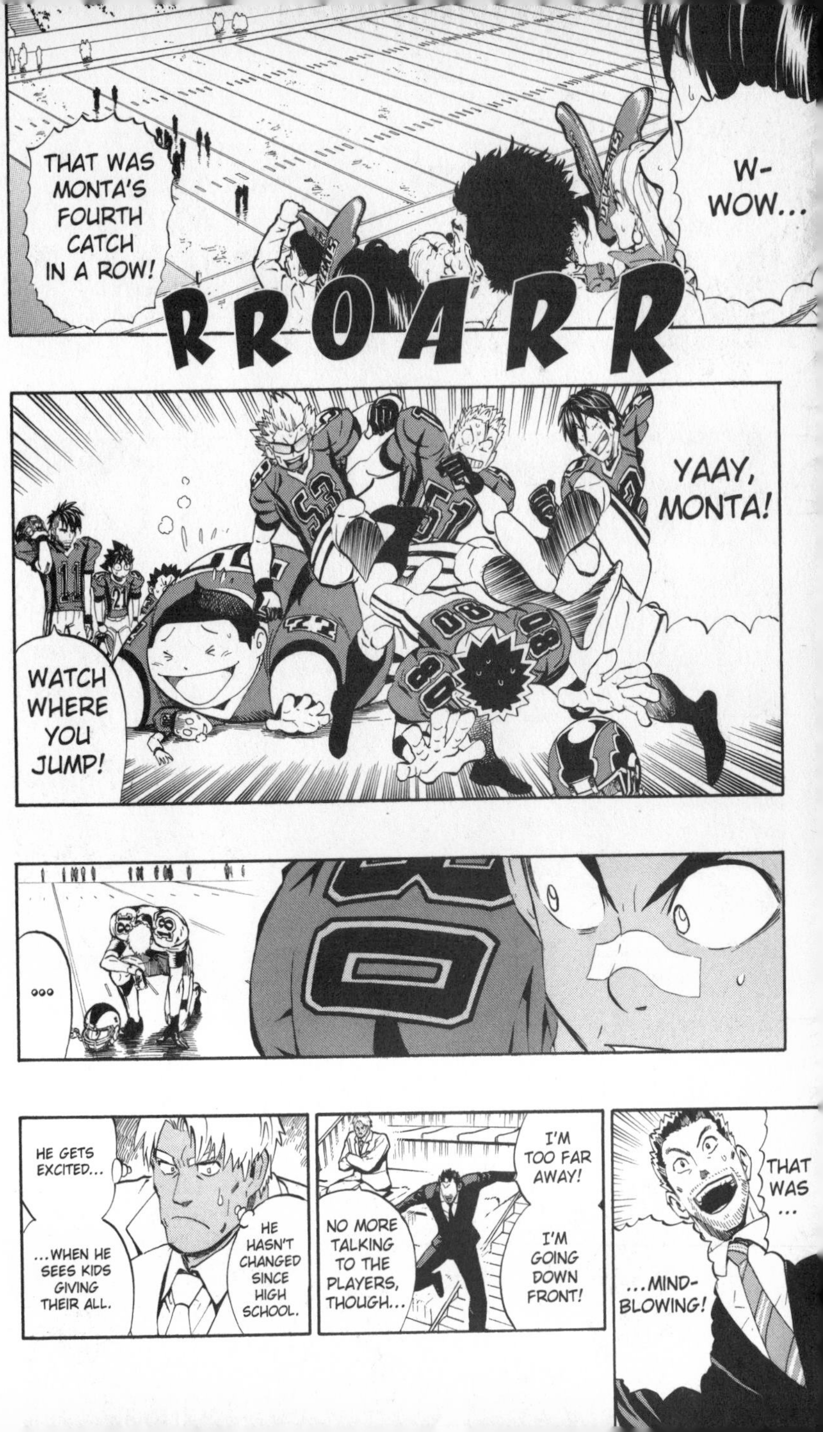
W- WOW...
THAT WAS MONTA'S FOURTH CATCH IN A ROW!
RROARR
YAAY, MONTA!
WATCH WHERE YOU JUMP!
...
THAT WAS ...
...MIND-BLOWING!
I'M TOO FAR AWAY!
I'M GOING DOWN FRONT!
NO MORE TALKING TO THE PLAYERS, THOUGH...
HE HASN'T CHANGED SINCE HIGH SCHOOL.
HE GETS EXCITED...
...WHEN HE SEES KIDS GIVING THEIR ALL.

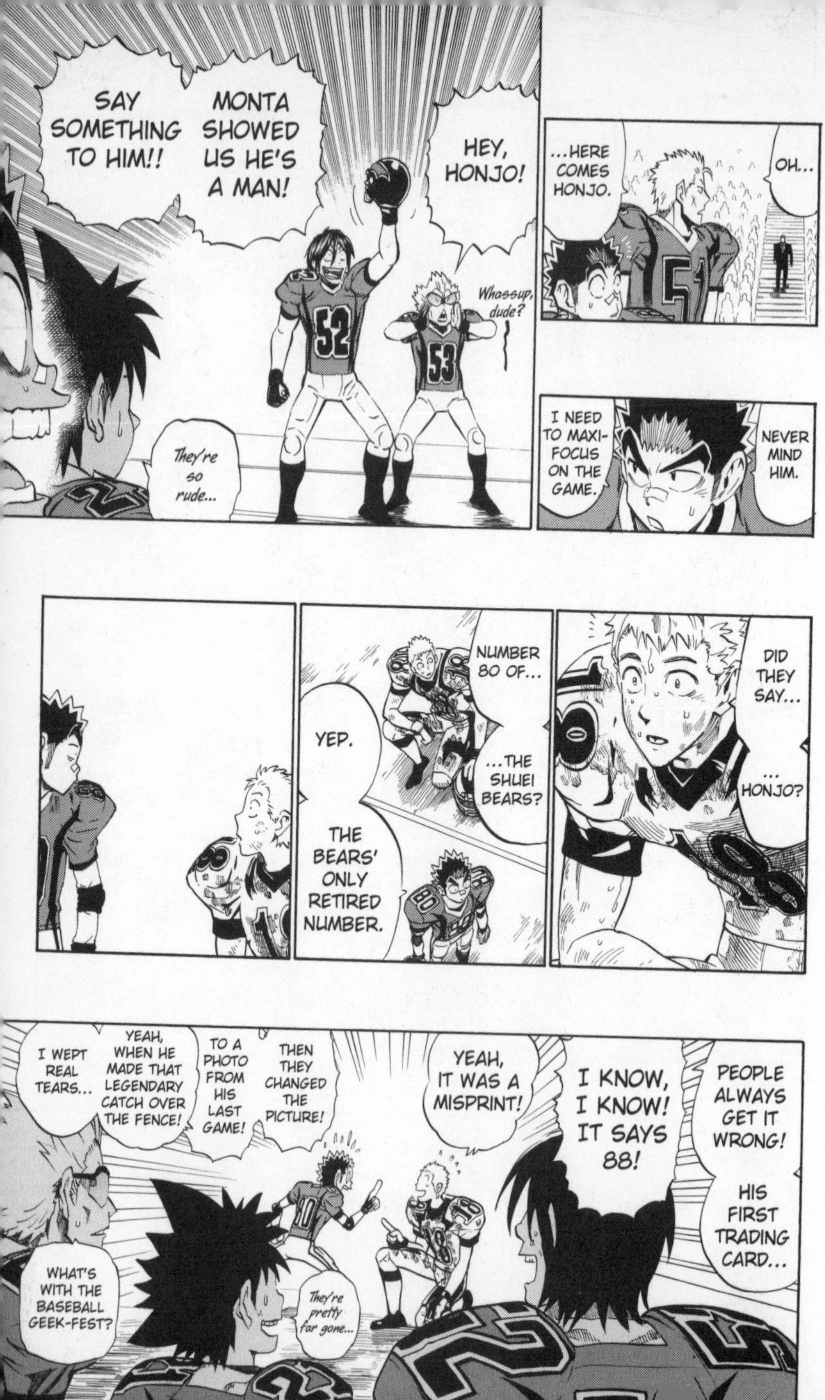
OH...
...HERE COMES HONJO.
NEVER MIND HIM.
I NEED TO MAXI-FOCUS ON THE GAME.
HEY, HONJO!
MONTA SHOWED US HE'S A MAN!
SAY SOMETHING TO HIM!!
Whassup, dude?
They're so rude...
DID THEY SAY...
...HONJO?
NUMBER 80 OF...
...THE SHUEI BEARS?
YEP.
THE BEARS' ONLY RETIRED NUMBER.
PEOPLE ALWAYS GET IT WRONG!
HIS FIRST TRADING CARD...
I KNOW, I KNOW! IT SAYS 88!
YEAH, IT WAS A MISPRINT!
THEN THEY CHANGED THE PICTURE!
TO A PHOTO FROM HIS LAST GAME!
YEAH, WHEN HE MADE THAT LEGENDARY CATCH OVER THE FENCE!
I WEPT REAL TEARS...
WHAT'S WITH THE BASEBALL GEEK-FEST?
They're pretty far gone...

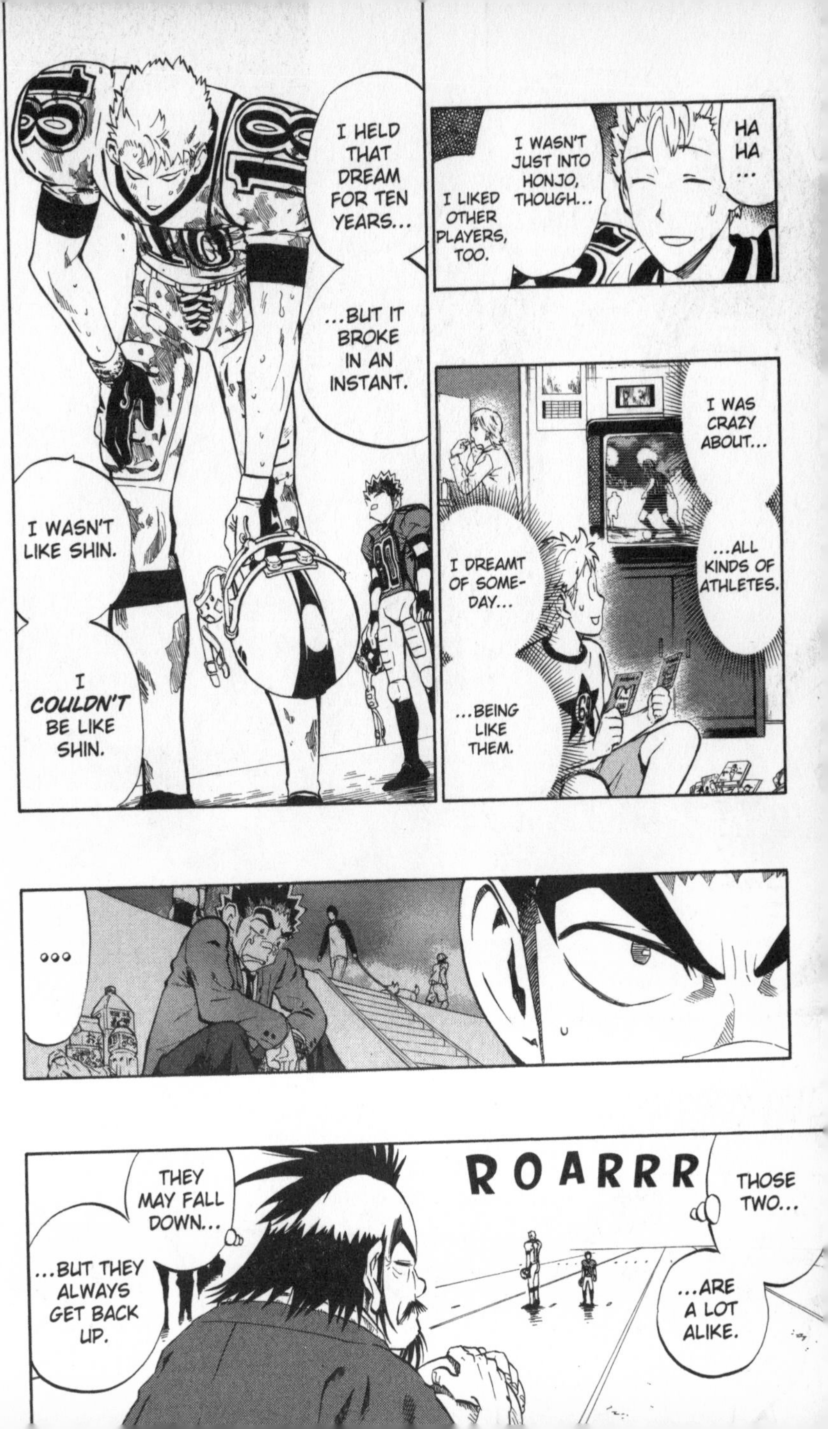
HA HA ...
I WASN'T JUST INTO HONJO, THOUGH...
I LIKED OTHER PLAYERS, TOO.
I WAS CRAZY ABOUT...
...ALL KINDS OF ATHLETES.
I DREAMT OF SOME-DAY...
...BEING LIKE THEM.
I HELD THAT DREAM FOR TEN YEARS...
...BUT IT BROKE IN AN INSTANT.
I WASN'T LIKE SHIN.
I *COULDN'T* BE LIKE SHIN.
...
ROARRR
THOSE TWO...
...ARE A LOT ALIKE.
THEY MAY FALL DOWN...
...BUT THEY ALWAYS GET BACK UP.

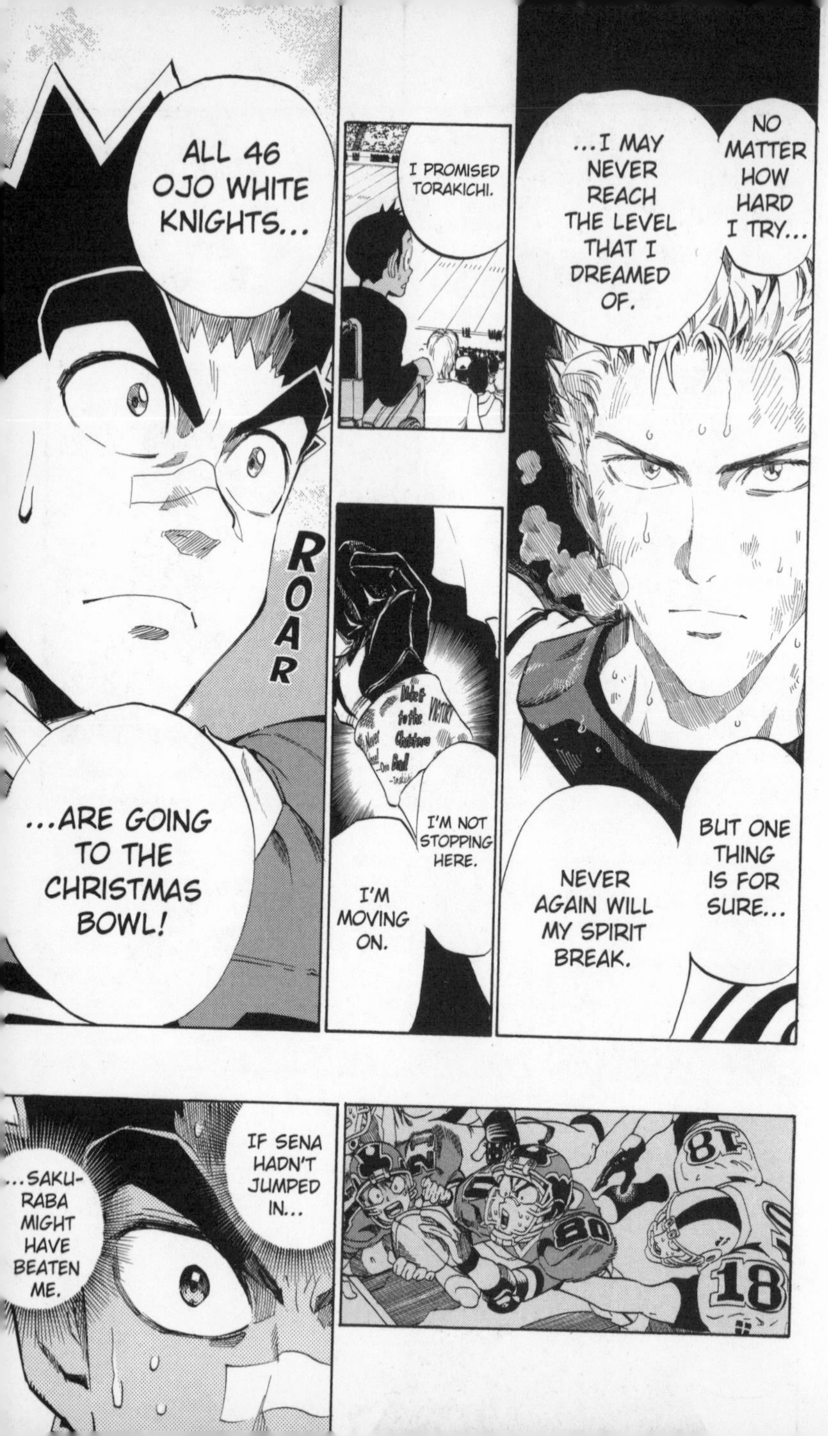
NO MATTER HOW HARD I TRY...
...I MAY NEVER REACH THE LEVEL THAT I DREAMED OF.
BUT ONE THING IS FOR SURE...
NEVER AGAIN WILL MY SPIRIT BREAK.
I PROMISED TORAKICHI.
I'M NOT STOPPING HERE.
I'M MOVING ON.
ALL 46 OJO WHITE KNIGHTS...
ROAR
...ARE GOING TO THE CHRISTMAS BOWL!
IF SENA HADN'T JUMPED IN...
...SAKU-RABA MIGHT HAVE BEATEN ME.

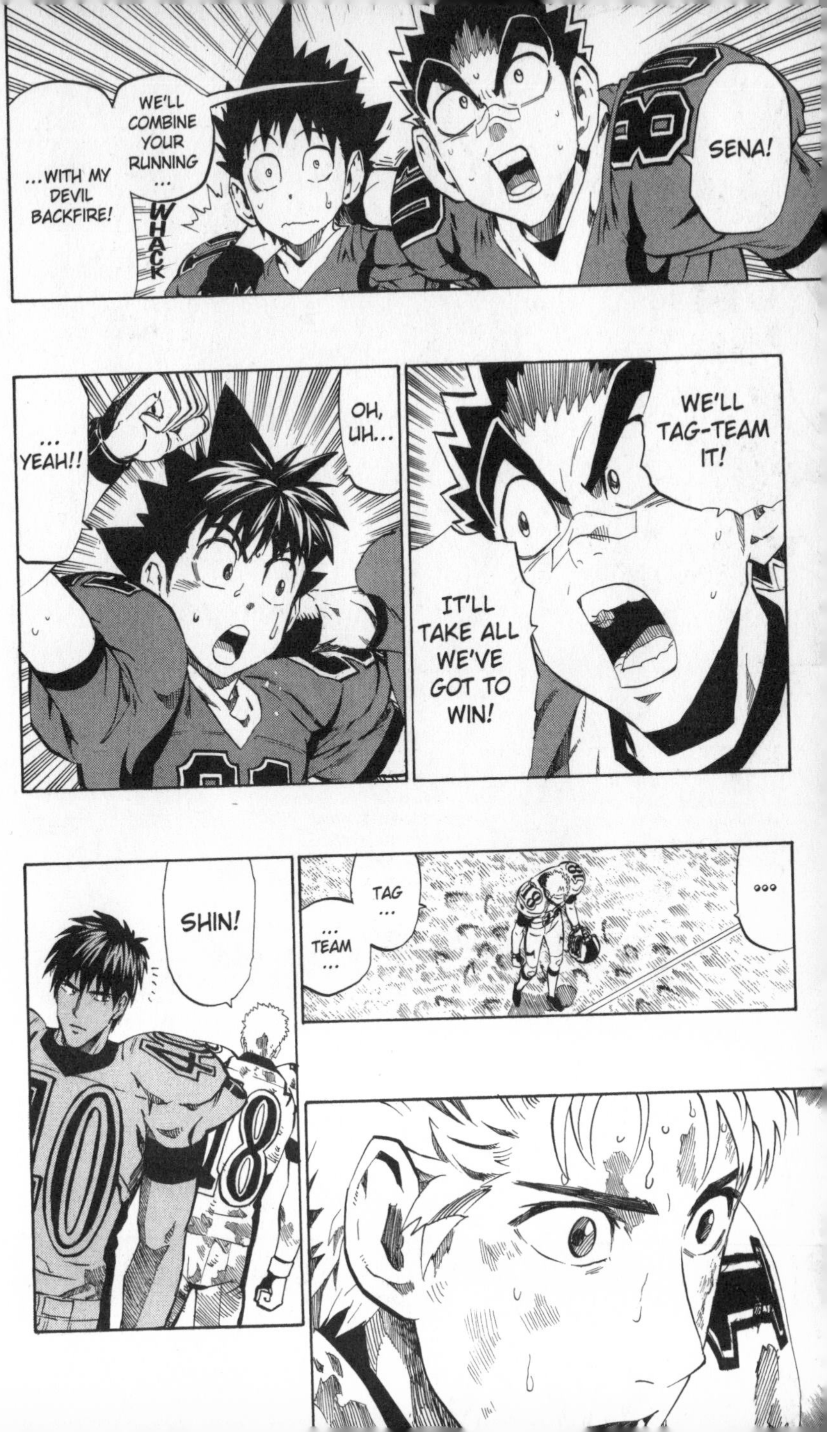
SENA!
WE'LL COMBINE YOUR RUNNING ...
...WITH MY DEVIL BACKFIRE!
WHACK
WE'LL TAG-TEAM IT!
IT'LL TAKE ALL WE'VE GOT TO WIN!
OH, UH...
... YEAH!!
...
TAG ...
... TEAM ...
SHIN!

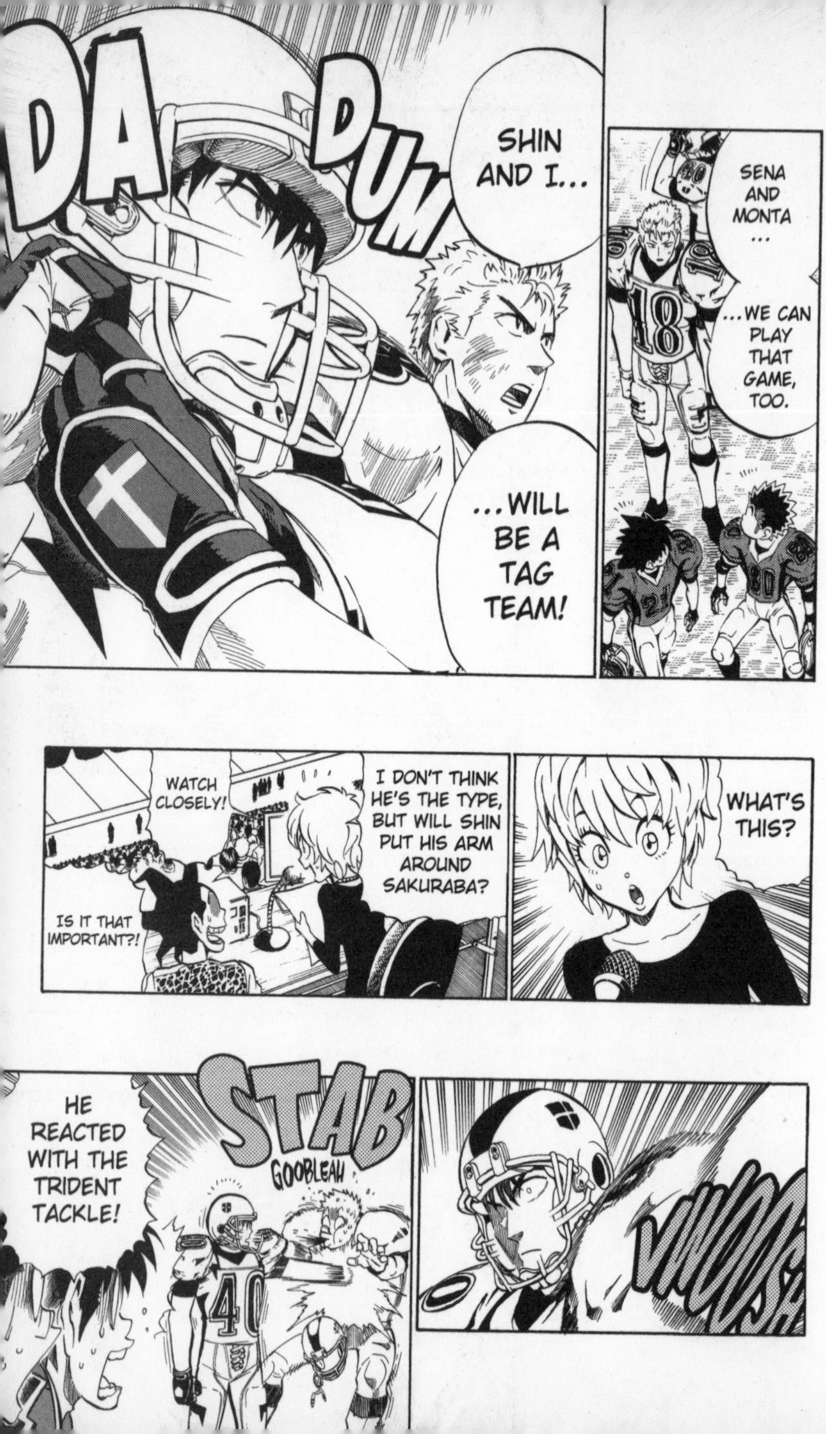
SENA AND MONTA ...
...WE CAN PLAY THAT GAME, TOO.
SHIN AND I...
DA DUM
...WILL BE A TAG TEAM!
WHAT'S THIS?
I DON'T THINK HE'S THE TYPE, BUT WILL SHIN PUT HIS ARM AROUND SAKURABA?
WATCH CLOSELY!
IS IT THAT IMPORTANT?!
STAB
GOOBLEAH
HE REACTED WITH THE TRIDENT TACKLE!

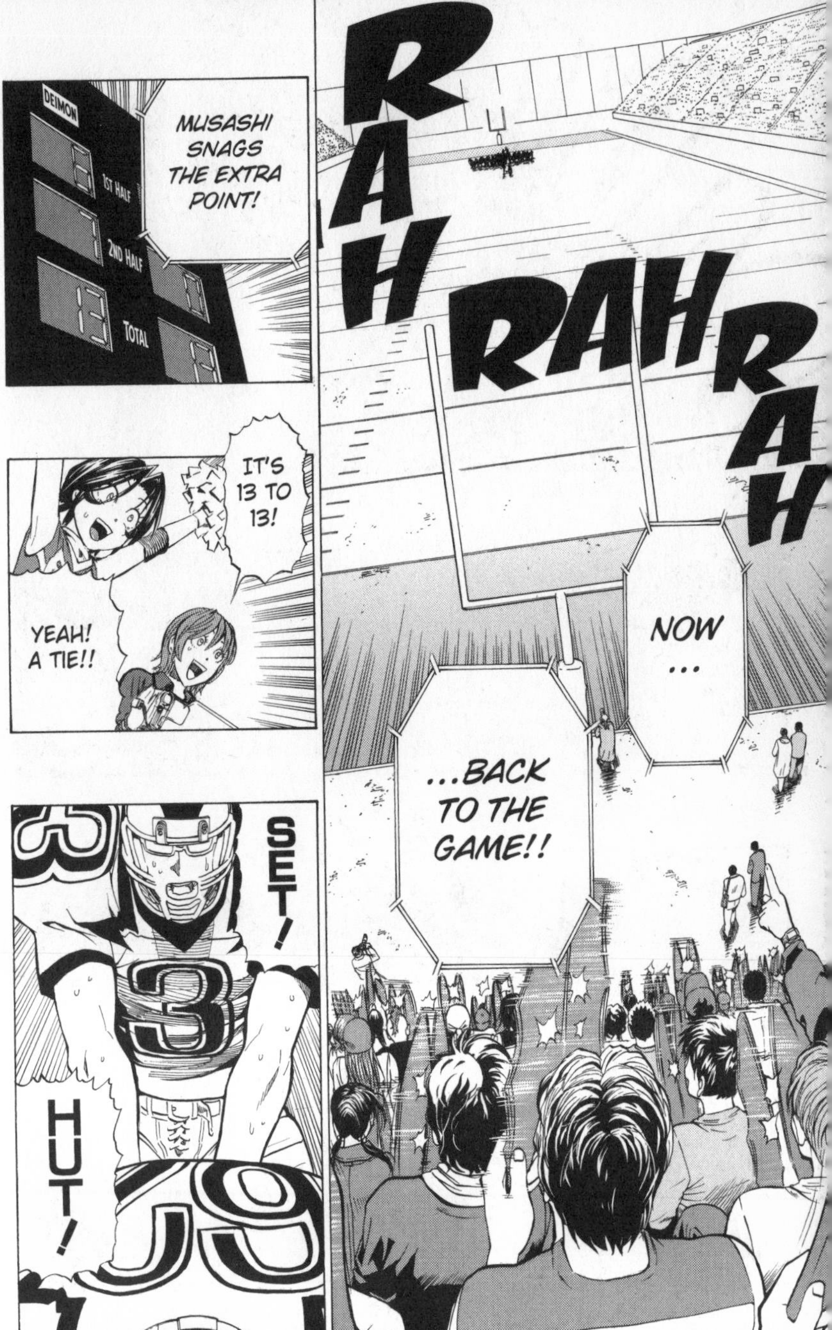
RAH RAH RAH
NOW...
...BACK TO THE GAME!!
MUSASHI SNAGS THE EXTRA POINT!
DEIMON
1ST HALF
2ND HALF
TOTAL
IT'S 13 TO 13!
YEAH! A TIE!!
SET!
HUT!

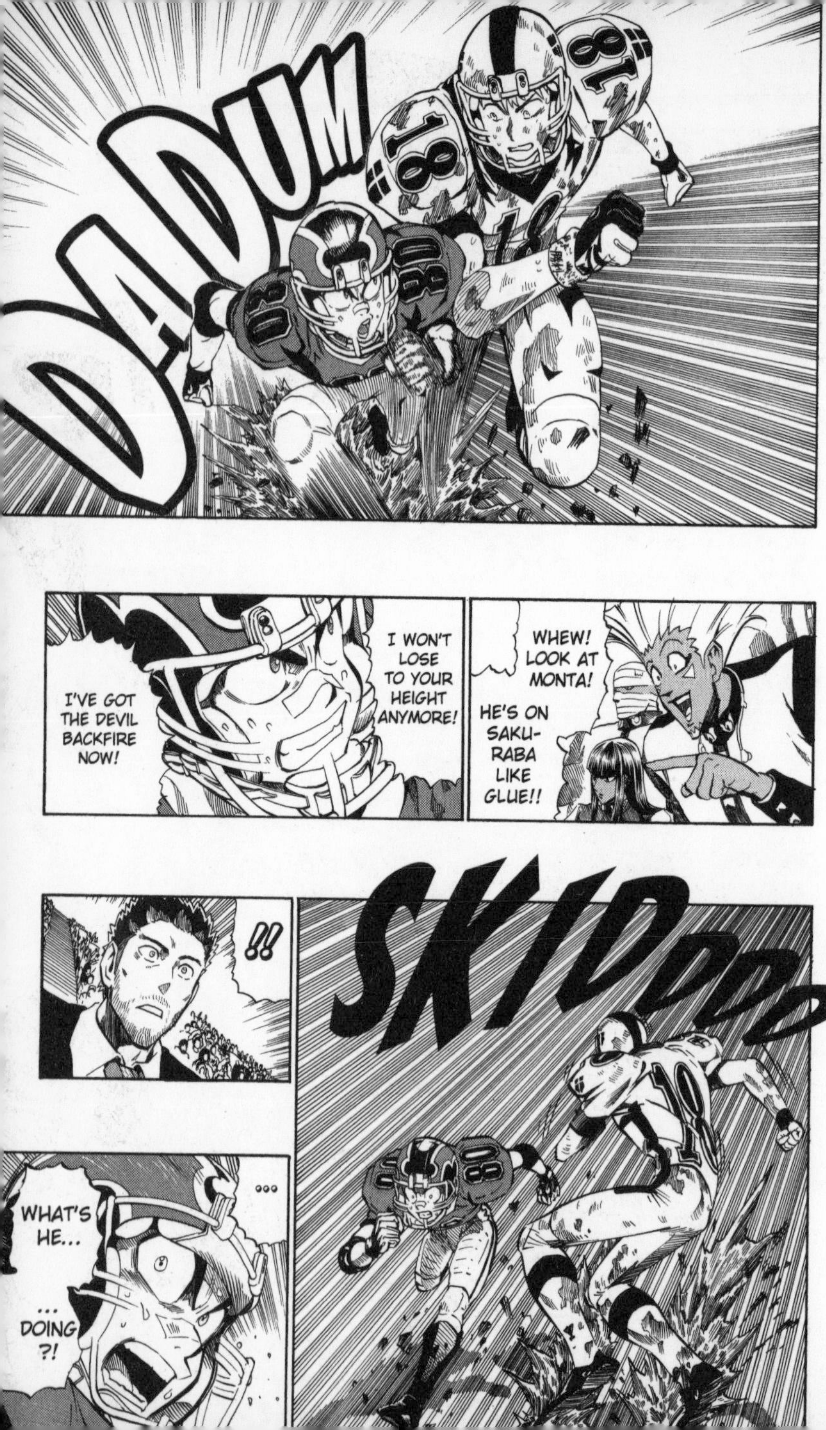
DADUM
WHEW! LOOK AT MONTA!
HE'S ON SAKU-RABA LIKE GLUE!!
I WON'T LOSE TO YOUR HEIGHT ANYMORE!
I'VE GOT THE DEVIL BACKFIRE NOW!
SKIDDDD
!!
...
WHAT'S HE...
...DOING?!

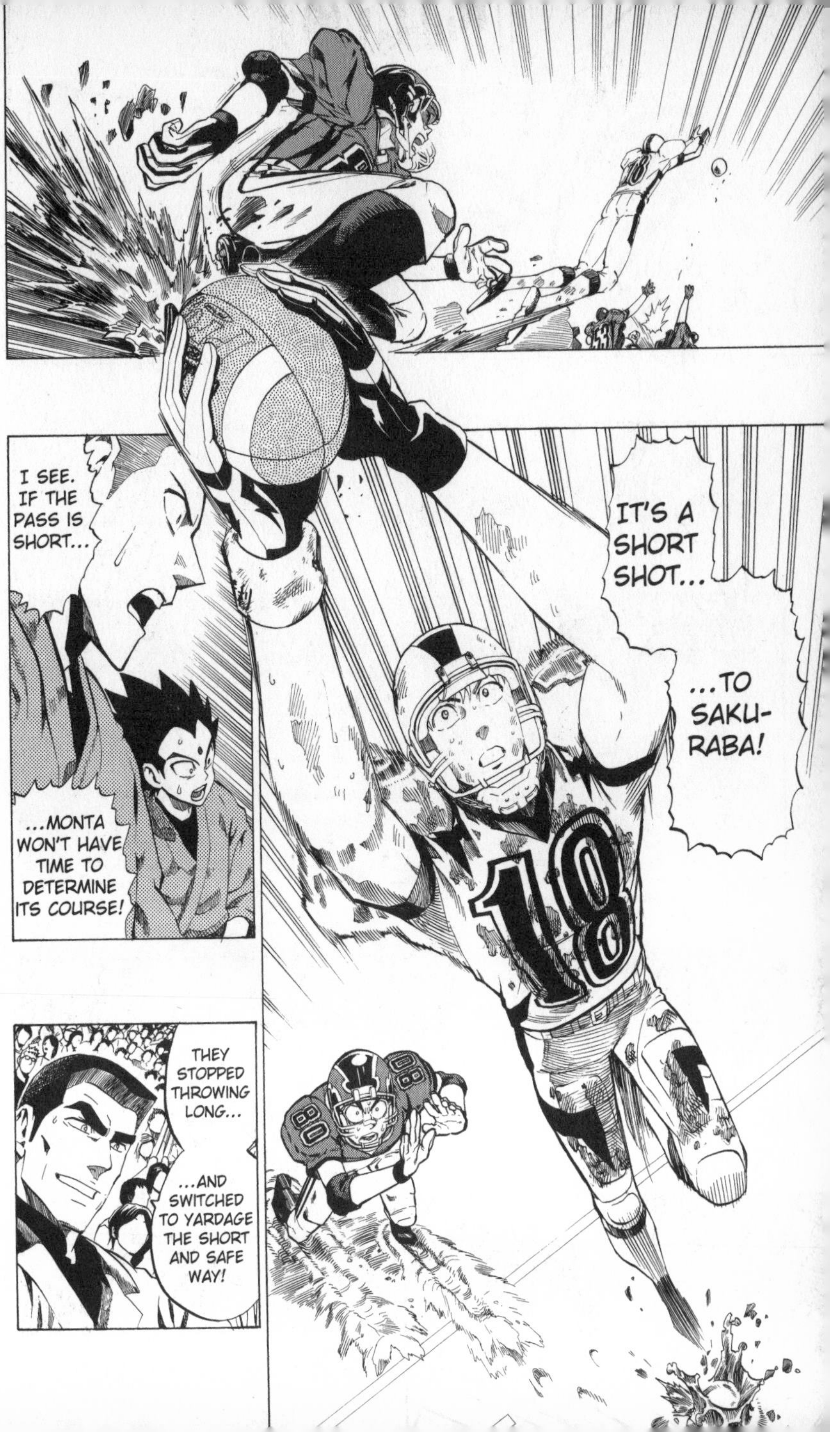
IT'S A SHORT SHOT...
...TO SAKU-RABA!
I SEE. IF THE PASS IS SHORT...
...MONTA WON'T HAVE TIME TO DETERMINE ITS COURSE!
THEY STOPPED THROWING LONG...
...AND SWITCHED TO YARDAGE THE SHORT AND SAFE WAY!

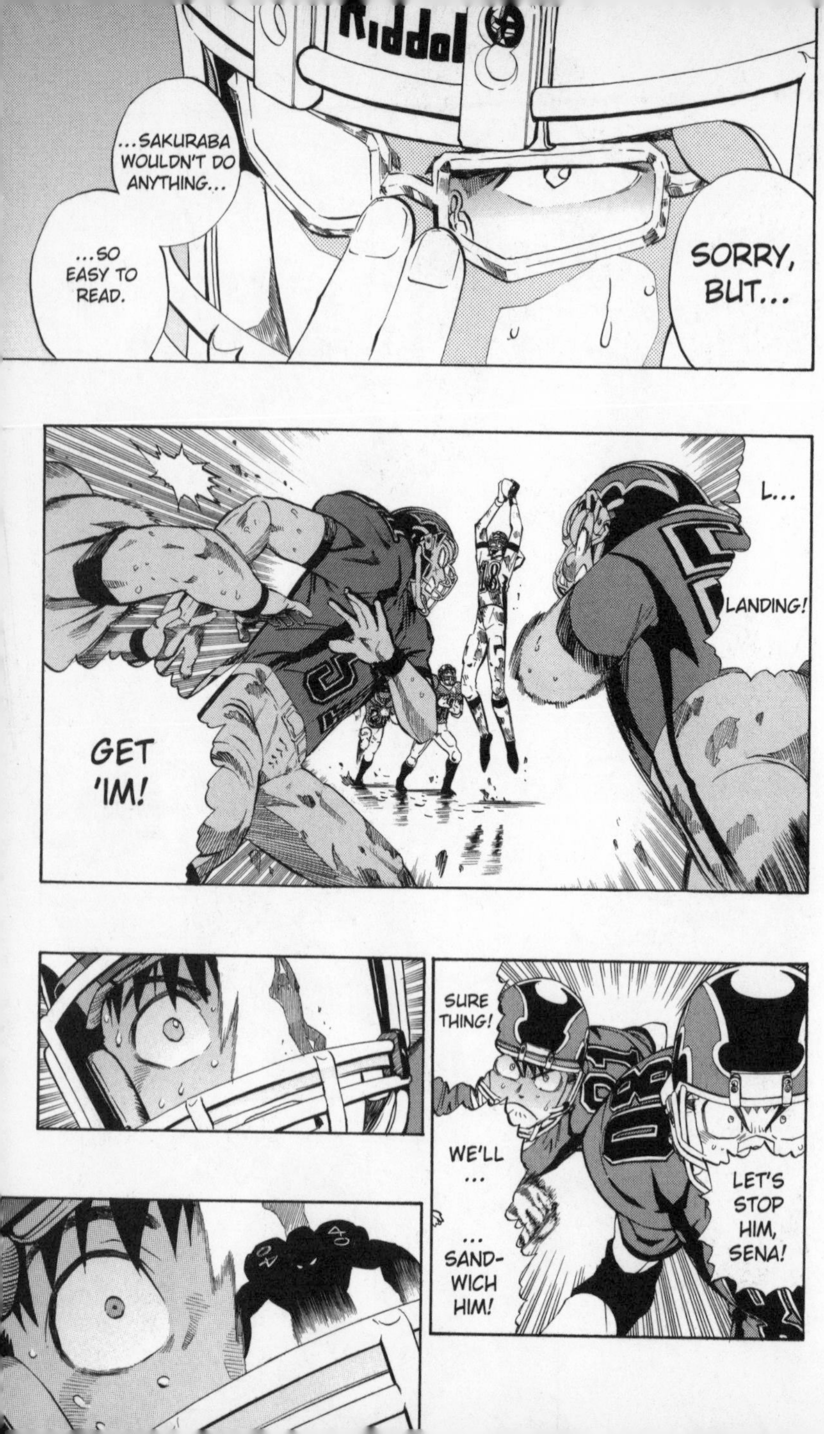
SORRY, BUT...
...SAKURABA WOULDN'T DO ANYTHING...
...SO EASY TO READ.
L...
LANDING!
GET 'IM!
LET'S STOP HIM, SENA!
SURE THING!
WE'LL...
...SANDWICH HIM!

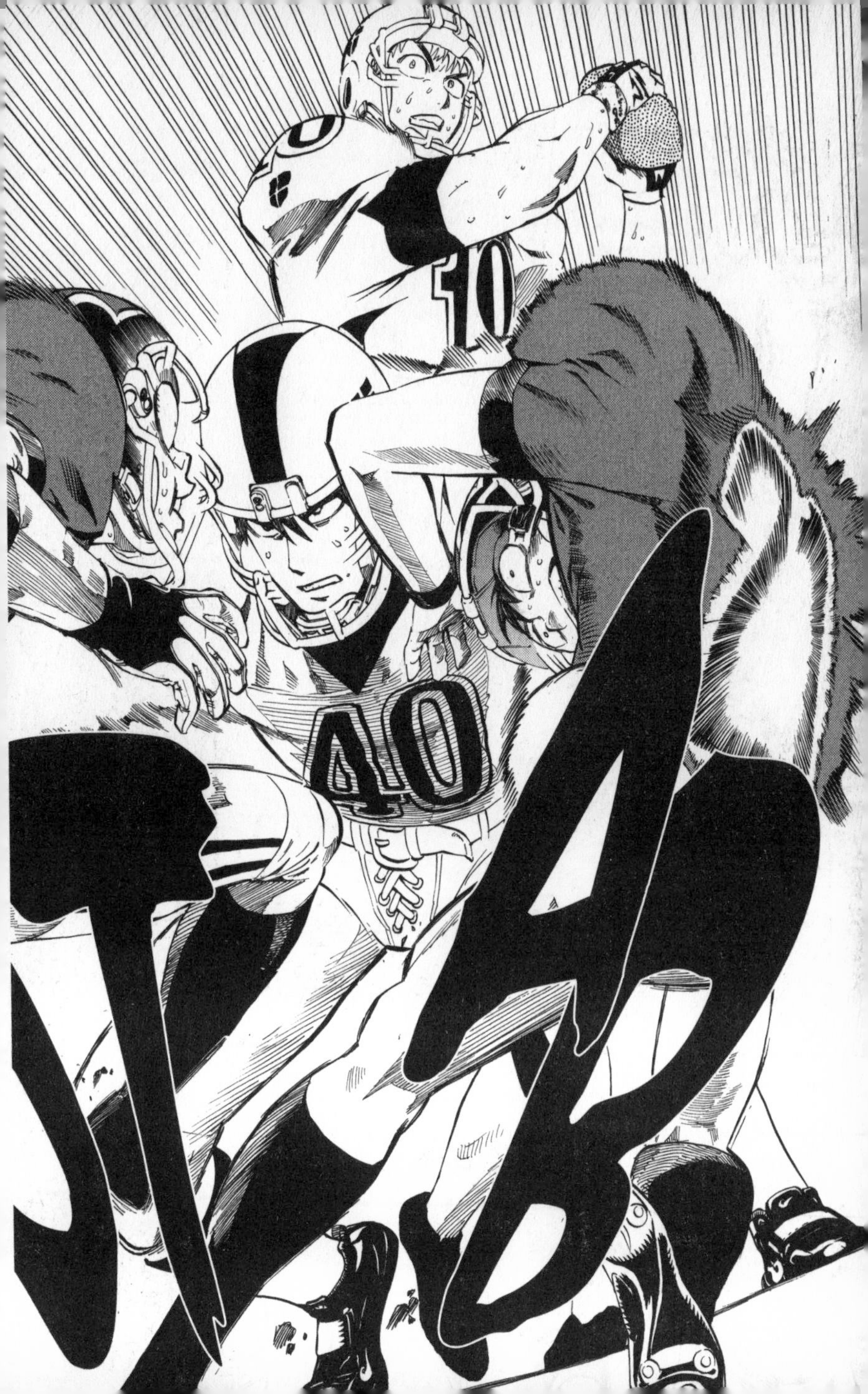

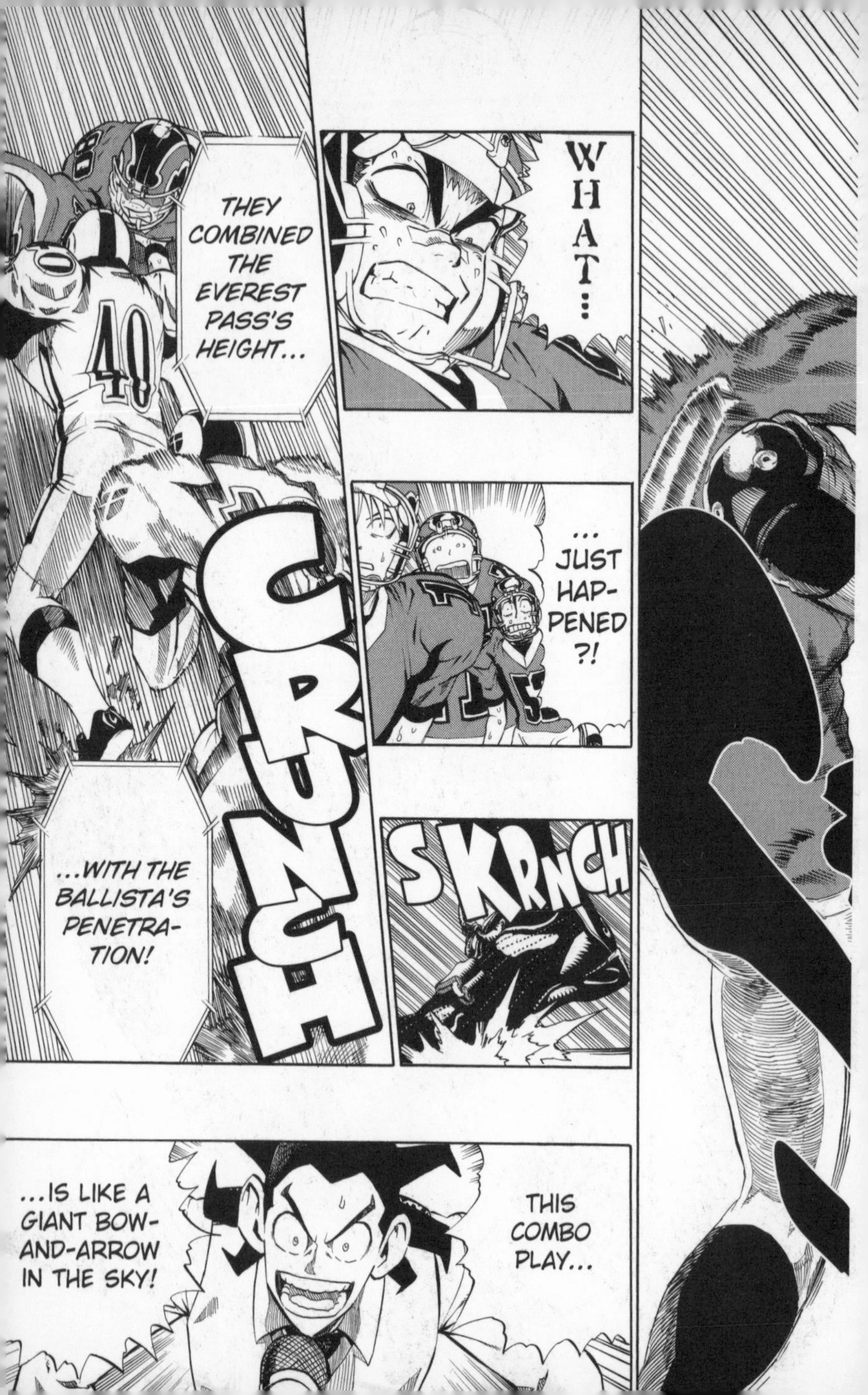
WHAT...
THEY COMBINED THE EVEREST PASS'S HEIGHT...
...JUST HAPPENED?!
CRUNCH
SKRNCH
...WITH THE BALLISTA'S PENETRATION!
THIS COMBO PLAY...
...IS LIKE A GIANT BOW-AND-ARROW IN THE SKY!

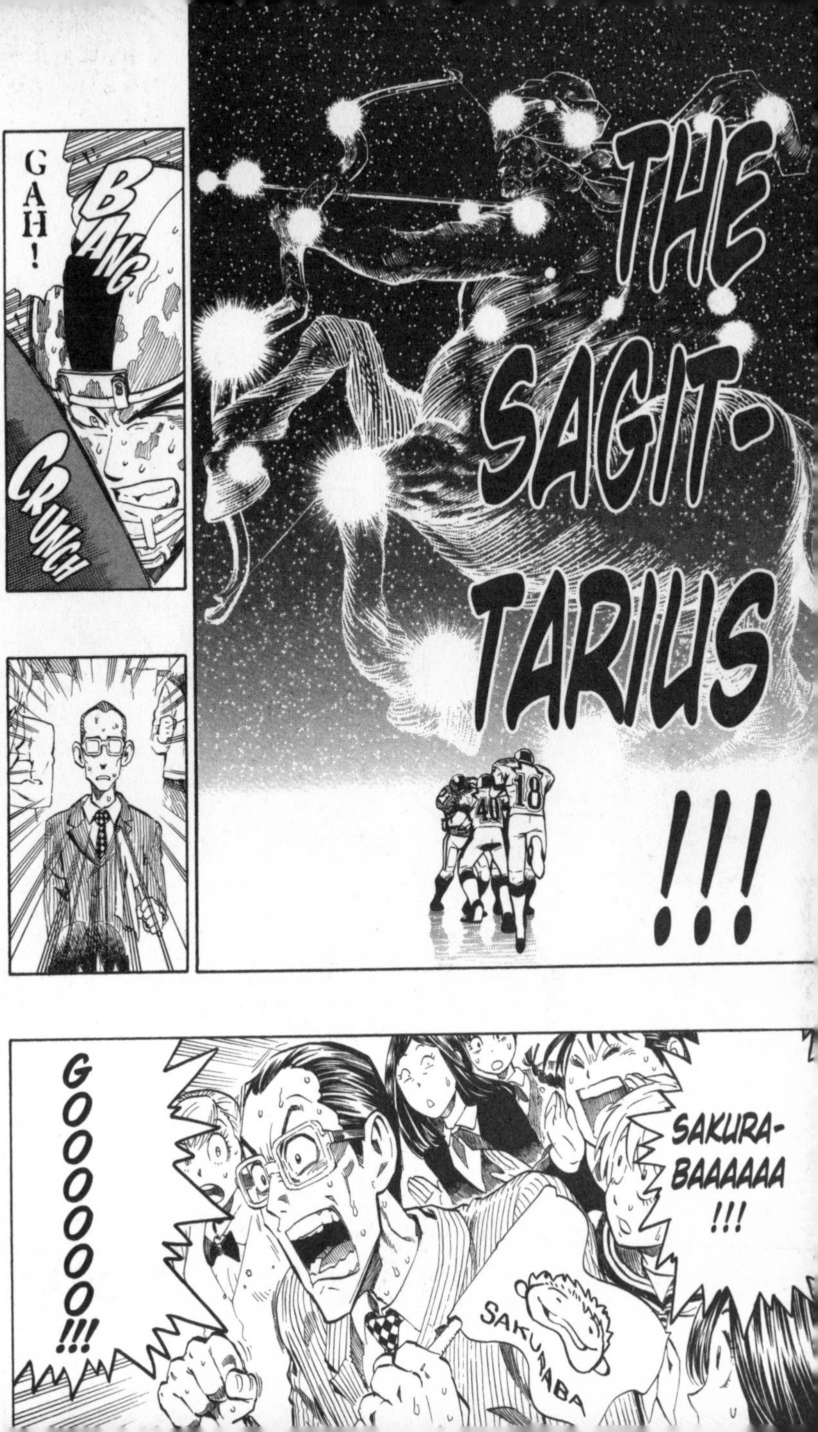
THE SAGIT-TARIUS!!!
BANG
GAH!
CRUNCH
SAKURA-BAAAAAA!!!
SAKURABA
GOOOOOOOO!!!

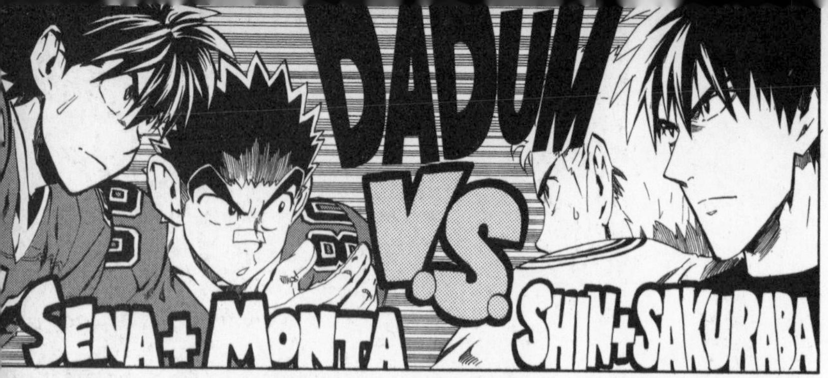
DADUM
V.S.
SHIN + SAKURABA
SENA + MONTA

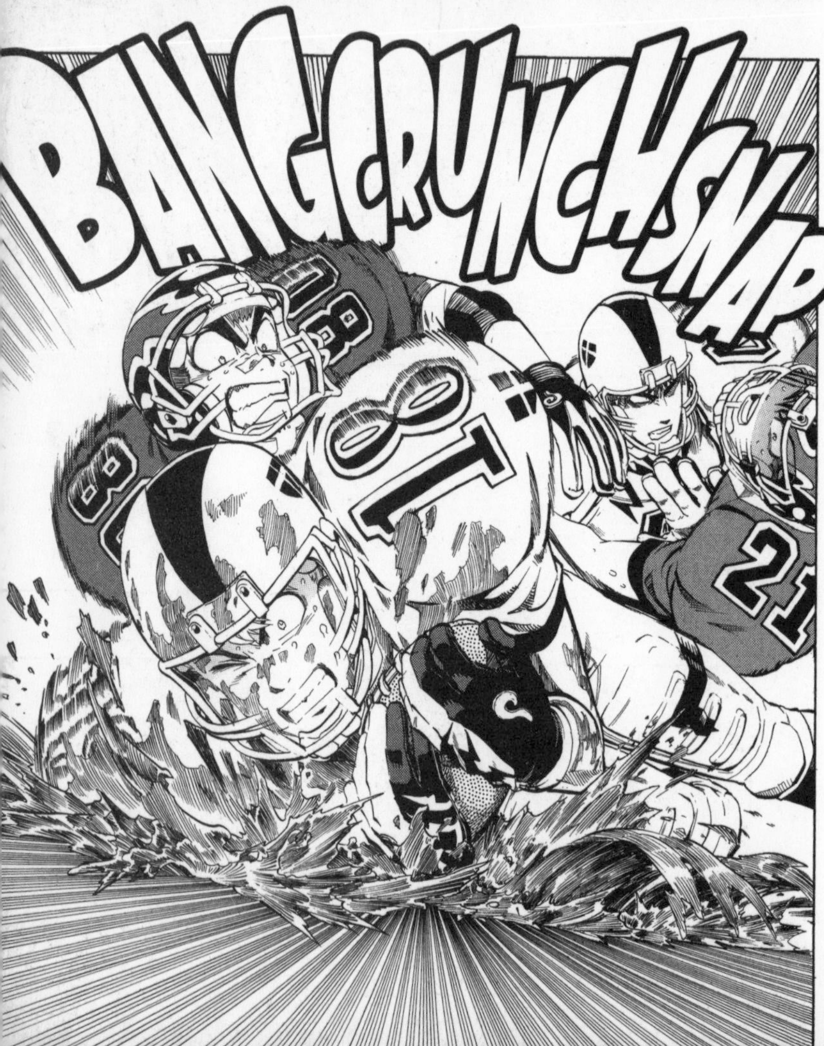
BANG CRUNCH SNAP

RIVAL BATTLE ★ DEIMON VS. OJO

SUPER MISCELLANY MATCH-UPS!!

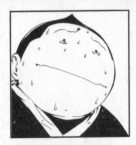

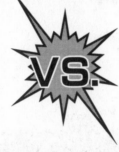

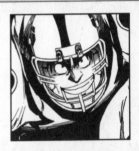

VS.

KURITA VS. **OTAWARA**

WIN | APPETITE |

| MAKING DOODY | WIN

VS.

JUMONJI VS. **IKARI**

| NUMBER OF FIGHTS PICKED | WIN

WIN | NUMBER OF TIMES SOMEONE PICKED A FIGHT WITH HIM |

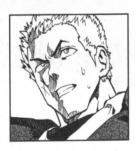

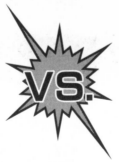

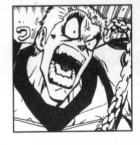

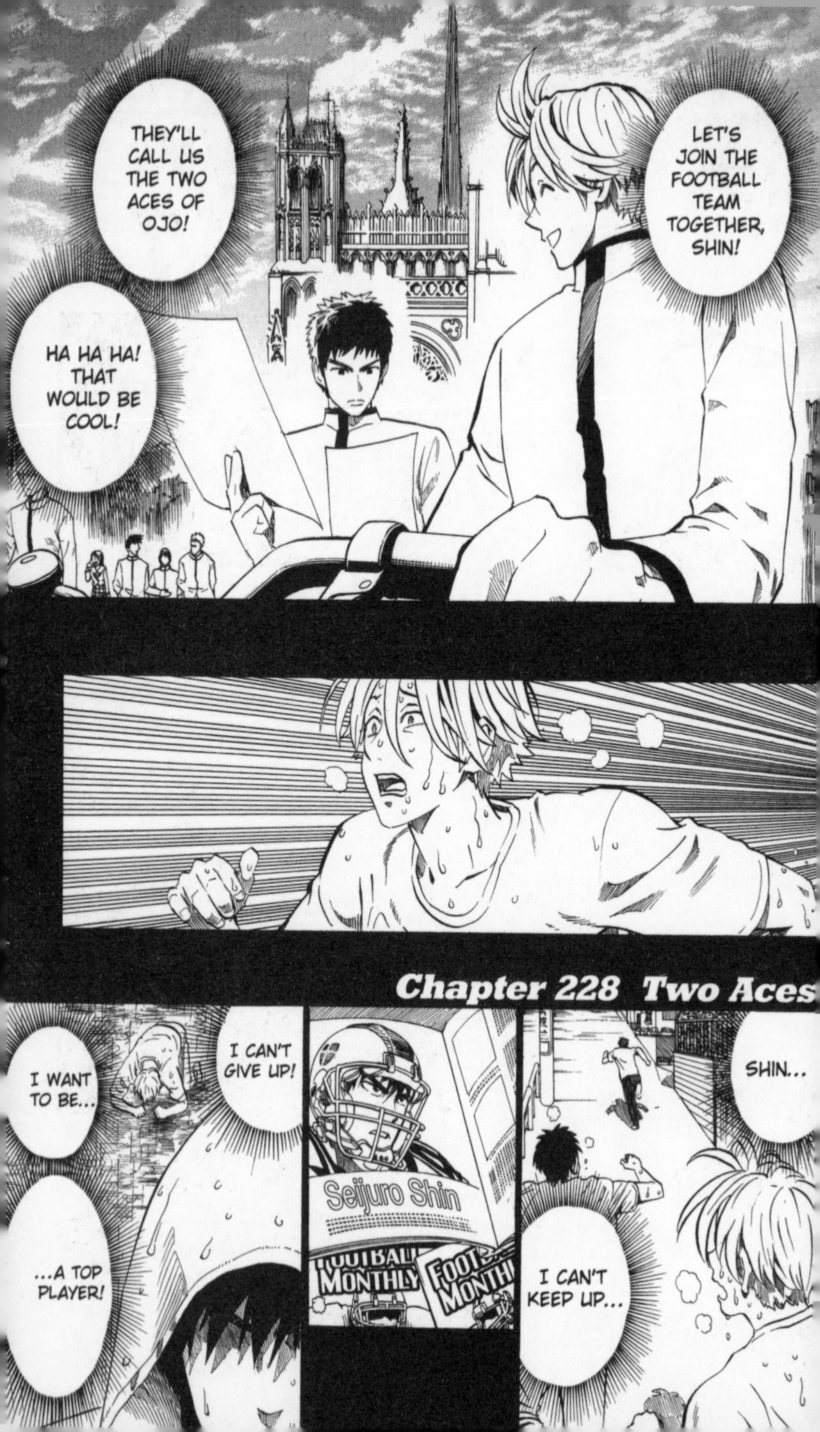
LET'S JOIN THE FOOTBALL TEAM TOGETHER, SHIN!
THEY'LL CALL US THE TWO ACES OF OJO!
HA HA HA! THAT WOULD BE COOL!
Chapter 228 Two Aces
SHIN...
I CAN'T KEEP UP...
Seijuro Shin
MONTHLY
I CAN'T GIVE UP!
I WANT TO BE...
...A TOP PLAYER!

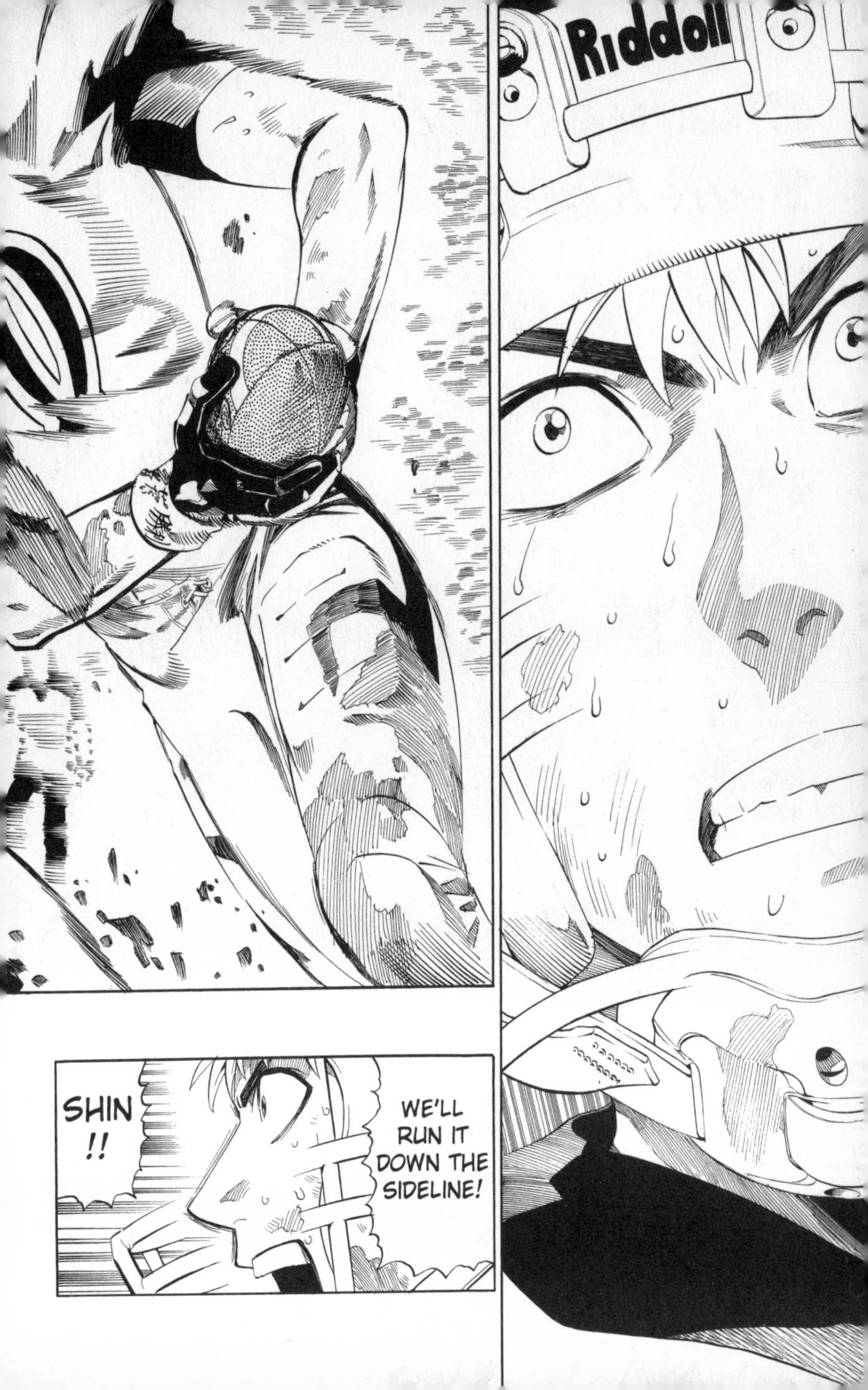
WE'LL RUN IT DOWN THE SIDELINE!
SHIN !!
Riddell

Chapter 228
Two Aces

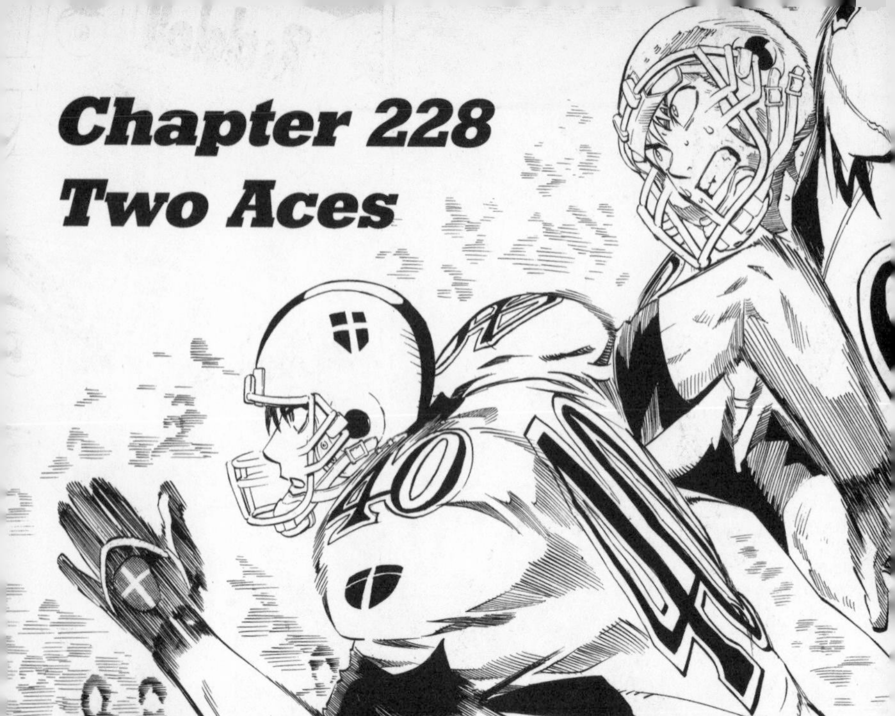

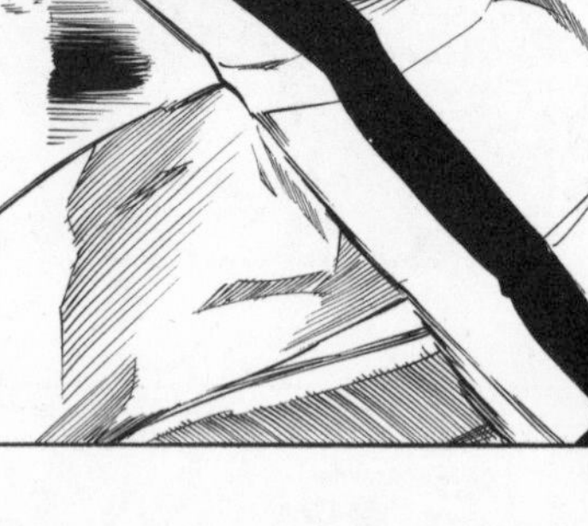
I HEAR YOU.
TOGETHER, WE'LL BREAK THROUGH.

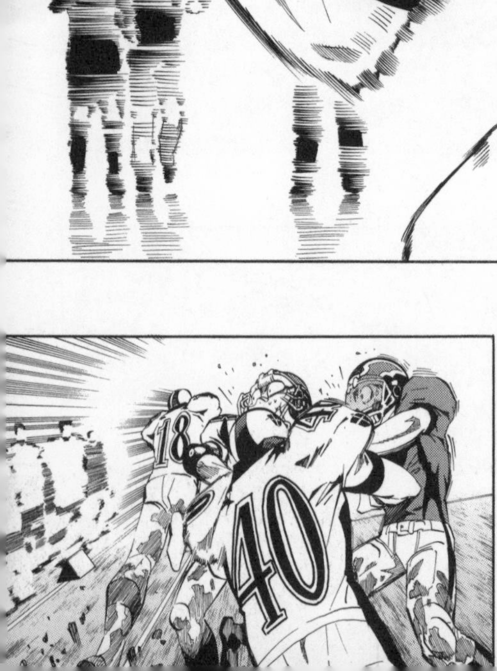

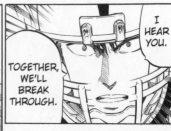

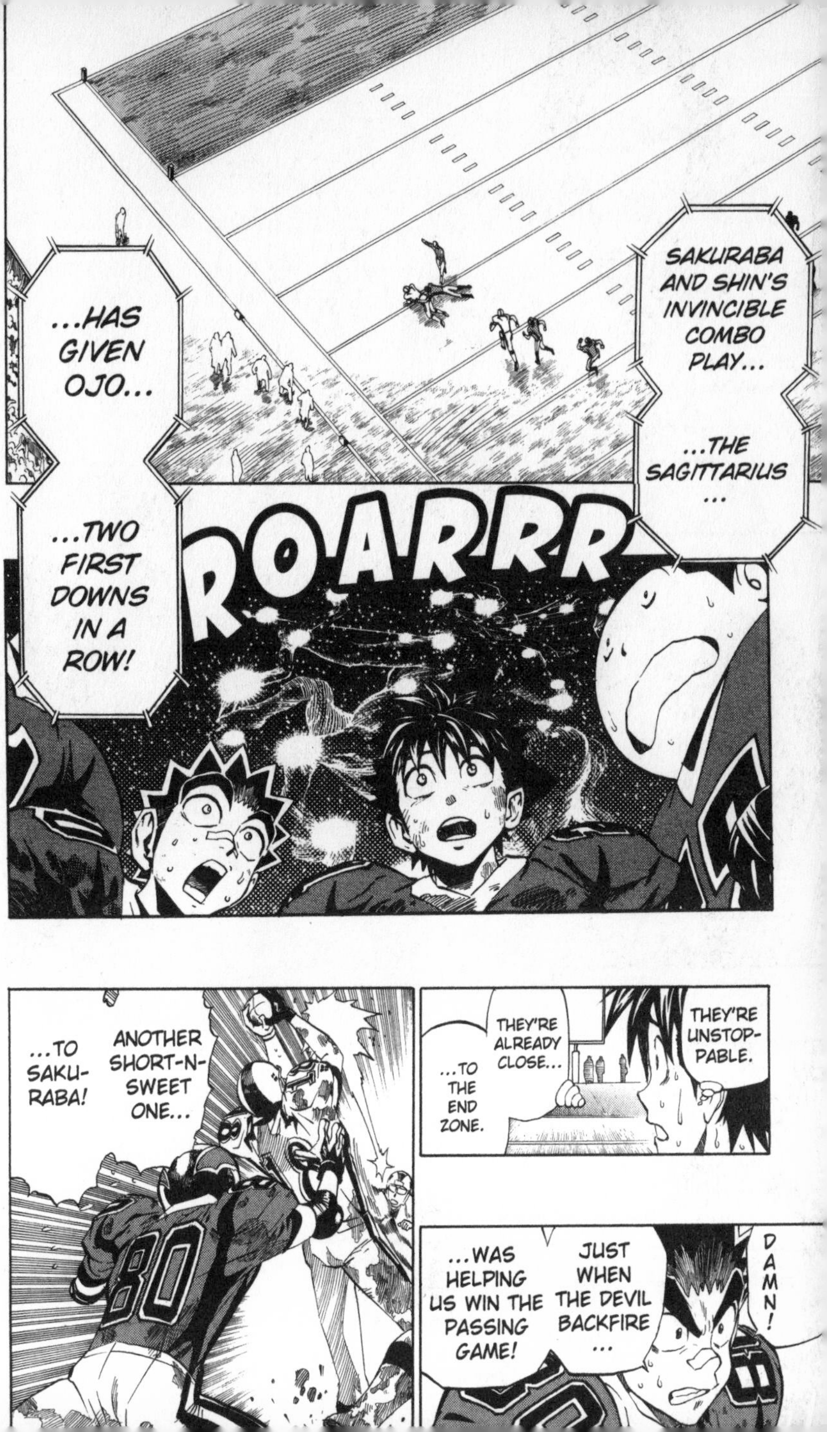
SAKURABA AND SHIN'S INVINCIBLE COMBO PLAY...
...THE SAGITTARIUS ...
...HAS GIVEN OJO...
...TWO FIRST DOWNS IN A ROW!
ROARRR
THEY'RE UNSTOP-PABLE.
THEY'RE ALREADY CLOSE...
...TO THE END ZONE.
DAMN!
JUST WHEN THE DEVIL BACKFIRE ...
...WAS HELPING US WIN THE PASSING GAME!
ANOTHER SHORT-N-SWEET ONE...
...TO SAKU-RABA!

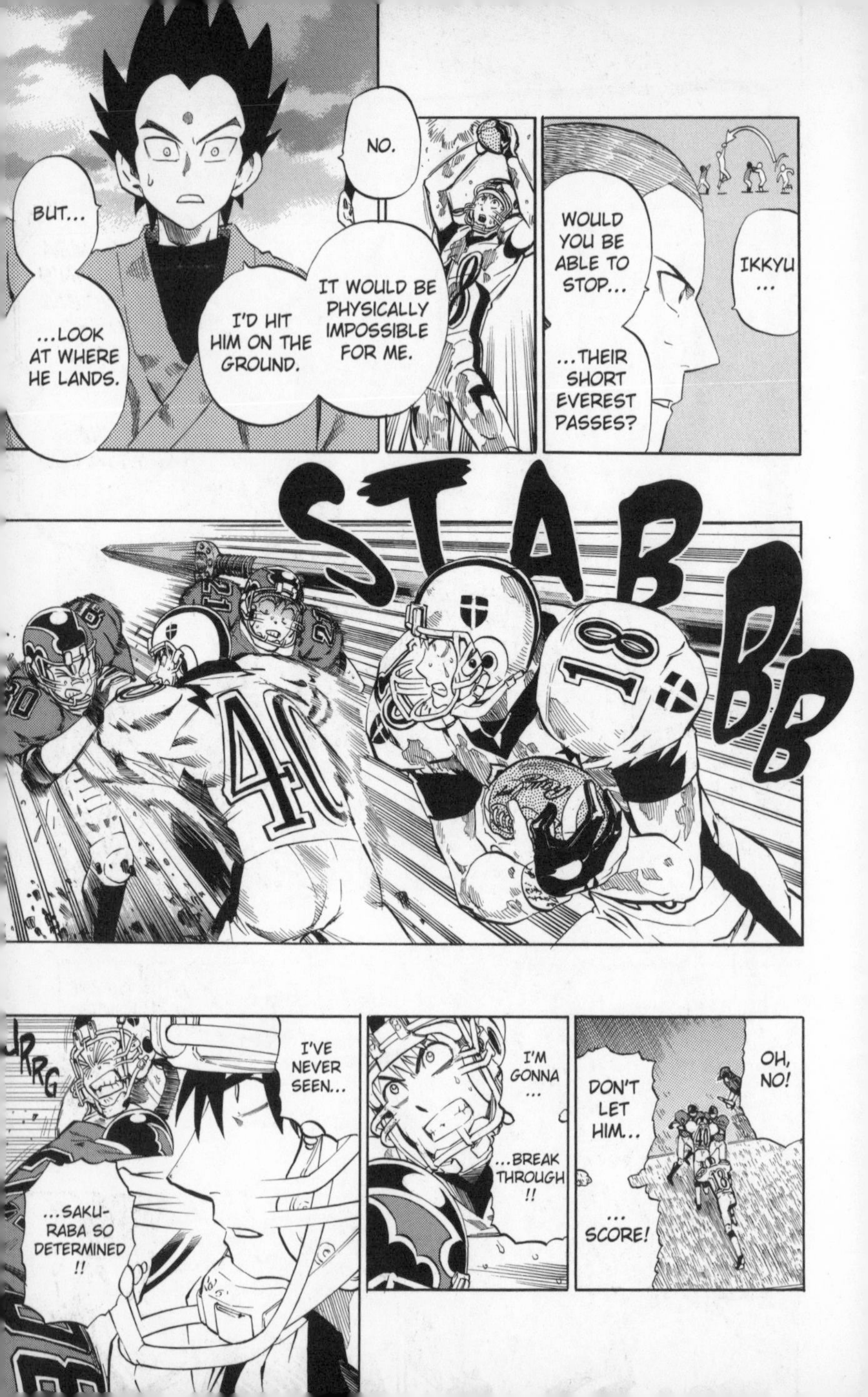
IKKYU ...
WOULD YOU BE ABLE TO STOP...
...THEIR SHORT EVEREST PASSES?
NO.
IT WOULD BE PHYSICALLY IMPOSSIBLE FOR ME.
I'D HIT HIM ON THE GROUND.
BUT...
...LOOK AT WHERE HE LANDS.
STABBB
OH, NO!
DON'T LET HIM...
... SCORE!
I'M GONNA ...
...BREAK THROUGH !!
I'VE NEVER SEEN...
...SAKU-RABA SO DETERMINED !!

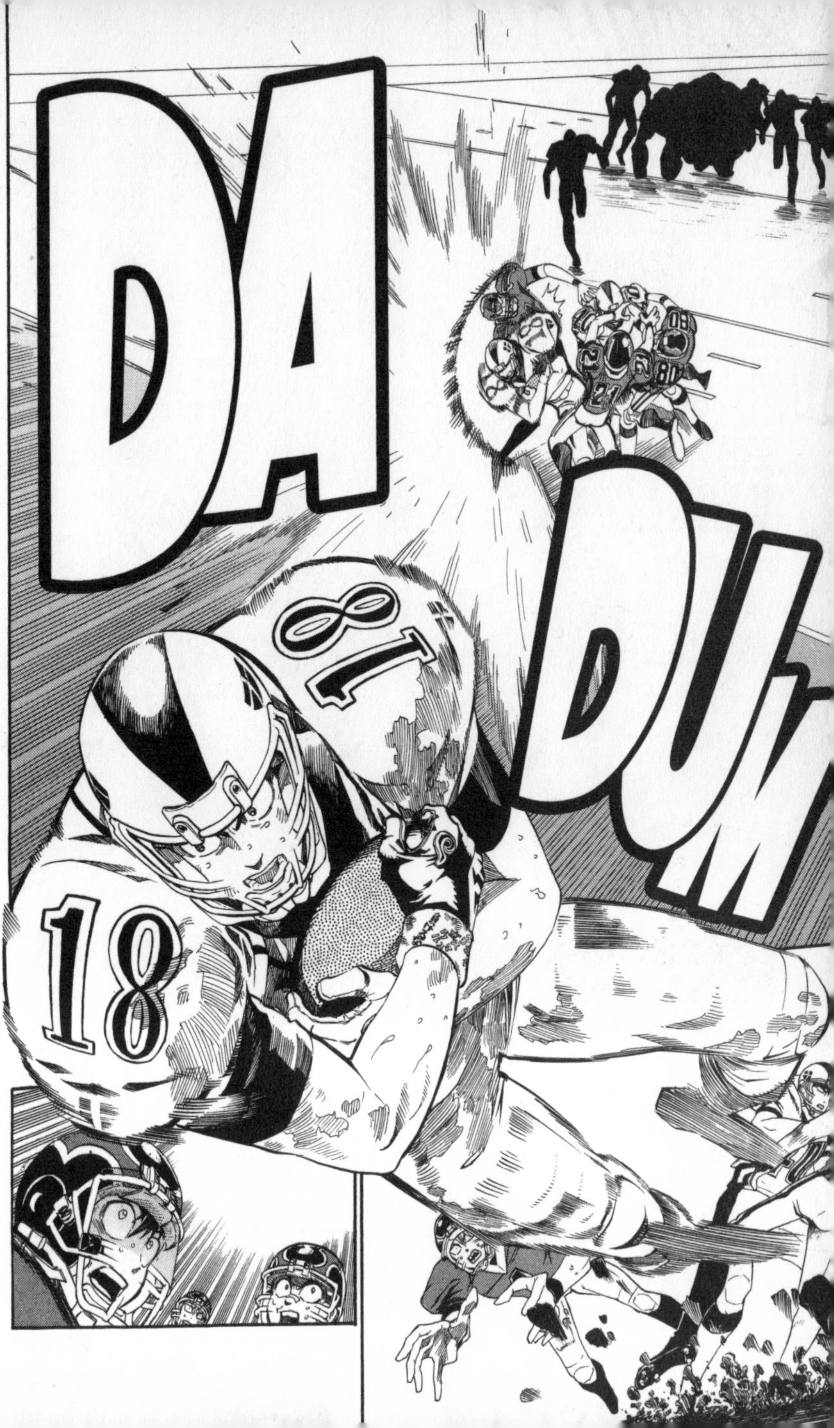
DA DUM

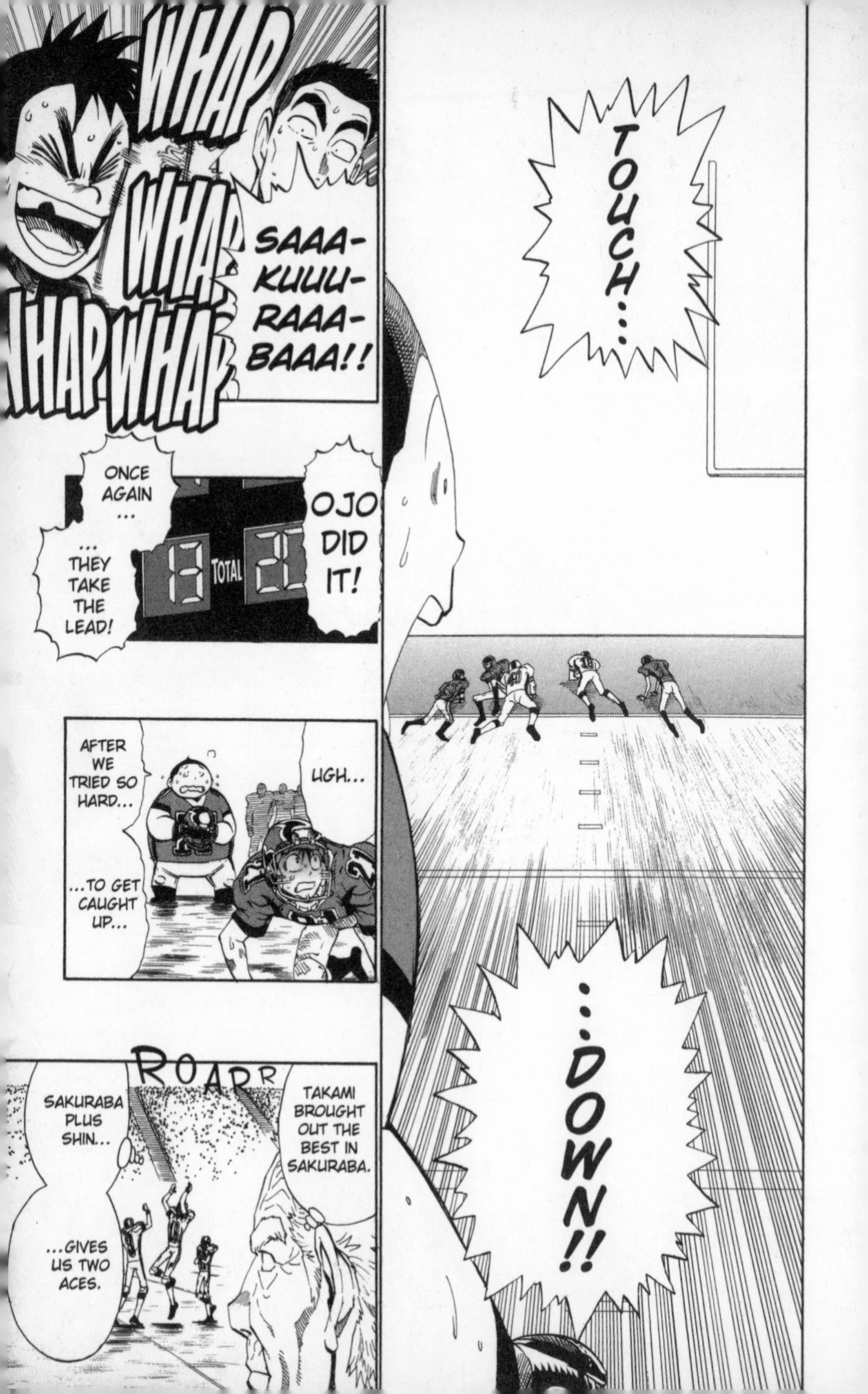
TOUCH...
...DOWN!!
WHAP
WHAP
WHAP WHAP
SAAAA-KUUUU-RAAA-BAAA!!
OJO DID IT!
ONCE AGAIN...
...THEY TAKE THE LEAD!
13 TOTAL 20
UGH...
AFTER WE TRIED SO HARD...
...TO GET CAUGHT UP...
ROARR
TAKAMI BROUGHT OUT THE BEST IN SAKURABA.
SAKURABA PLUS SHIN...
...GIVES US TWO ACES.

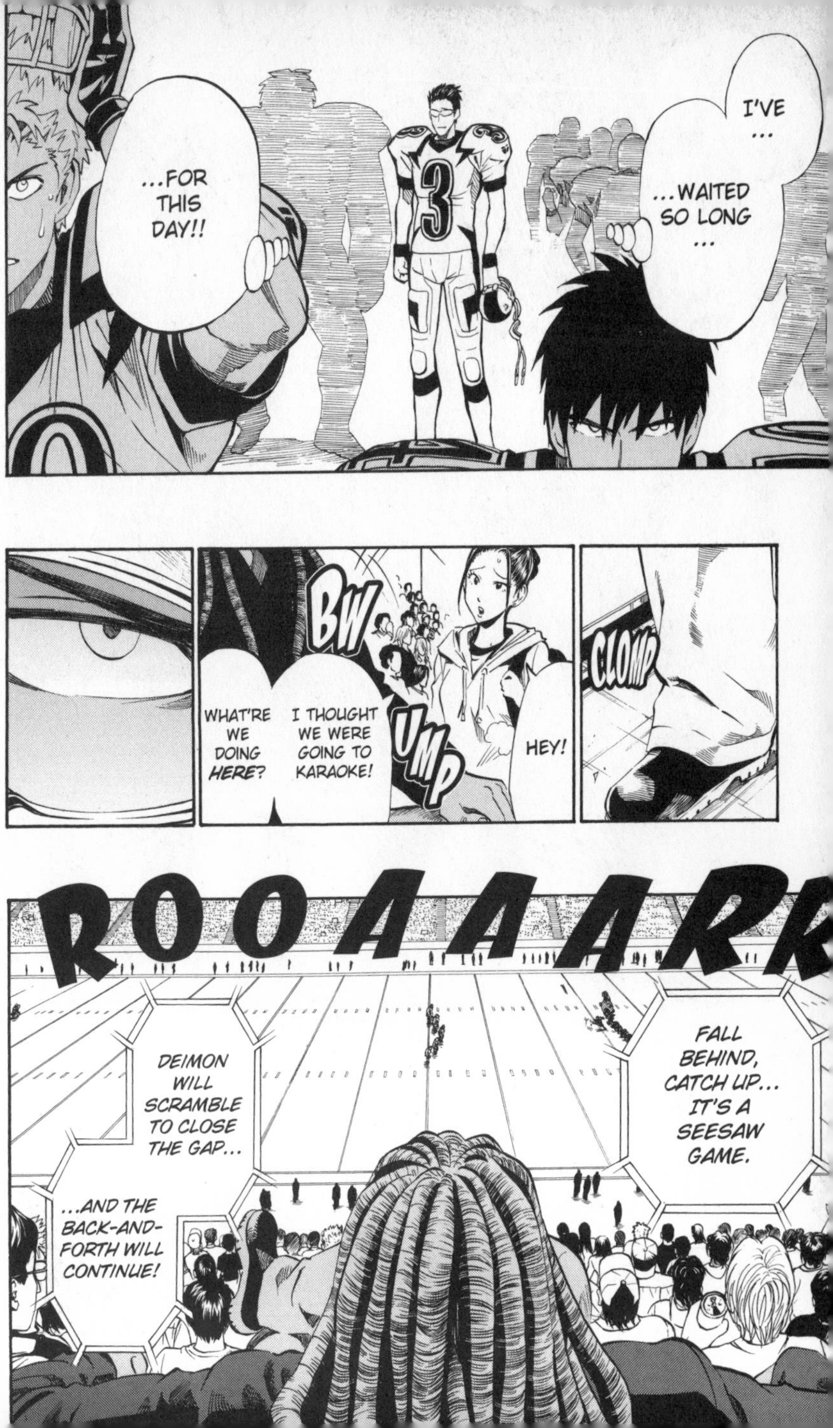
I'VE ...
...WAITED SO LONG ...
...FOR THIS DAY!!
CLOMP
HEY!
BWUMP
I THOUGHT WE WERE GOING TO KARAOKE!
WHAT'RE WE DOING HERE?
ROOAAARR
FALL BEHIND, CATCH UP... IT'S A SEESAW GAME.
DEIMON WILL SCRAMBLE TO CLOSE THE GAP...
...AND THE BACK-AND-FORTH WILL CONTINUE!

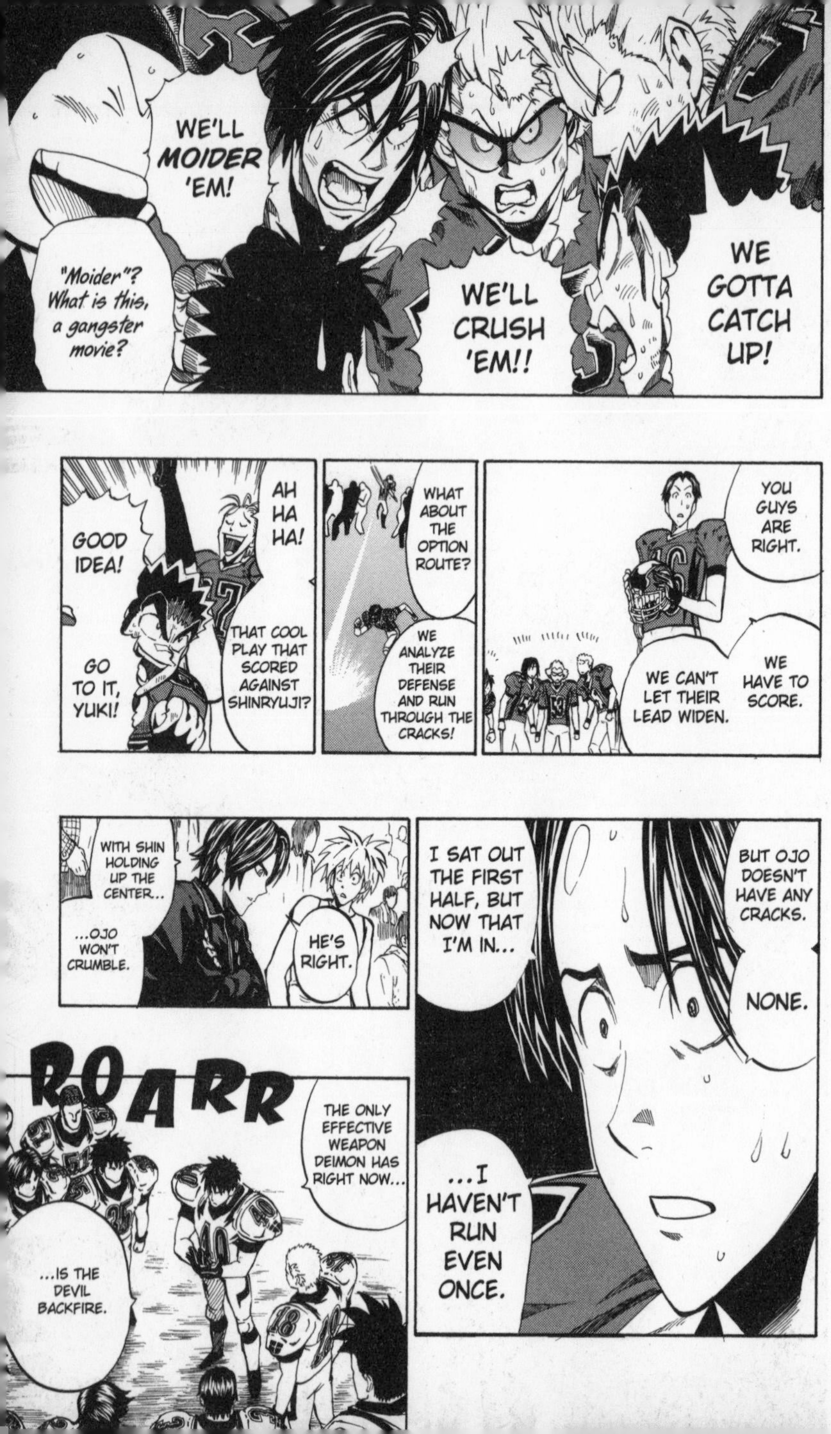
WE GOTTA CATCH UP!
WE'LL CRUSH 'EM!!
WE'LL MOIDER 'EM!
"Moider"? What is this, a gangster movie?
YOU GUYS ARE RIGHT.
WE HAVE TO SCORE.
WE CAN'T LET THEIR LEAD WIDEN.
WHAT ABOUT THE OPTION ROUTE?
WE ANALYZE THEIR DEFENSE AND RUN THROUGH THE CRACKS!
AH HA HA!
THAT COOL PLAY THAT SCORED AGAINST SHINRYUJI?
GOOD IDEA!
GO TO IT, YUKI!
BUT OJO DOESN'T HAVE ANY CRACKS.
NONE.
I SAT OUT THE FIRST HALF, BUT NOW THAT I'M IN...
...I HAVEN'T RUN EVEN ONCE.
WITH SHIN HOLDING UP THE CENTER...
...OJO WON'T CRUMBLE.
HE'S RIGHT.
ROARR
THE ONLY EFFECTIVE WEAPON DEIMON HAS RIGHT NOW...
...IS THE DEVIL BACKFIRE.

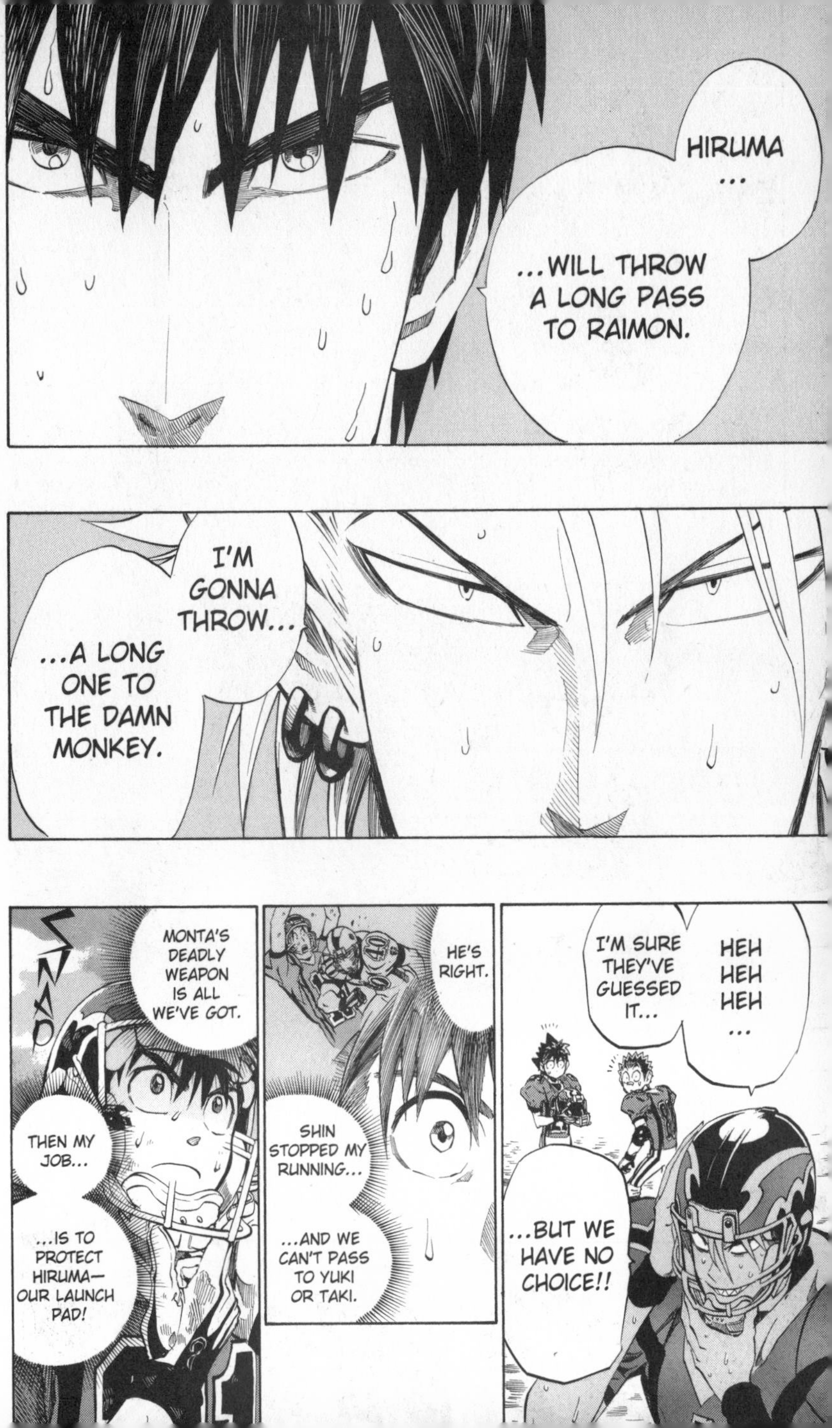
HIRUMA ...
...WILL THROW A LONG PASS TO RAIMON.
I'M GONNA THROW...
...A LONG ONE TO THE DAMN MONKEY.
HEH HEH HEH ...
I'M SURE THEY'VE GUESSED IT...
...BUT WE HAVE NO CHOICE!!
HE'S RIGHT.
SHIN STOPPED MY RUNNING...
...AND WE CAN'T PASS TO YUKI OR TAKI.
SNAP
MONTA'S DEADLY WEAPON IS ALL WE'VE GOT.
THEN MY JOB...
...IS TO PROTECT HIRUMA—OUR LAUNCH PAD!

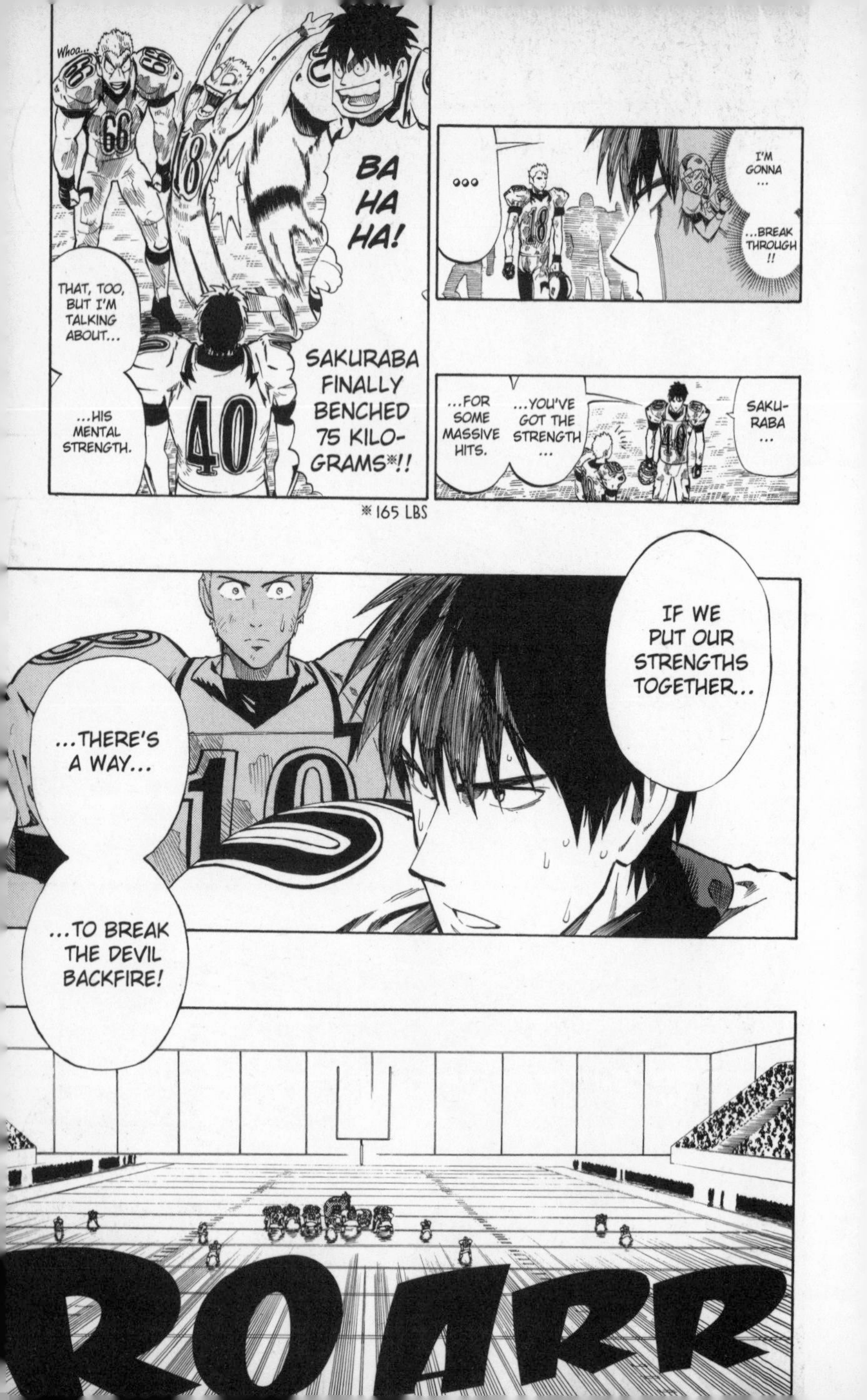
I'M GONNA ...
...BREAK THROUGH !!
...
SAKU-RABA ...
...YOU'VE GOT THE STRENGTH ...
...FOR SOME MASSIVE HITS.
Whoa...
BA HA HA!
THAT, TOO, BUT I'M TALKING ABOUT...
...HIS MENTAL STRENGTH.
SAKURABA FINALLY BENCHED 75 KILO-GRAMS※!!
IF WE PUT OUR STRENGTHS TOGETHER...
...THERE'S A WAY...
...TO BREAK THE DEVIL BACKFIRE!
ROARR

※165 LBS

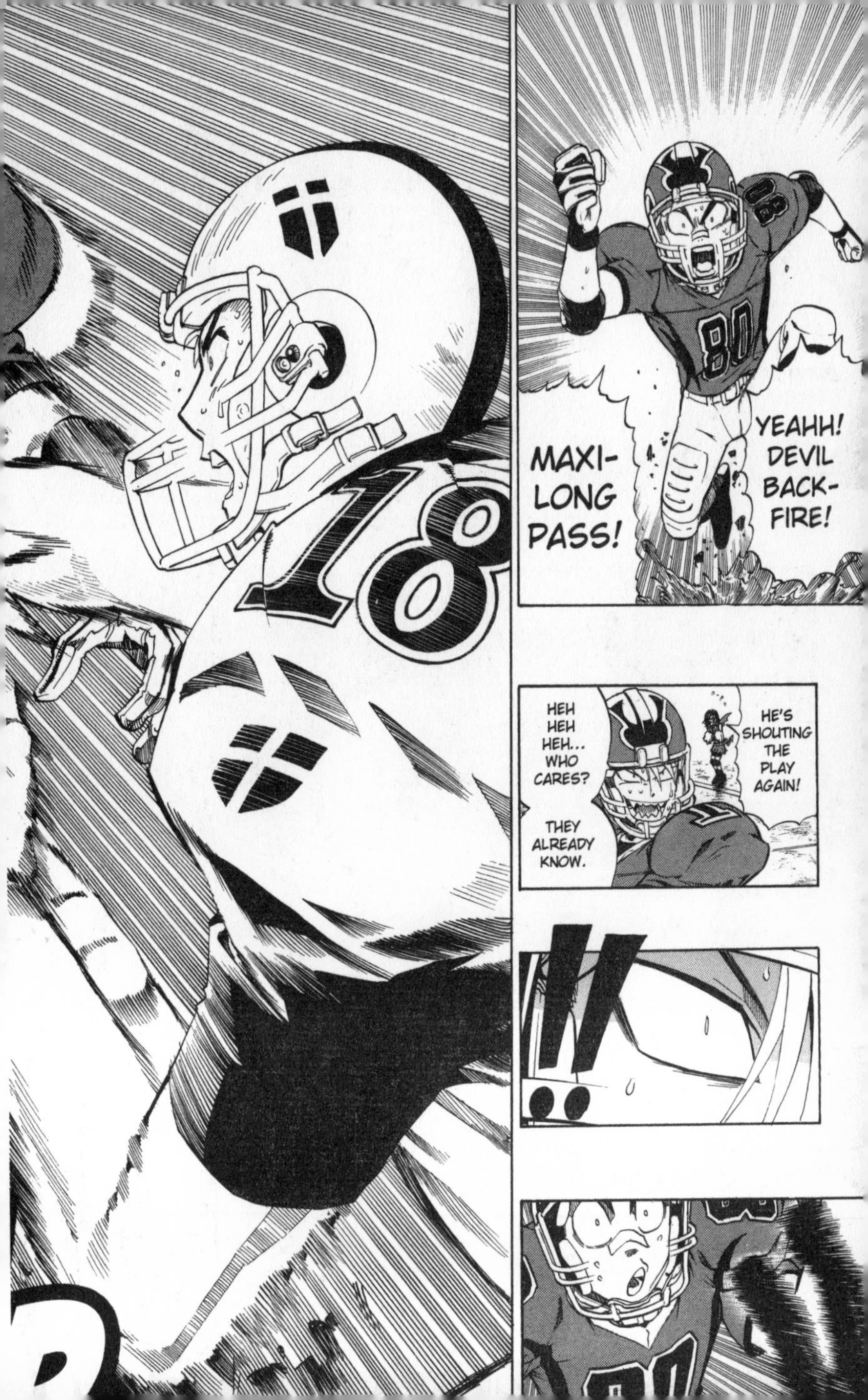
YEAHH! DEVIL BACK-FIRE!
MAXI-LONG PASS!
HE'S SHOUTING THE PLAY AGAIN!
HEH HEH HEH... WHO CARES?
THEY ALREADY KNOW.

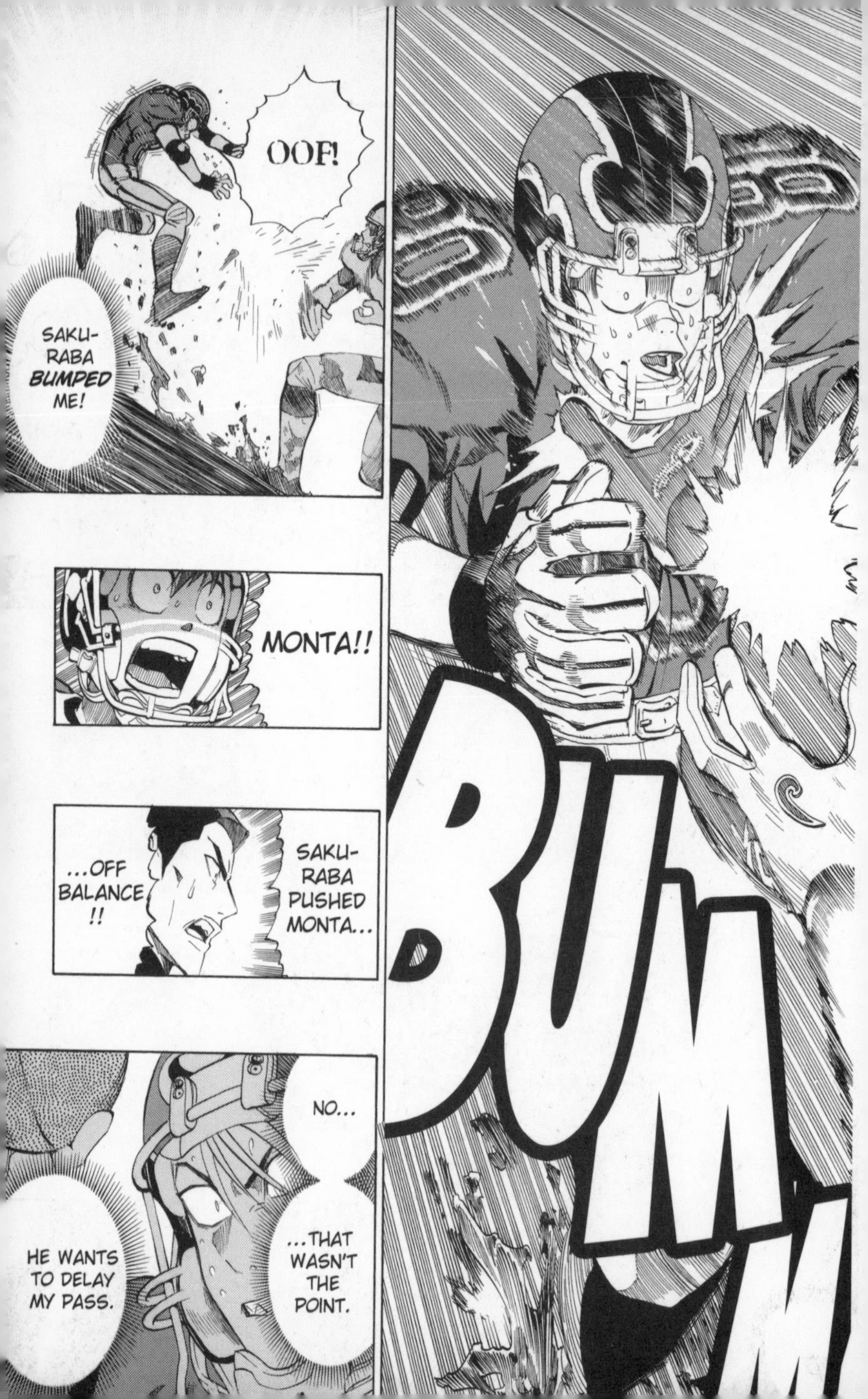
BUMM
OOF!
SAKU-RABA BUMPED ME!
MONTA!!
SAKU-RABA PUSHED MONTA...
...OFF BALANCE!!
NO...
...THAT WASN'T THE POINT.
HE WANTS TO DELAY MY PASS.

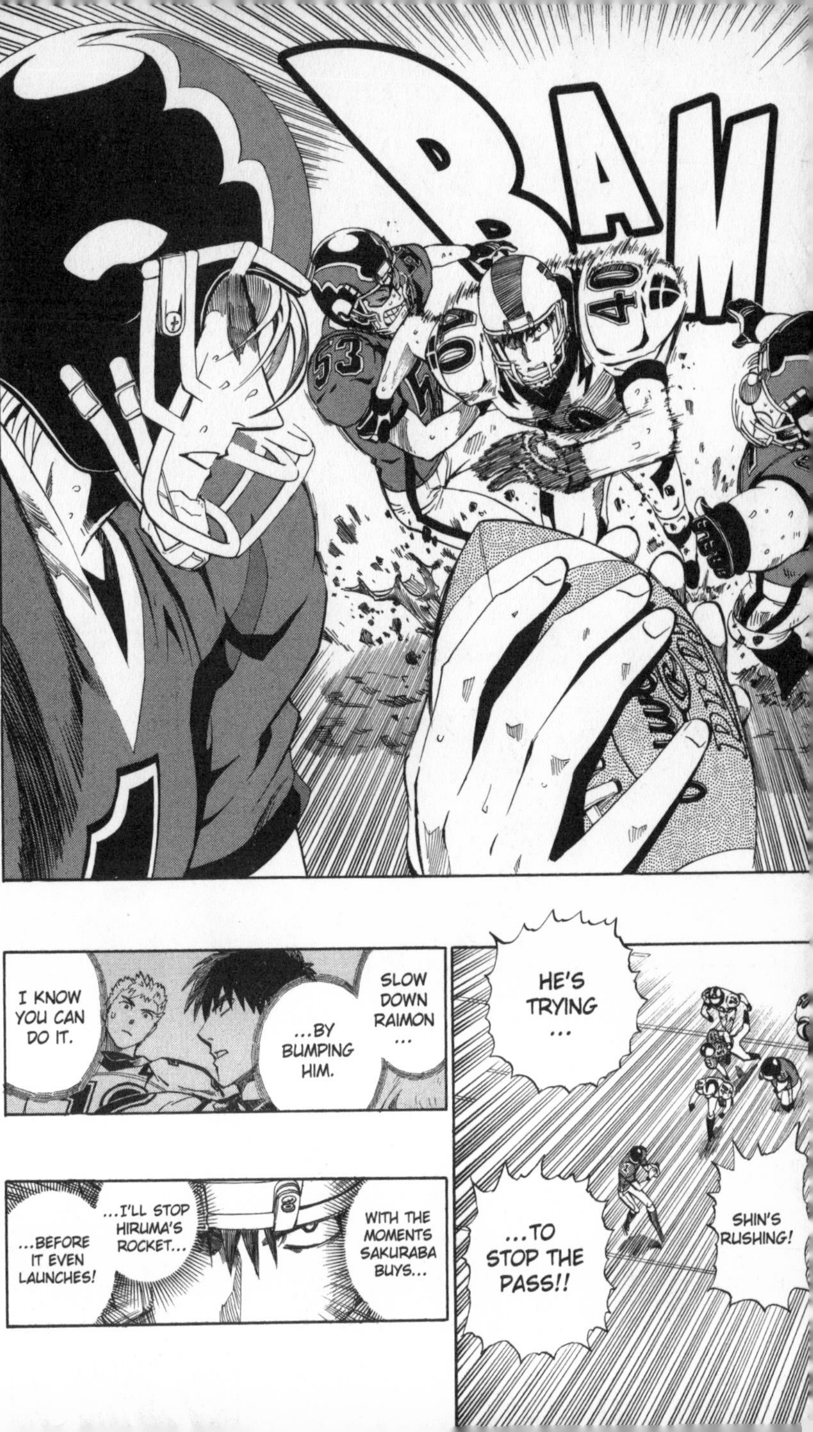
BAM
HE'S TRYING...
SHIN'S RUSHING!
...TO STOP THE PASS!!
SLOW DOWN RAIMON...
...BY BUMPING HIM.
I KNOW YOU CAN DO IT.
WITH THE MOMENTS SAKURABA BUYS...
...I'LL STOP HIRUMA'S ROCKET...
...BEFORE IT EVEN LAUNCHES!

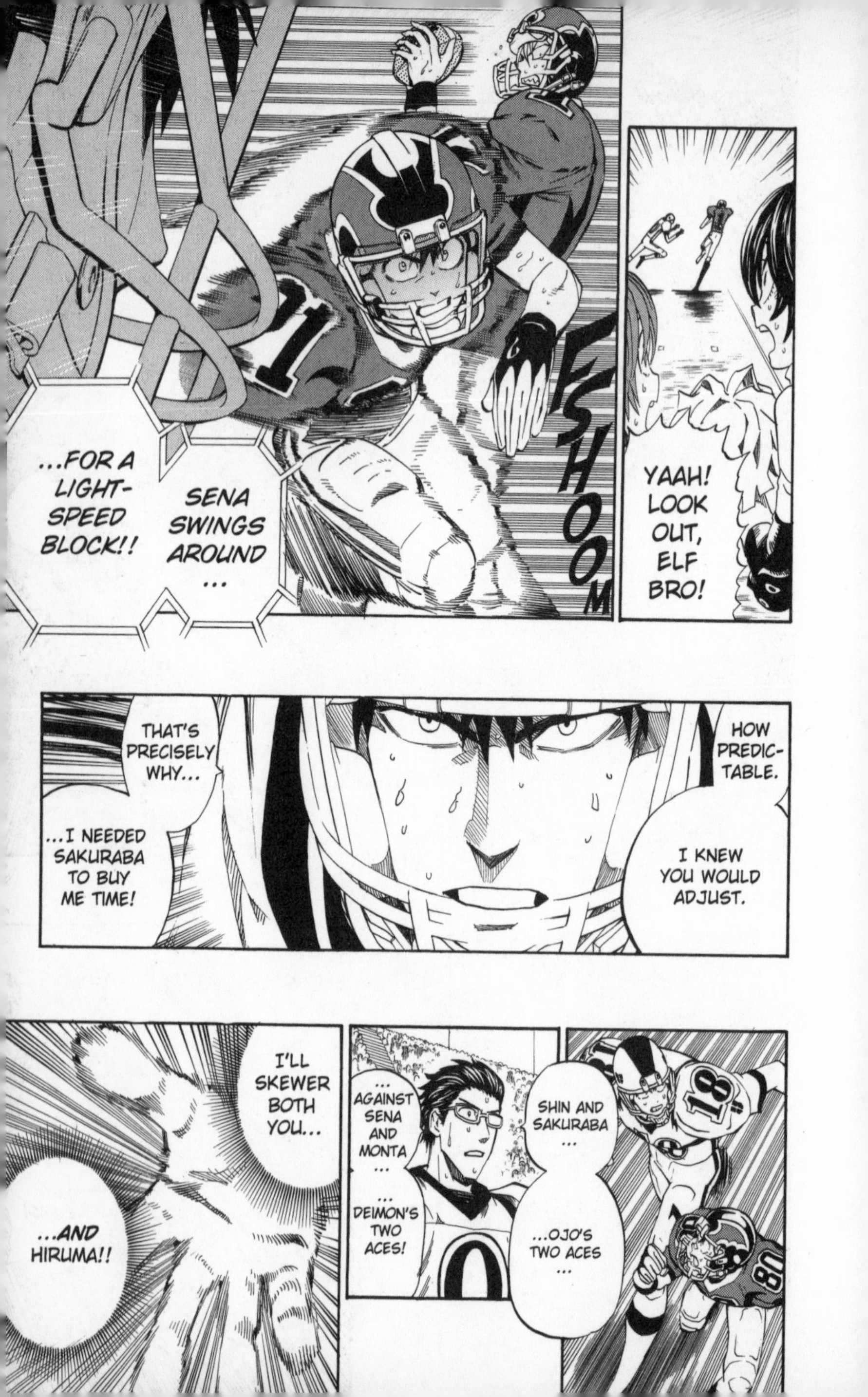

YAAH! LOOK OUT, ELF BRO!
FSHOOM
SENA SWINGS AROUND ...
...FOR A LIGHT-SPEED BLOCK!!
HOW PREDIC-TABLE.
I KNEW YOU WOULD ADJUST.
THAT'S PRECISELY WHY...
...I NEEDED SAKURABA TO BUY ME TIME!
SHIN AND SAKURABA ...
...OJO'S TWO ACES ...
... AGAINST SENA AND MONTA ...
... DEIMON'S TWO ACES!
I'LL SKEWER BOTH YOU...
...AND HIRUMA!!

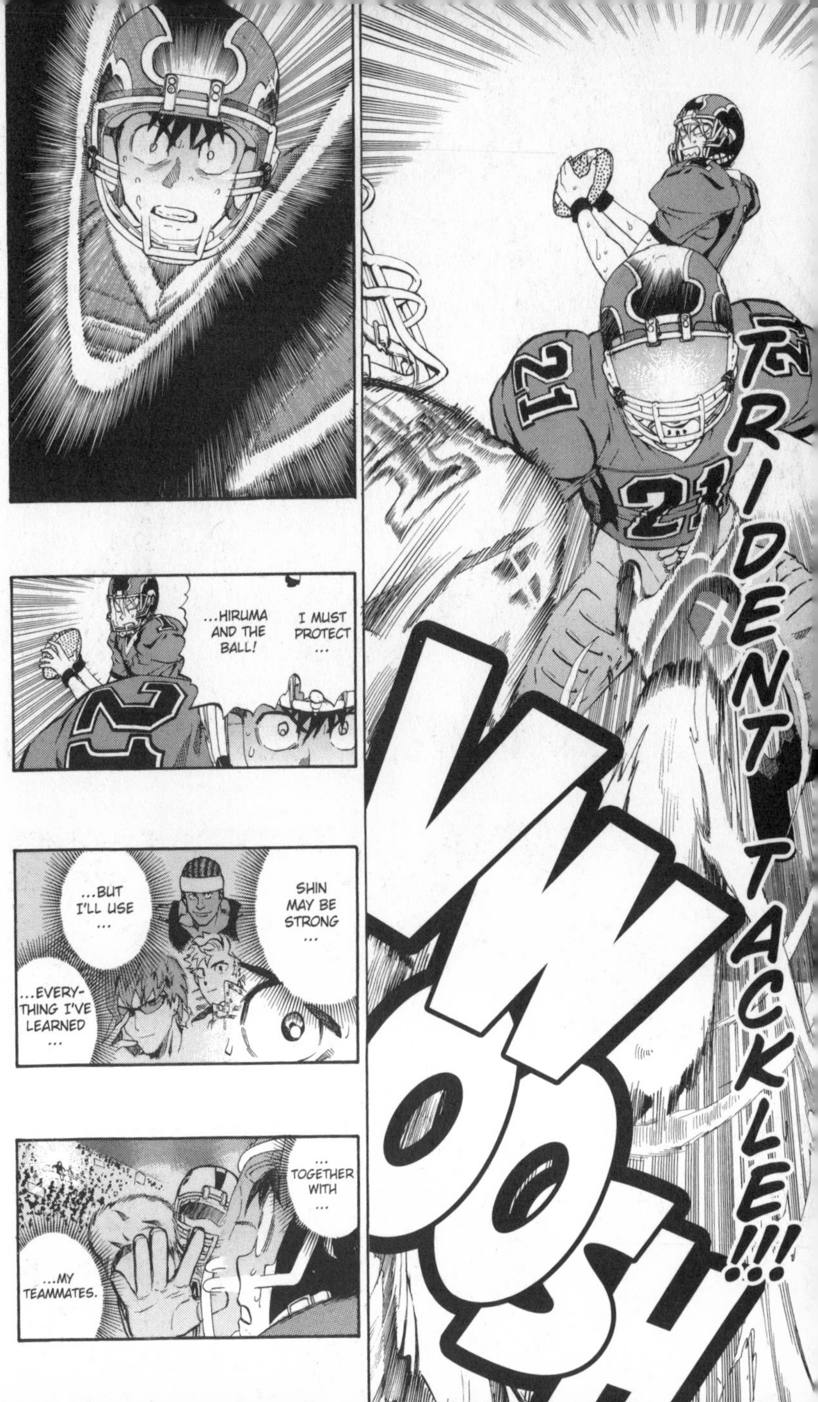
TRIDENT TACKLE!!!
WHOOSH!
I MUST PROTECT ...
...HIRUMA AND THE BALL!
SHIN MAY BE STRONG ...
...BUT I'LL USE ...
...EVERY-THING I'VE LEARNED ...
... TOGETHER WITH ...
...MY TEAMMATES.

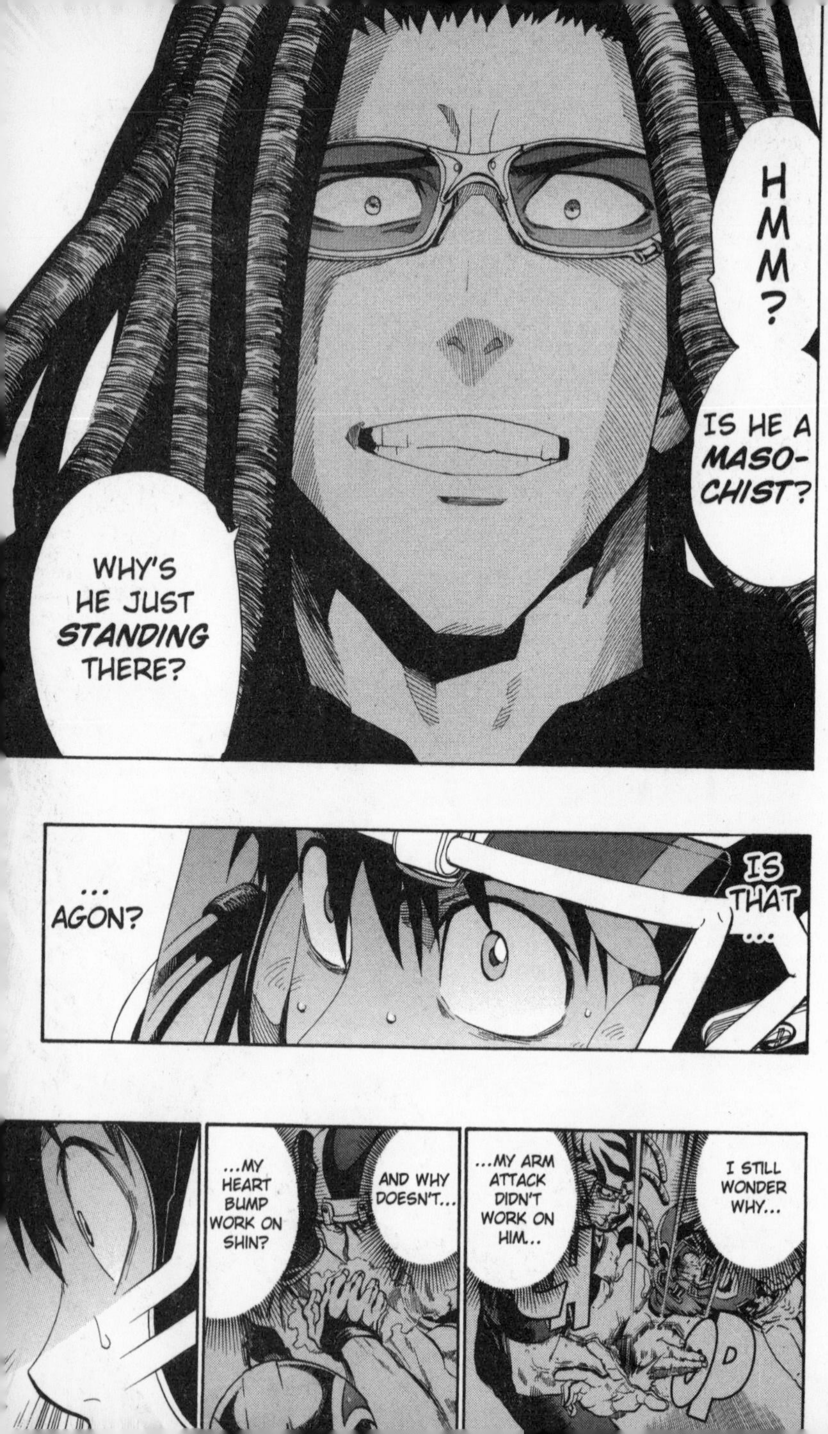
HMM?
IS HE A MASOCHIST?
WHY'S HE JUST STANDING THERE?
IS THAT...
...AGON?
I STILL WONDER WHY...
...MY ARM ATTACK DIDN'T WORK ON HIM..
AND WHY DOESN'T...
...MY HEART BUMP WORK ON SHIN?

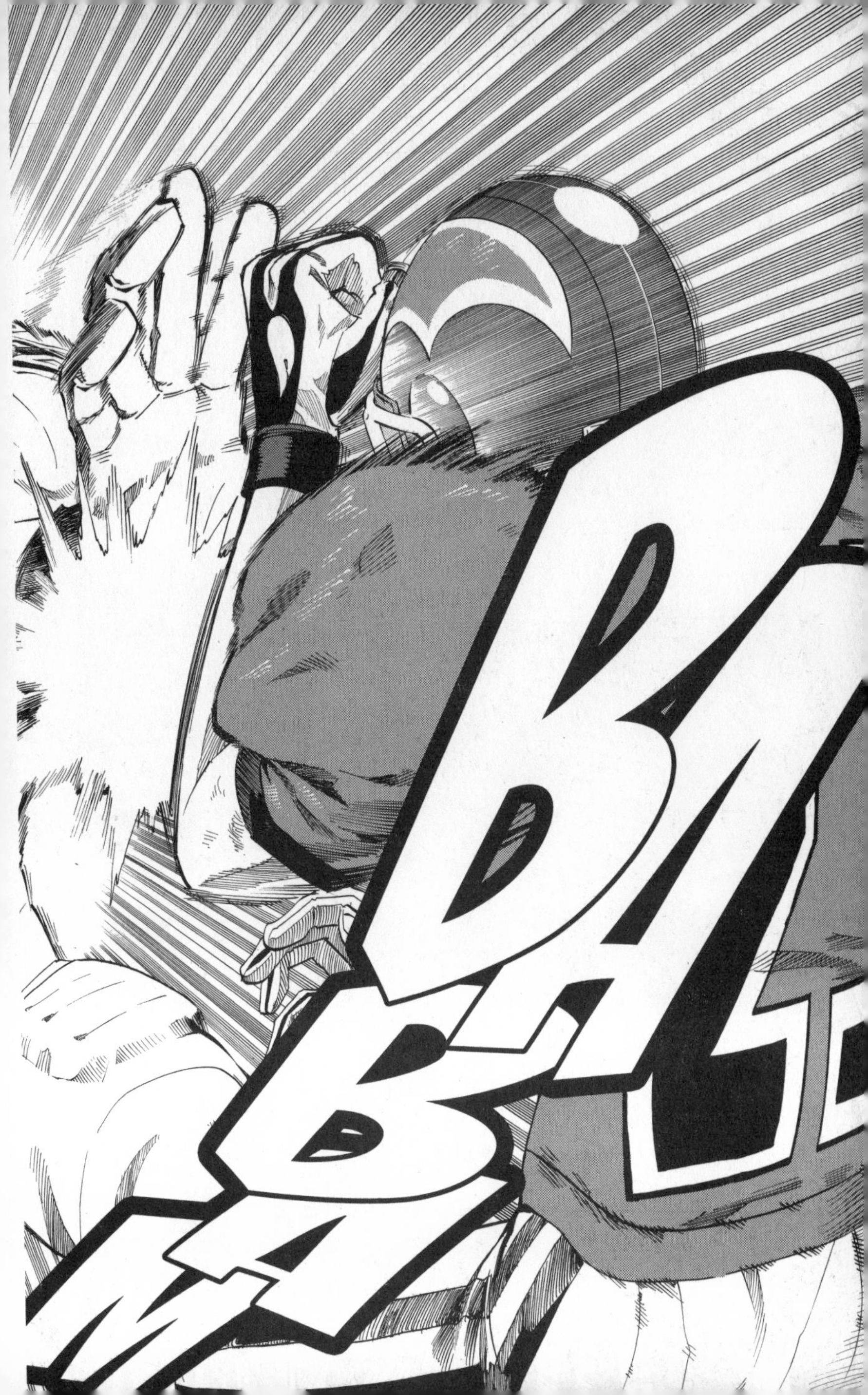

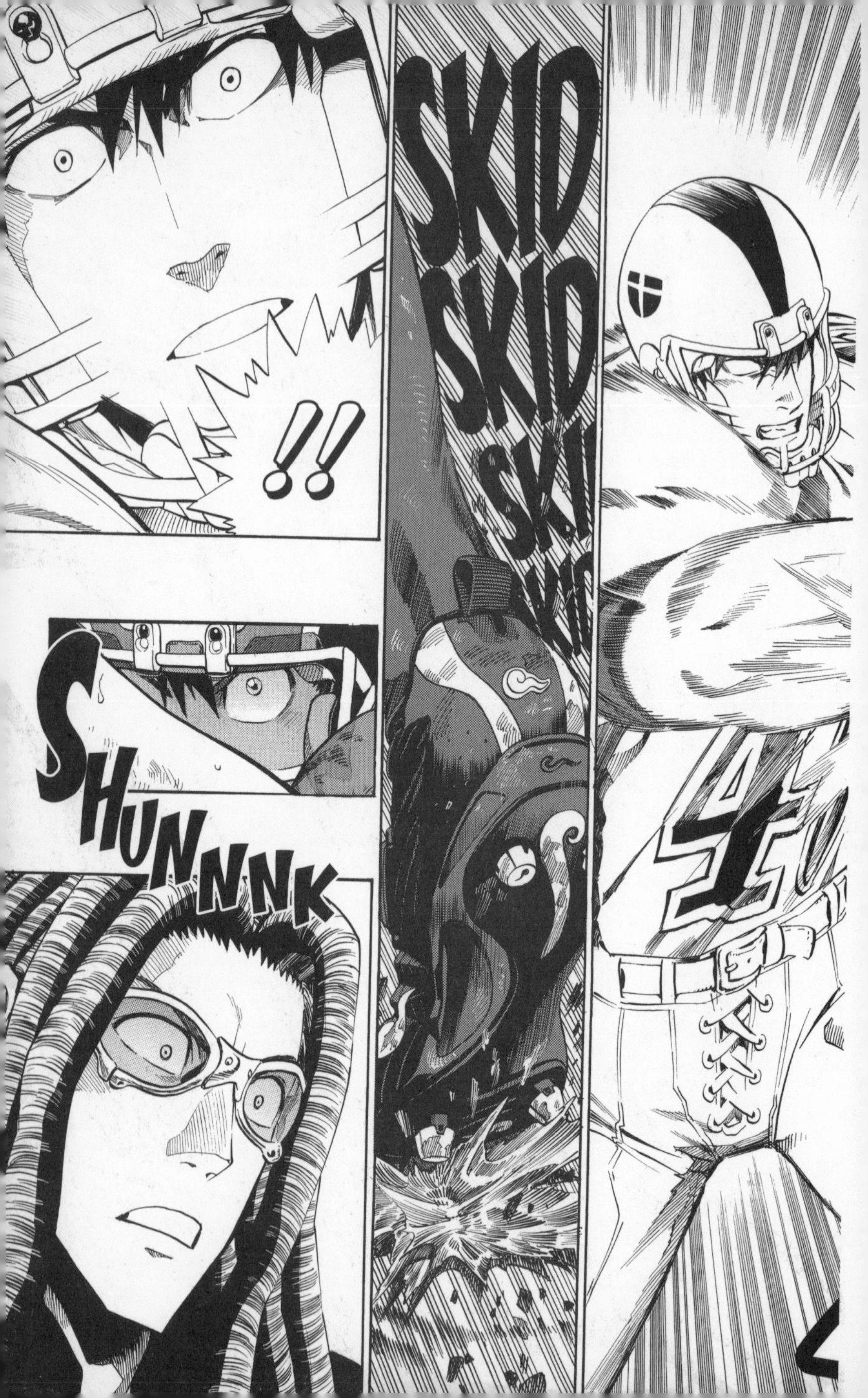

SKID SKID SKI SKI
!!
SHUNNNK

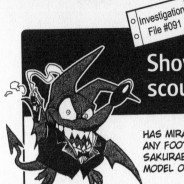

Investigation File #091

Show us Jari Productions' scouting info!!

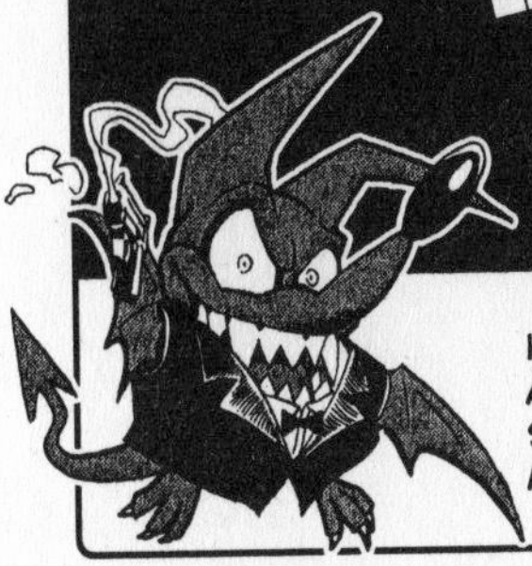

HAS MIRACLE ITO EVER SCOUTED ANY FOOTBALL PLAYERS BESIDES SAKURABA OR AKABA TO BE A MODEL OR PERFORMER?

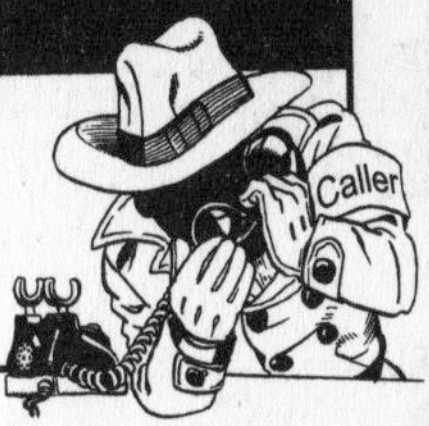
Caller

Caller name: Vector in Tokyo

Miracle Ito's (SECRET) Scout Notes

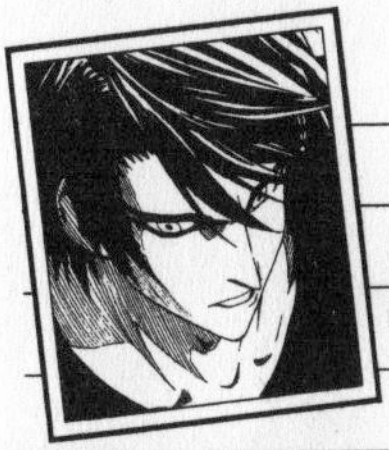

Shun Kakei

Such height! And almond-shaped eyes! Perfect for modeling!! But he's probably only interested in football and might quit and take Sakuraba with him. Hmm...

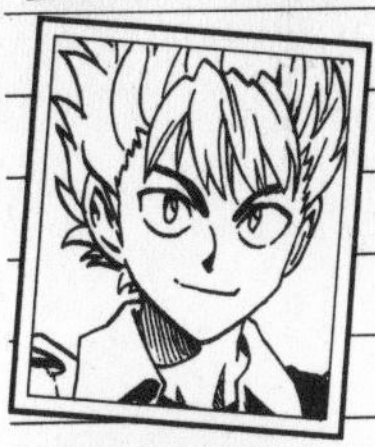

Riku Kaitani

He's cool, but maybe too short. Maybe a pair of secret platform shoes would work?

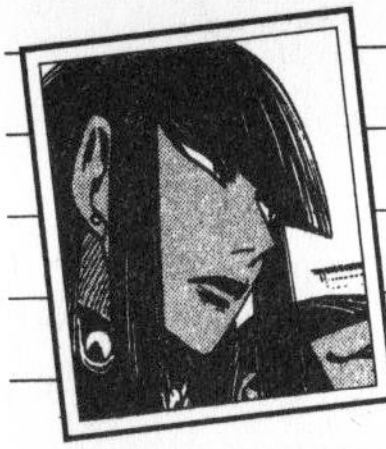

Kiminari Harao

Quite a hottie.
He might need a stylist to do something about his hair and makeup, though.
Or maybe it's all right the way it is?

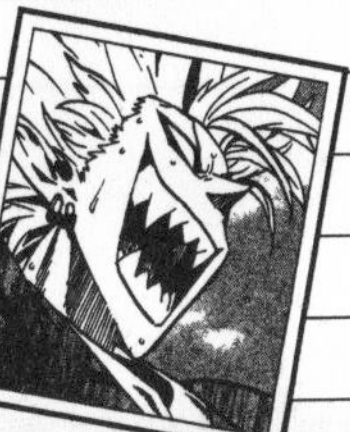

Yoichi Hiruma

I thought maybe he'd make an intelligent talking head on TV, but I don't think there's any way I could ever control him...

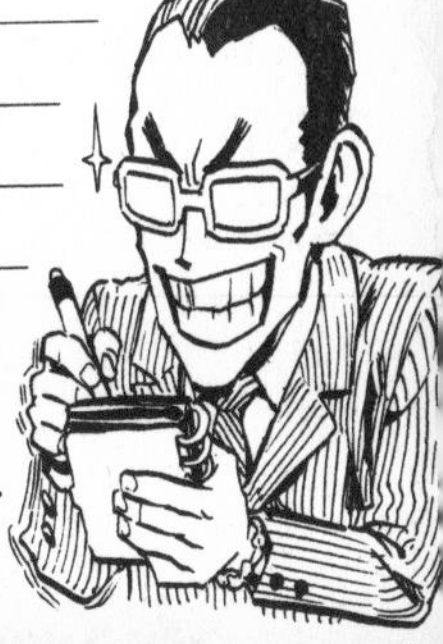

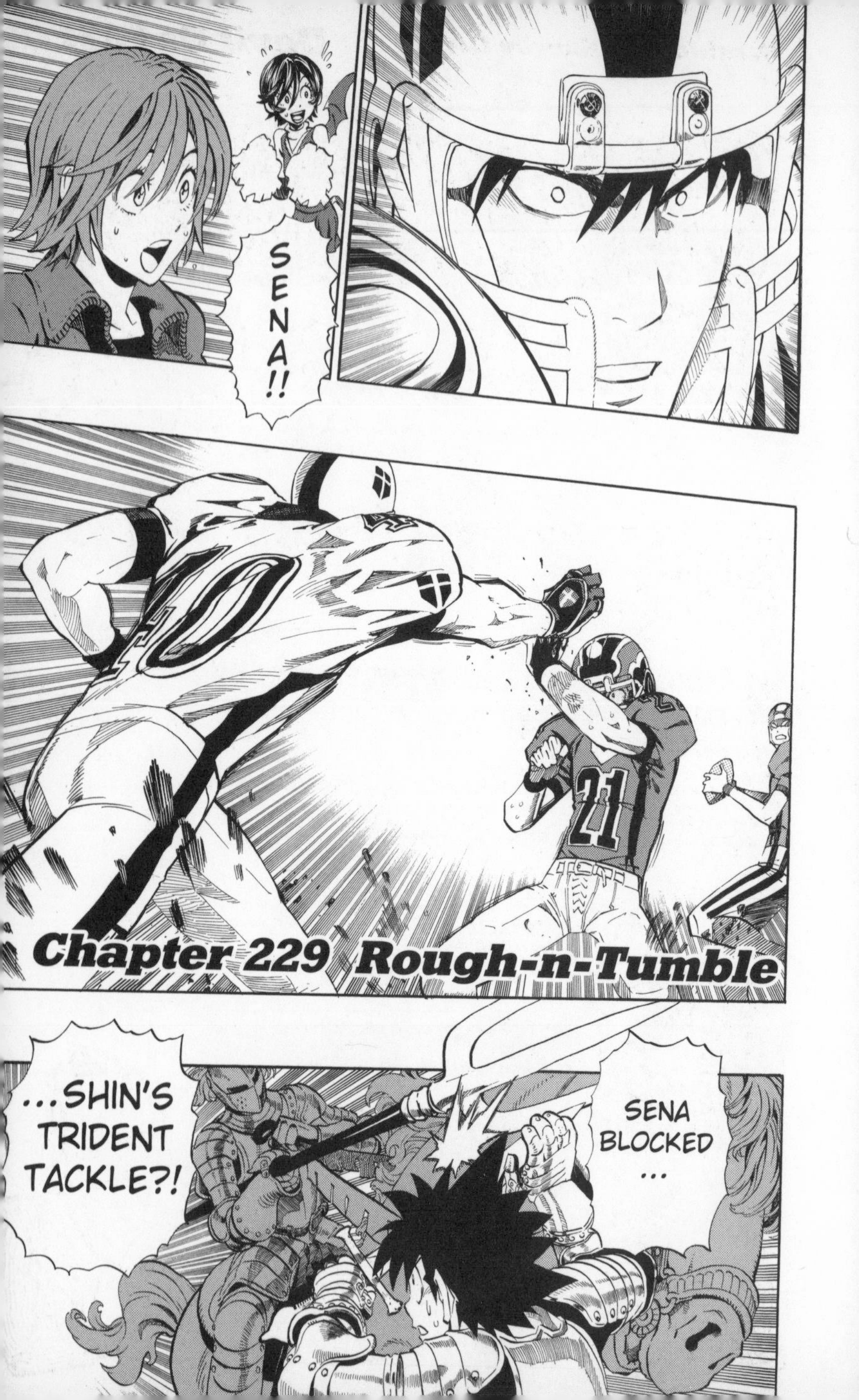
SENA!!
Chapter 229 Rough-n-Tumble
SENA BLOCKED ...
...SHIN'S TRIDENT TACKLE?!

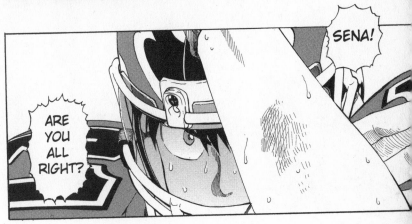

SENA!

ARE YOU ALL RIGHT?

OW!

OWW!

OWWWWW!!

AGH!

OUCH!

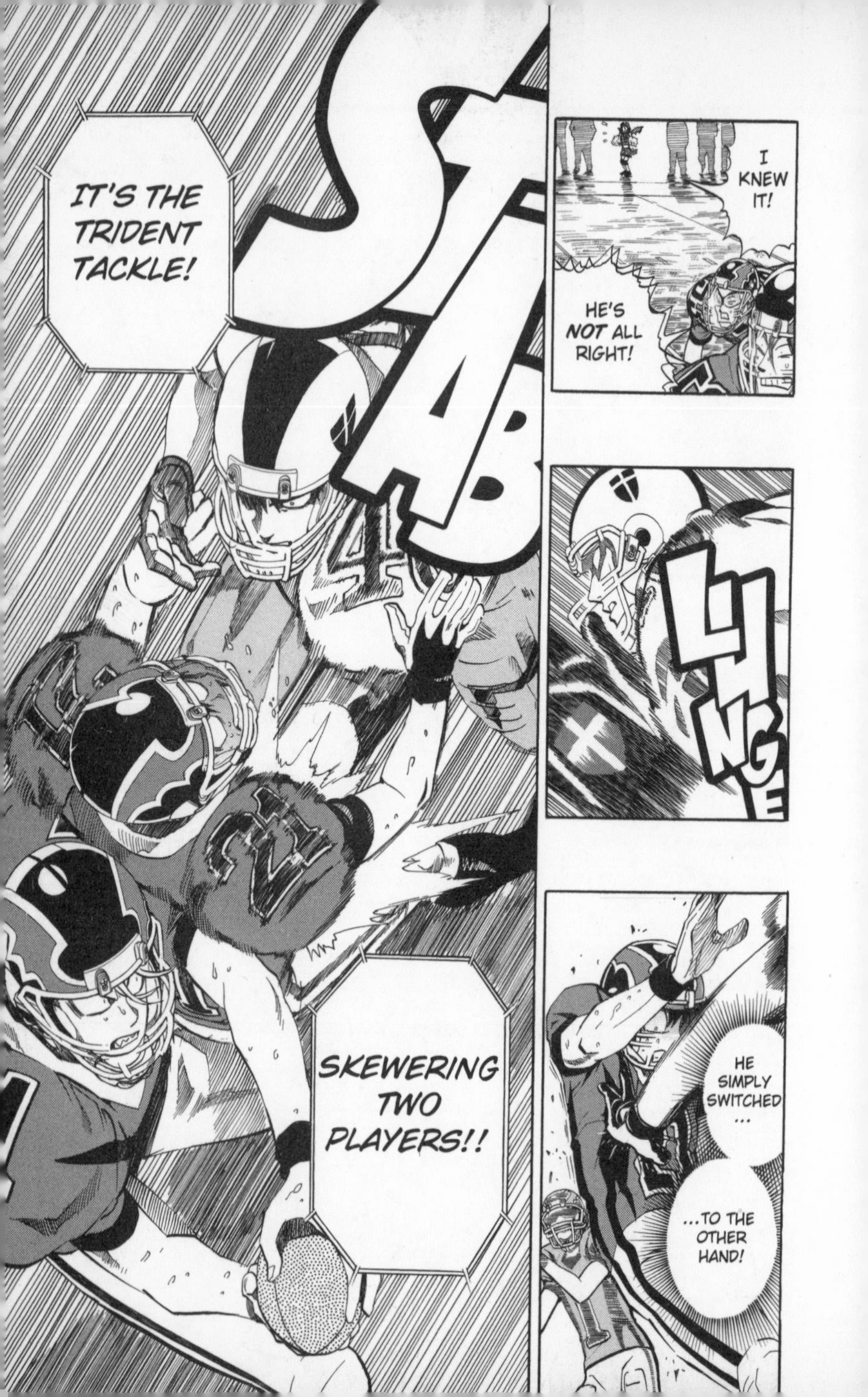
I KNEW IT!
HE'S *NOT* ALL RIGHT!
LUNGE
HE SIMPLY SWITCHED...
...TO THE OTHER HAND!
STAB
IT'S THE TRIDENT TACKLE!
SKEWERING TWO PLAYERS!!

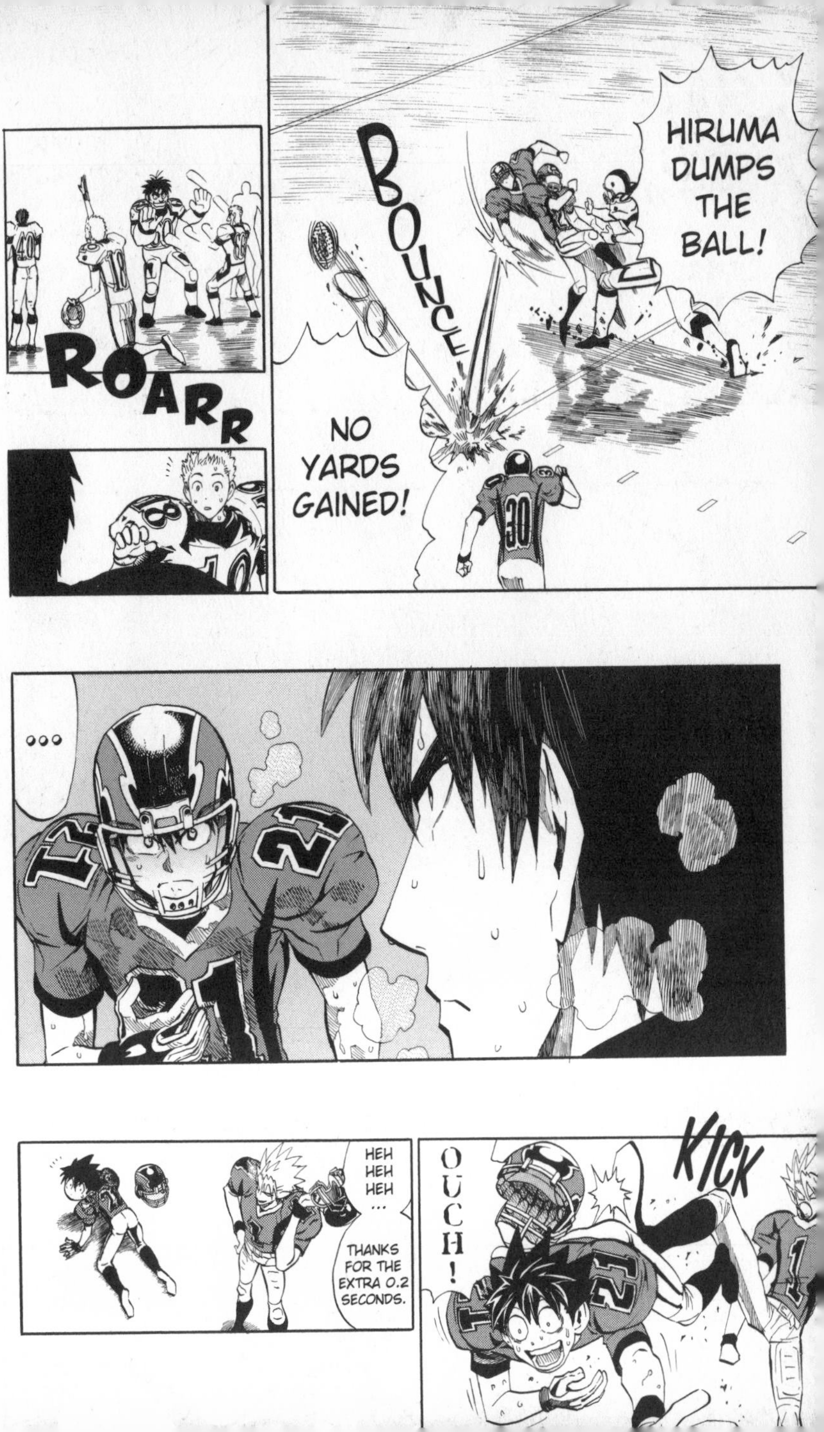
HIRUMA DUMPS THE BALL!
BOUNCE
NO YARDS GAINED!
ROARR
...
KICK
OUCH!
HEH HEH HEH ...
THANKS FOR THE EXTRA 0.2 SECONDS.

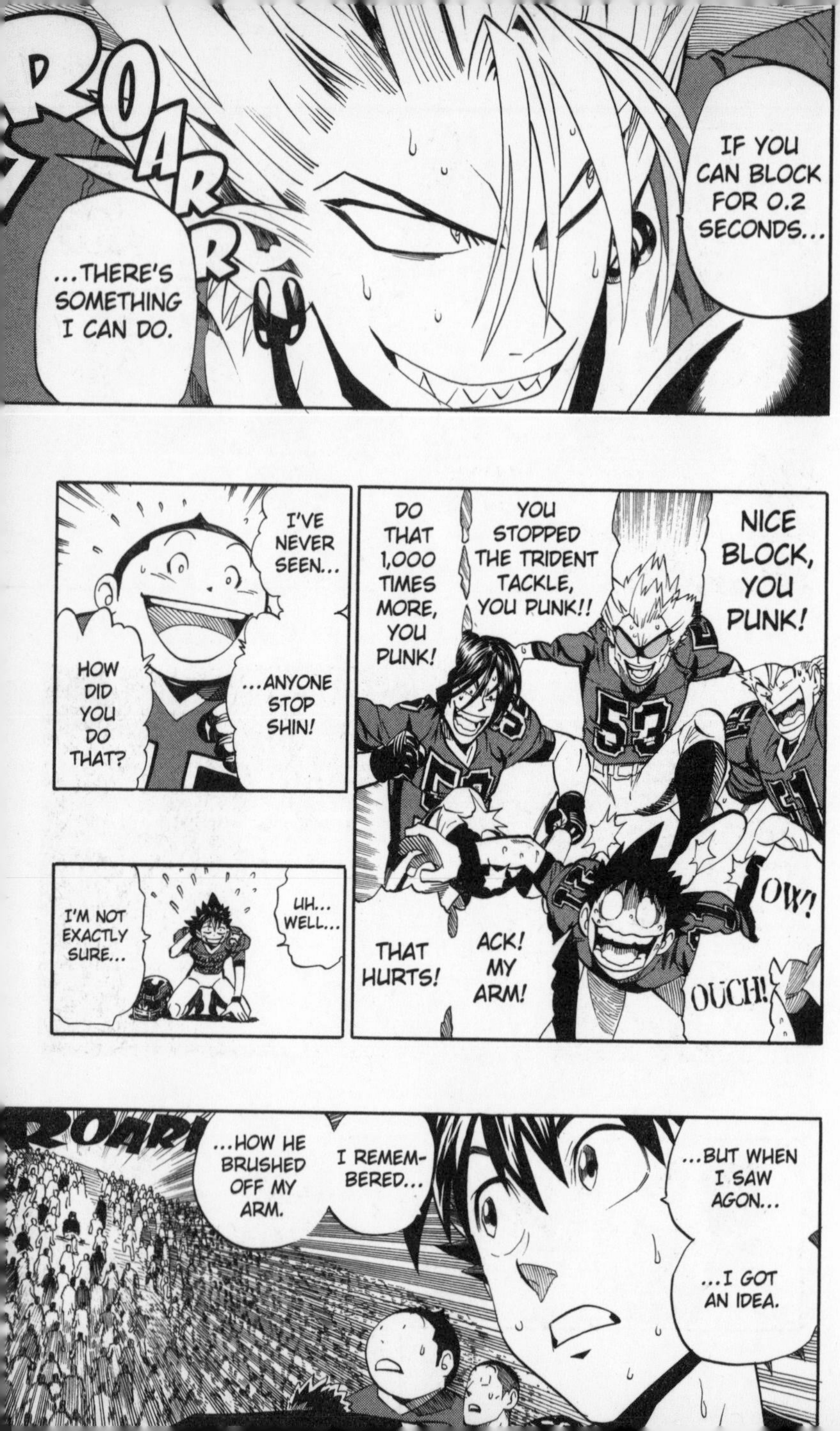
IF YOU CAN BLOCK FOR 0.2 SECONDS...
ROAAR
...THERE'S SOMETHING I CAN DO.
NICE BLOCK, YOU PUNK!
YOU STOPPED THE TRIDENT TACKLE, YOU PUNK!!
DO THAT 1,000 TIMES MORE, YOU PUNK!
OW!
OUCH!
ACK! MY ARM!
THAT HURTS!
I'VE NEVER SEEN...
...ANYONE STOP SHIN!
HOW DID YOU DO THAT?
UH... WELL...
I'M NOT EXACTLY SURE...
...BUT WHEN I SAW AGON...
...I GOT AN IDEA.
I REMEMBERED...
...HOW HE BRUSHED OFF MY ARM.
ROAR

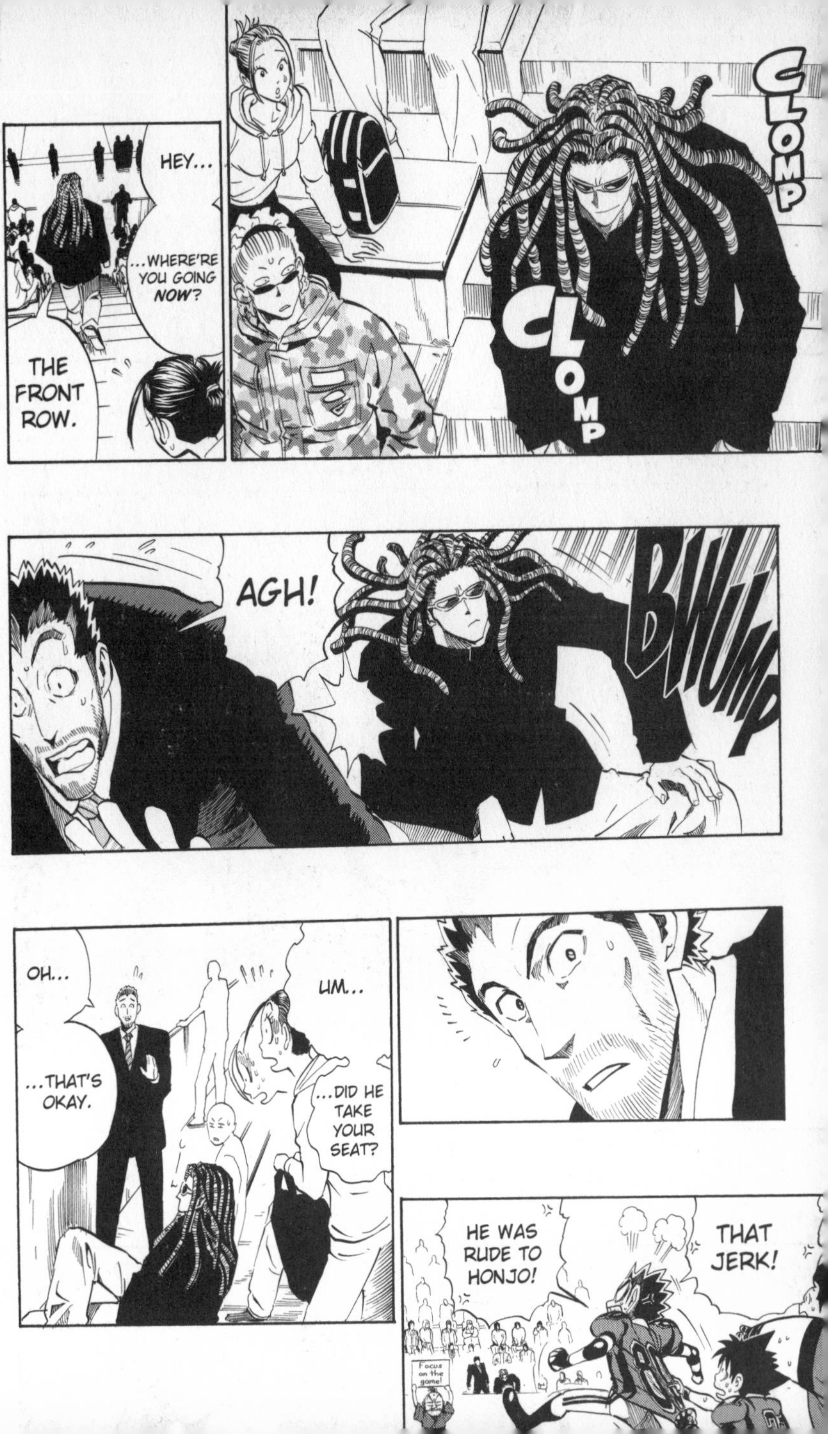
CLOMP
CLOMP
HEY...
...WHERE'RE YOU GOING NOW?
THE FRONT ROW.
AGH!
BWUMP
UM...
...DID HE TAKE YOUR SEAT?
OH...
...THAT'S OKAY.
THAT JERK!
HE WAS RUDE TO HONJO!
Focus on the game!

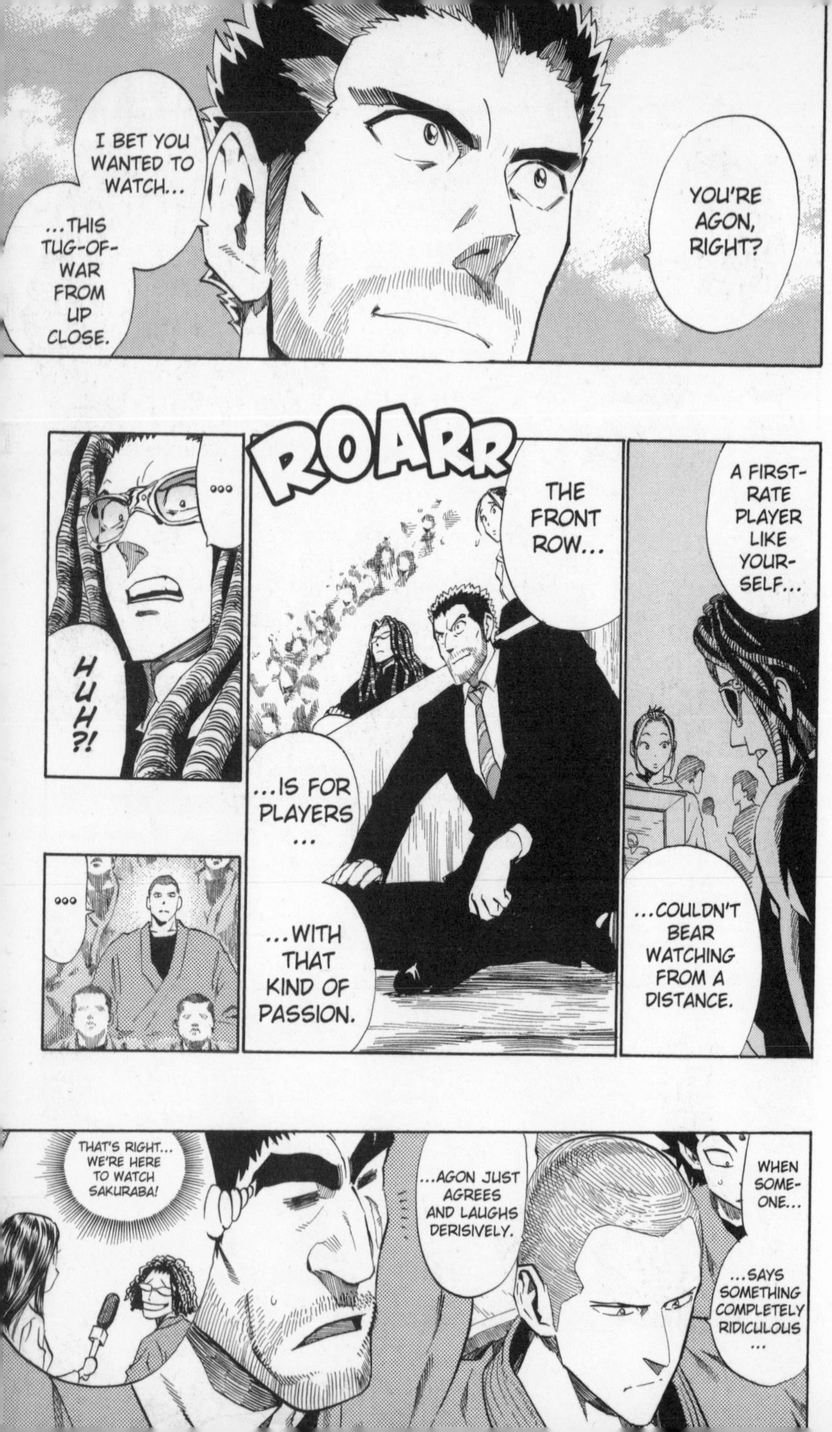
YOU'RE AGON, RIGHT?
I BET YOU WANTED TO WATCH...
...THIS TUG-OF-WAR FROM UP CLOSE.
A FIRST-RATE PLAYER LIKE YOURSELF...
...COULDN'T BEAR WATCHING FROM A DISTANCE.
ROARR
THE FRONT ROW...
...IS FOR PLAYERS...
...WITH THAT KIND OF PASSION.
...
HUH?!
...
WHEN SOME-ONE...
...SAYS SOMETHING COMPLETELY RIDICULOUS...
...AGON JUST AGREES AND LAUGHS DERISIVELY.
THAT'S RIGHT... WE'RE HERE TO WATCH SAKURABA!

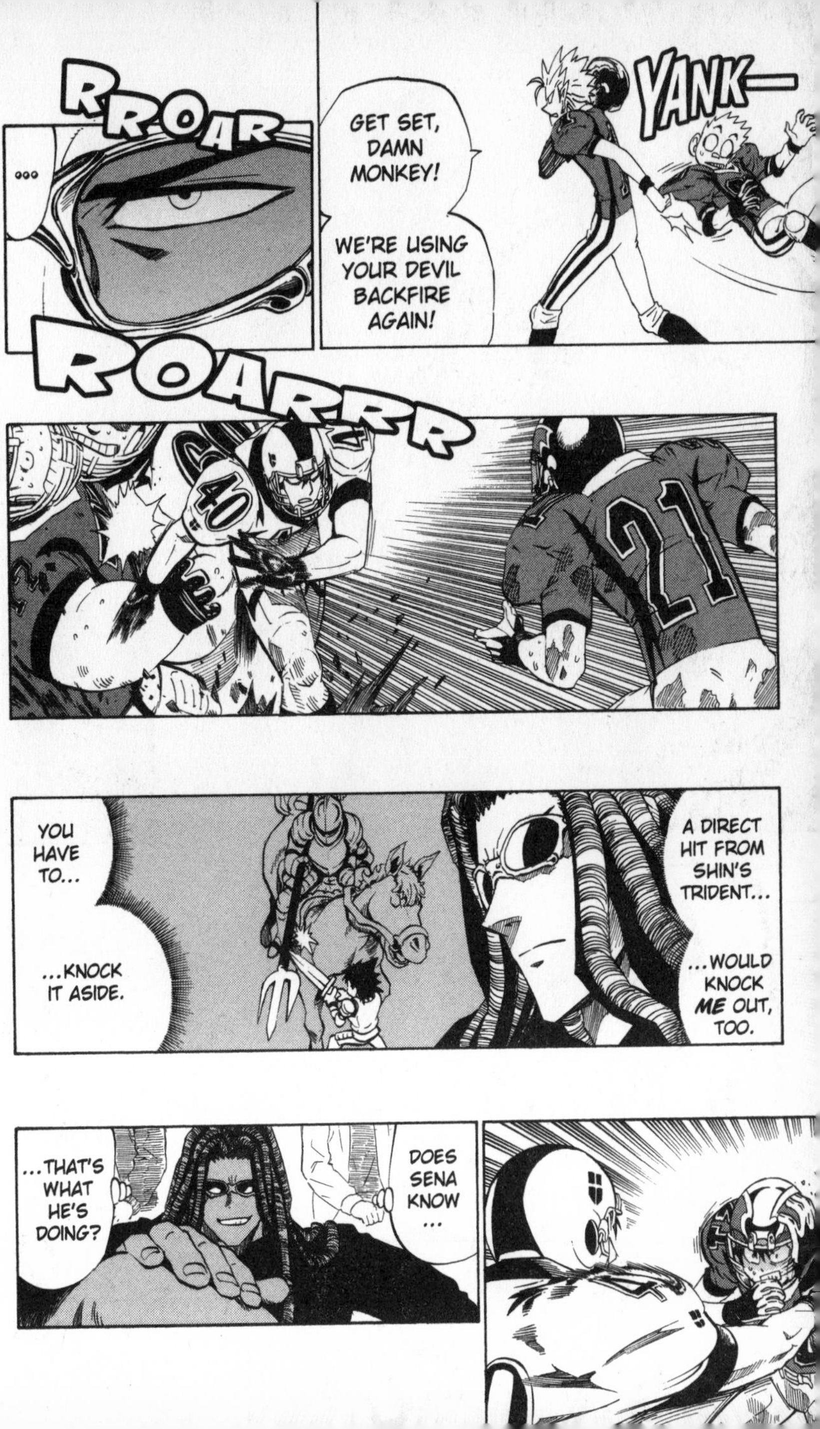
YANK—
GET SET, DAMN MONKEY!
WE'RE USING YOUR DEVIL BACKFIRE AGAIN!
RROAR
...
ROARRRR
A DIRECT HIT FROM SHIN'S TRIDENT...
...WOULD KNOCK *ME* OUT, TOO.
YOU HAVE TO...
...KNOCK IT ASIDE.
DOES SENA KNOW...
...THAT'S WHAT HE'S DOING?

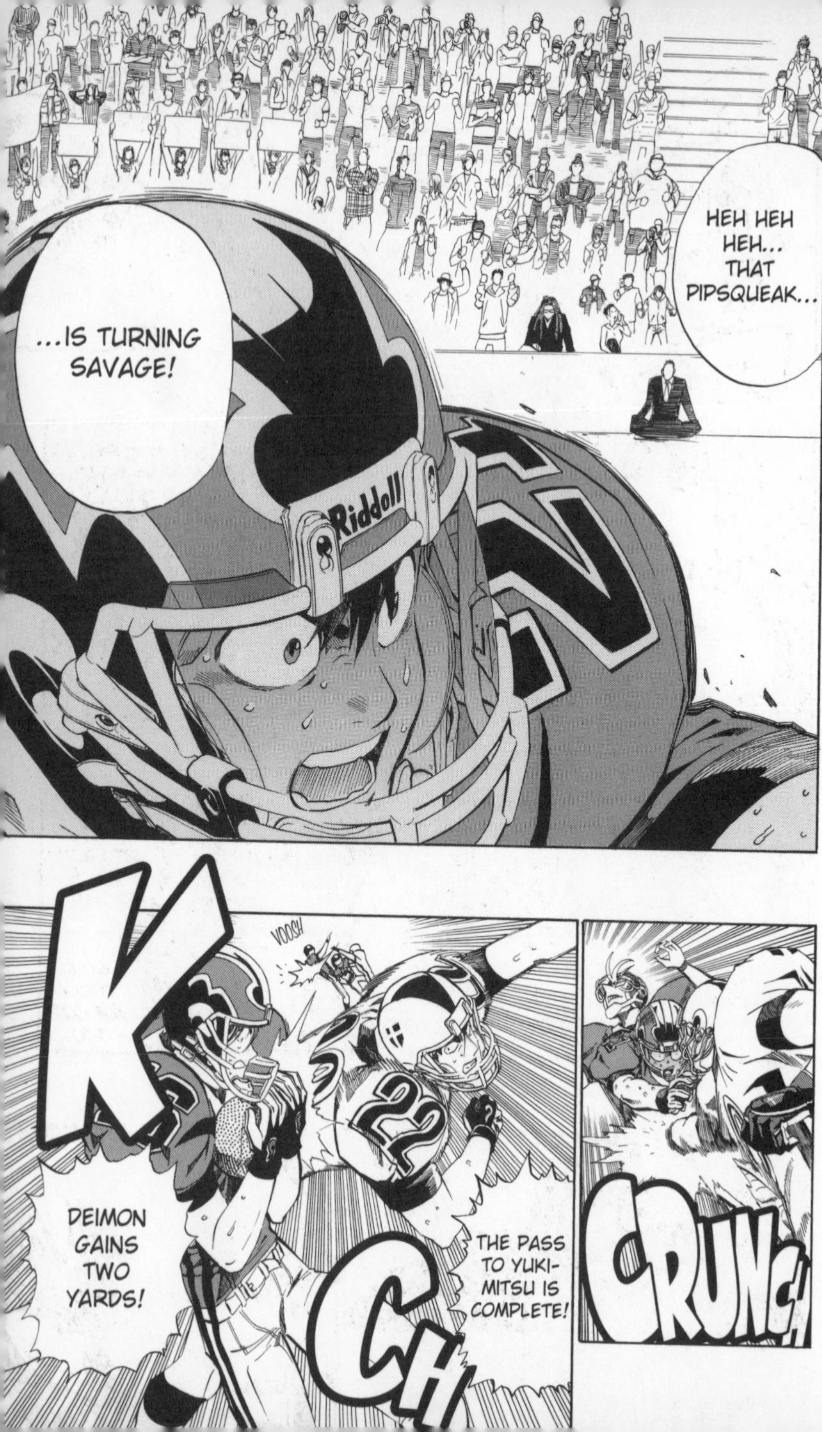
HEH HEH HEH... THAT PIPSQUEAK...
...IS TURNING SAVAGE!
Riddoll
CRUNCH
VOOSH
K
THE PASS TO YUKI-MITSU IS COMPLETE!
DEIMON GAINS TWO YARDS!
CH

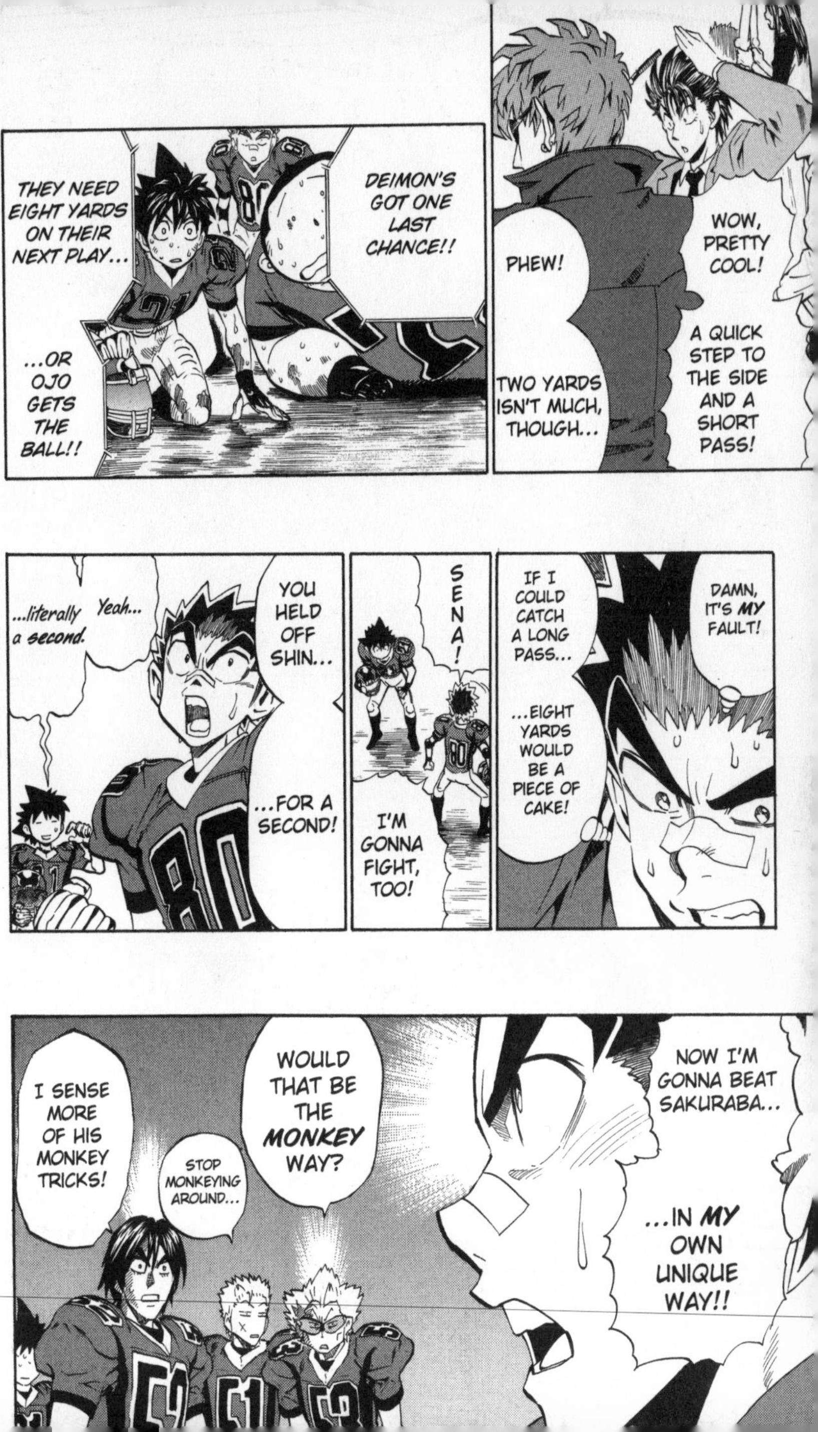
WOW, PRETTY COOL!
A QUICK STEP TO THE SIDE AND A SHORT PASS!
PHEW!
TWO YARDS ISN'T MUCH, THOUGH...
DEIMON'S GOT ONE LAST CHANCE!!
THEY NEED EIGHT YARDS ON THEIR NEXT PLAY...
...OR OJO GETS THE BALL!!
DAMN, IT'S *MY* FAULT!
IF I COULD CATCH A LONG PASS...
...EIGHT YARDS WOULD BE A PIECE OF CAKE!
SENA!
I'M GONNA FIGHT, TOO!
YOU HELD OFF SHIN...
...FOR A SECOND!
Yeah...
...literally a *second*.
NOW I'M GONNA BEAT SAKURABA...
...IN *MY* OWN UNIQUE WAY!!
WOULD THAT BE THE *MONKEY* WAY?
STOP MONKEYING AROUND...
I SENSE MORE OF HIS MONKEY TRICKS!

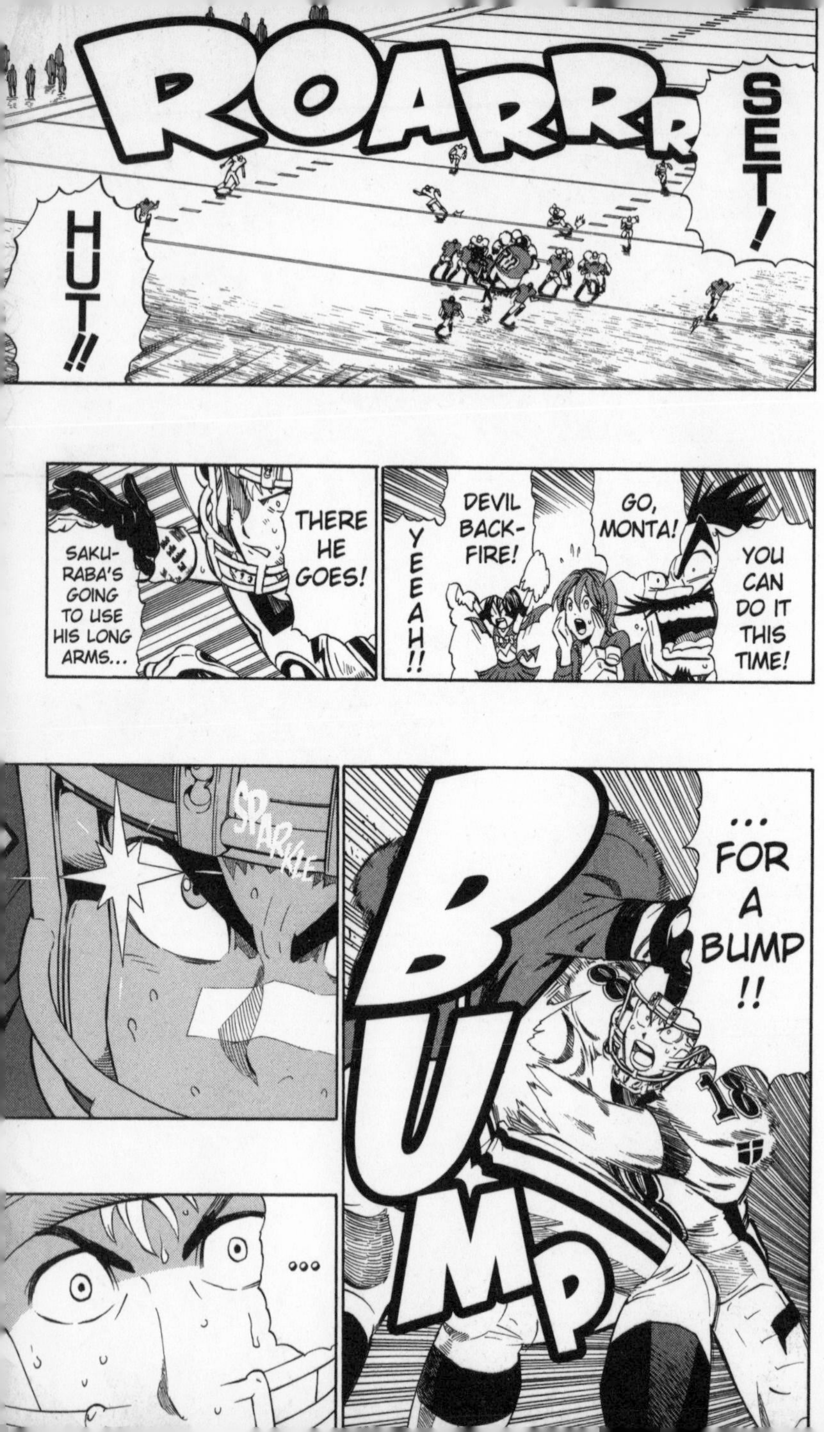
SET!
ROARRR
HUT!!
YOU CAN DO IT THIS TIME!
GO, MONTA!
DEVIL BACK-FIRE!
YEEAH!!
THERE HE GOES!
SAKU-RABA'S GOING TO USE HIS LONG ARMS...
BUMP
... FOR A BUMP !!
SPARKLE
...

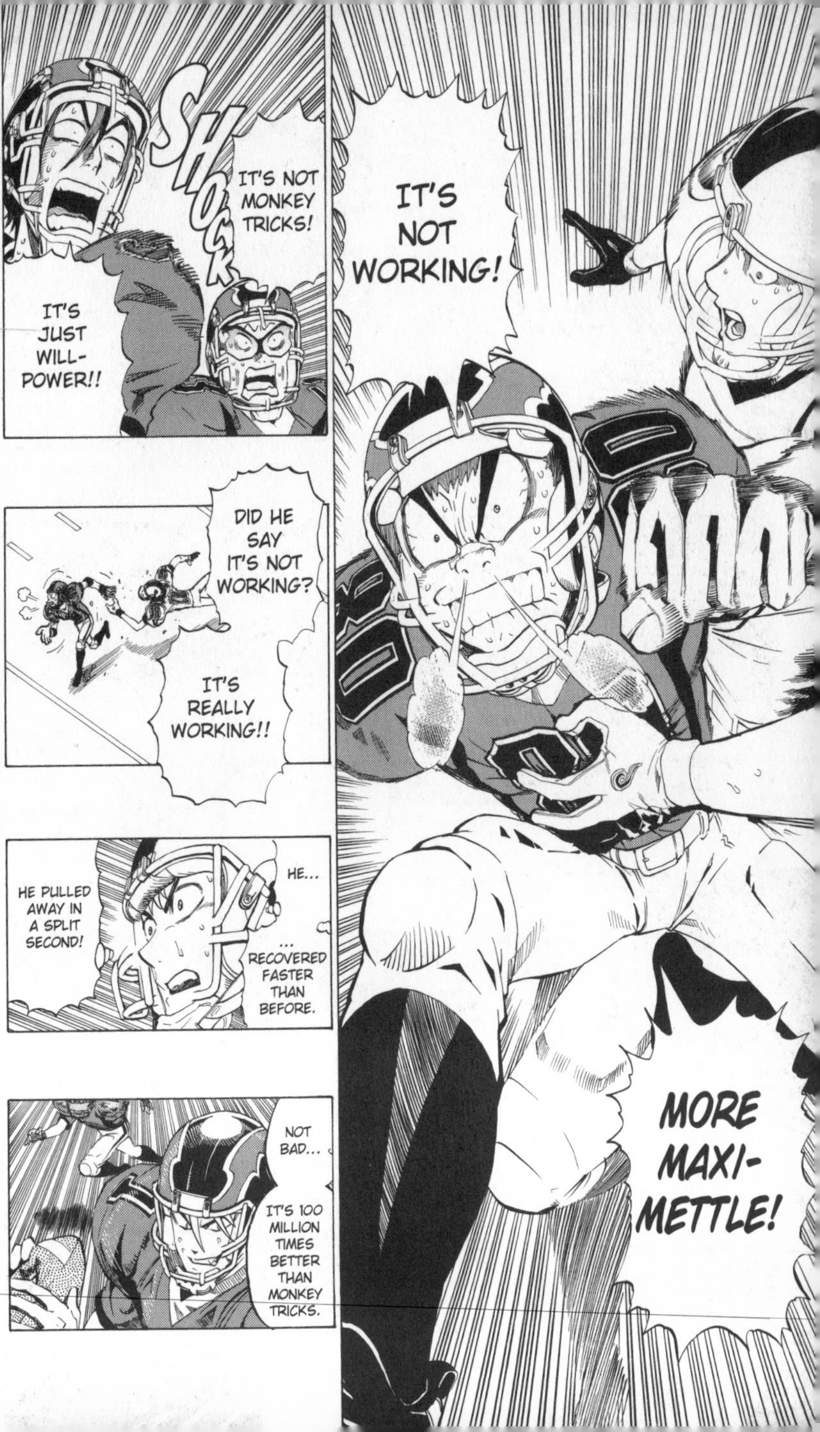
IT'S NOT WORKING!
MORE MAXI-METTLE!
SHOCK
IT'S NOT MONKEY TRICKS!
IT'S JUST WILL-POWER!!
DID HE SAY IT'S NOT WORKING?
IT'S REALLY WORKING!!
HE...
...RECOVERED FASTER THAN BEFORE.
HE PULLED AWAY IN A SPLIT SECOND!
NOT BAD...
IT'S 100 MILLION TIMES BETTER THAN MONKEY TRICKS.

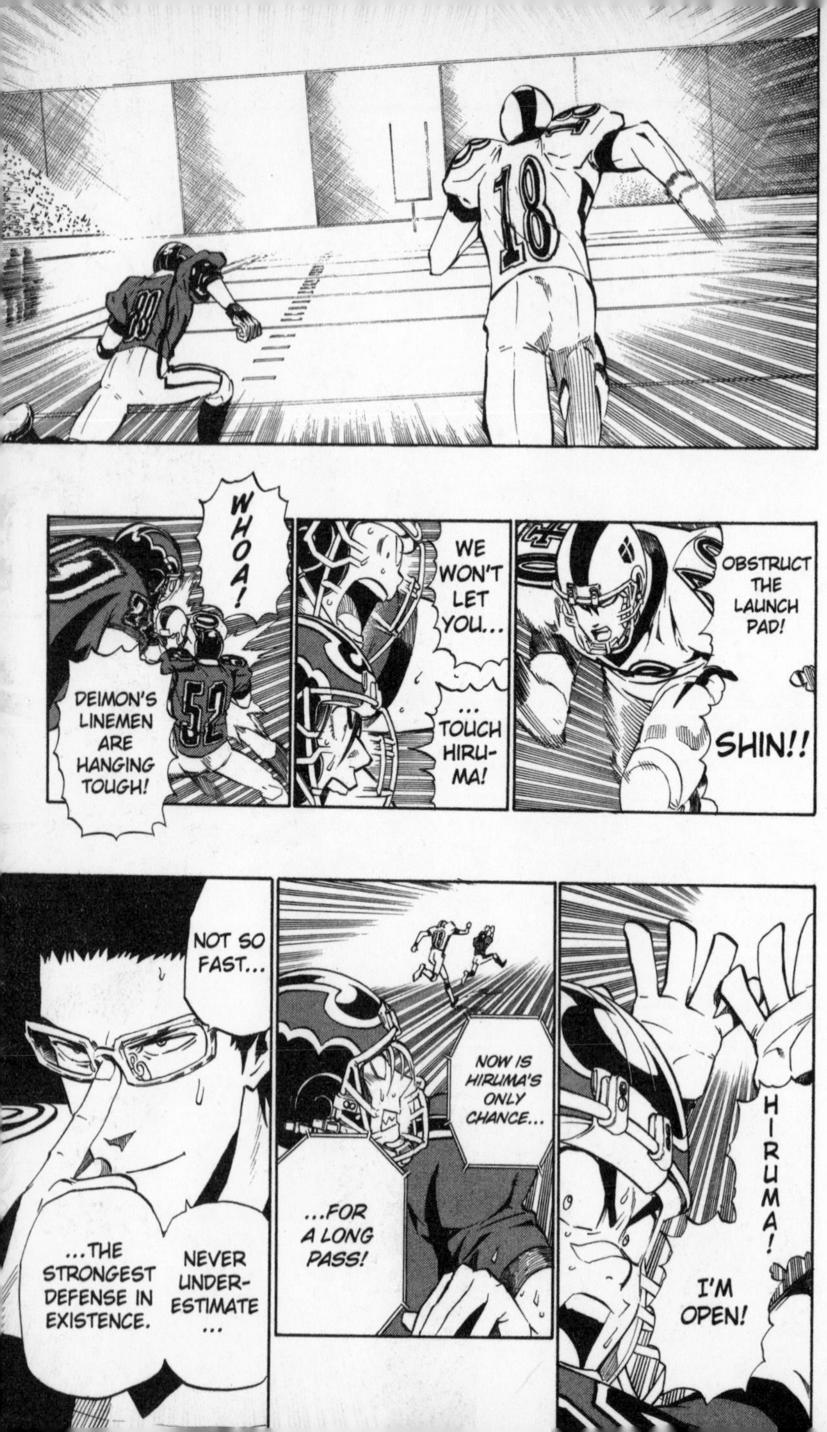
OBSTRUCT THE LAUNCH PAD!
SHIN!!
WE WON'T LET YOU...
...TOUCH HIRUMA!
WHOA!
DEIMON'S LINEMEN ARE HANGING TOUGH!
HIRUMA!
I'M OPEN!
NOW IS HIRUMA'S ONLY CHANCE...
...FOR A LONG PASS!
NOT SO FAST...
NEVER UNDER-ESTIMATE...
...THE STRONGEST DEFENSE IN EXISTENCE.

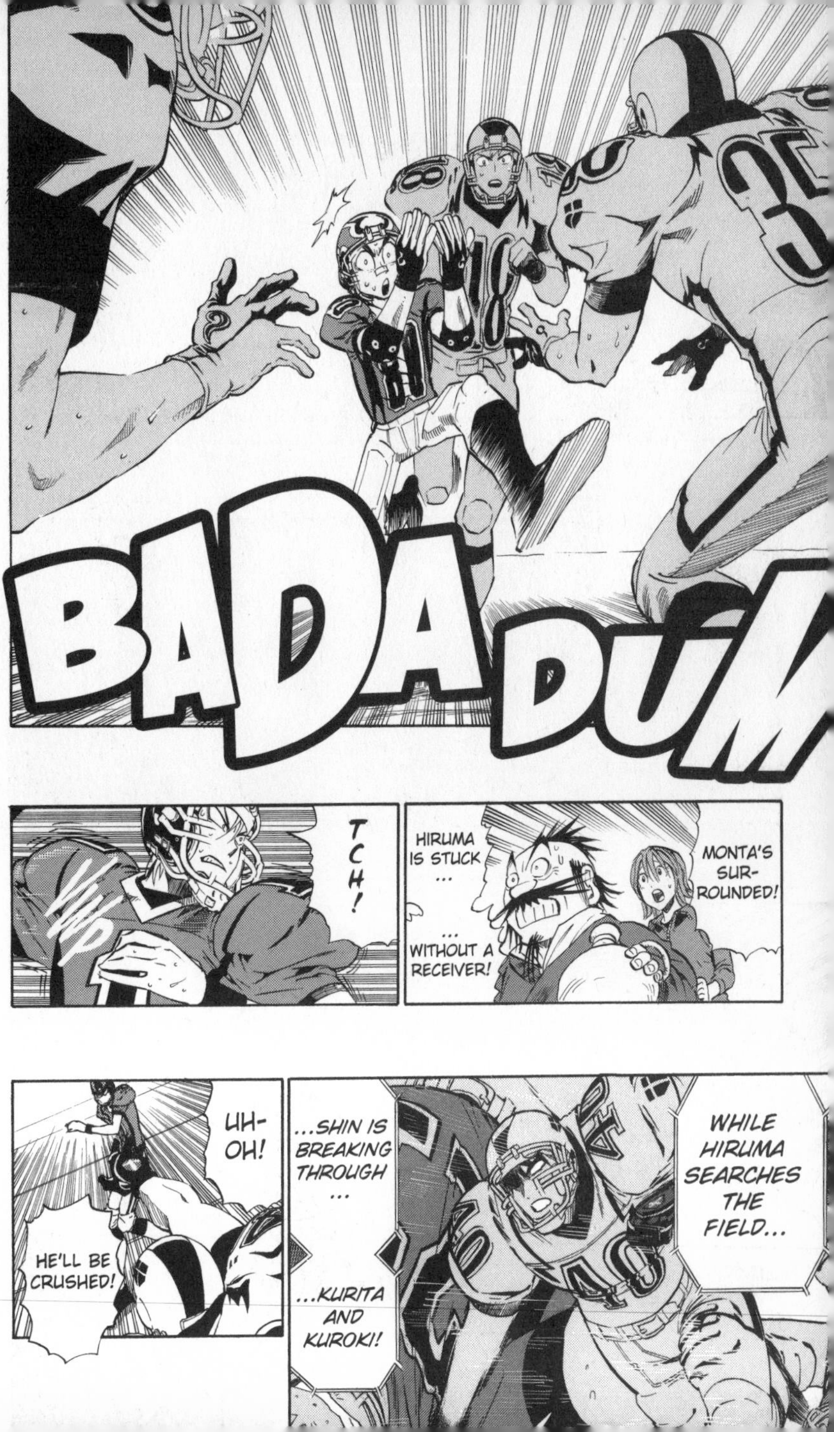
BADA DUM
MONTA'S SUR-ROUNDED!
HIRUMA IS STUCK ...
... WITHOUT A RECEIVER!
TCH!
WHILE HIRUMA SEARCHES THE FIELD...
...SHIN IS BREAKING THROUGH ...
...KURITA AND KUROKI!
UH-OH!
HE'LL BE CRUSHED!

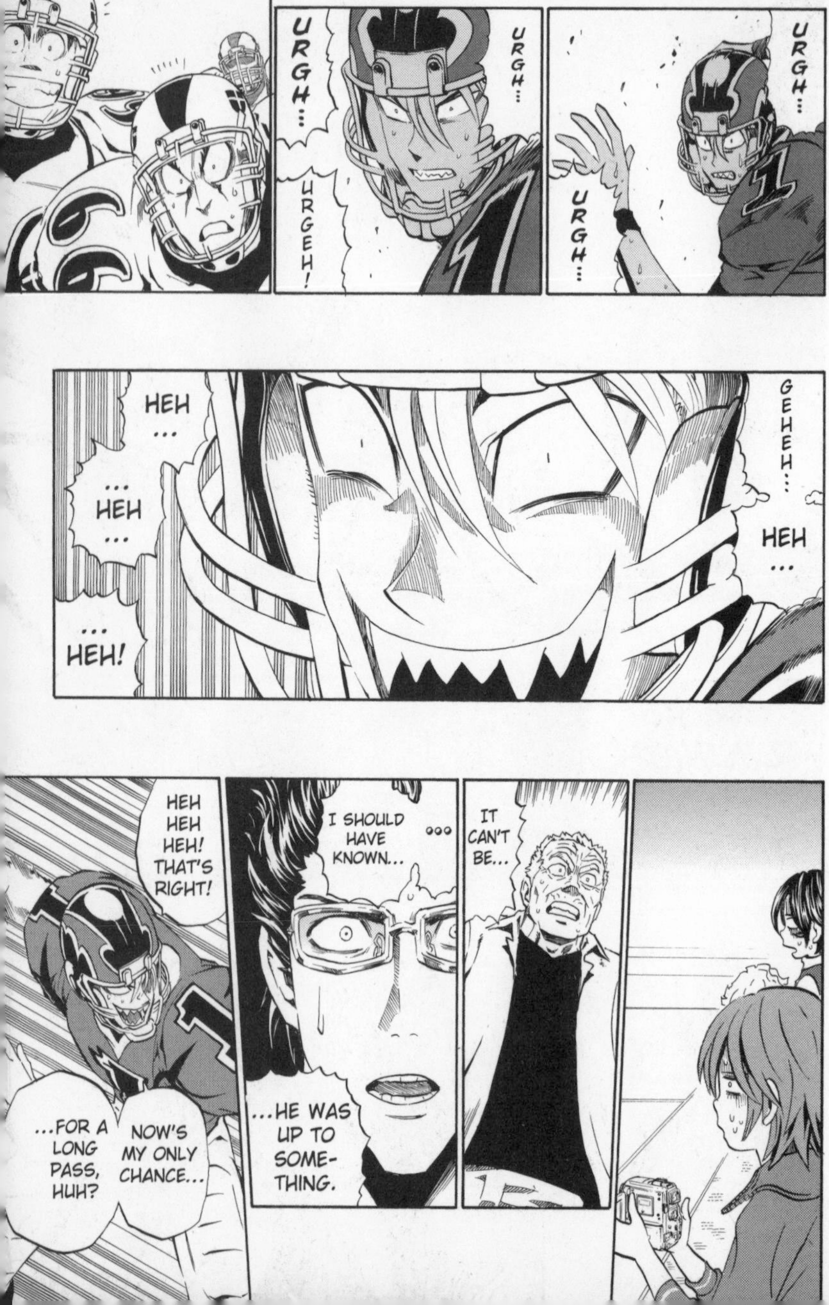
URGH...
URGH...
URGH...
URGH...
URGEH!
URGH...
GEHEH...
HEH...
HEH...
...HEH...
...HEH!
IT CAN'T BE...
...
I SHOULD HAVE KNOWN...
...HE WAS UP TO SOMETHING.
HEH HEH HEH! THAT'S RIGHT!
NOW'S MY ONLY CHANCE...
...FOR A LONG PASS, HUH?

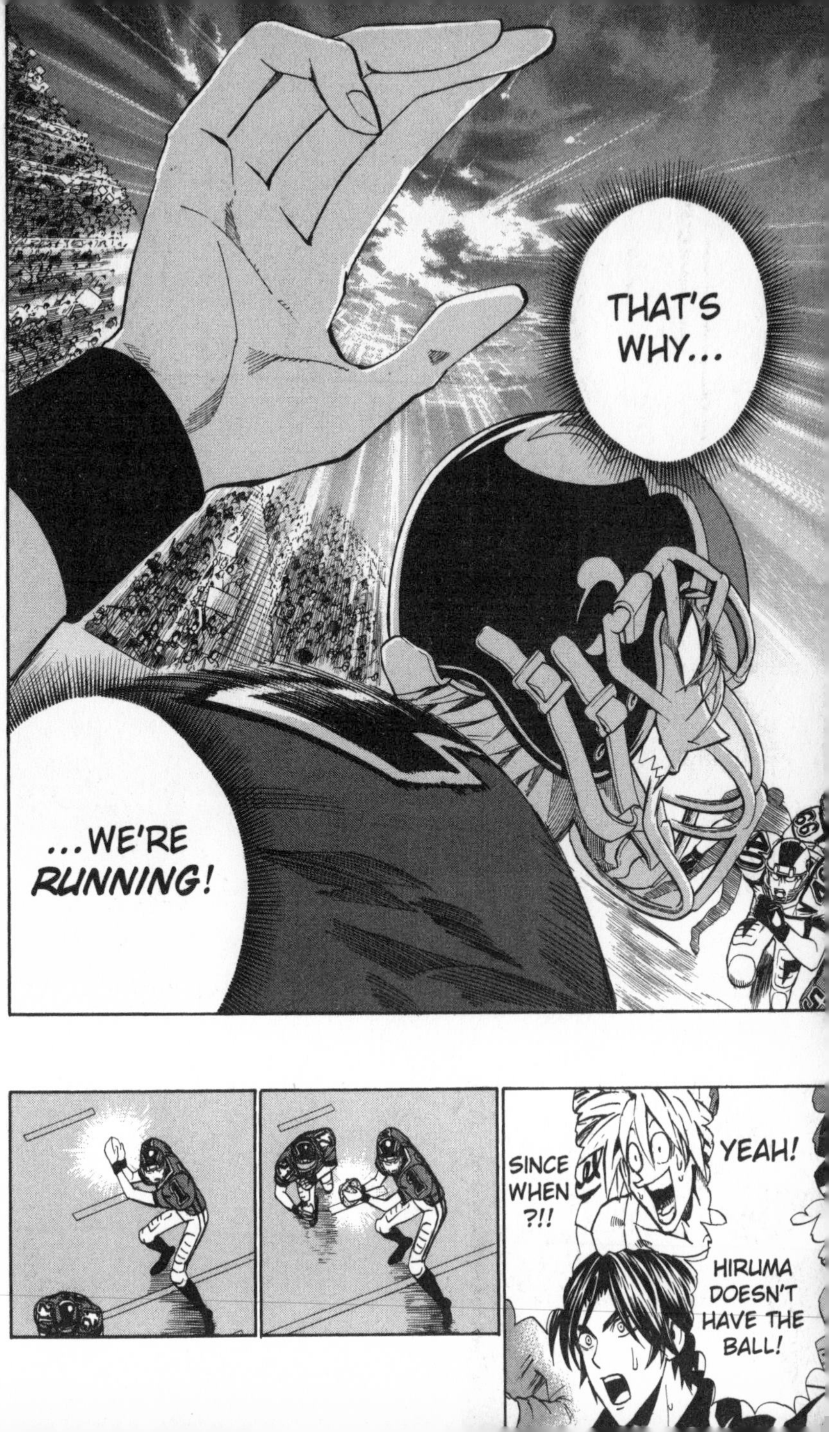
THAT'S WHY...
...WE'RE *RUNNING*!
YEAH!
SINCE WHEN ?!!
HIRUMA DOESN'T HAVE THE BALL!

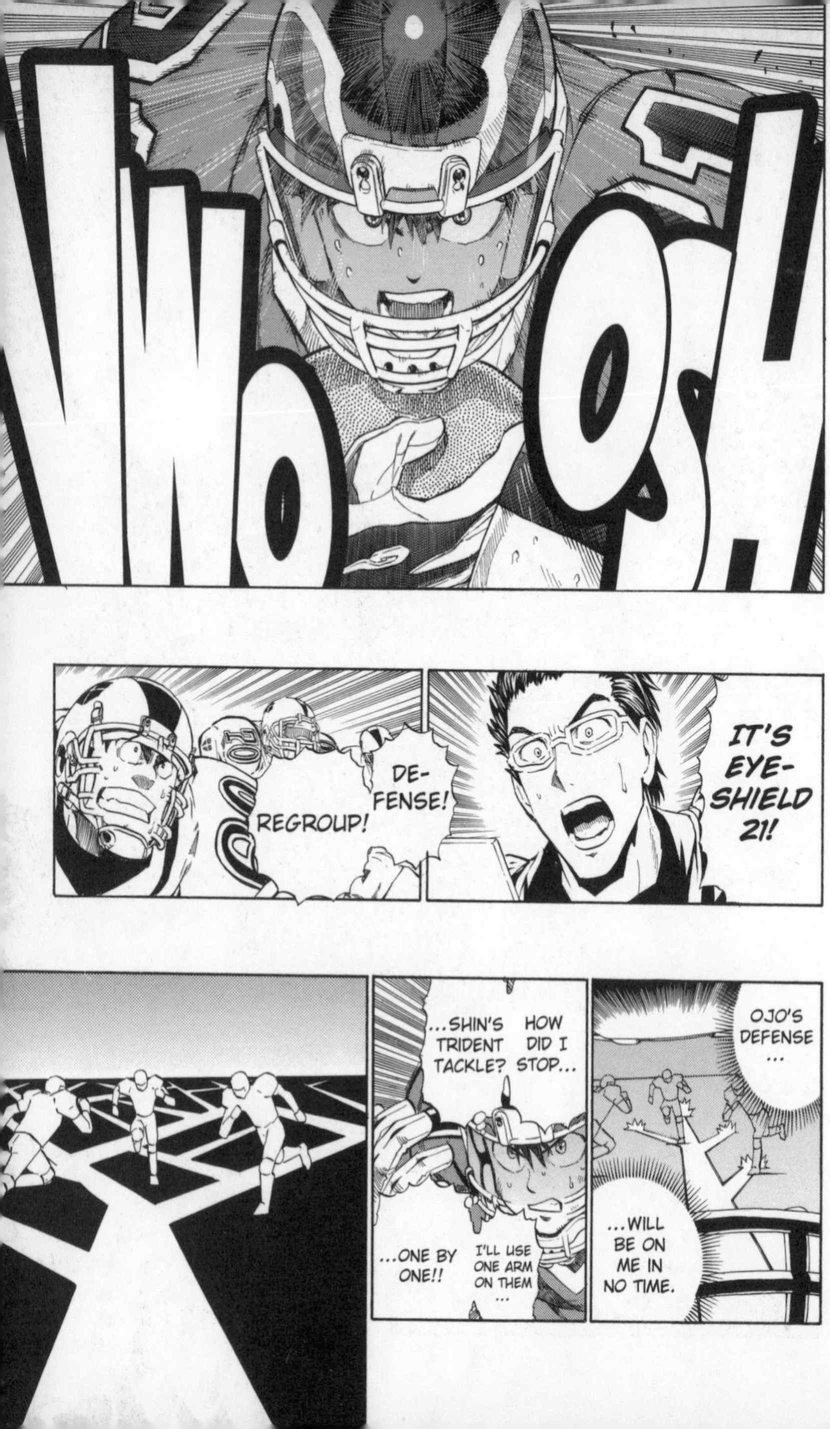
WHOOSH!
IT'S EYE-SHIELD 21!
DE-FENSE!
REGROUP!
OJO'S DEFENSE ...
...WILL BE ON ME IN NO TIME.
HOW DID I STOP...
...SHIN'S TRIDENT TACKLE?
I'LL USE ONE ARM ON THEM ...
...ONE BY ONE!!

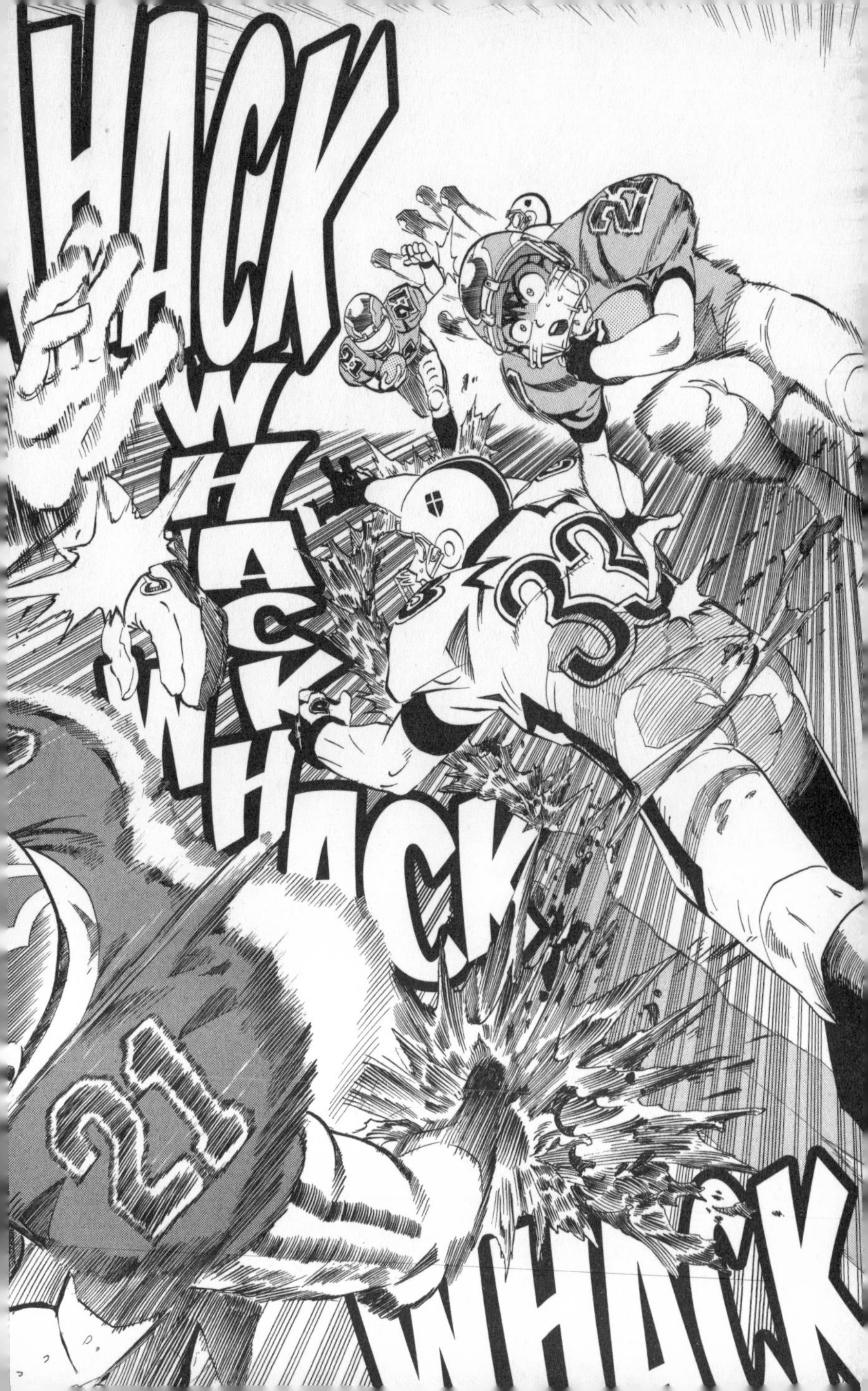
HACK
WHACK
WHACK
WHACK

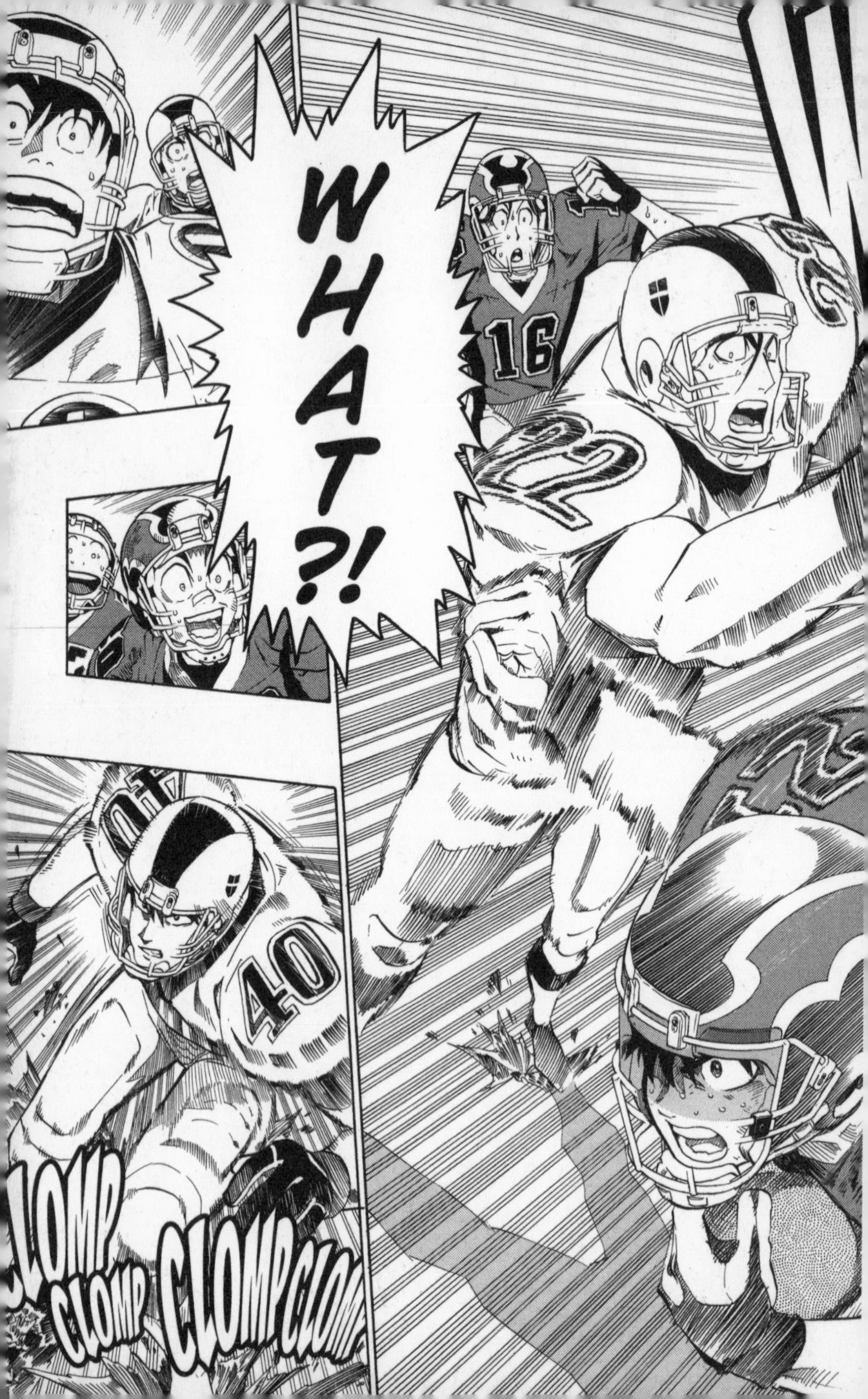
WHAT?!
CLOMP
CLOMP
CLOMPCLOM

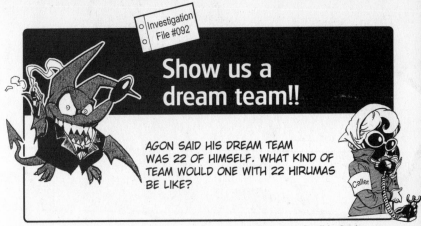

Investigation File #092

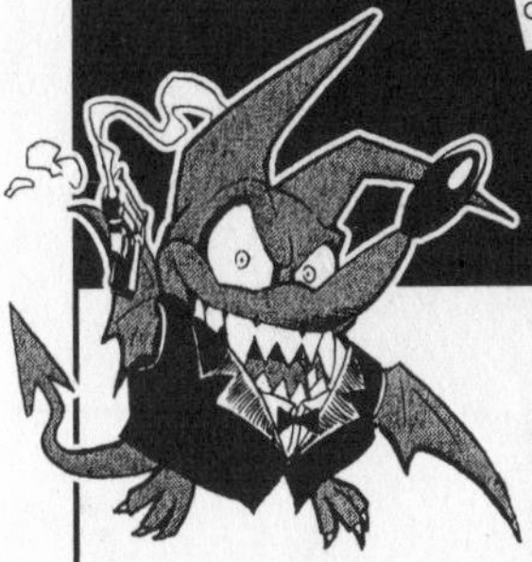

Show us a dream team!!

AGON SAID HIS DREAM TEAM WAS 22 OF HIMSELF. WHAT KIND OF TEAM WOULD ONE WITH 22 HIRUMAS BE LIKE?

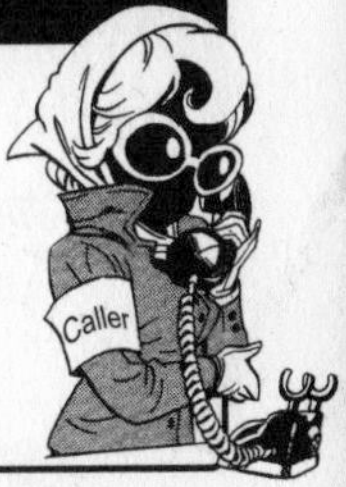
Caller

Caller name: Devil in Osaka

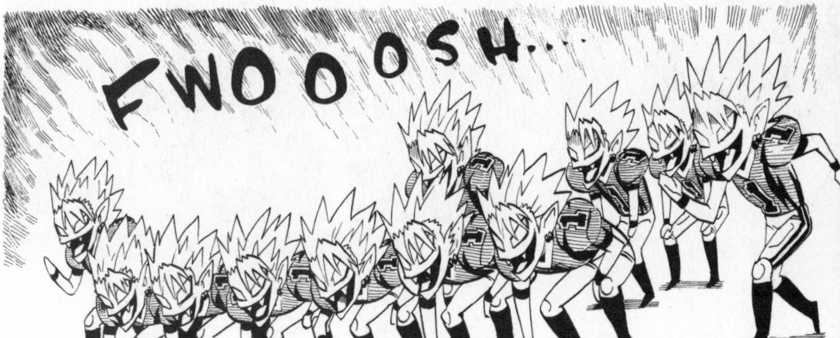
FWOOOSH...

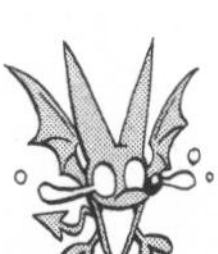

YEEEEEEEK!
I DON'T EVEN WANT TO IMAGINE THAT!!

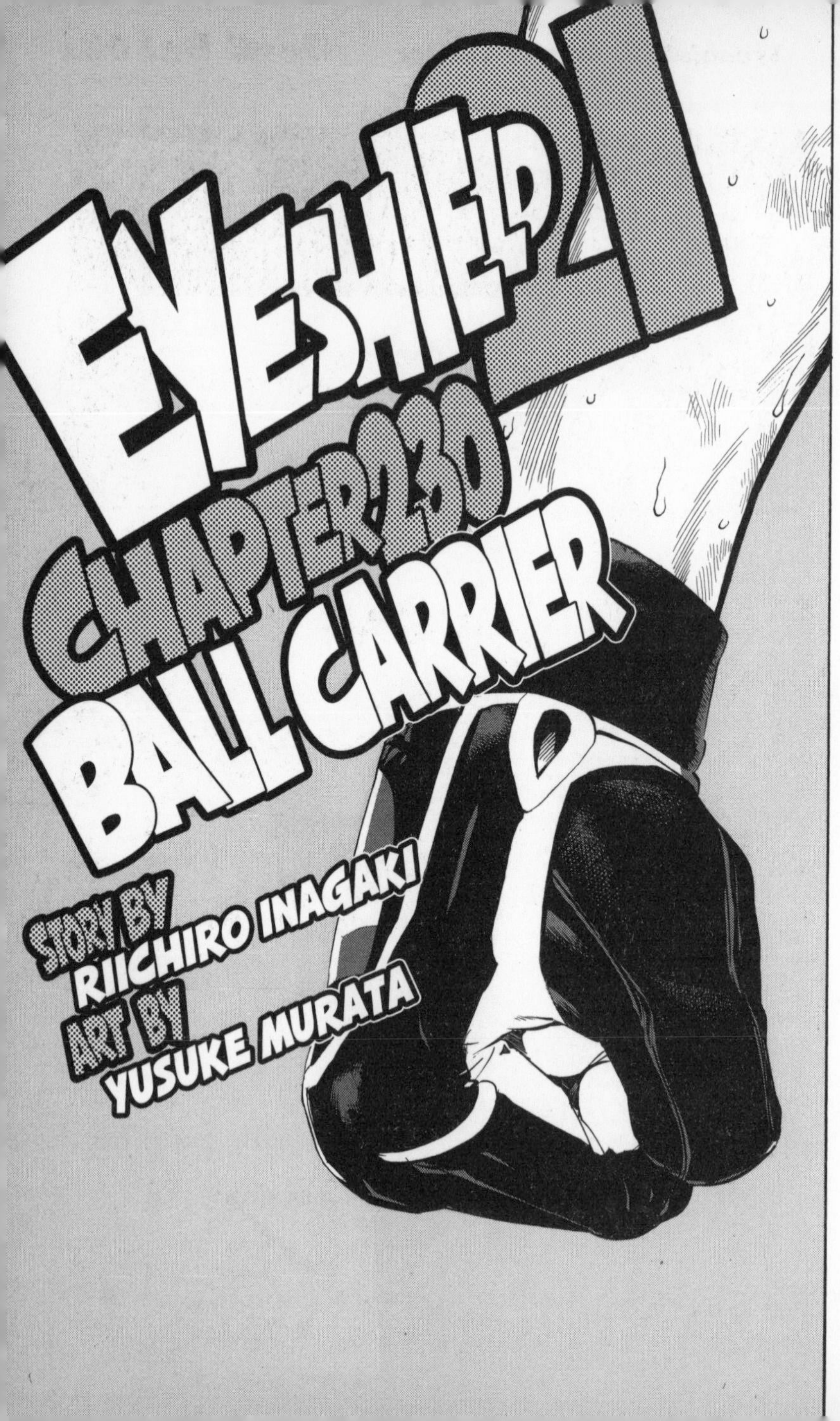
EYESHIELD 21
CHAPTER 230
BALL CARRIER
STORY BY
RIICHIRO INAGAKI
ART BY
YUSUKE MURATA

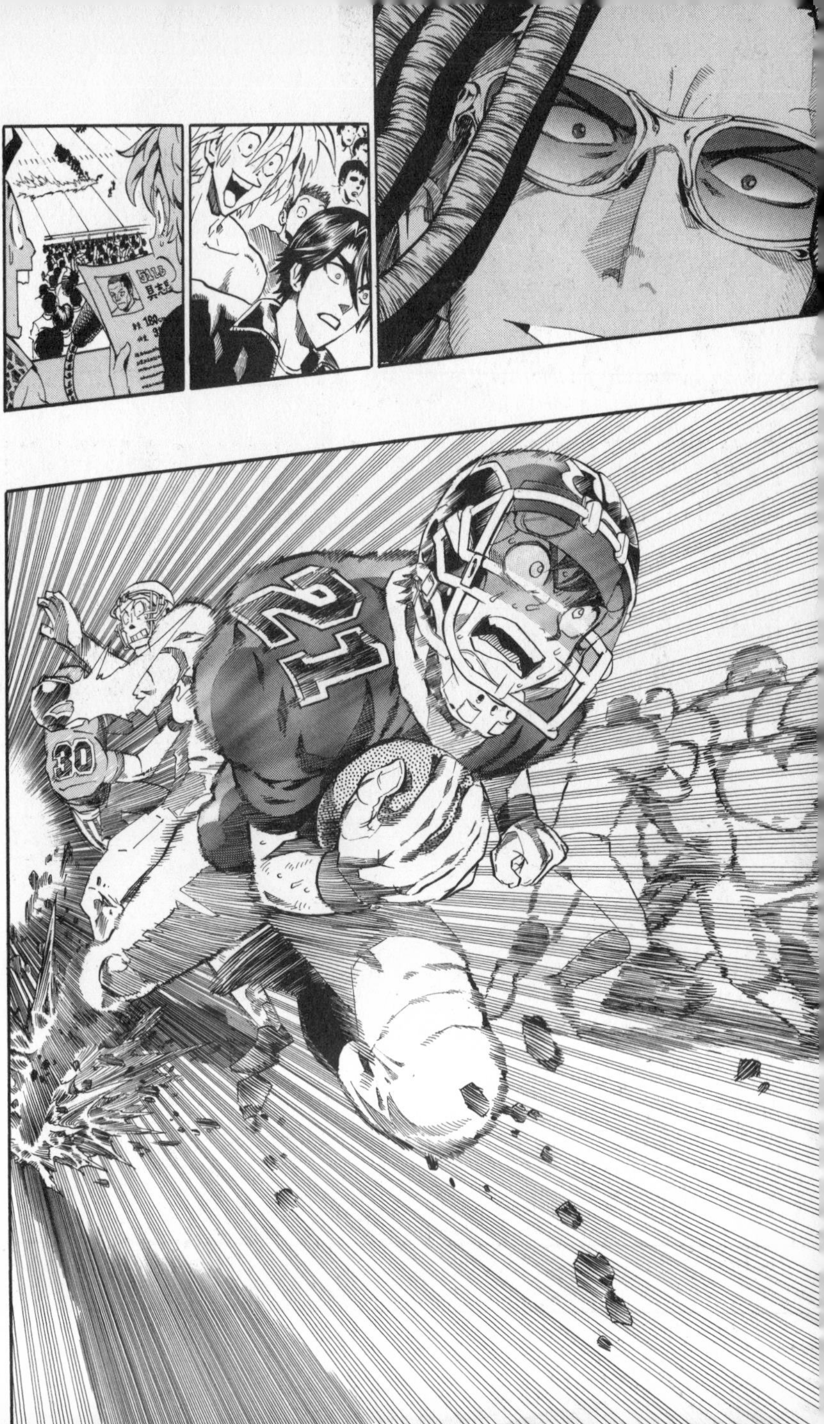

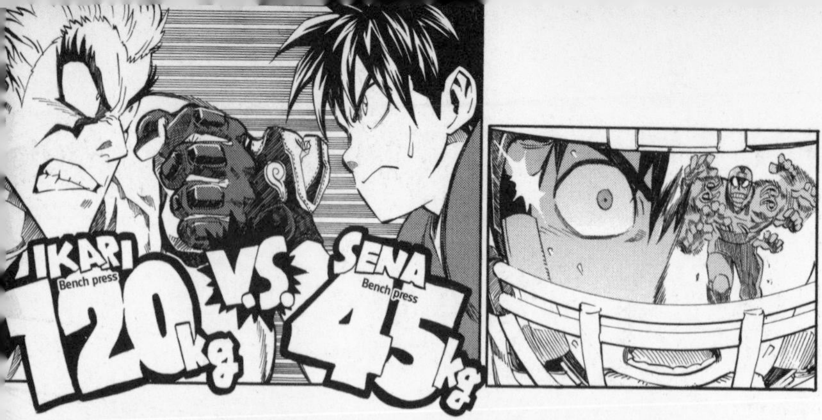
IKARI
Bench press
120kg
V.S.
SENA
Bench press
45kg

120 KG = 264 LBS AND 45KG = 99 LBS

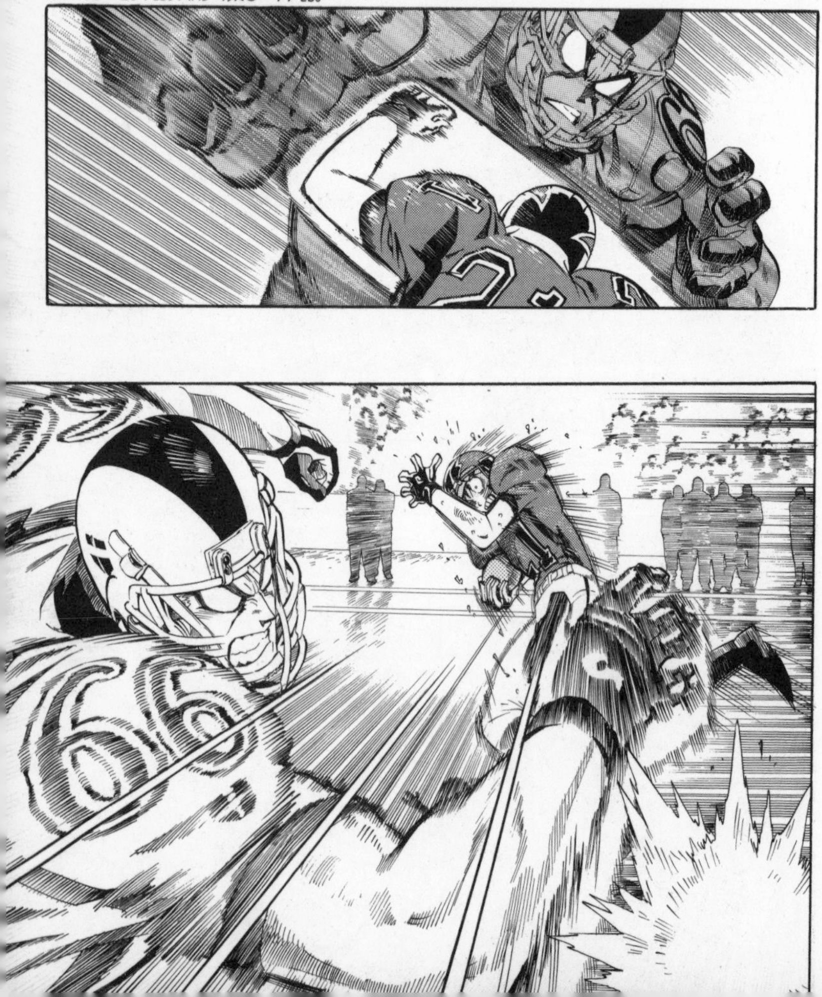

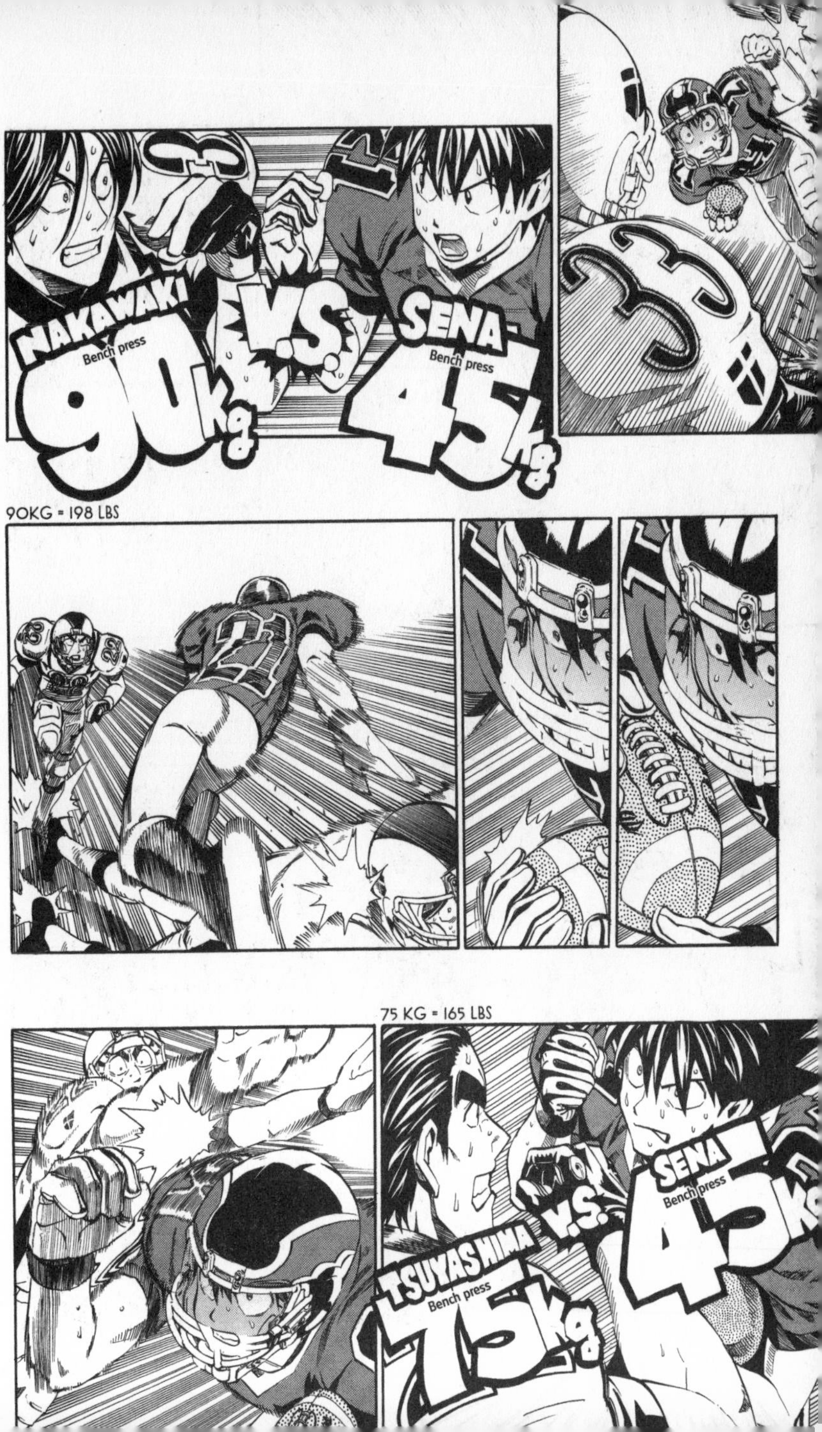
SENA
Bench press
45kg
V.S.
NAKAWAKI
Bench press
90kg
90KG = 198 LBS
75 KG = 165 LBS
SENA
Bench press
45kg
V.S.
TSUYASHIMA
Bench press
75kg

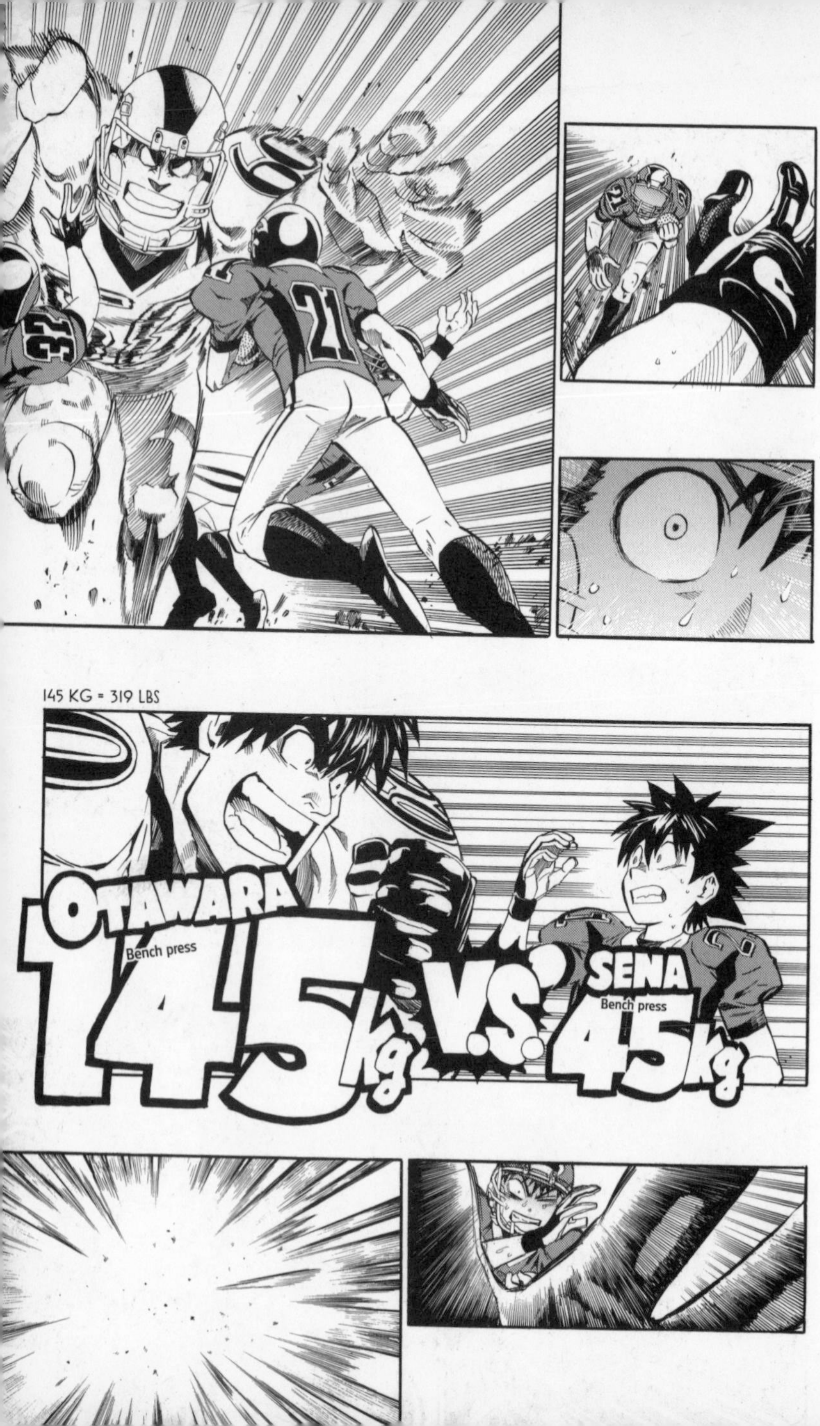
145 KG = 319 LBS
OTAWARA
Bench press
145 kg
V.S.
SENA
Bench press
45 kg

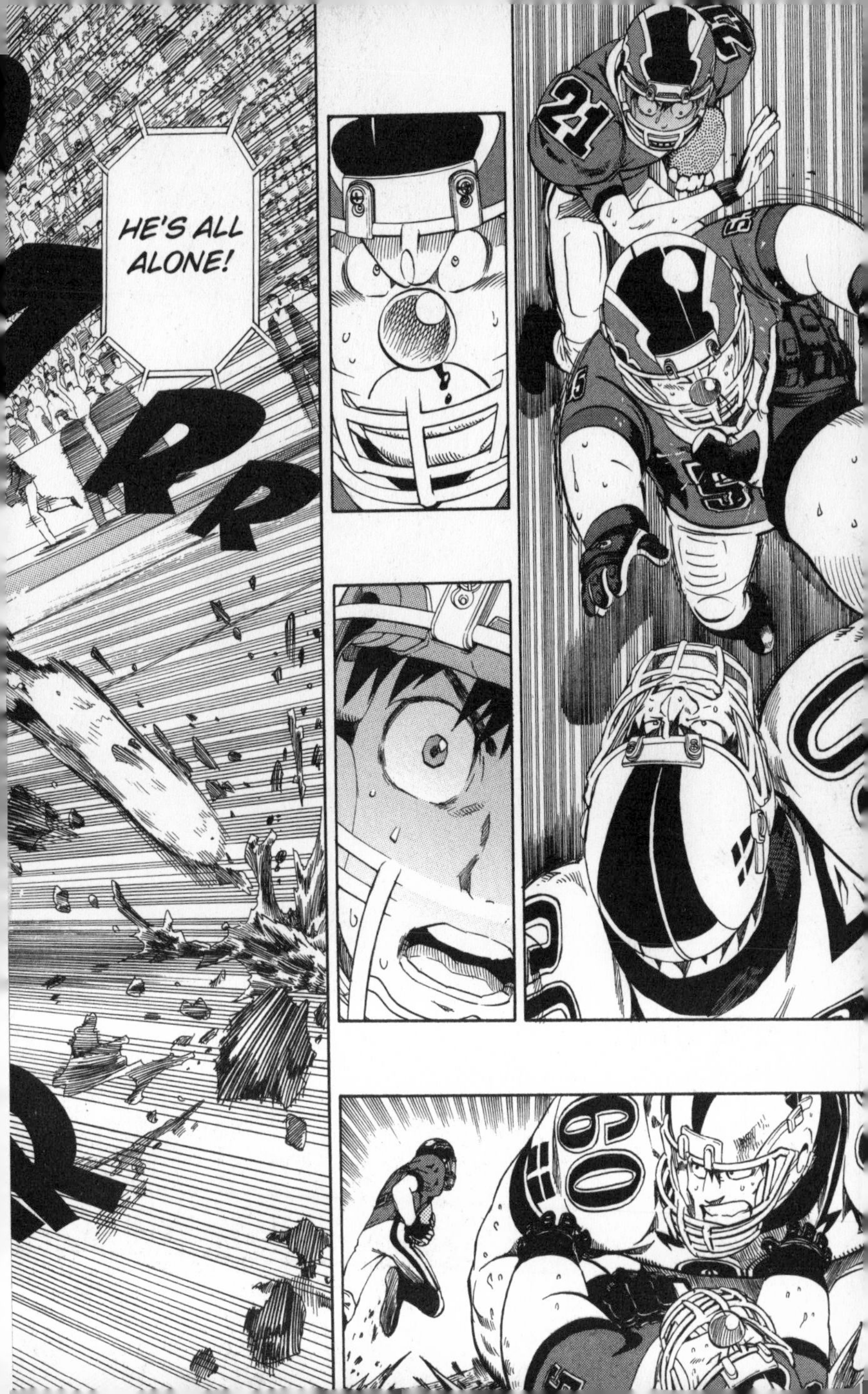
HE'S ALL ALONE!
RR

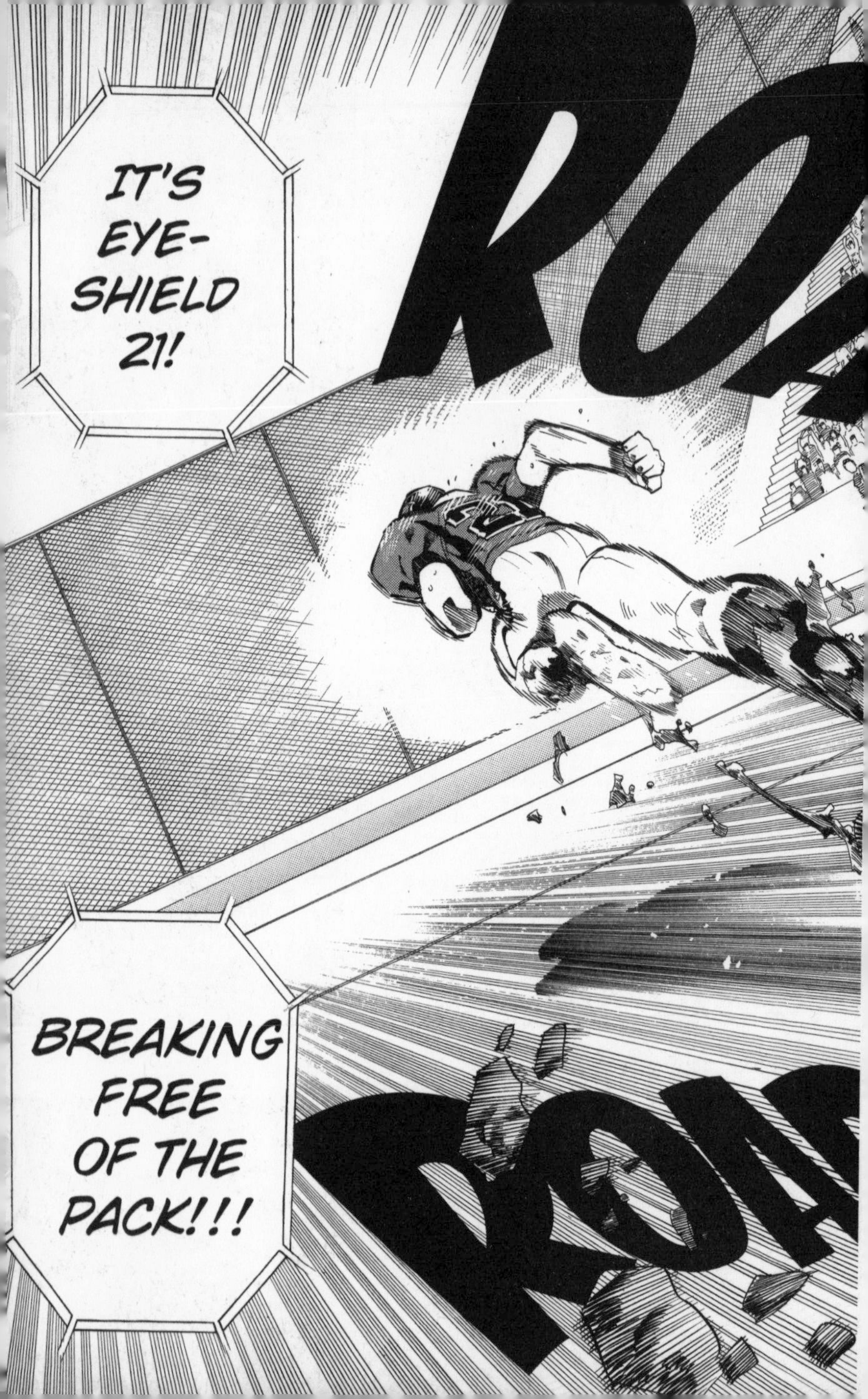
IT'S EYE-SHIELD 21!
BREAKING FREE OF THE PACK!!!

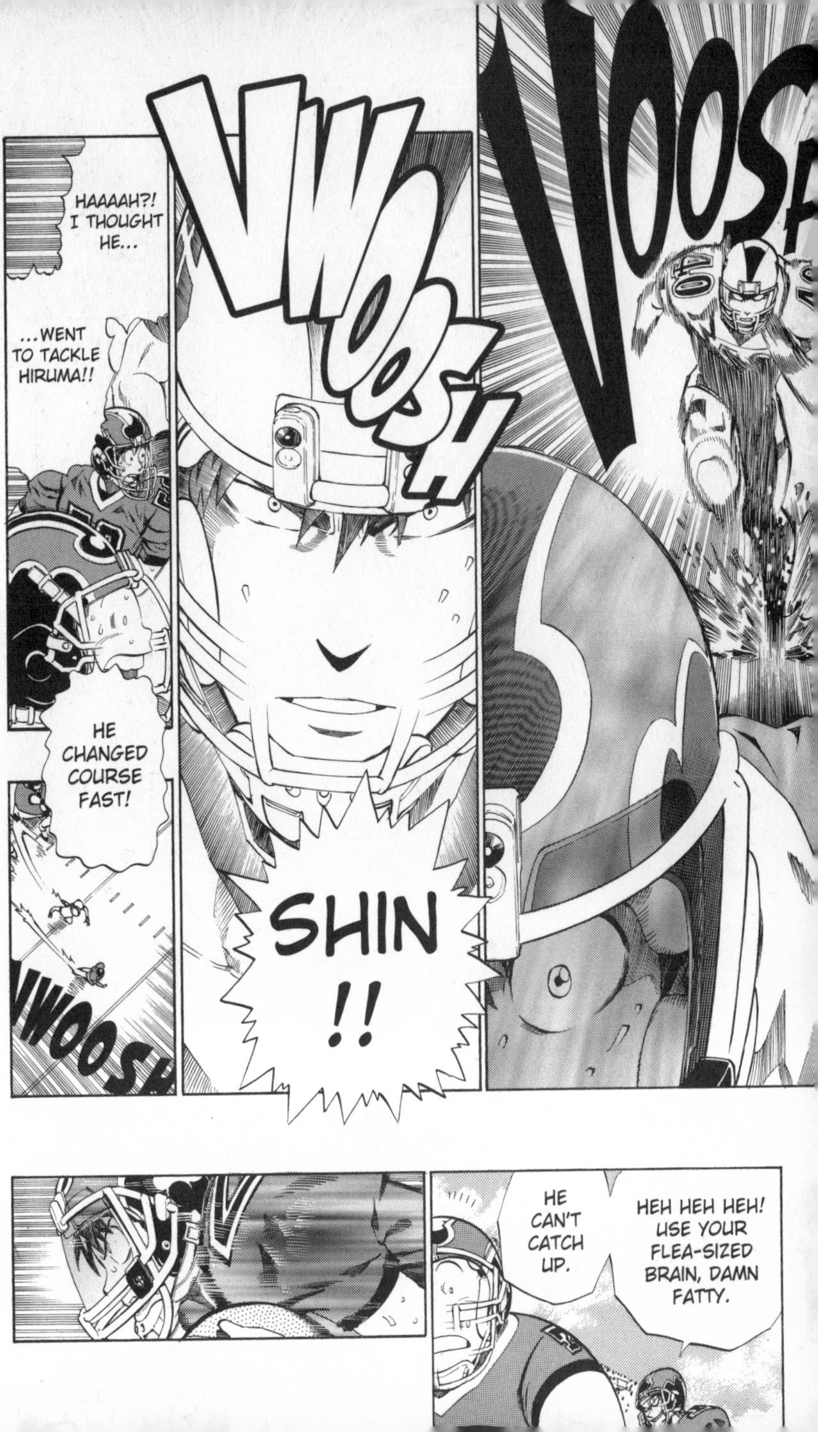
VOOS
VWOOSH
SHIN !!
HAAAAH?! I THOUGHT HE...
...WENT TO TACKLE HIRUMA!!
HE CHANGED COURSE FAST!
WWOOS
HEH HEH HEH! USE YOUR FLEA-SIZED BRAIN, DAMN FATTY.
HE CAN'T CATCH UP.

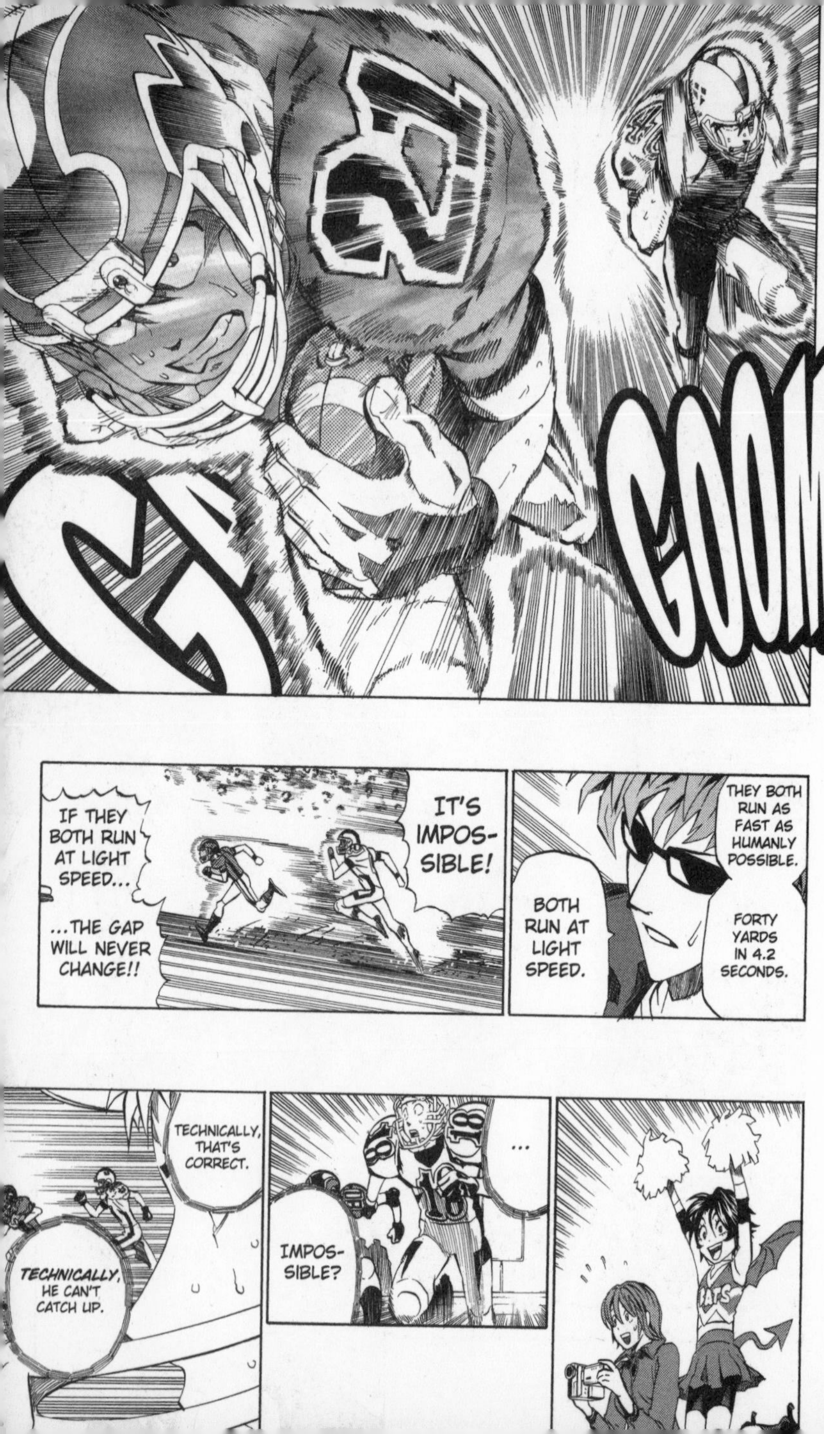
GOOM
THEY BOTH RUN AS FAST AS HUMANLY POSSIBLE.
FORTY YARDS IN 4.2 SECONDS.
BOTH RUN AT LIGHT SPEED.
IT'S IMPOSSIBLE!
IF THEY BOTH RUN AT LIGHT SPEED...
...THE GAP WILL NEVER CHANGE!!
...
IMPOSSIBLE?
TECHNICALLY, THAT'S CORRECT.
TECHNICALLY, HE CAN'T CATCH UP.

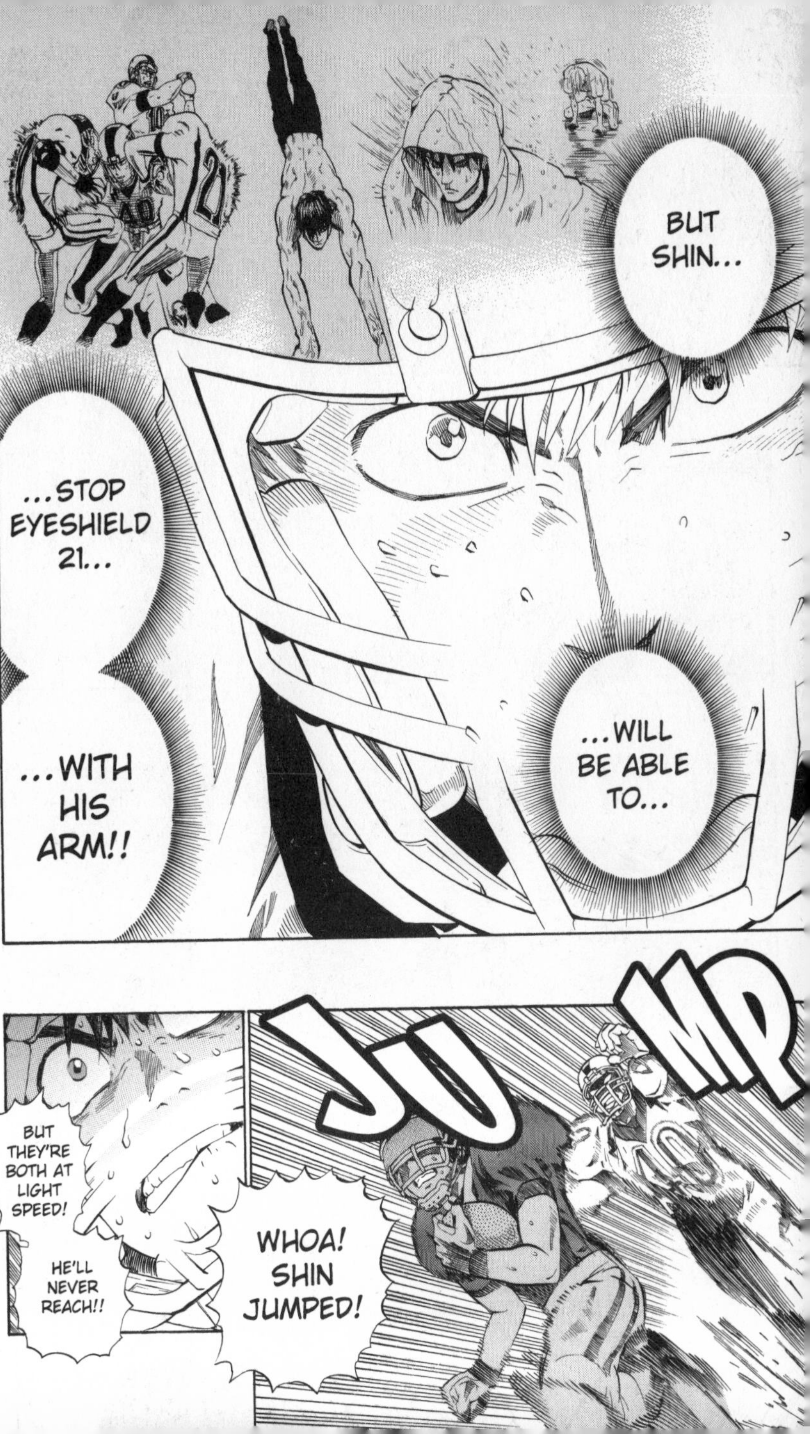
BUT SHIN...
...WILL BE ABLE TO...
...STOP EYESHIELD 21...
...WITH HIS ARM!!
JUMP
WHOA! SHIN JUMPED!
BUT THEY'RE BOTH AT LIGHT SPEED!
HE'LL NEVER REACH!!

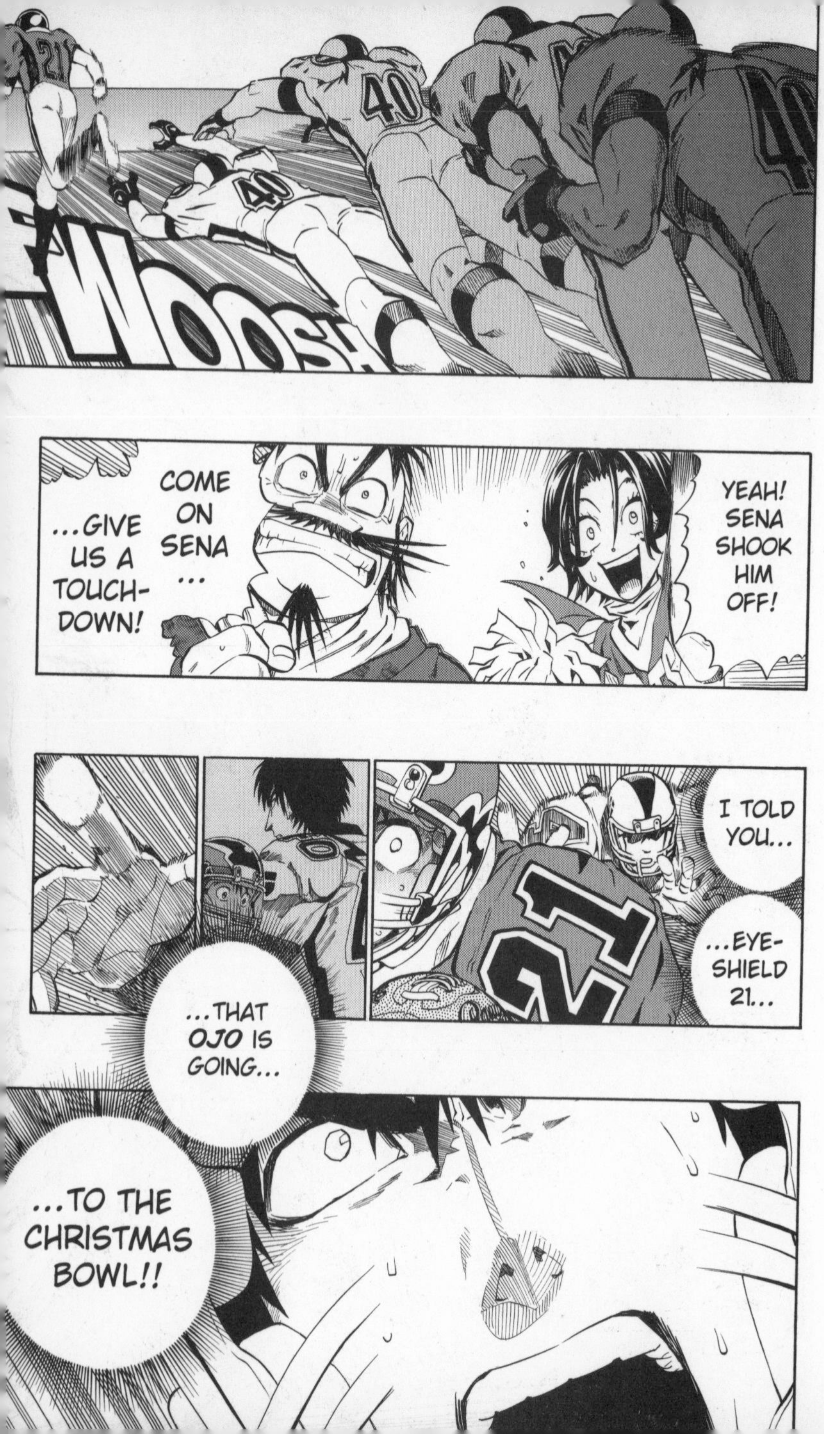
WOOSH
YEAH! SENA SHOOK HIM OFF!
COME ON SENA...
...GIVE US A TOUCH-DOWN!
I TOLD YOU...
...EYE-SHIELD 21...
...THAT OJO IS GOING...
...TO THE CHRISTMAS BOWL!!

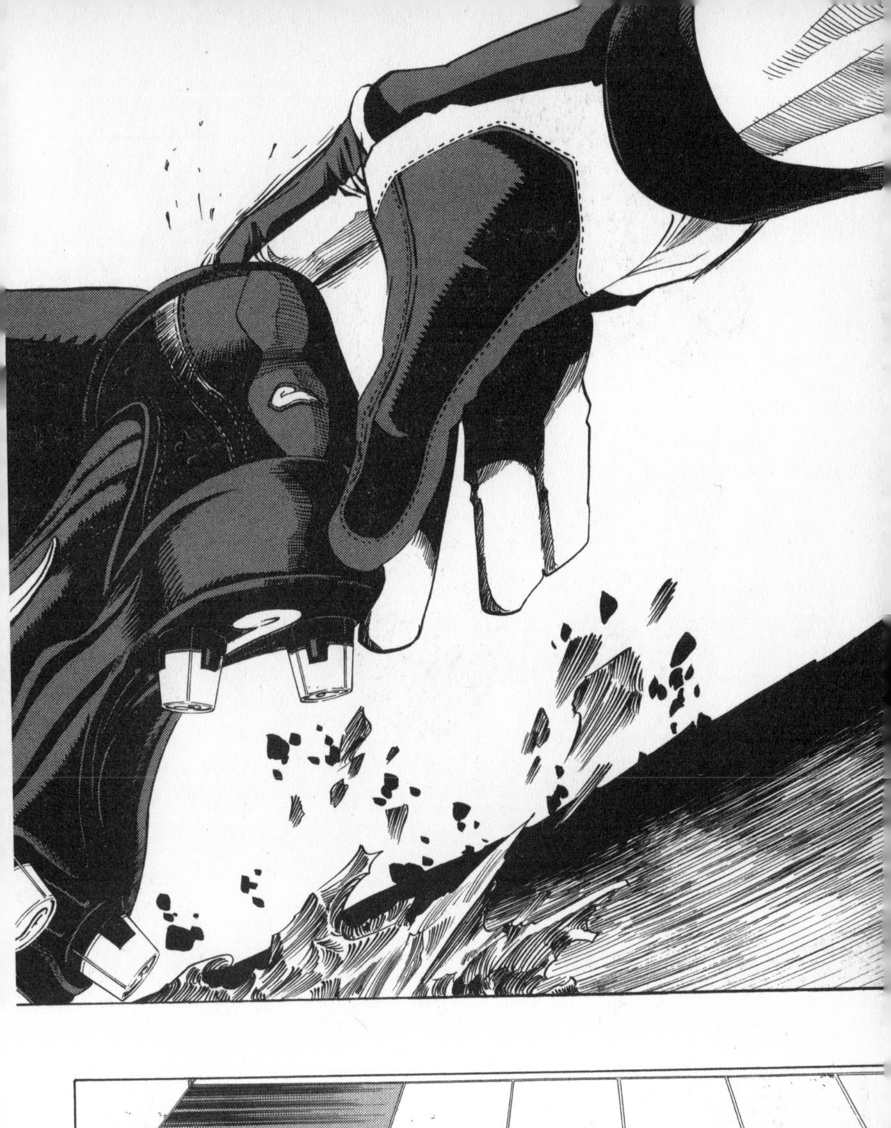
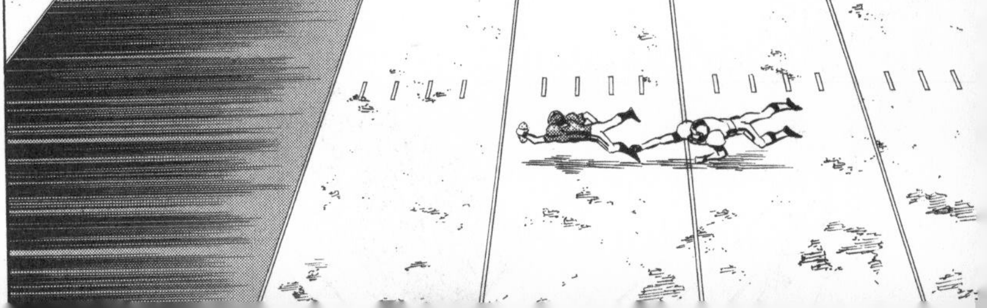

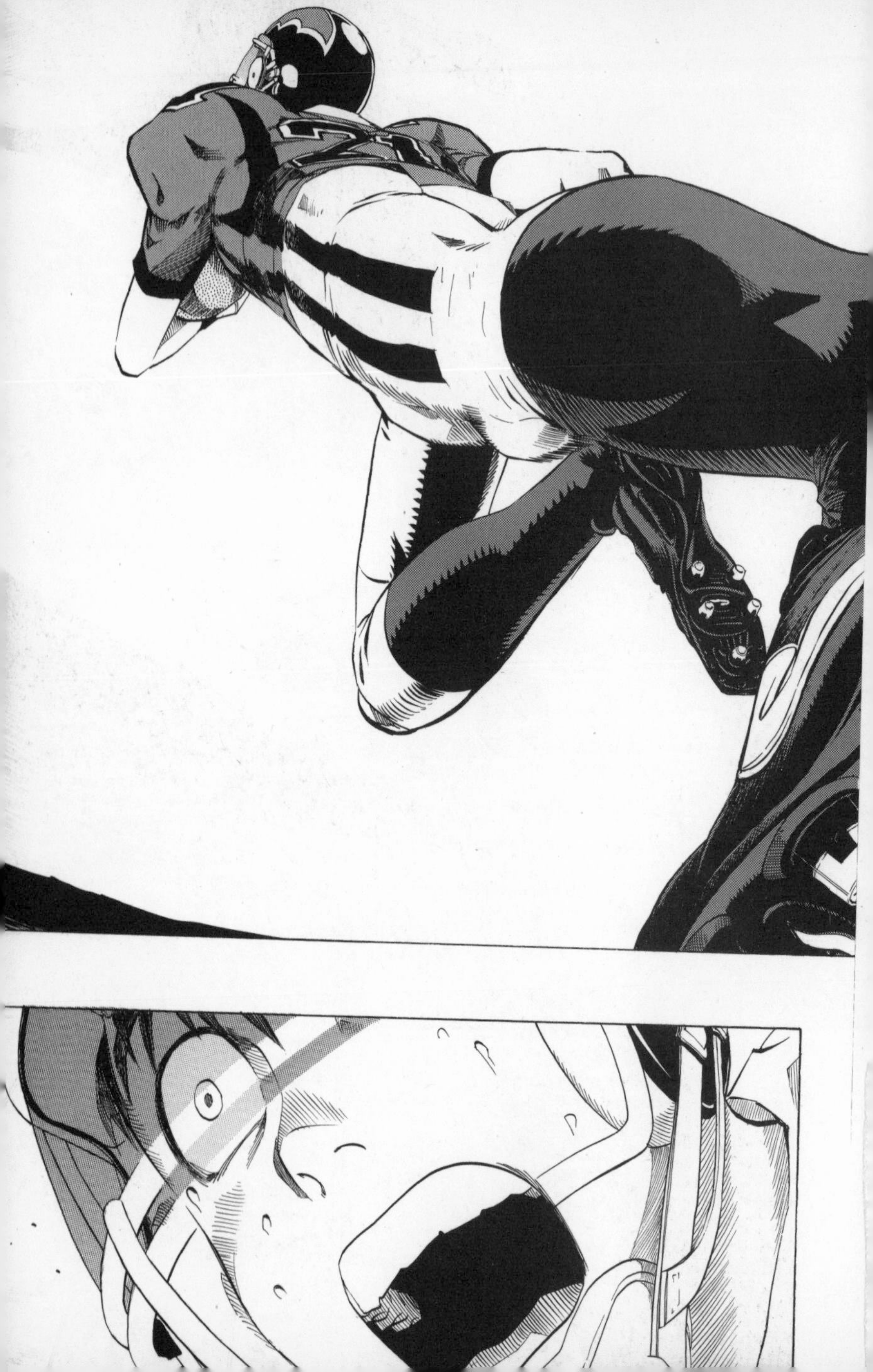

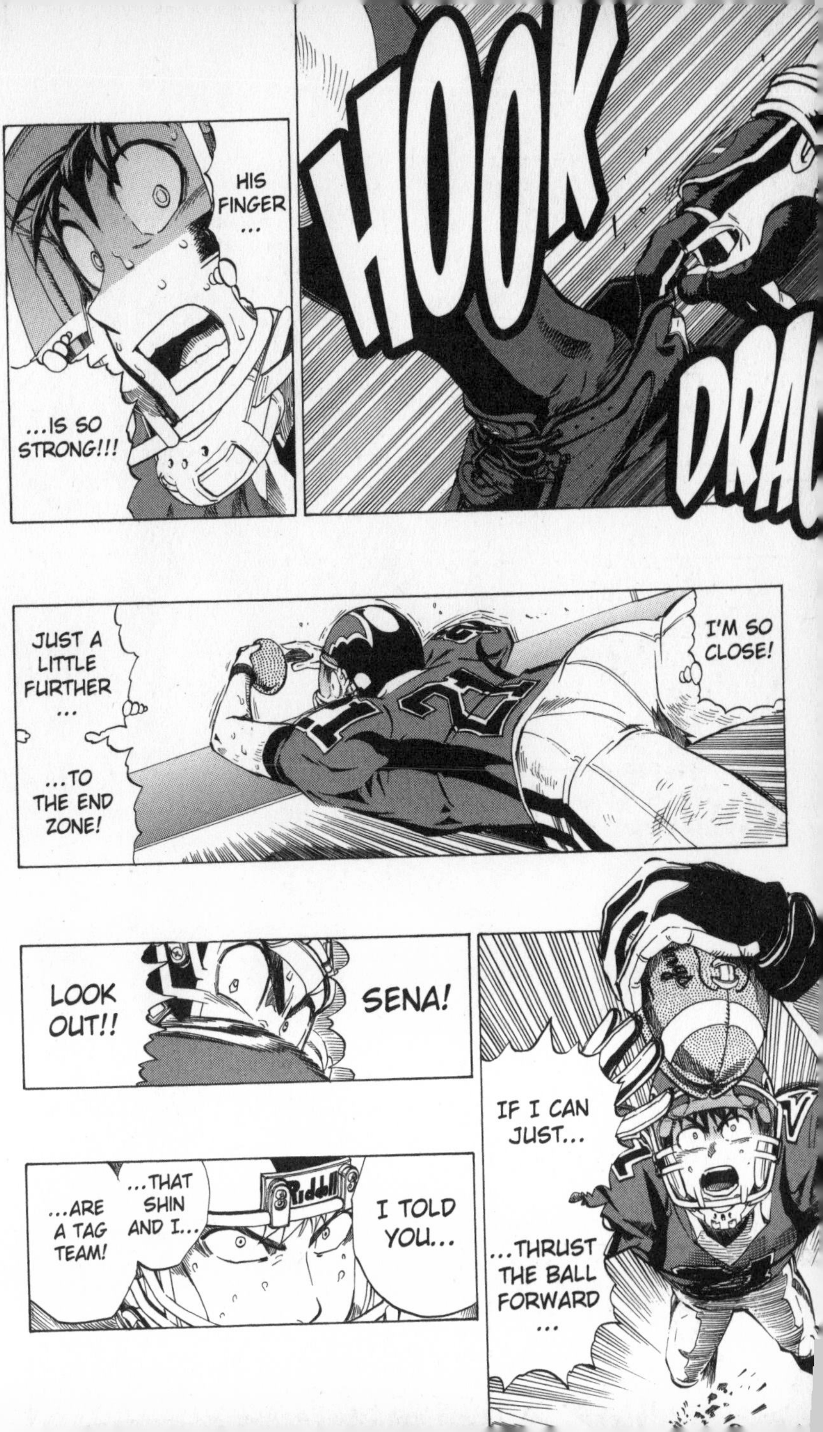
HOOK
DRA
HIS FINGER ...
...IS SO STRONG!!!
I'M SO CLOSE!
JUST A LITTLE FURTHER ...
...TO THE END ZONE!
IF I CAN JUST...
...THRUST THE BALL FORWARD ...
SENA!
LOOK OUT!!
I TOLD YOU...
...THAT SHIN AND I...
...ARE A TAG TEAM!

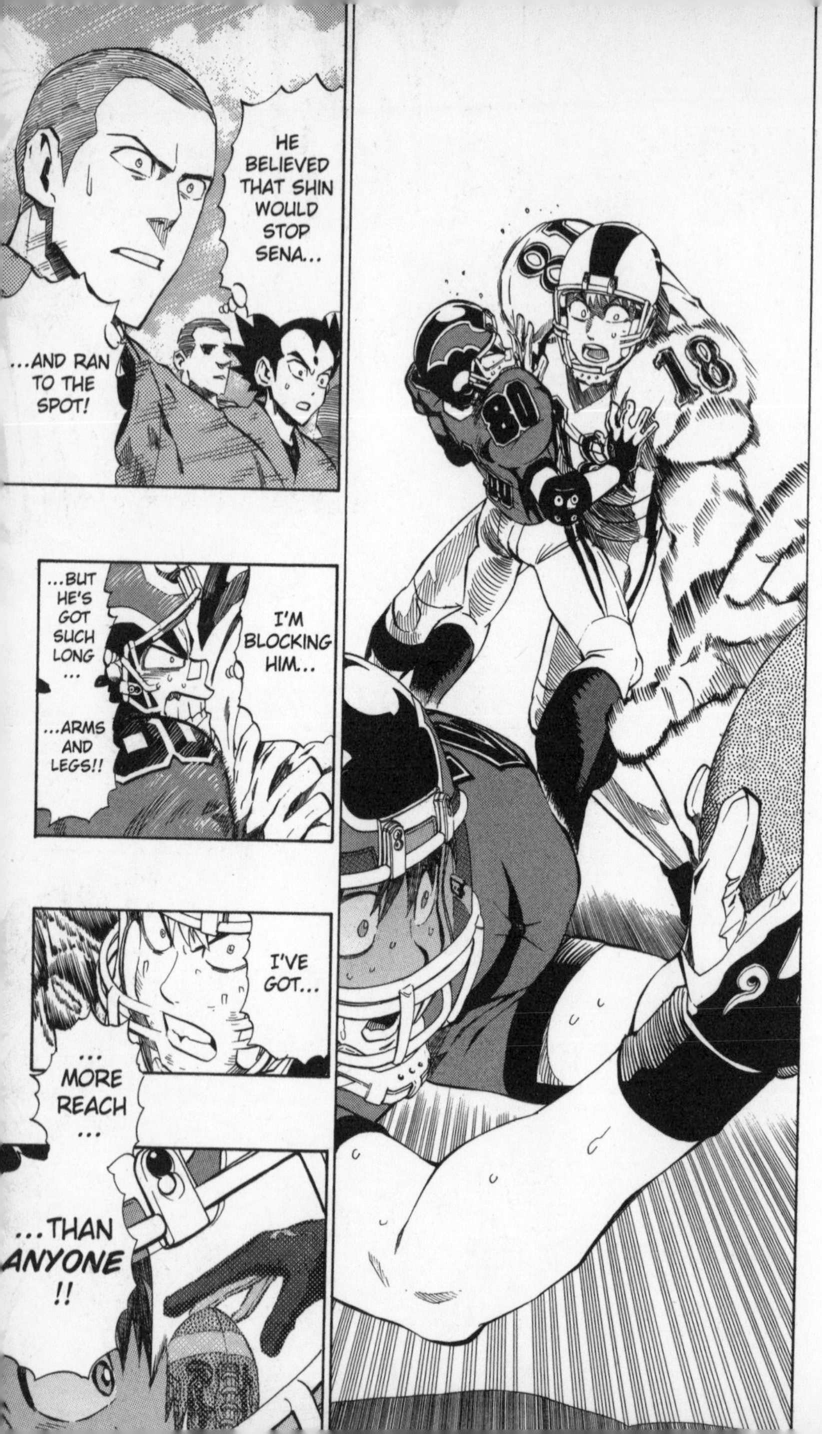
HE BELIEVED THAT SHIN WOULD STOP SENA...
...AND RAN TO THE SPOT!
I'M BLOCKING HIM...
...BUT HE'S GOT SUCH LONG...
...ARMS AND LEGS!!
I'VE GOT...
...MORE REACH...
...THAN ANYONE!!

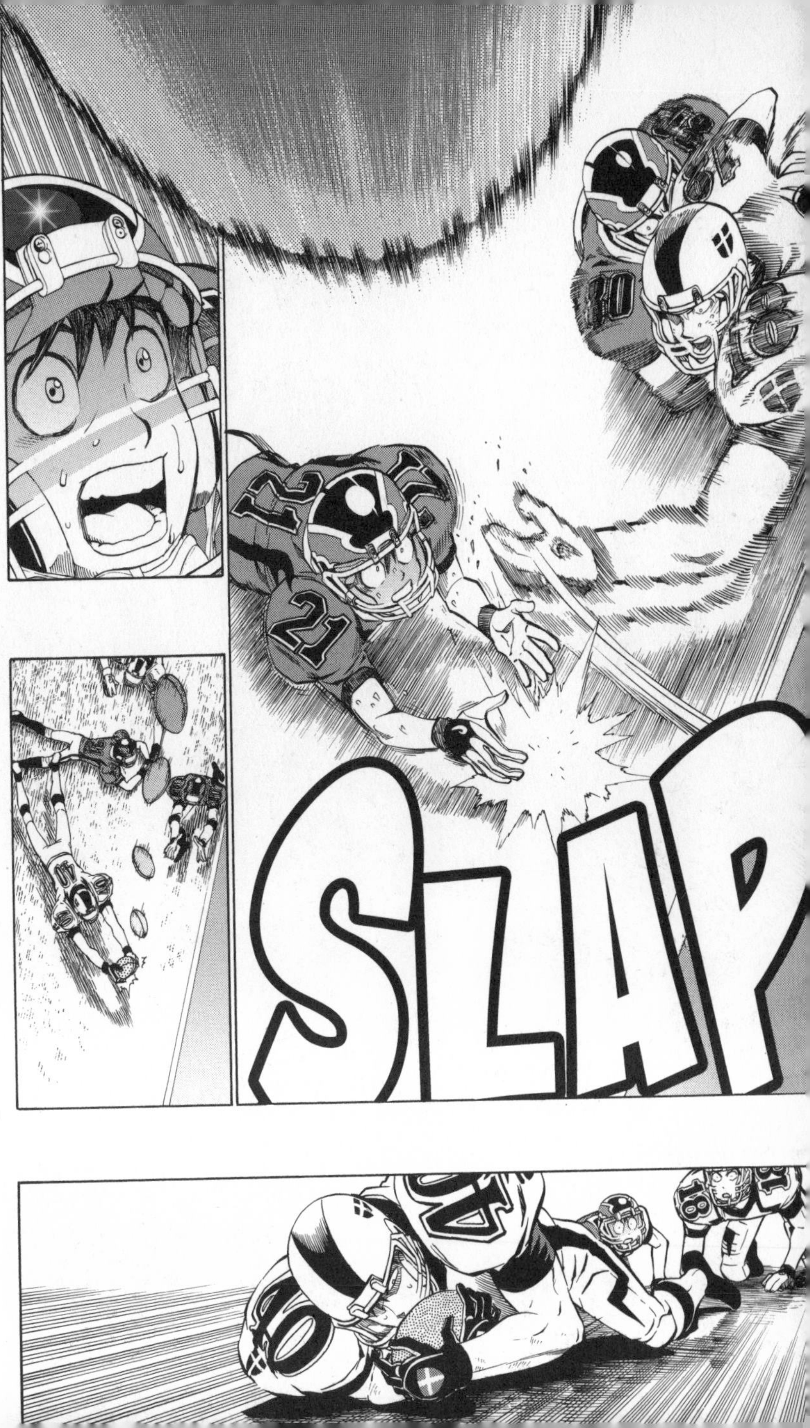
SLAP

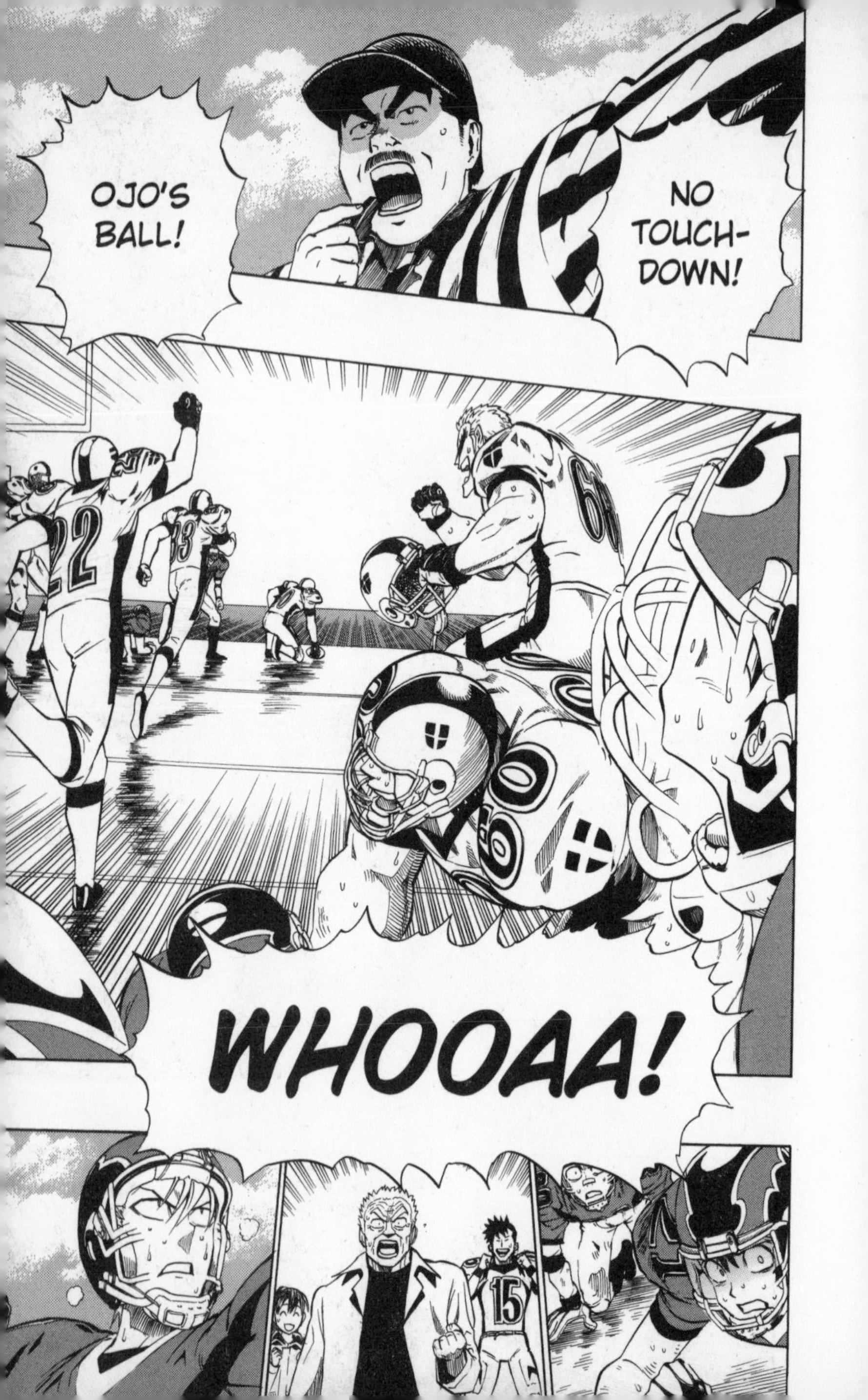
NO TOUCH-DOWN!
OJO'S BALL!
WHOOAA!

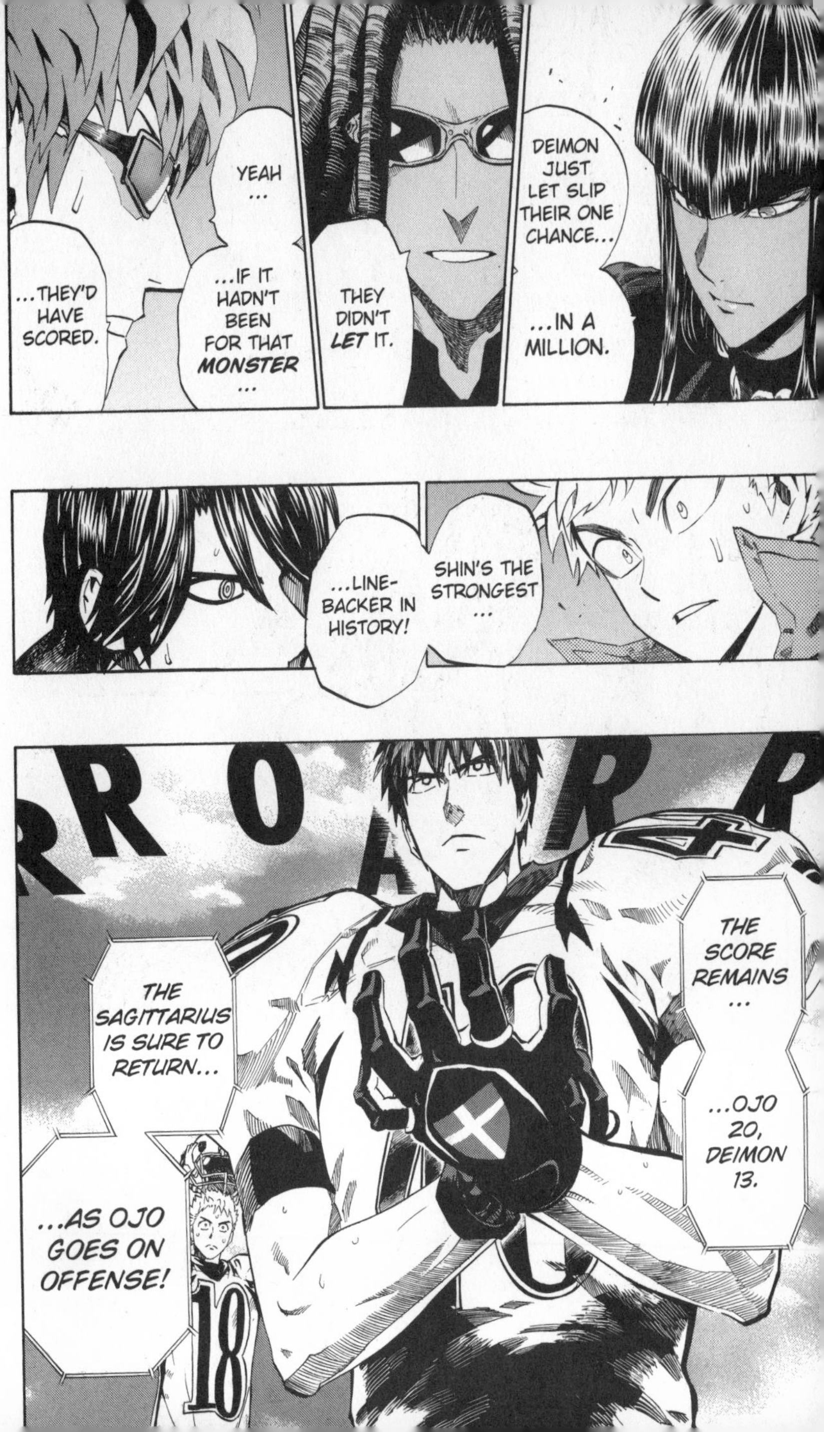
DEIMON JUST LET SLIP THEIR ONE CHANCE...
...IN A MILLION.
THEY DIDN'T LET IT.
YEAH...
...IF IT HADN'T BEEN FOR THAT MONSTER...
...THEY'D HAVE SCORED.
SHIN'S THE STRONGEST...
...LINE-BACKER IN HISTORY!
RROARR
THE SCORE REMAINS...
...OJO 20, DEIMON 13.
THE SAGITTARIUS IS SURE TO RETURN...
...AS OJO GOES ON OFFENSE!

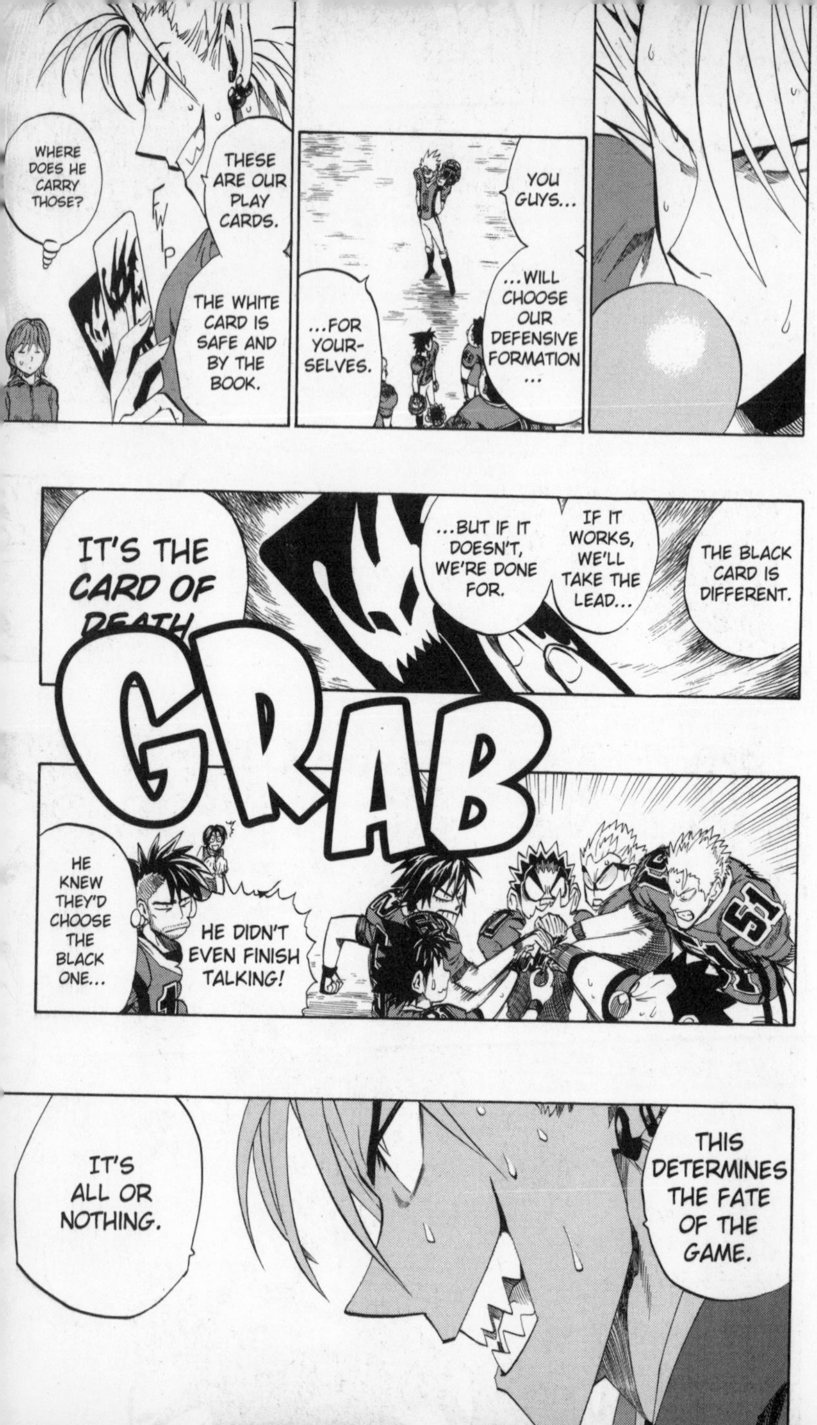
YOU GUYS...
...WILL CHOOSE OUR DEFENSIVE FORMATION...
...FOR YOURSELVES.
THESE ARE OUR PLAY CARDS.
FWIP
WHERE DOES HE CARRY THOSE?
THE WHITE CARD IS SAFE AND BY THE BOOK.
THE BLACK CARD IS DIFFERENT.
IF IT WORKS, WE'LL TAKE THE LEAD...
...BUT IF IT DOESN'T, WE'RE DONE FOR.
IT'S THE CARD OF
GRAB
HE DIDN'T EVEN FINISH TALKING!
HE KNEW THEY'D CHOOSE THE BLACK ONE...
THIS DETERMINES THE FATE OF THE GAME.
IT'S ALL OR NOTHING.

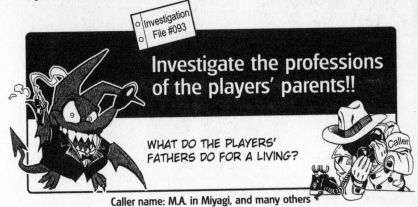

○ Investigation File #093

Investigate the professions of the players' parents!!

WHAT DO THE PLAYERS' FATHERS DO FOR A LIVING?

Caller

Caller name: M.A. in Miyagi, and many others

BOSS! THEY WON'T ALL FIT HERE!!

DON'T SWEAT IT. HERE'S THE SCOOP ON THE TWO TEAMS PLAYING NOW, OJO AND DEIMON.

	Sena's Father	Office Worker		Ishimaru's Father	Pencil-pusher
	Monta's Father	Construction		Sakuraba's Father	Advertising
	Jumonji's Father	Judge		Otawara's Father	Gym teacher
	Taki's Father	Salesman		Takami's Father	Government official
	Mamori's Father	Pilot		Ikari's Father	Sailor

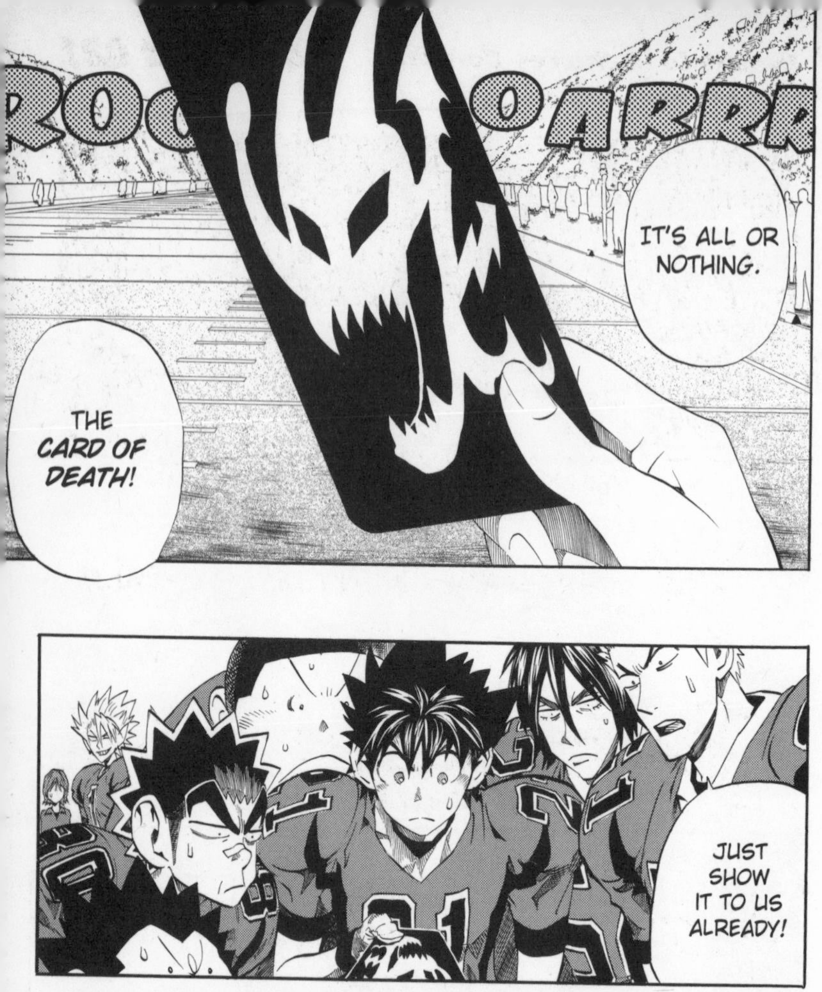
ROO OARRR
IT'S ALL OR NOTHING.
THE CARD OF DEATH!
JUST SHOW IT TO US ALREADY!

Chapter 231 Death Card

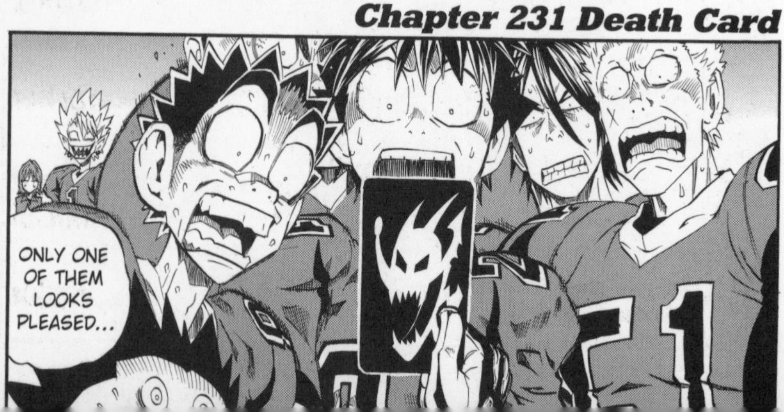
ONLY ONE OF THEM LOOKS PLEASED...

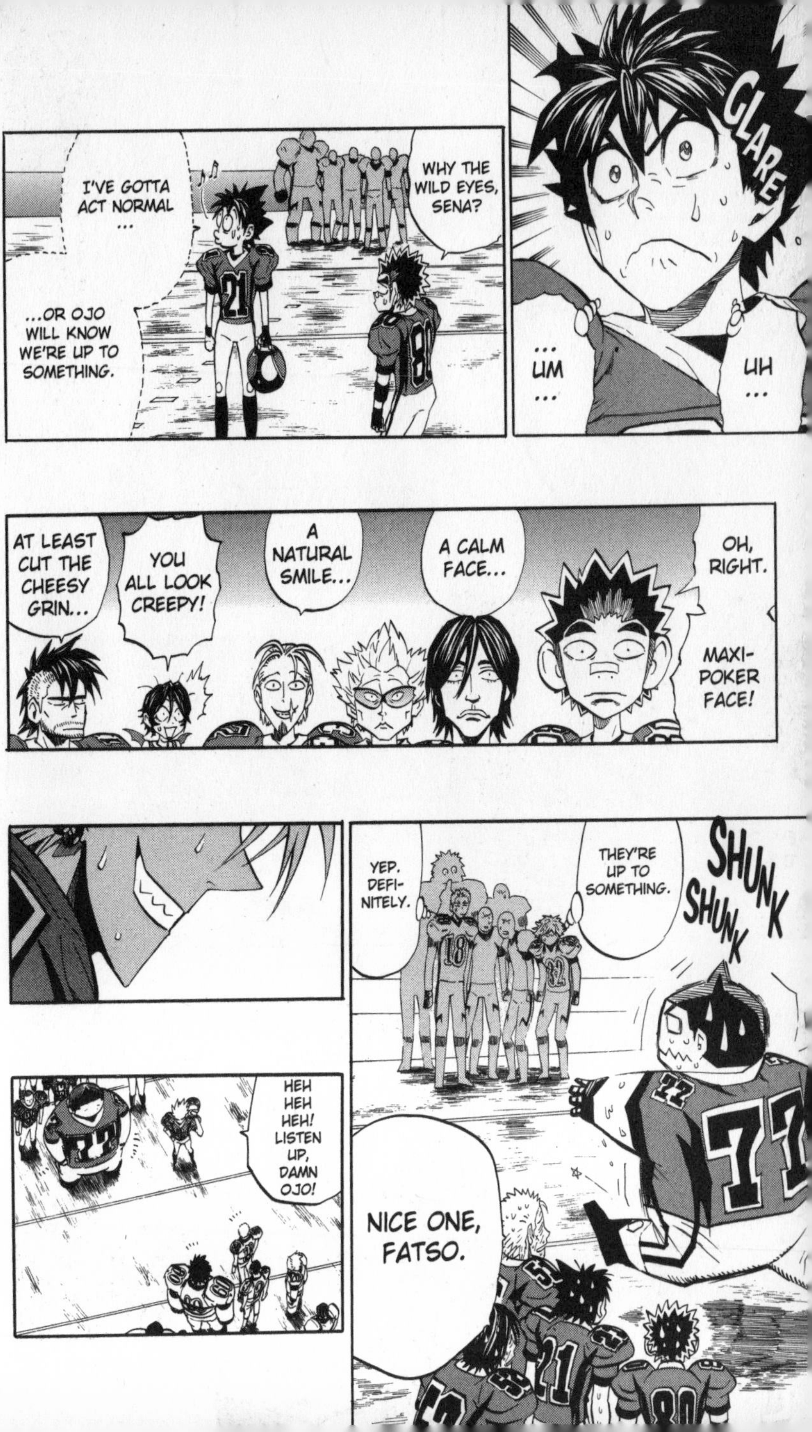
GLARE
UH ...
... UM ...
WHY THE WILD EYES, SENA?
I'VE GOTTA ACT NORMAL ...
...OR OJO WILL KNOW WE'RE UP TO SOMETHING.
OH, RIGHT.
MAXI-POKER FACE!
A CALM FACE...
A NATURAL SMILE...
YOU ALL LOOK CREEPY!
AT LEAST CUT THE CHEESY GRIN...
SHUNK
SHUNK
THEY'RE UP TO SOMETHING.
YEP. DEFI-NITELY.
NICE ONE, FATSO.
HEH HEH HEH! LISTEN UP, DAMN OJO!

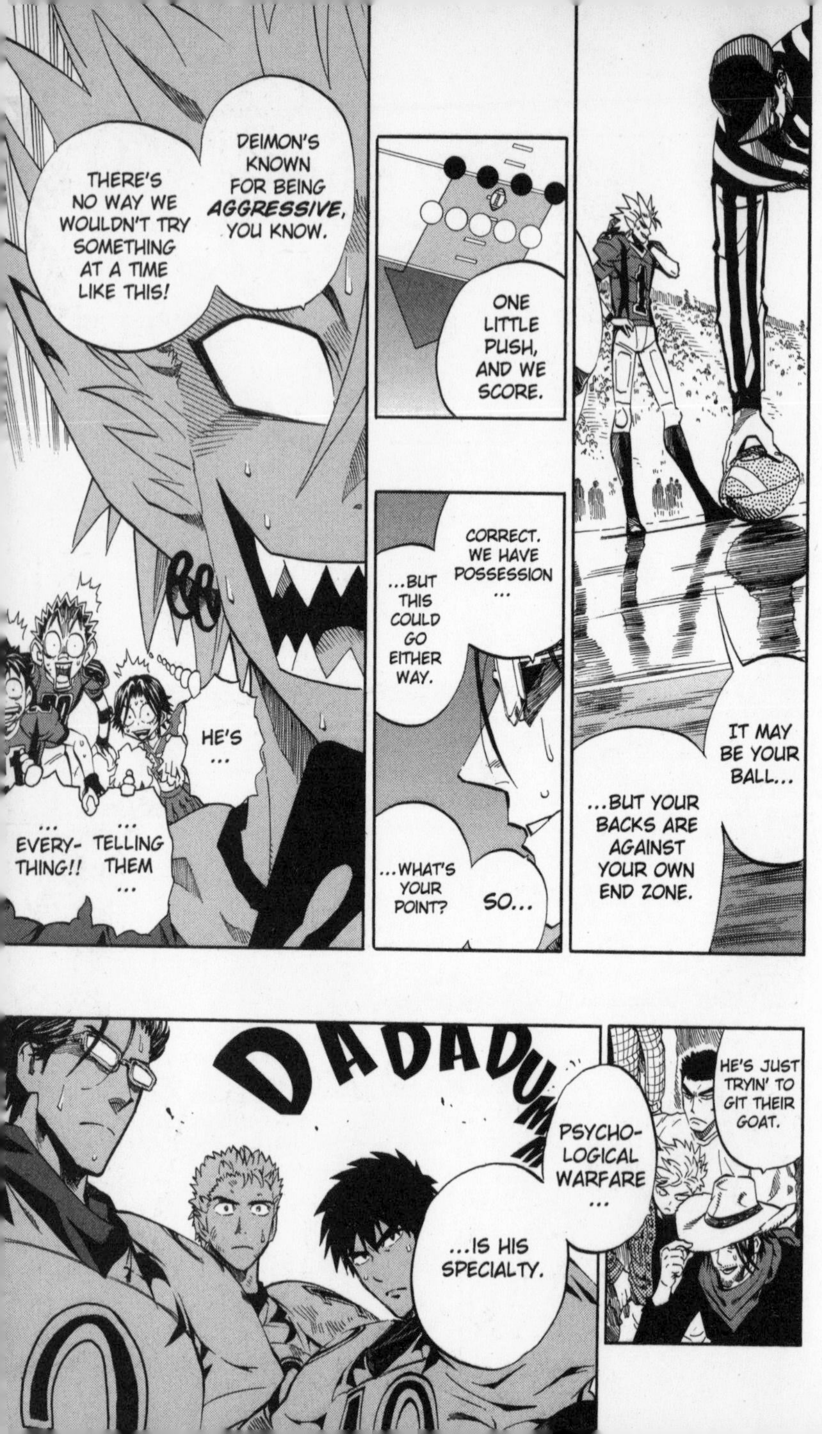
IT MAY BE YOUR BALL...
...BUT YOUR BACKS ARE AGAINST YOUR OWN END ZONE.
ONE LITTLE PUSH, AND WE SCORE.
CORRECT. WE HAVE POSSESSION...
...BUT THIS COULD GO EITHER WAY.
SO...
...WHAT'S YOUR POINT?
DEIMON'S KNOWN FOR BEING *AGGRESSIVE*, YOU KNOW.
THERE'S NO WAY WE WOULDN'T TRY SOMETHING AT A TIME LIKE THIS!
HE'S...
...TELLING THEM...
...EVERYTHING!!
HE'S JUST TRYIN' TO GIT THEIR GOAT.
DADADUMM
PSYCHOLOGICAL WARFARE...
...IS HIS SPECIALTY.

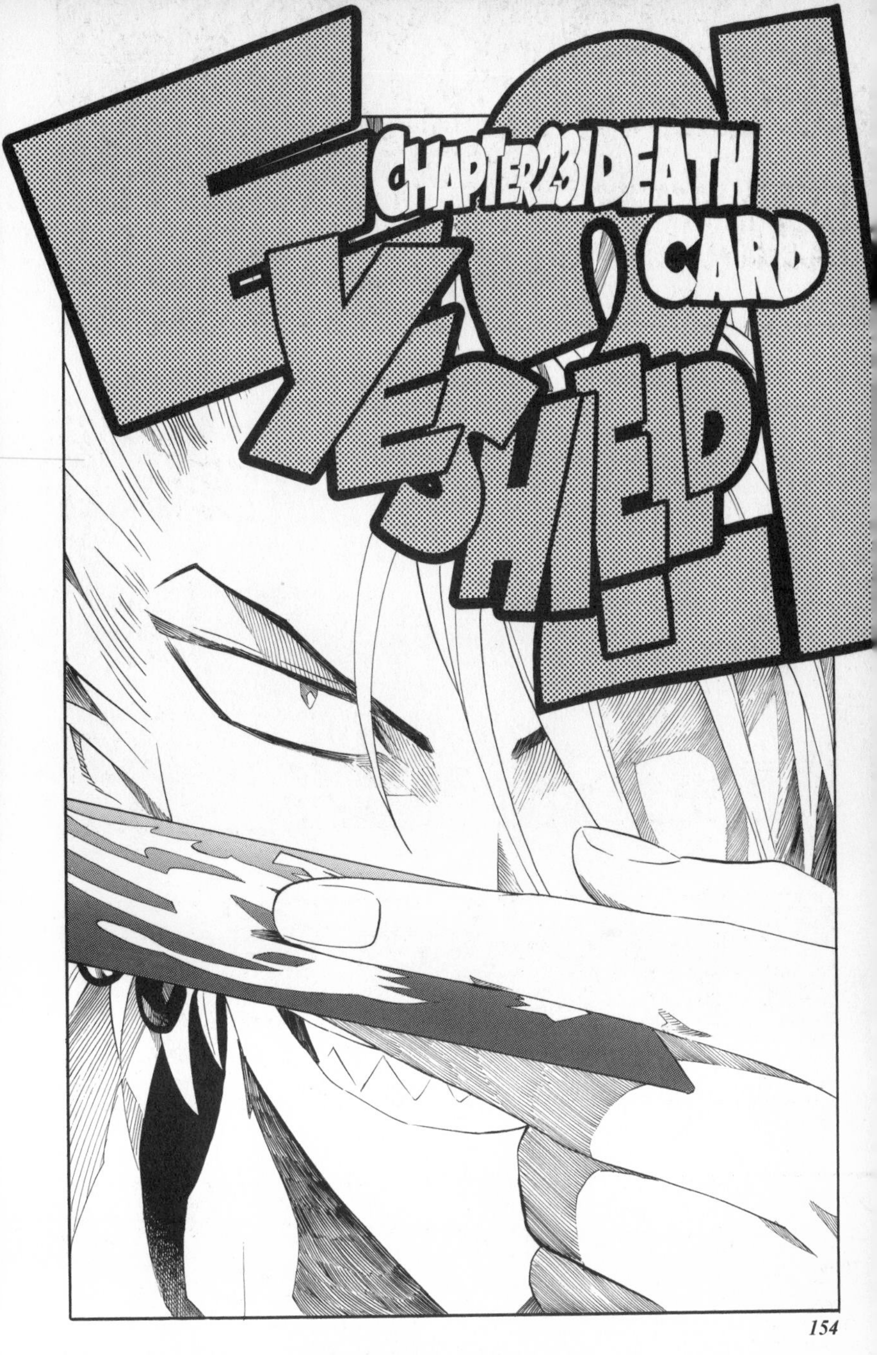
CHAPTER 231 DEATH CARD
EYESHIELD!

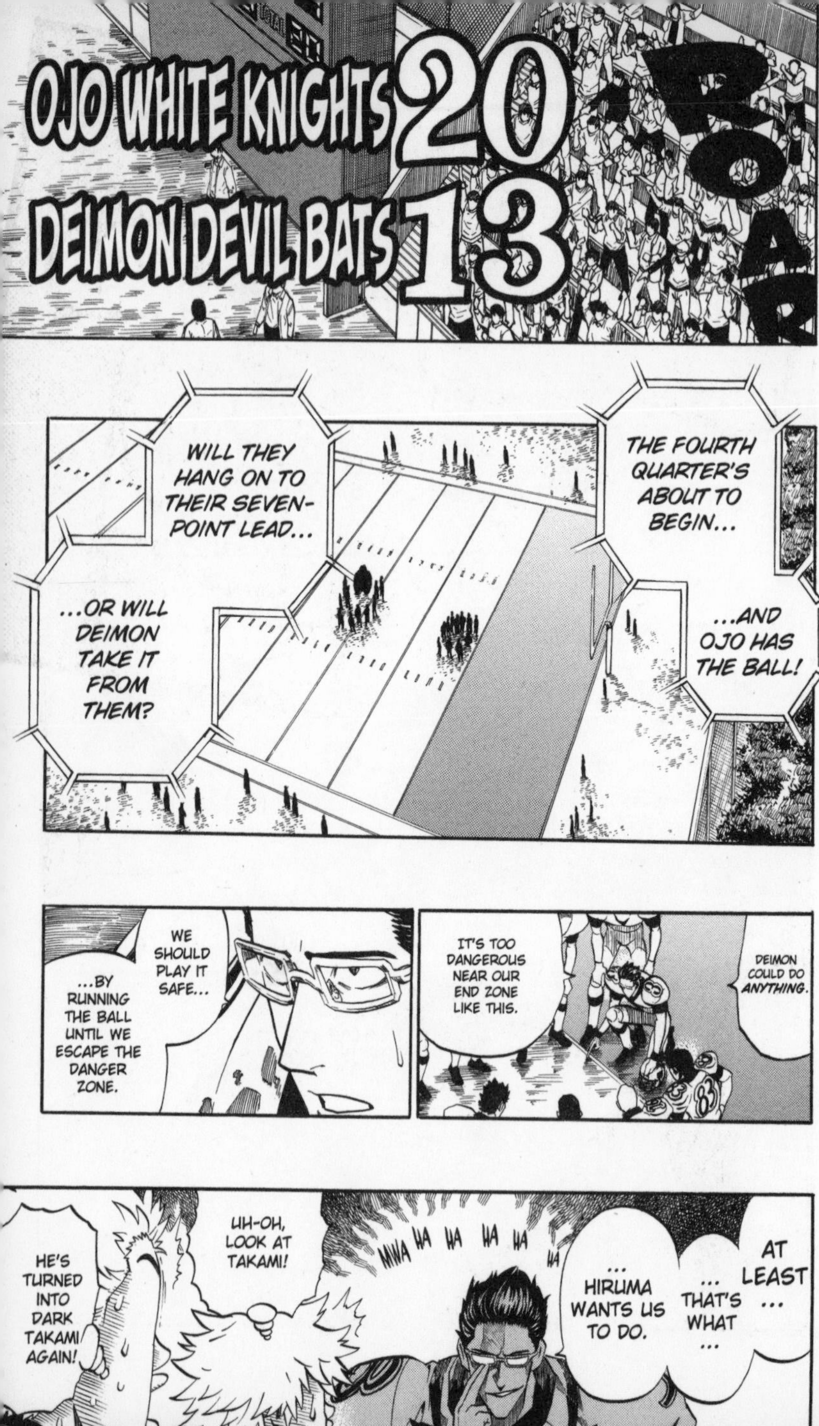
OJO WHITE KNIGHTS 20
DEIMON DEVIL BATS 13
ROAR
THE FOURTH QUARTER'S ABOUT TO BEGIN...
...AND OJO HAS THE BALL!
WILL THEY HANG ON TO THEIR SEVEN-POINT LEAD...
...OR WILL DEIMON TAKE IT FROM THEM?
DEIMON COULD DO *ANYTHING*.
IT'S TOO DANGEROUS NEAR OUR END ZONE LIKE THIS.
WE SHOULD PLAY IT SAFE...
...BY RUNNING THE BALL UNTIL WE ESCAPE THE DANGER ZONE.
AT LEAST...
...THAT'S WHAT...
...HIRUMA WANTS US TO DO.
MWA HA HA HA HA HA
UH-OH, LOOK AT TAKAMI!
HE'S TURNED INTO DARK TAKAMI AGAIN!

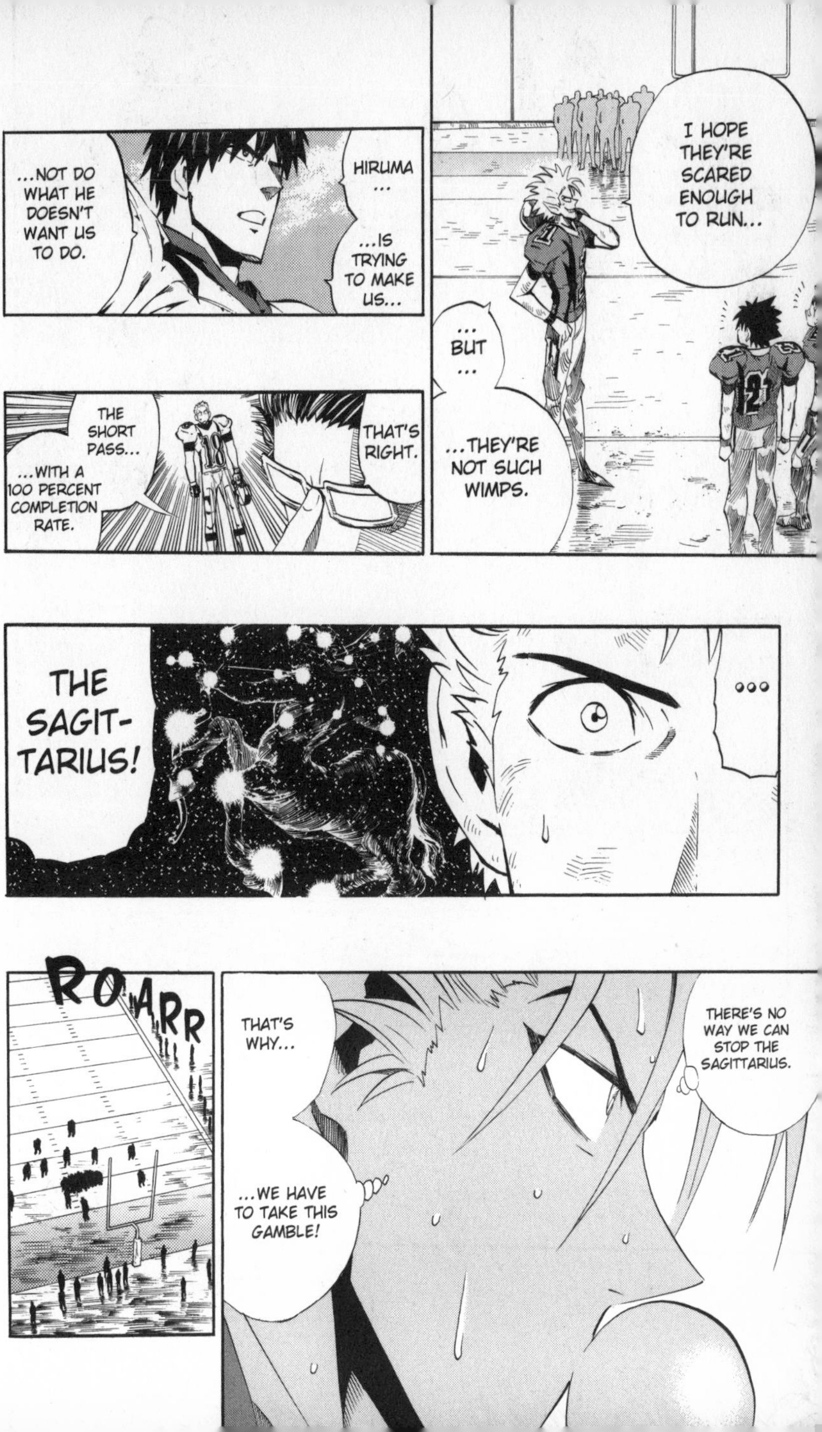
I HOPE THEY'RE SCARED ENOUGH TO RUN...
...BUT...
...THEY'RE NOT SUCH WIMPS.
HIRUMA...
...IS TRYING TO MAKE US...
...NOT DO WHAT HE DOESN'T WANT US TO DO.
THAT'S RIGHT.
THE SHORT PASS...
...WITH A 100 PERCENT COMPLETION RATE.
...
THE SAGIT-TARIUS!
THERE'S NO WAY WE CAN STOP THE SAGITTARIUS.
THAT'S WHY...
...WE HAVE TO TAKE THIS GAMBLE!
ROARR

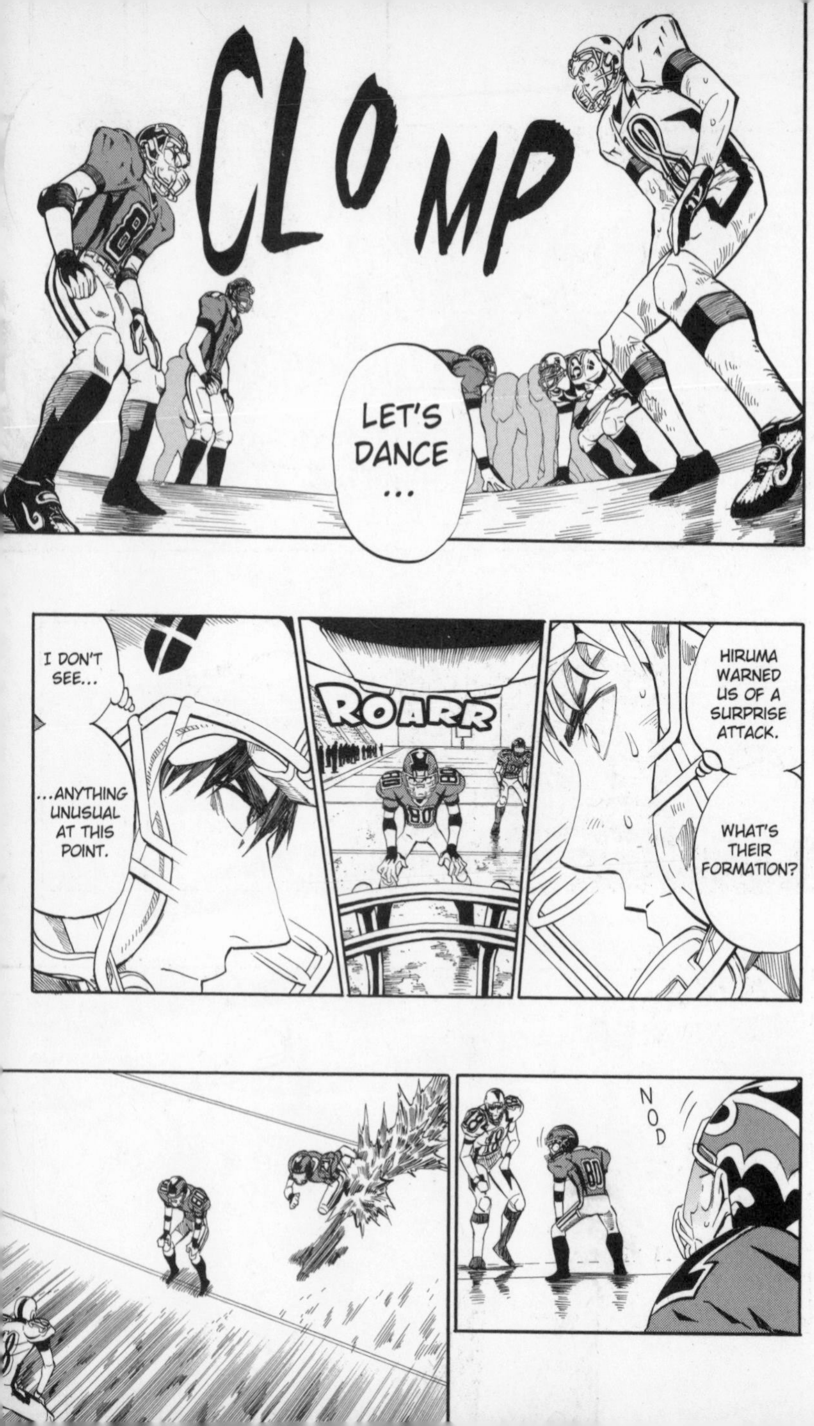
CLOMP
LET'S DANCE ...
HIRUMA WARNED US OF A SURPRISE ATTACK.
WHAT'S THEIR FORMATION?
ROARR
I DON'T SEE...
...ANYTHING UNUSUAL AT THIS POINT.
NOD

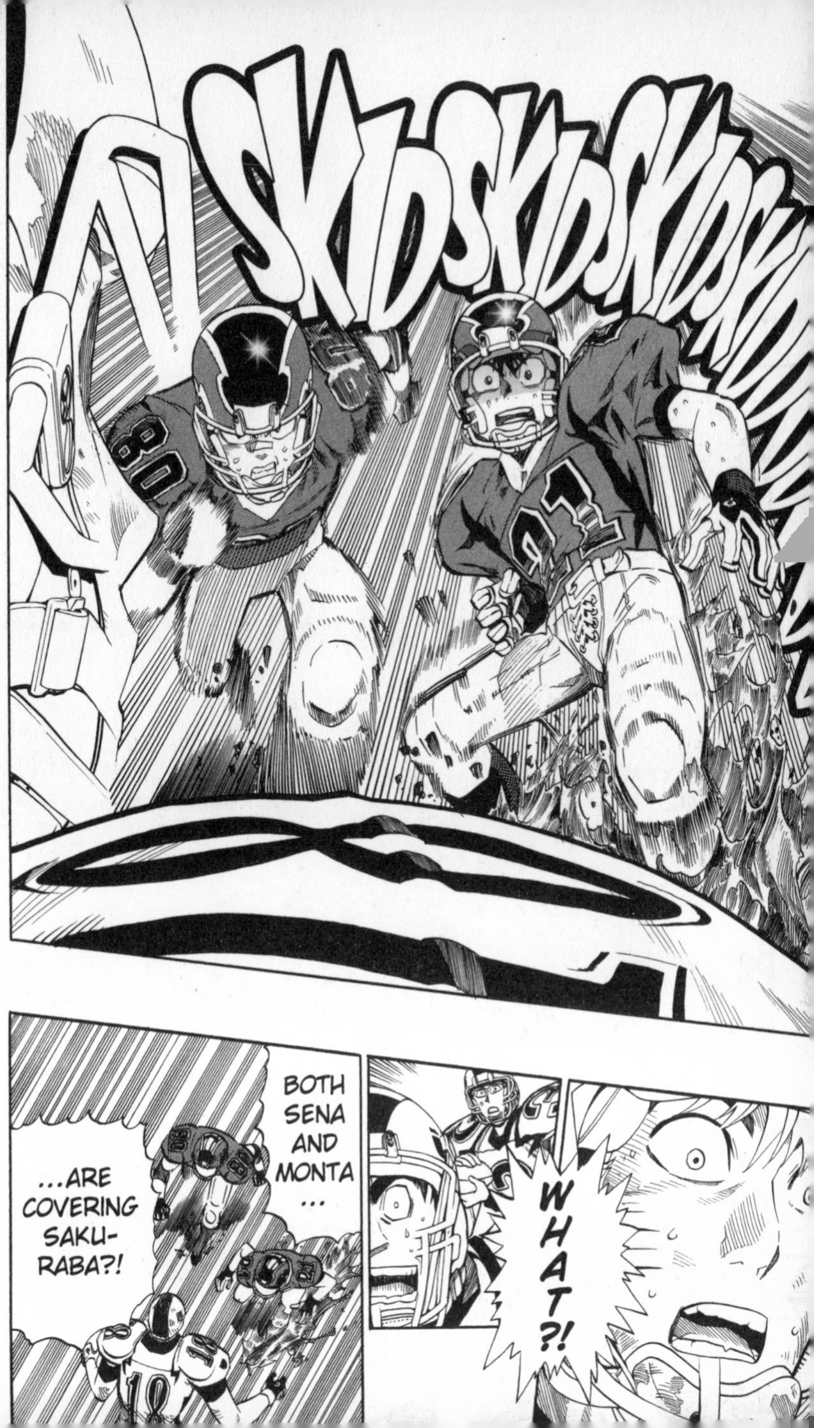
DSKIDSKIDSKIDSKID
WHAT?!
BOTH SENA AND MONTA...
...ARE COVERING SAKURABA?!

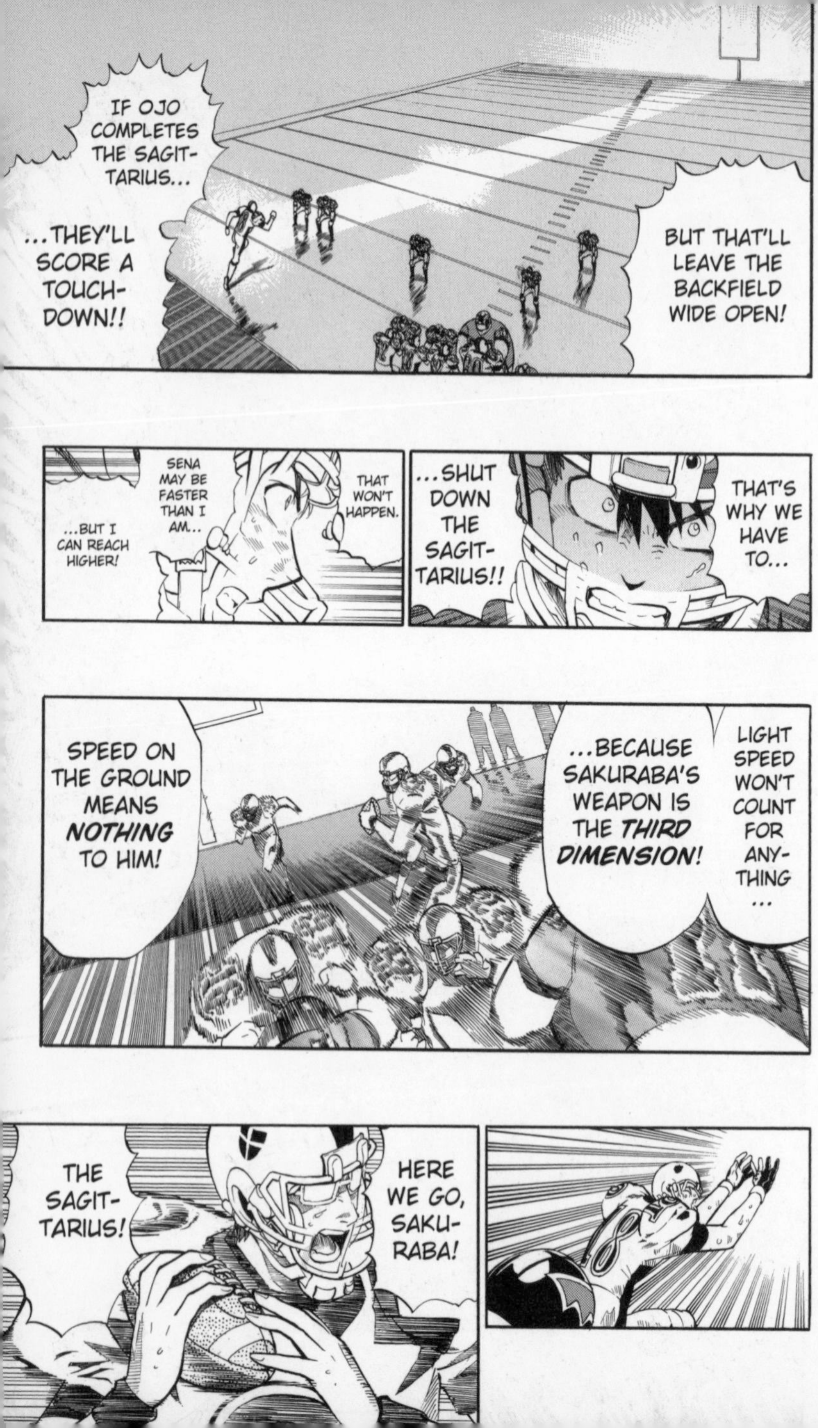
IF OJO COMPLETES THE SAGIT-TARIUS...
...THEY'LL SCORE A TOUCH-DOWN!!
BUT THAT'LL LEAVE THE BACKFIELD WIDE OPEN!
THAT'S WHY WE HAVE TO...
...SHUT DOWN THE SAGIT-TARIUS!!
THAT WON'T HAPPEN.
SENA MAY BE FASTER THAN I AM...
...BUT I CAN REACH HIGHER!
LIGHT SPEED WON'T COUNT FOR ANY-THING...
...BECAUSE SAKURABA'S WEAPON IS THE *THIRD DIMENSION*!
SPEED ON THE GROUND MEANS *NOTHING* TO HIM!
HERE WE GO, SAKU-RABA!
THE SAGIT-TARIUS!

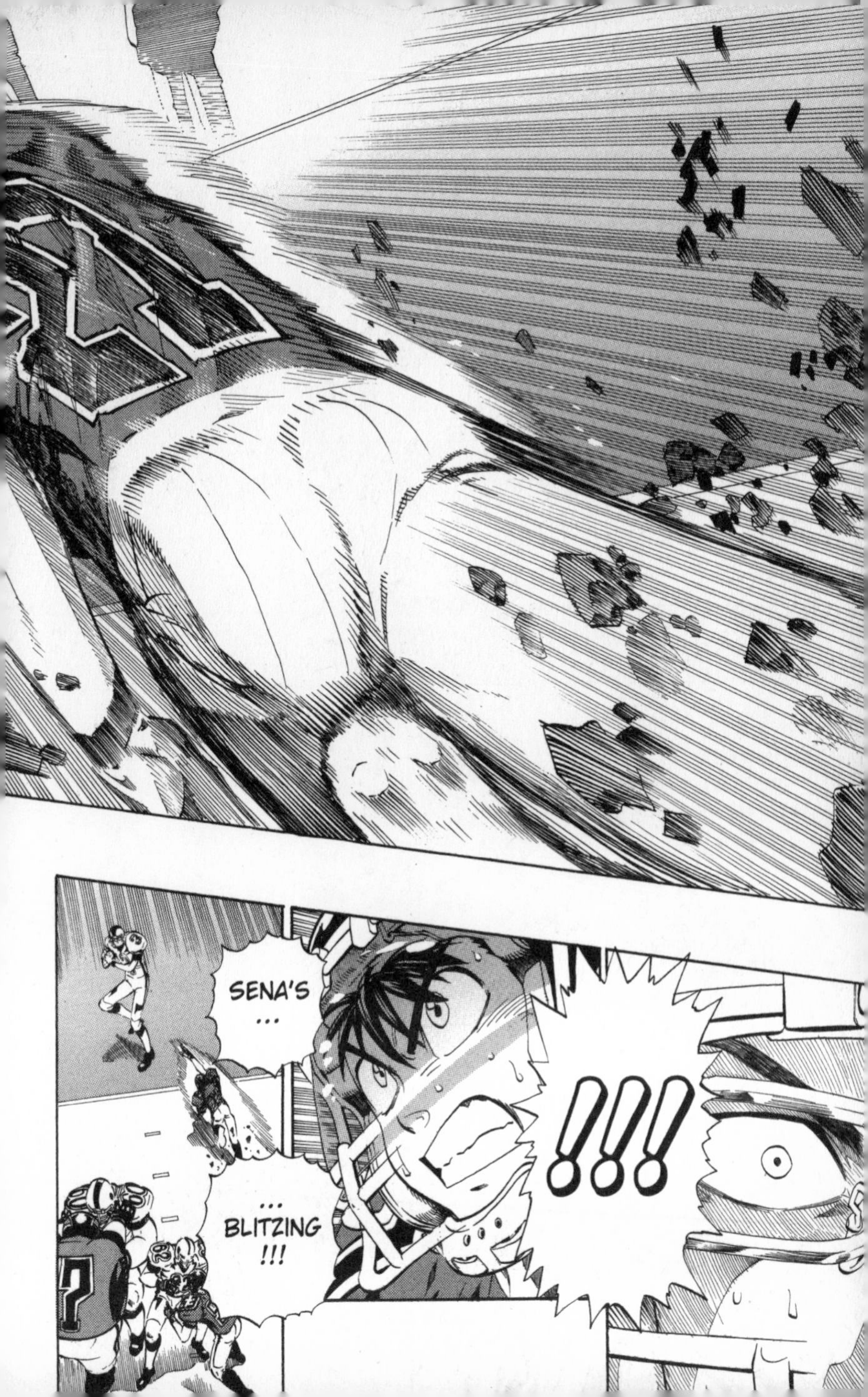
!!!
SENA'S ...
... BLITZING !!!

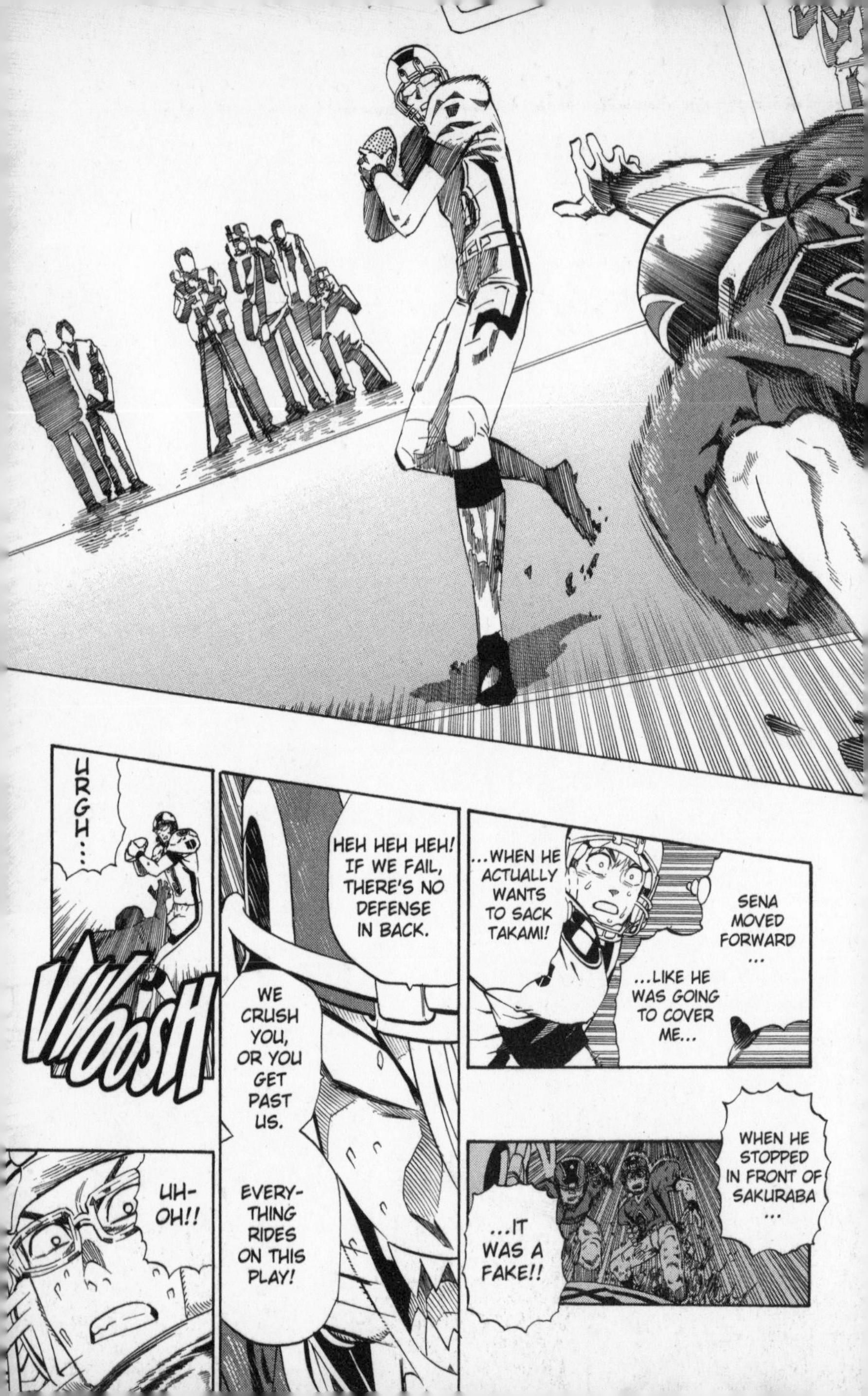
SENA MOVED FORWARD...
...LIKE HE WAS GOING TO COVER ME...
...WHEN HE ACTUALLY WANTS TO SACK TAKAMI!
WHEN HE STOPPED IN FRONT OF SAKURABA...
...IT WAS A FAKE!!
HEH HEH HEH! IF WE FAIL, THERE'S NO DEFENSE IN BACK.
WE CRUSH YOU, OR YOU GET PAST US.
EVERYTHING RIDES ON THIS PLAY!
URGH...
VWOOSH
UH-OH!!

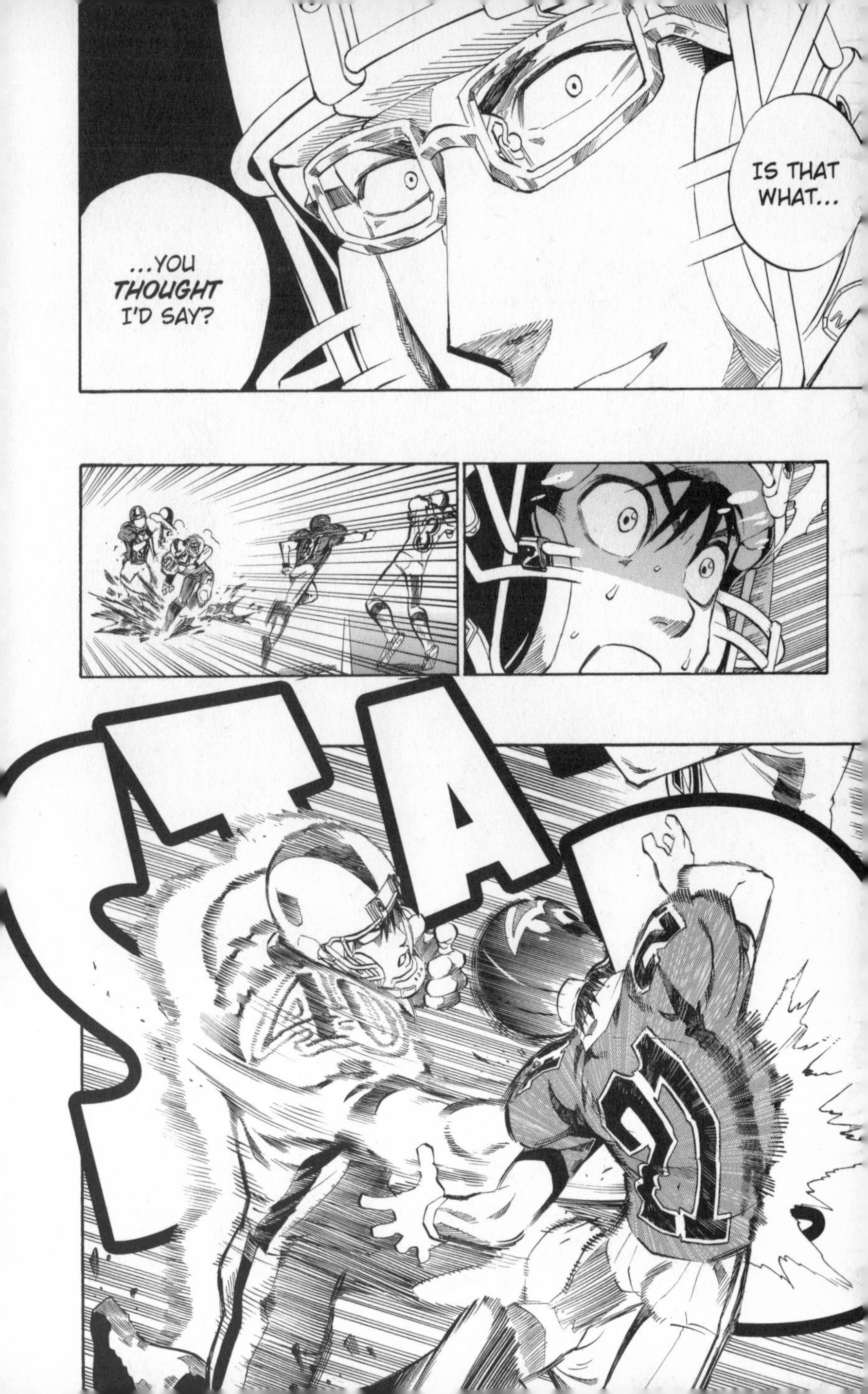
IS THAT WHAT...
...YOU THOUGHT I'D SAY?
SLAP

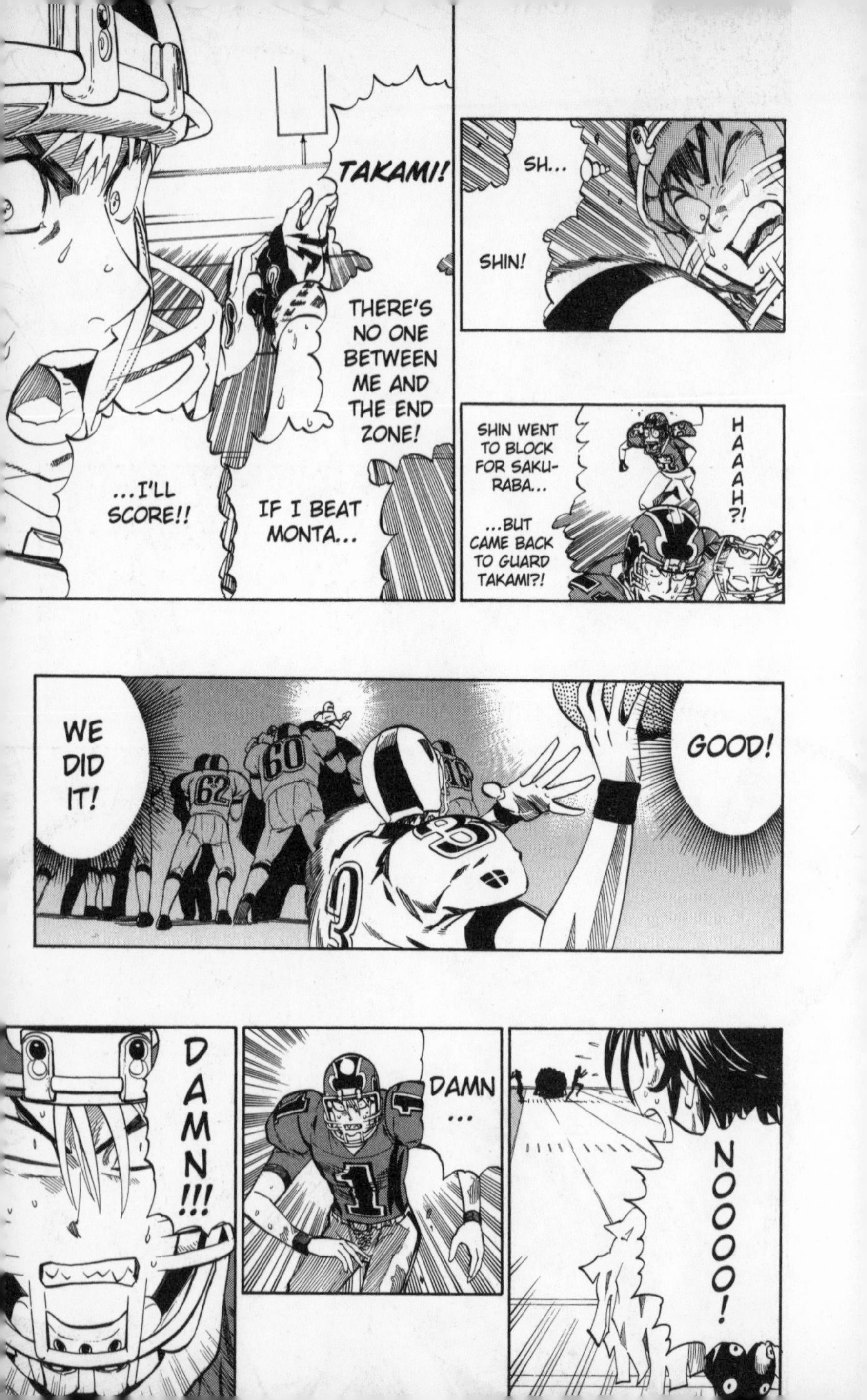
SH...
SHIN!
HAAAAH?!
SHIN WENT TO BLOCK FOR SAKU-RABA...
...BUT CAME BACK TO GUARD TAKAMI?!
TAKAMI!
THERE'S NO ONE BETWEEN ME AND THE END ZONE!
IF I BEAT MONTA...
...I'LL SCORE!!
GOOD!
WE DID IT!
NOOOO!
DAMN...
DAMN!!!

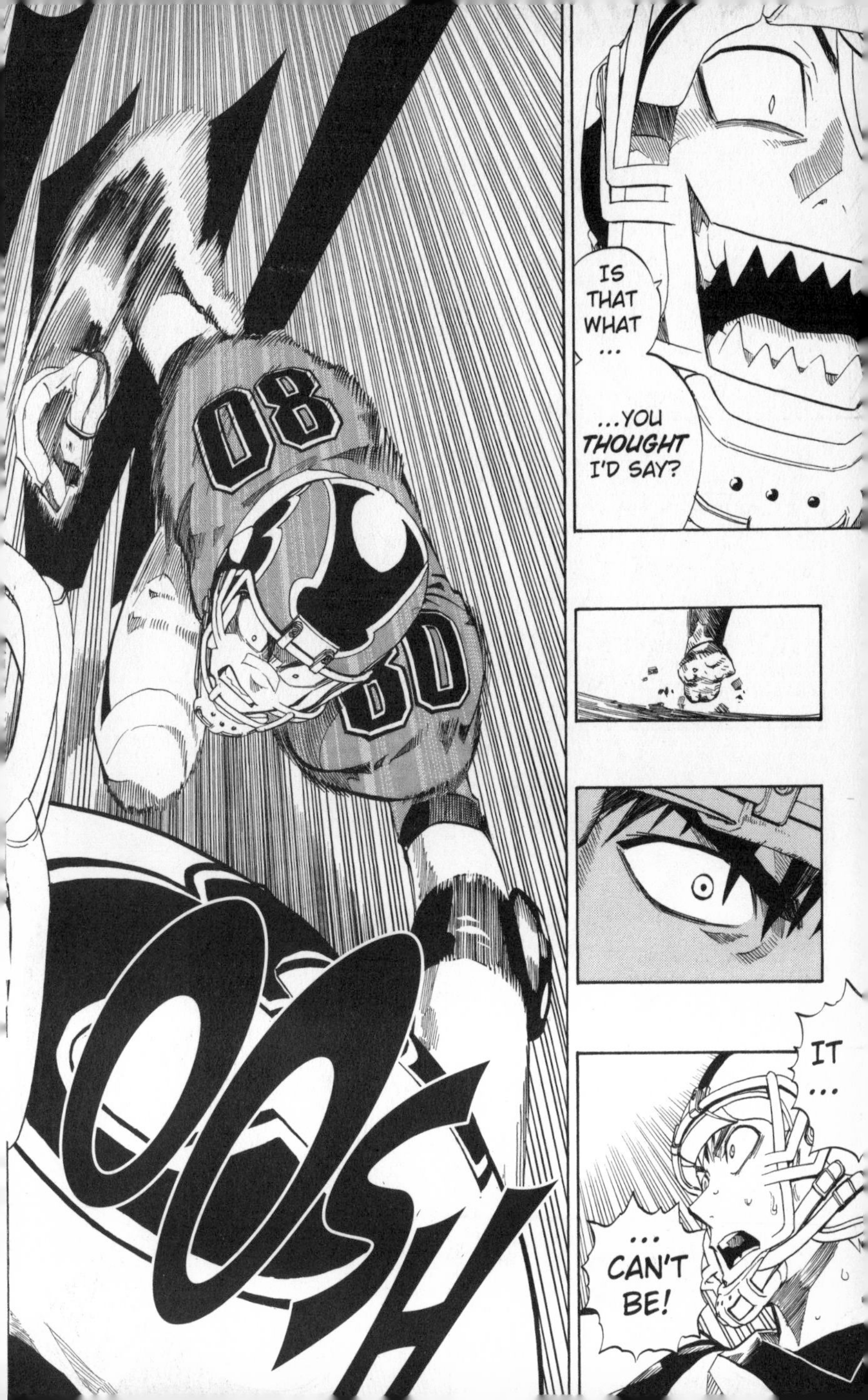
IS THAT WHAT ...
...YOU *THOUGHT* I'D SAY?
IT ...
... CAN'T BE!
WOOSH

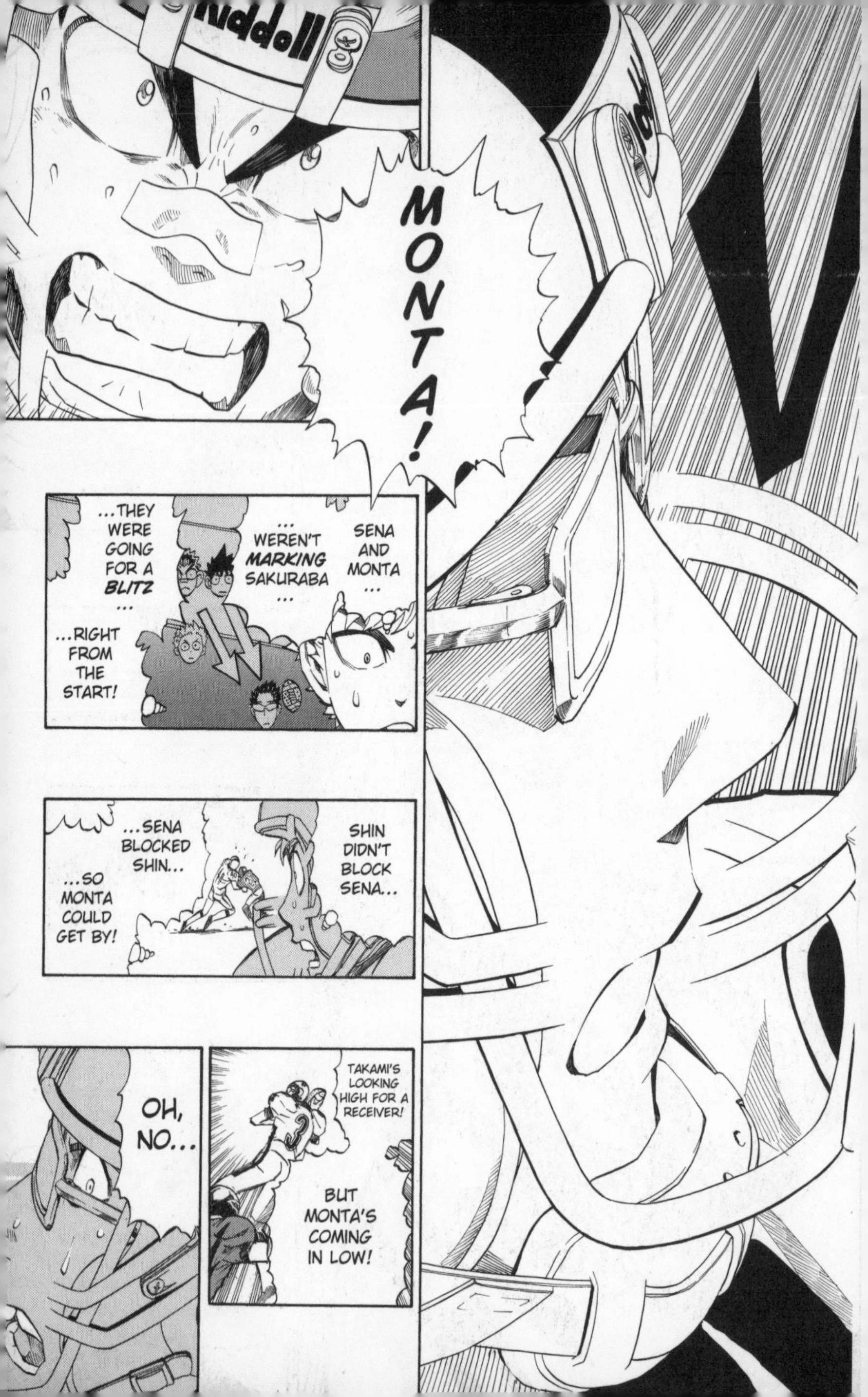
MONTA!
SENA AND MONTA...
...WEREN'T MARKING SAKURABA...
...THEY WERE GOING FOR A BLITZ...
...RIGHT FROM THE START!
SHIN DIDN'T BLOCK SENA...
...SENA BLOCKED SHIN...
...SO MONTA COULD GET BY!
TAKAMI'S LOOKING HIGH FOR A RECEIVER!
BUT MONTA'S COMING IN LOW!
OH, NO...

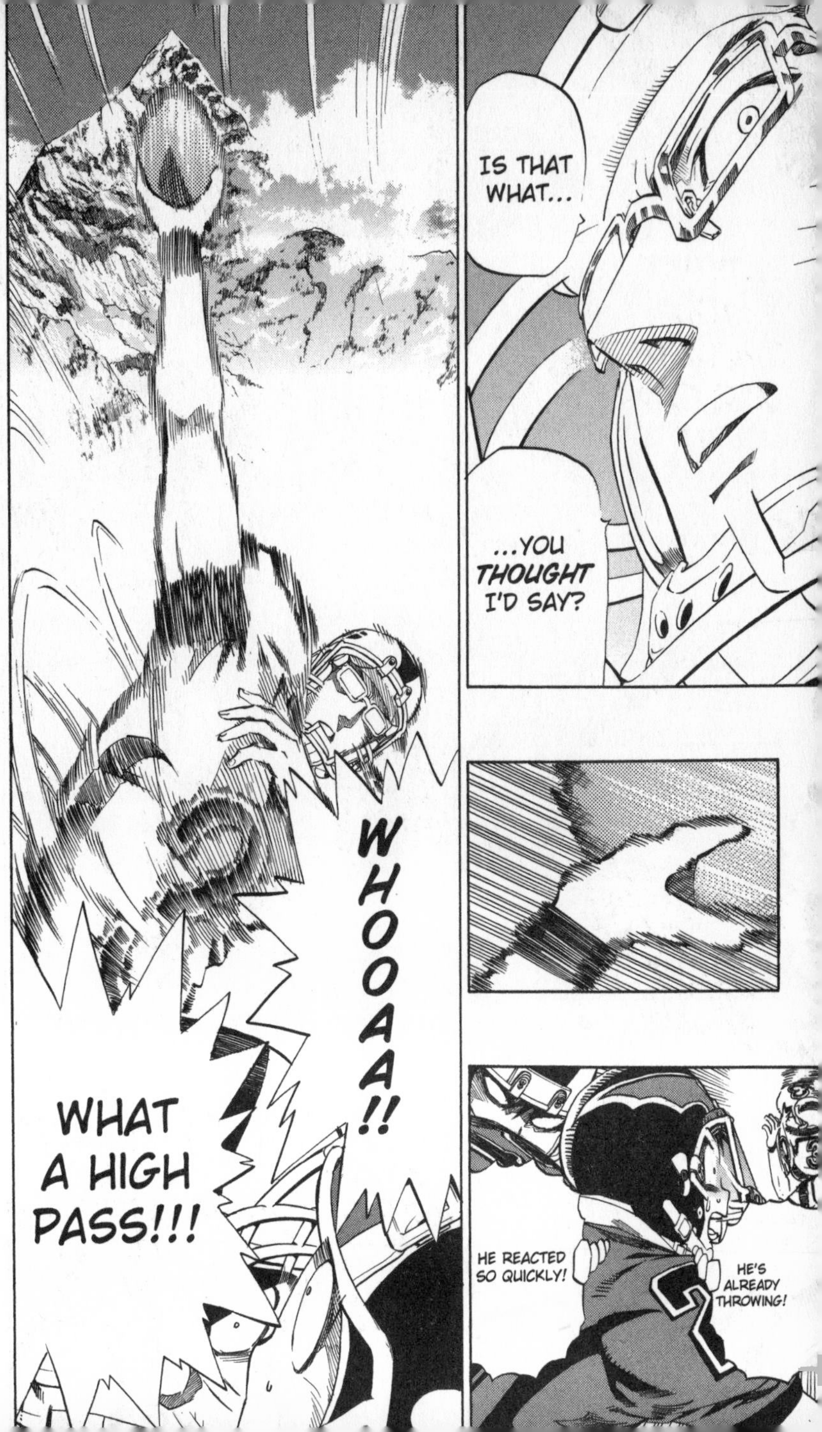
IS THAT WHAT...
...YOU *THOUGHT* I'D SAY?
HE'S ALREADY THROWING!
HE REACTED SO QUICKLY!
WHOOAAA!!
WHAT A HIGH PASS!!!

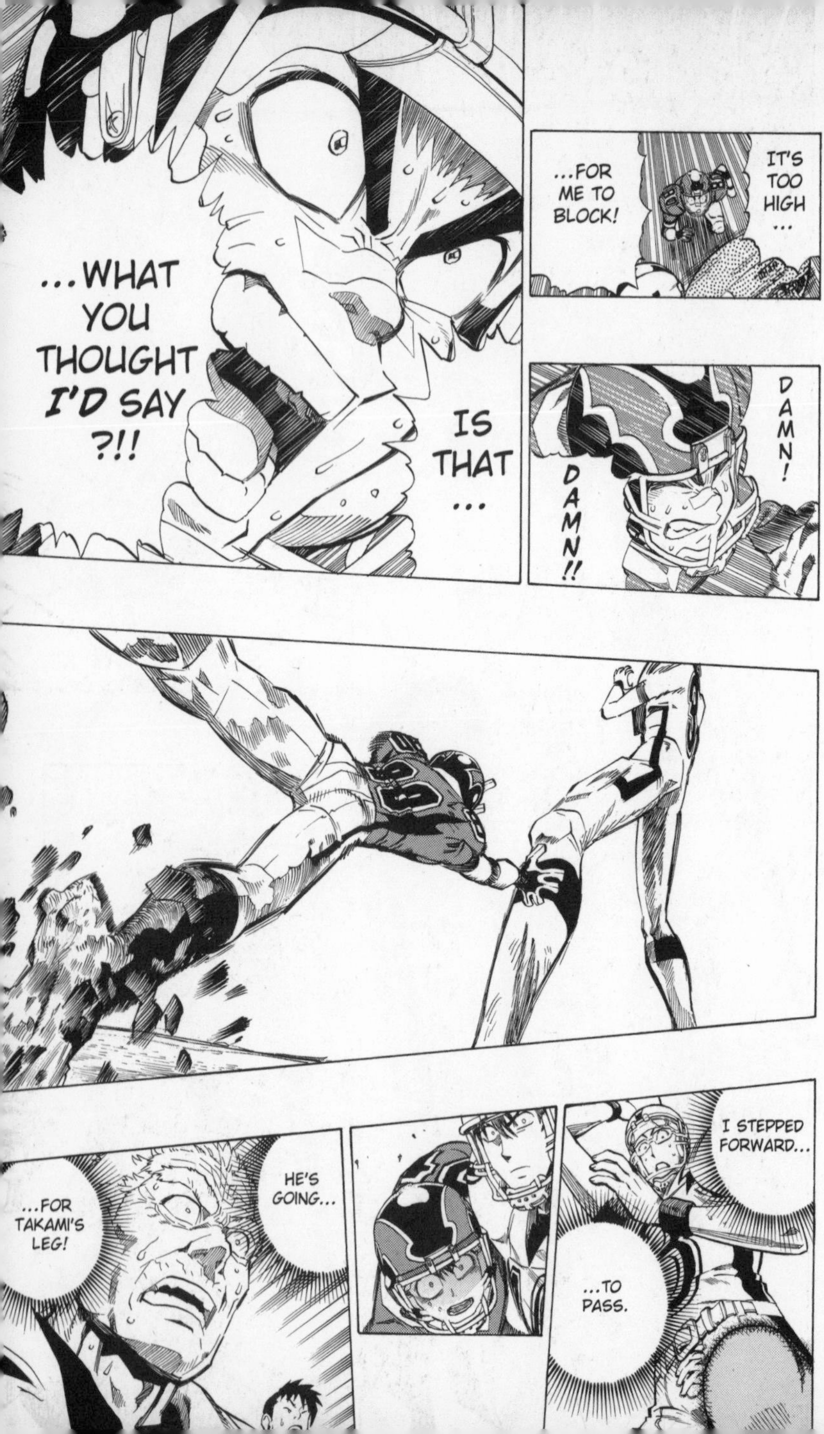
IT'S TOO HIGH...
...FOR ME TO BLOCK!
DAMN!
DAMN!!
IS THAT...
...WHAT YOU THOUGHT I'D SAY?!!
I STEPPED FORWARD...
...TO PASS.
HE'S GOING...
...FOR TAKAMI'S LEG!

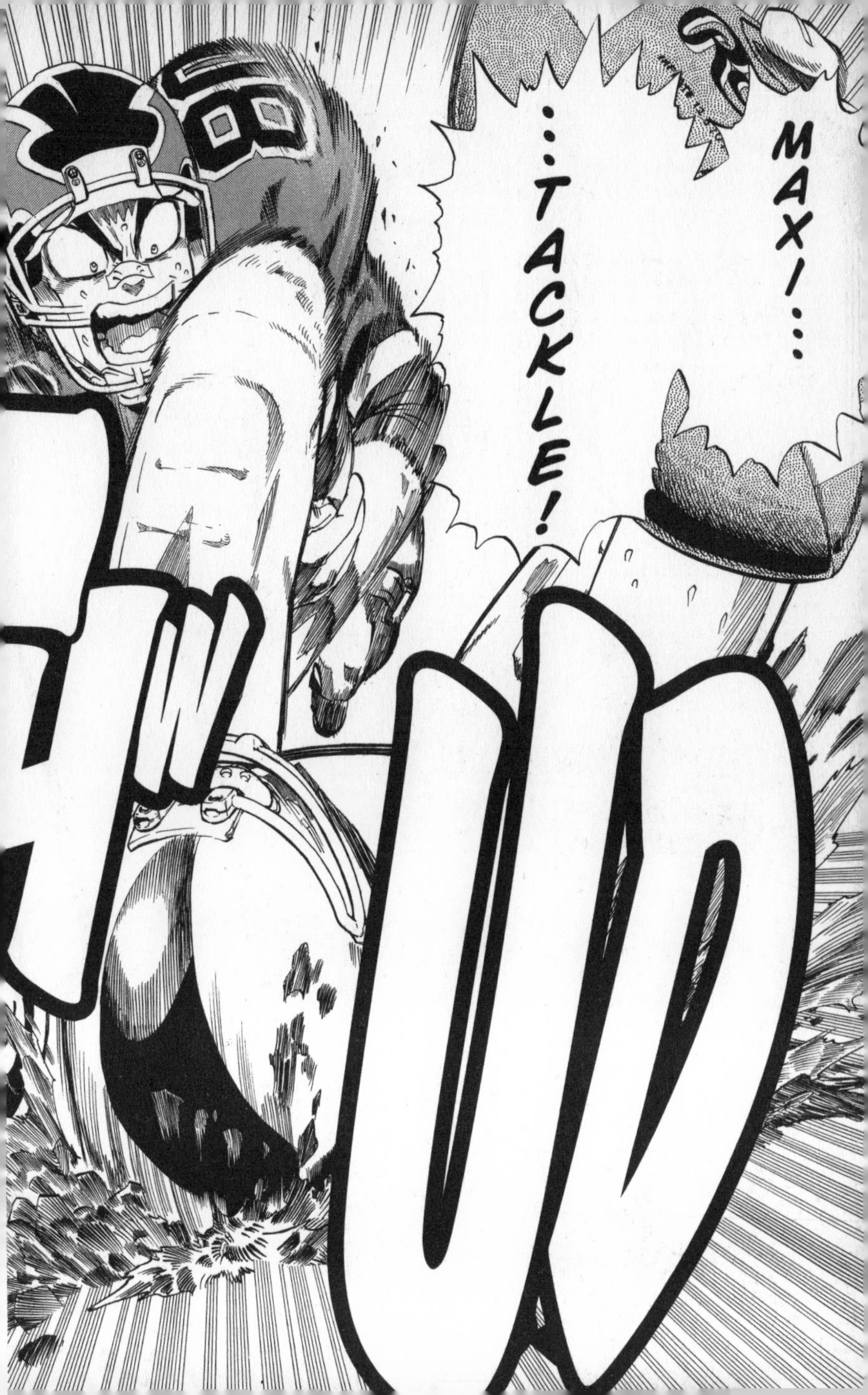
MAXI...
...TACKLE!

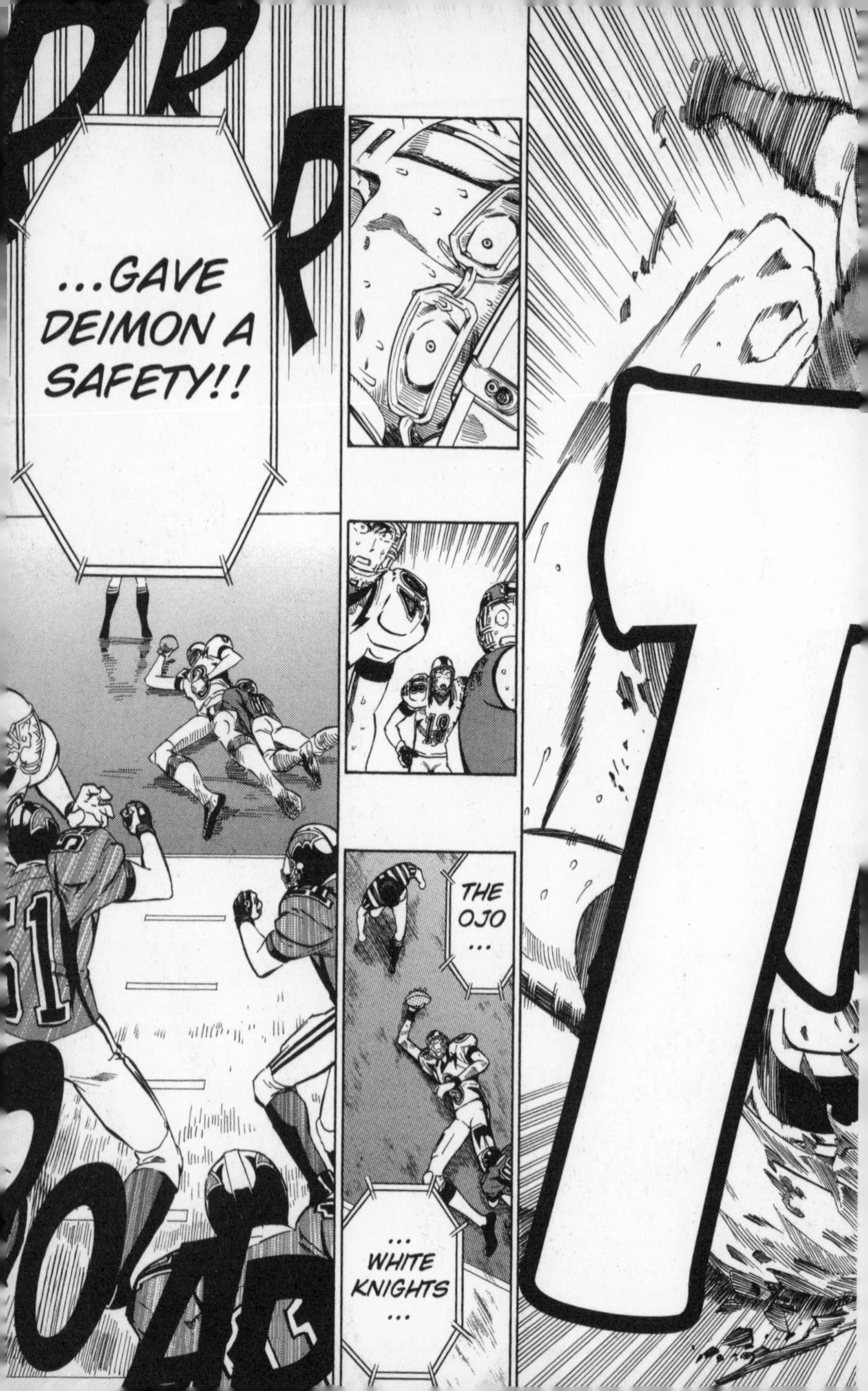
THE OJO ...
... WHITE KNIGHTS ...
...GAVE DEIMON A SAFETY!!

Eyeshield 21 Survey Corner

Devil Bat 021

Investigation File #094

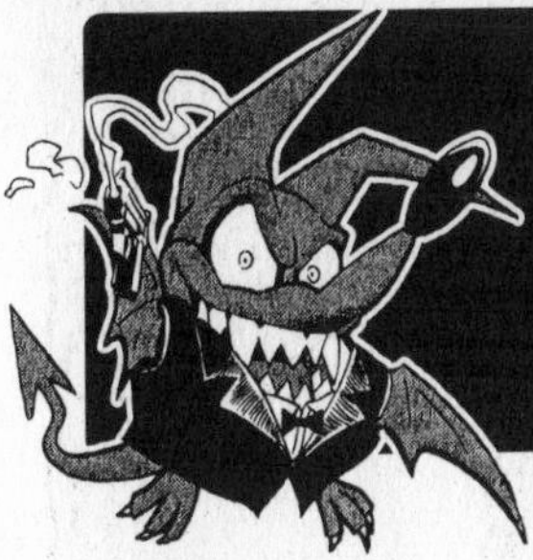

Show us the results for Taki's high school entrance exam!!

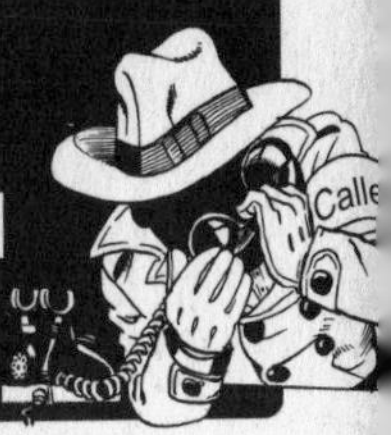

Caller name: Fox-like Human

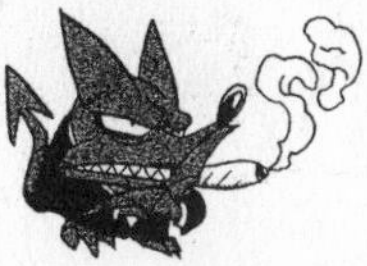

SORRY, ALL TAKI GAVE US WAS A LONG EXPLANATION OF HOW COOL HE IS.

Send your queries for Devil Bat 021 here!!

Devil Bat 021
Shonen Jump Advanced/Eyeshield 21
c/o VIZ Media, LLC
P.O. Box 77010
San Francisco, CA 94107

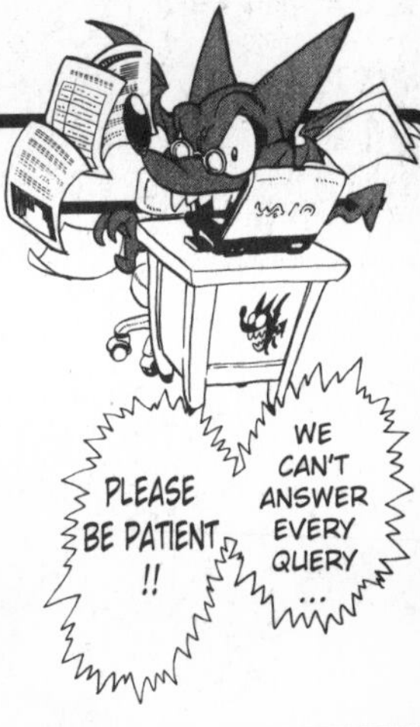
PLEASE BE PATIENT!!
WE CAN'T ANSWER EVERY QUERY...

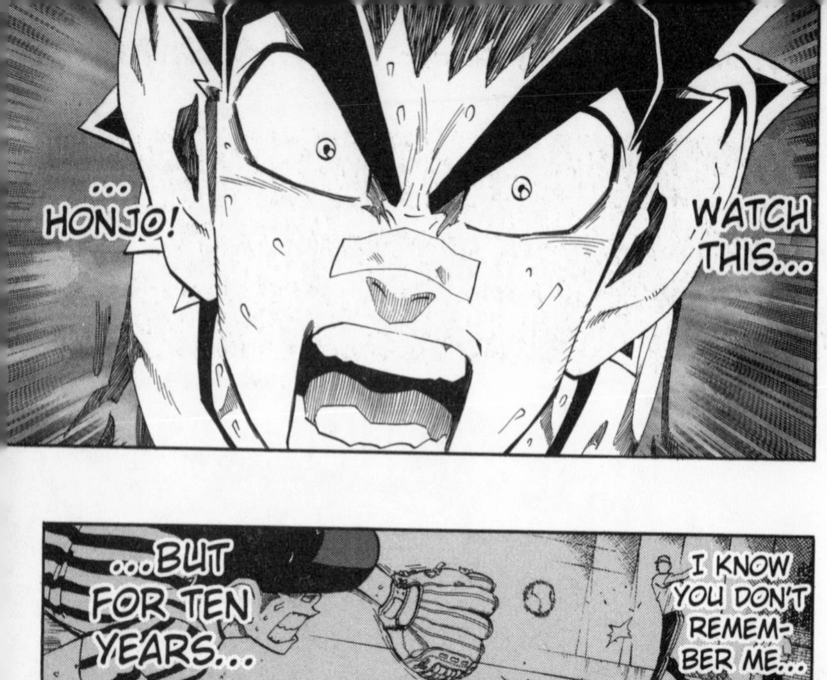
WATCH THIS...
...HONJO!
I KNOW YOU DON'T REMEM-BER ME...
...BUT FOR TEN YEARS...
...I'VE WANTED TO BE A CATCHING SUPER-HERO...
...JUST LIKE YOU!!

Chapter 232 Death Game

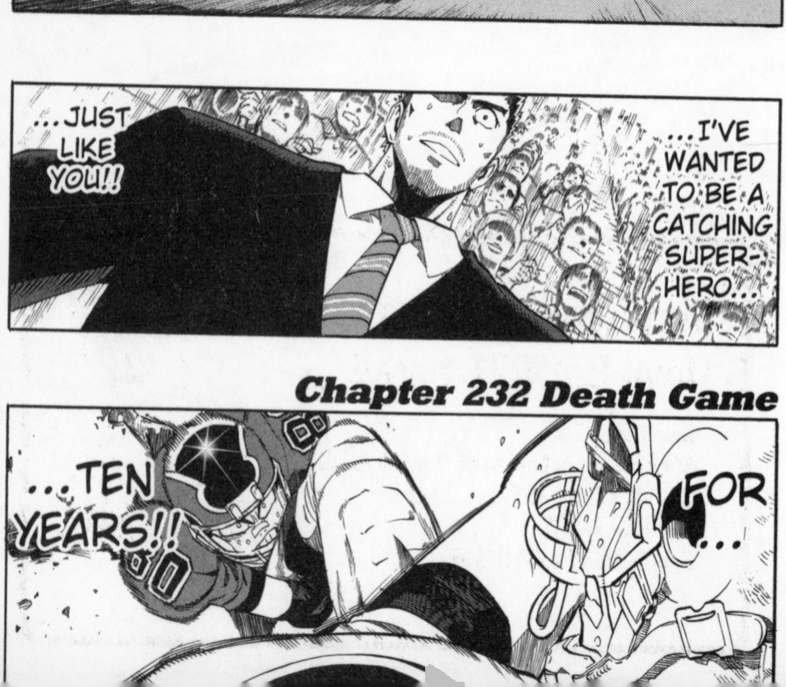
FOR...
...TEN YEARS!!

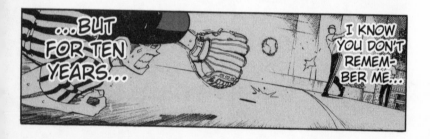

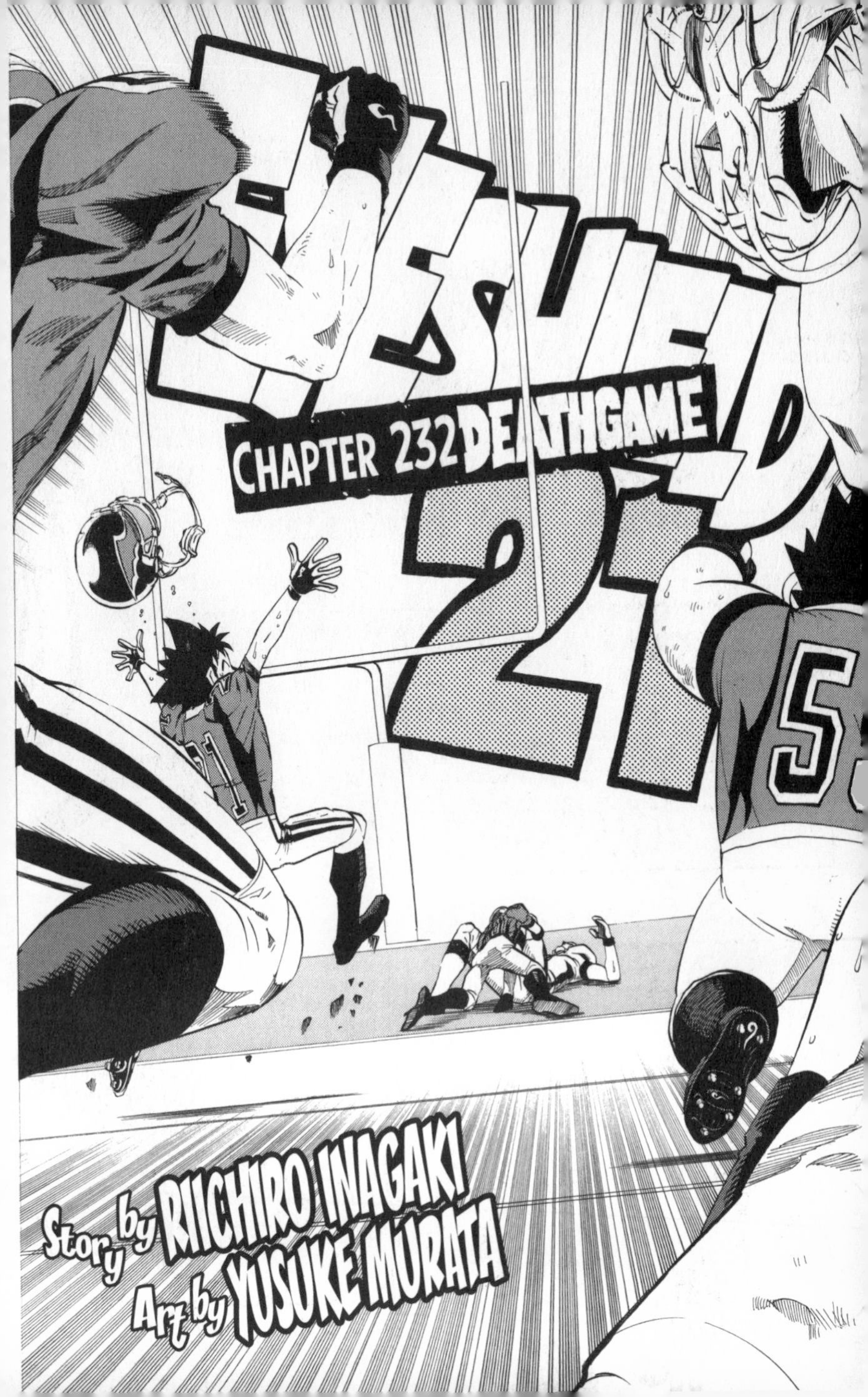
Eyeshield 21
CHAPTER 232 DEATHGAME
Story by RIICHIRO INAGAKI
Art by YUSUKE MURATA

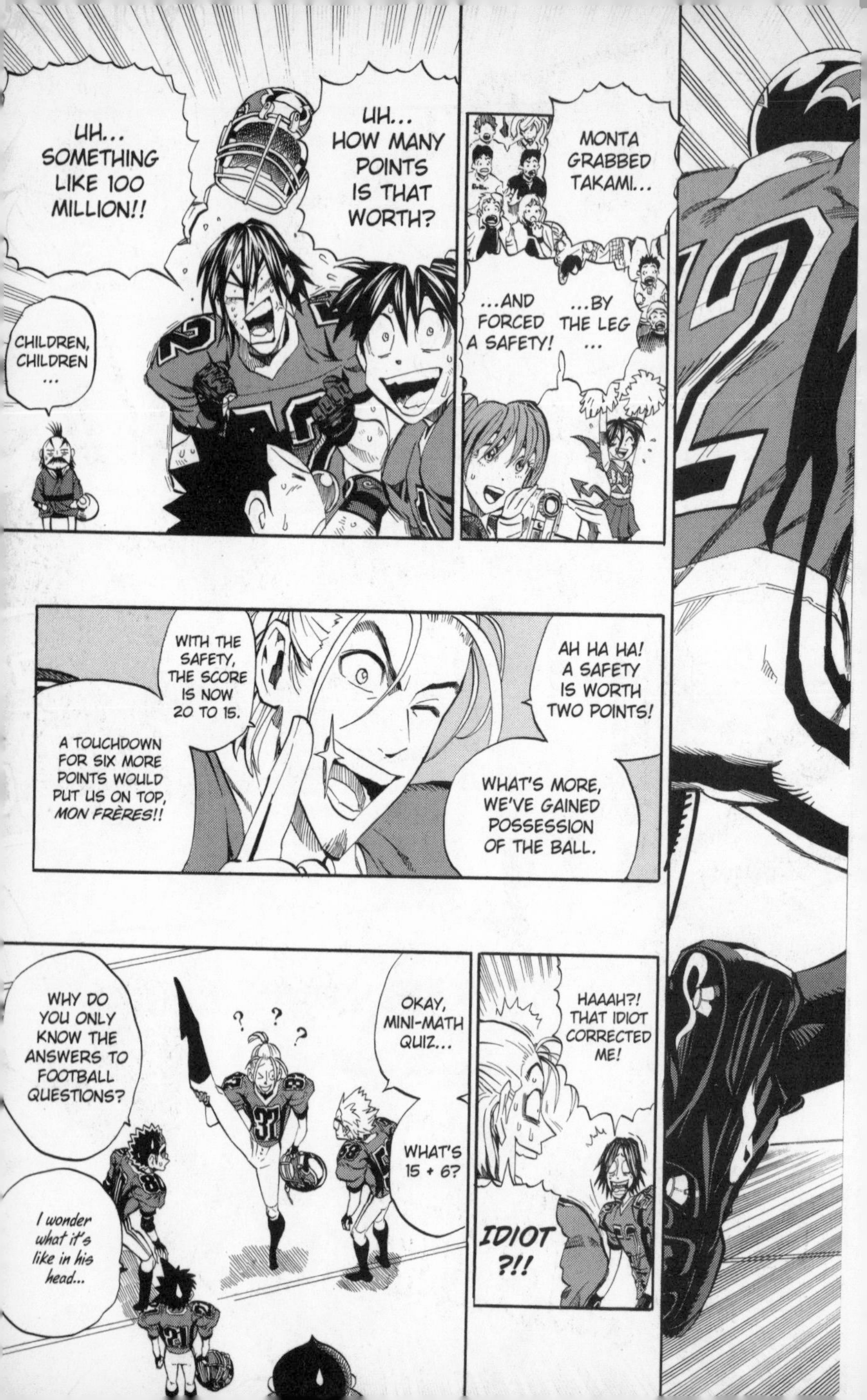
MONTA GRABBED TAKAMI...
...BY THE LEG...
...AND FORCED A SAFETY!
UH... HOW MANY POINTS IS THAT WORTH?
UH... SOMETHING LIKE 100 MILLION!!
CHILDREN, CHILDREN...
AH HA HA! A SAFETY IS WORTH TWO POINTS!
WHAT'S MORE, WE'VE GAINED POSSESSION OF THE BALL.
WITH THE SAFETY, THE SCORE IS NOW 20 TO 15.
A TOUCHDOWN FOR SIX MORE POINTS WOULD PUT US ON TOP, *MON FRÈRES*!!
HAAAH?! THAT IDIOT CORRECTED ME!
IDIOT ?!!
OKAY, MINI-MATH QUIZ...
WHAT'S 15 + 6?
WHY DO YOU ONLY KNOW THE ANSWERS TO FOOTBALL QUESTIONS?
I wonder what it's like in his head...

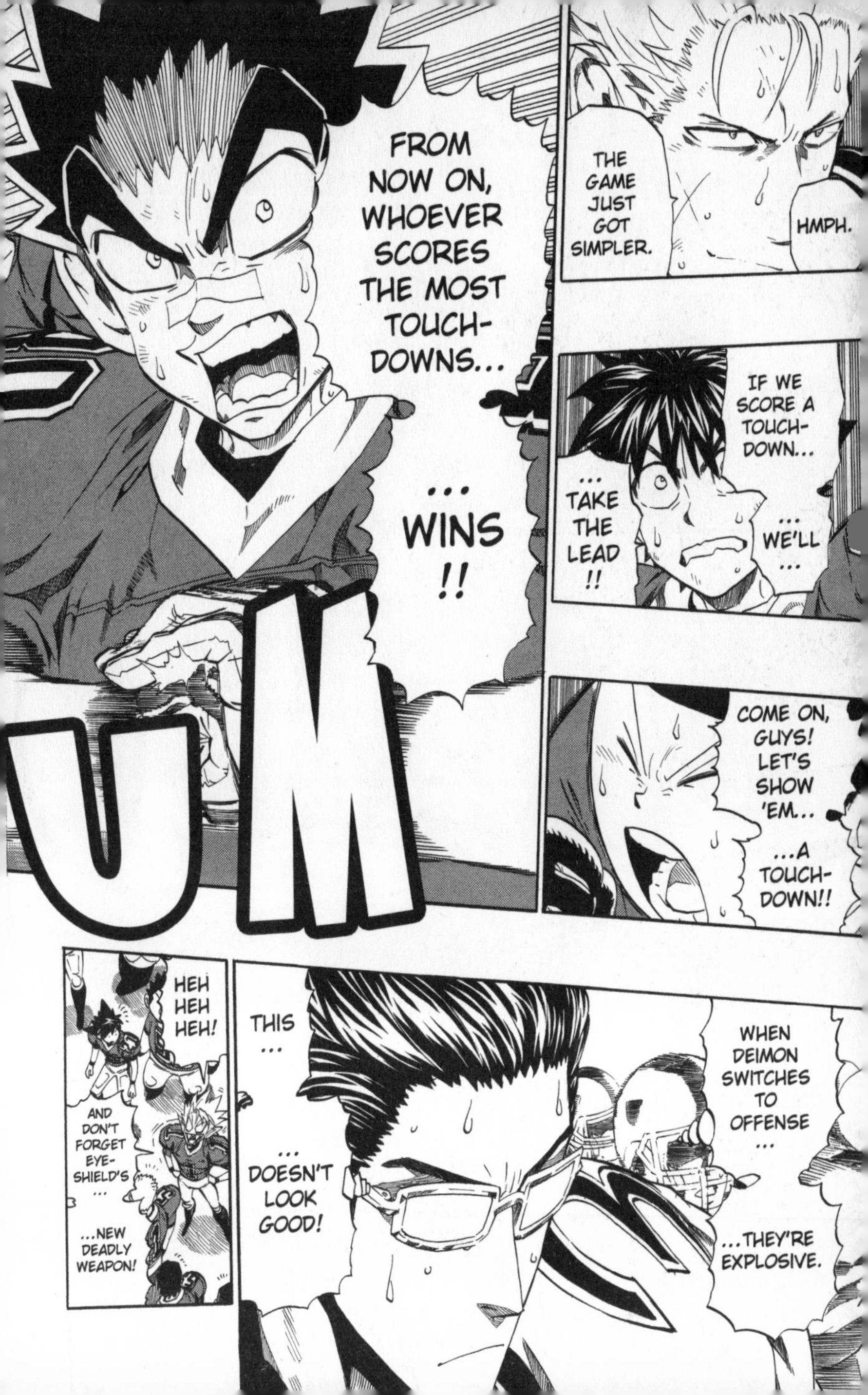
THE GAME JUST GOT SIMPLER.
HMPH.
IF WE SCORE A TOUCH-DOWN...
...WE'LL...
...TAKE THE LEAD!!
COME ON, GUYS! LET'S SHOW 'EM...
...A TOUCH-DOWN!!
FROM NOW ON, WHOEVER SCORES THE MOST TOUCH-DOWNS...
...WINS!!
UM
WHEN DEIMON SWITCHES TO OFFENSE...
...THEY'RE EXPLOSIVE.
THIS...
...DOESN'T LOOK GOOD!
HEH HEH HEH!
AND DON'T FORGET EYE-SHIELD'S...
...NEW DEADLY WEAPON!

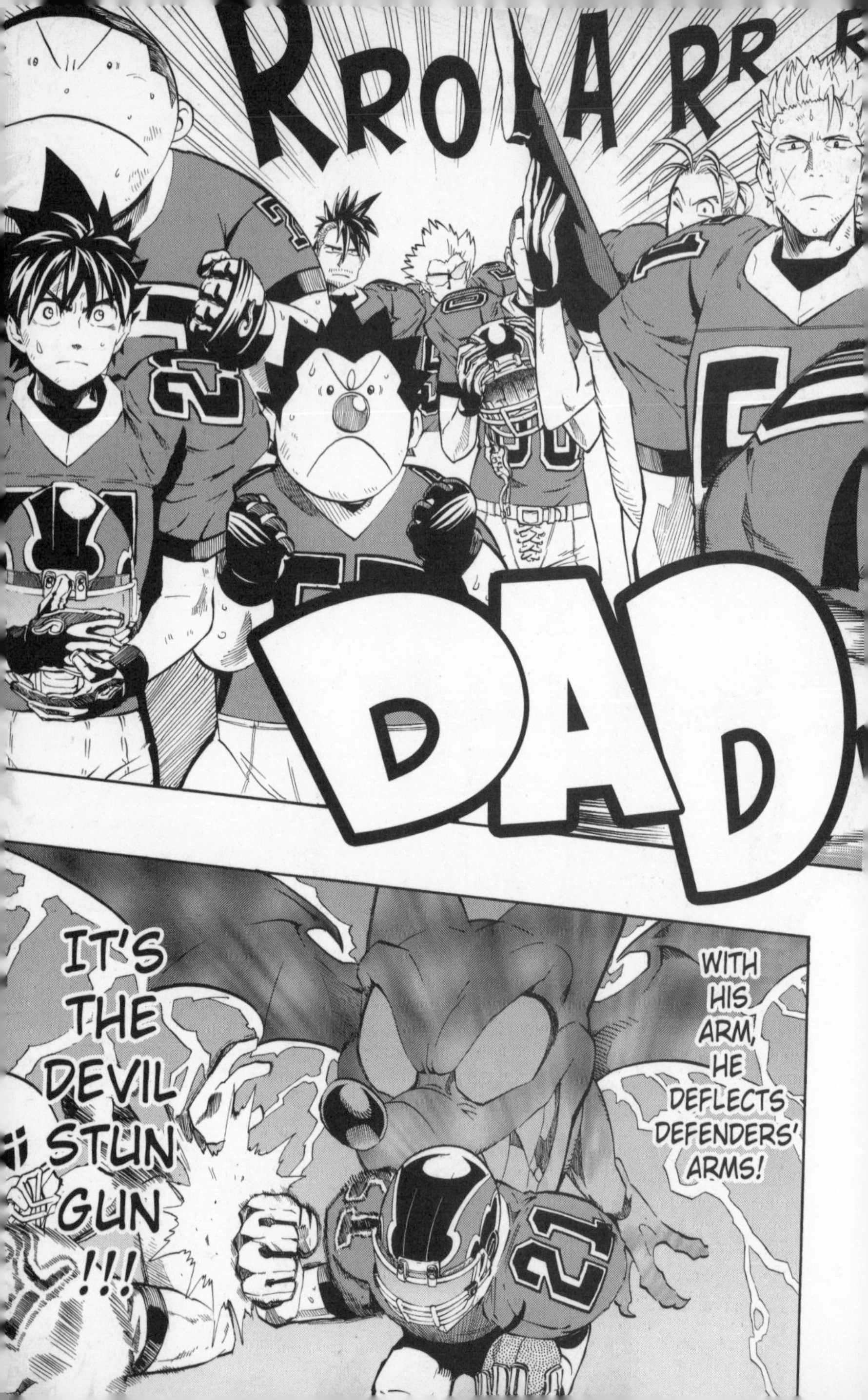
KRROAARRR
DAD
WITH HIS ARM, HE DEFLECTS DEFENDERS' ARMS!
IT'S THE DEVIL STUN GUN!!!

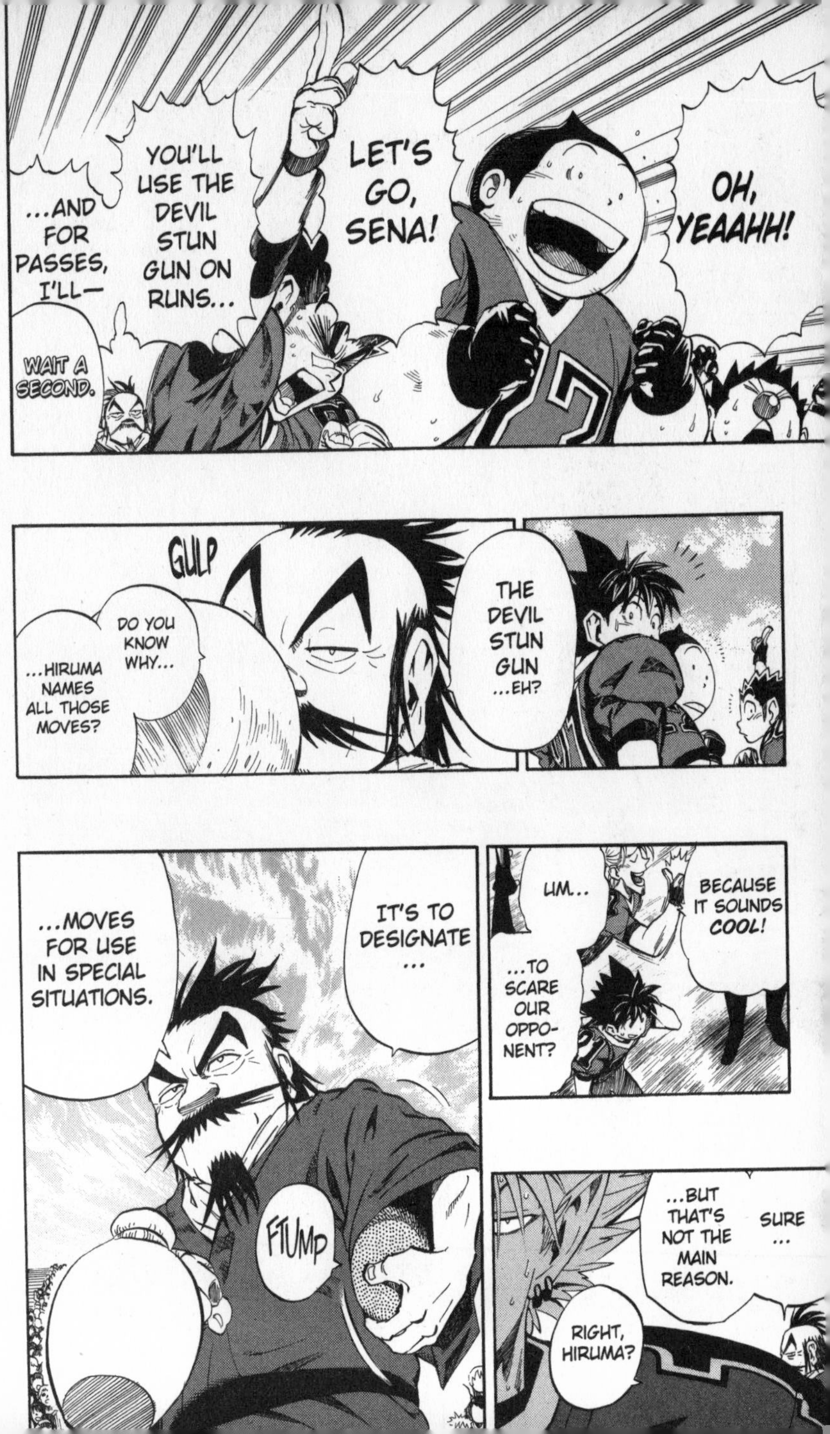
OH, YEAAHH!
LET'S GO, SENA!
YOU'LL USE THE DEVIL STUN GUN ON RUNS...
...AND FOR PASSES, I'LL—
WAIT A SECOND.
THE DEVIL STUN GUN ...EH?
GULP
DO YOU KNOW WHY...
...HIRUMA NAMES ALL THOSE MOVES?
BECAUSE IT SOUNDS COOL!
UM...
...TO SCARE OUR OPPONENT?
SURE ...
...BUT THAT'S NOT THE MAIN REASON.
RIGHT, HIRUMA?
IT'S TO DESIGNATE ...
...MOVES FOR USE IN SPECIAL SITUATIONS.
FTUMP

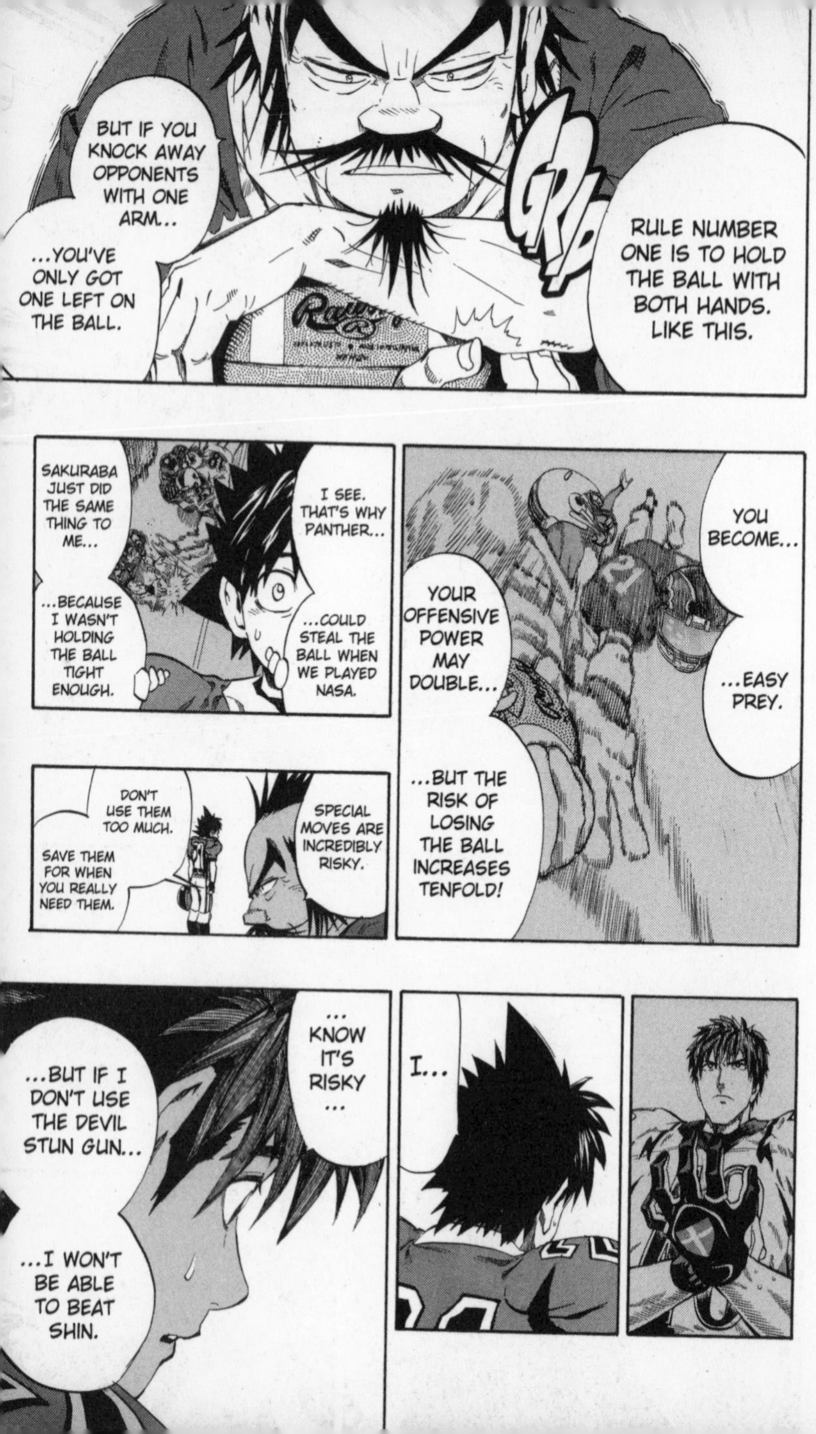
GRIP
RULE NUMBER ONE IS TO HOLD THE BALL WITH BOTH HANDS. LIKE THIS.
BUT IF YOU KNOCK AWAY OPPONENTS WITH ONE ARM...
...YOU'VE ONLY GOT ONE LEFT ON THE BALL.
YOU BECOME...
...EASY PREY.
YOUR OFFENSIVE POWER MAY DOUBLE...
...BUT THE RISK OF LOSING THE BALL INCREASES TENFOLD!
I SEE. THAT'S WHY PANTHER...
...COULD STEAL THE BALL WHEN WE PLAYED NASA.
SAKURABA JUST DID THE SAME THING TO ME...
...BECAUSE I WASN'T HOLDING THE BALL TIGHT ENOUGH.
SPECIAL MOVES ARE INCREDIBLY RISKY.
DON'T USE THEM TOO MUCH.
SAVE THEM FOR WHEN YOU REALLY NEED THEM.
I...
... KNOW IT'S RISKY ...
...BUT IF I DON'T USE THE DEVIL STUN GUN...
...I WON'T BE ABLE TO BEAT SHIN.

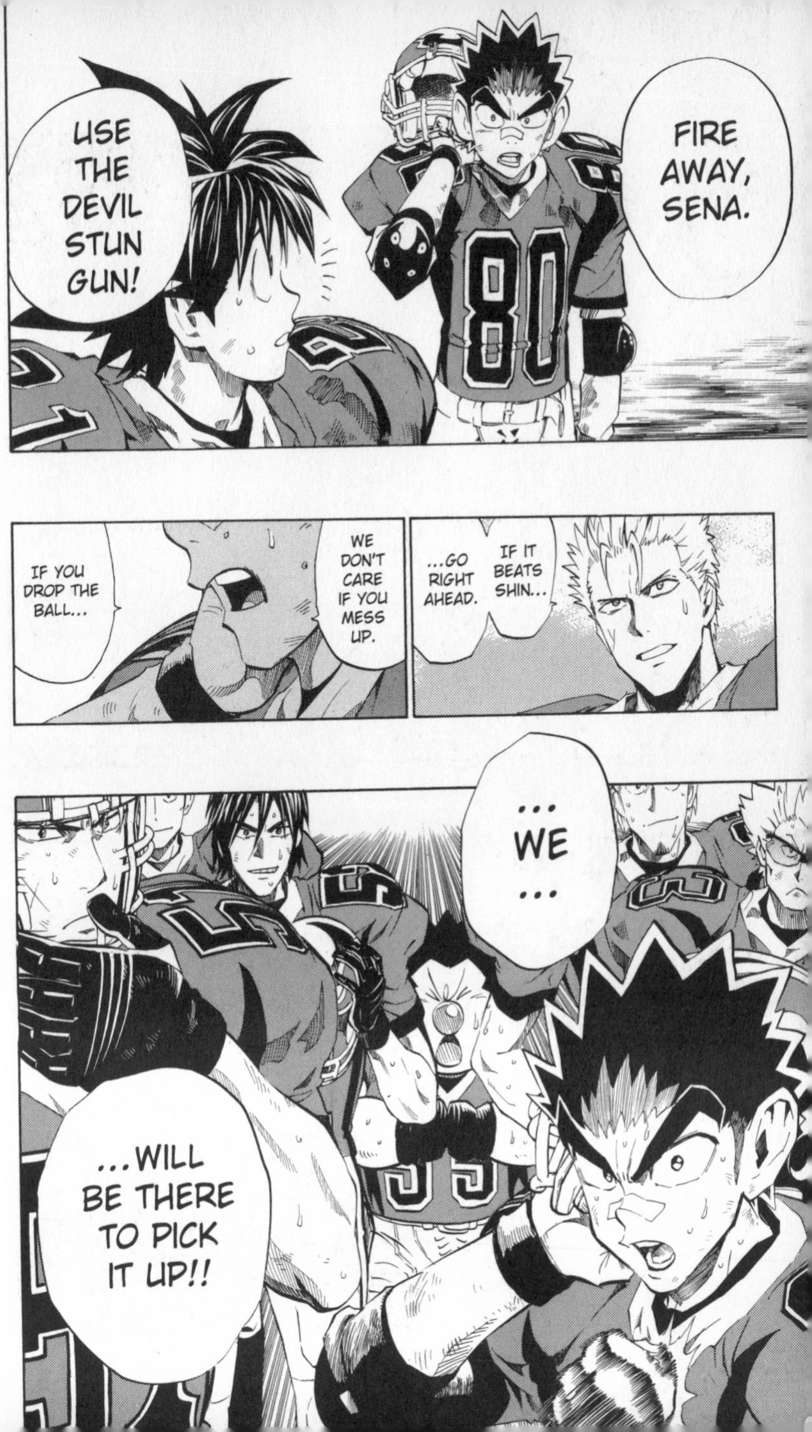
FIRE AWAY, SENA.
USE THE DEVIL STUN GUN!
IF IT BEATS SHIN...
...GO RIGHT AHEAD.
WE DON'T CARE IF YOU MESS UP.
IF YOU DROP THE BALL...
... WE ...
...WILL BE THERE TO PICK IT UP!!

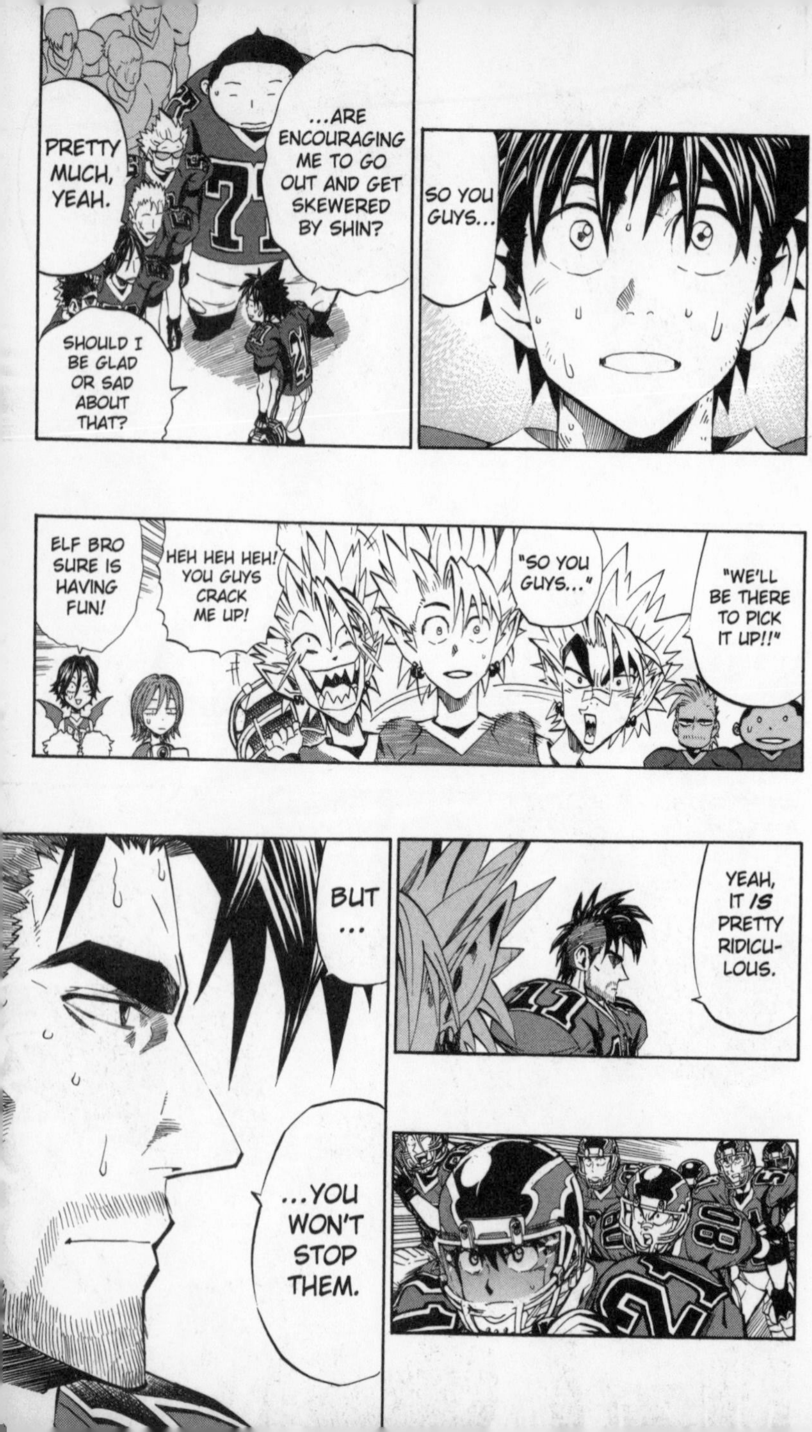
SO YOU GUYS...
...ARE ENCOURAGING ME TO GO OUT AND GET SKEWERED BY SHIN?
PRETTY MUCH, YEAH.
SHOULD I BE GLAD OR SAD ABOUT THAT?
"WE'LL BE THERE TO PICK IT UP!!"
"SO YOU GUYS..."
HEH HEH HEH! YOU GUYS CRACK ME UP!
ELF BRO SURE IS HAVING FUN!
YEAH, IT *IS* PRETTY RIDICULOUS.
BUT ...
...YOU WON'T STOP THEM.

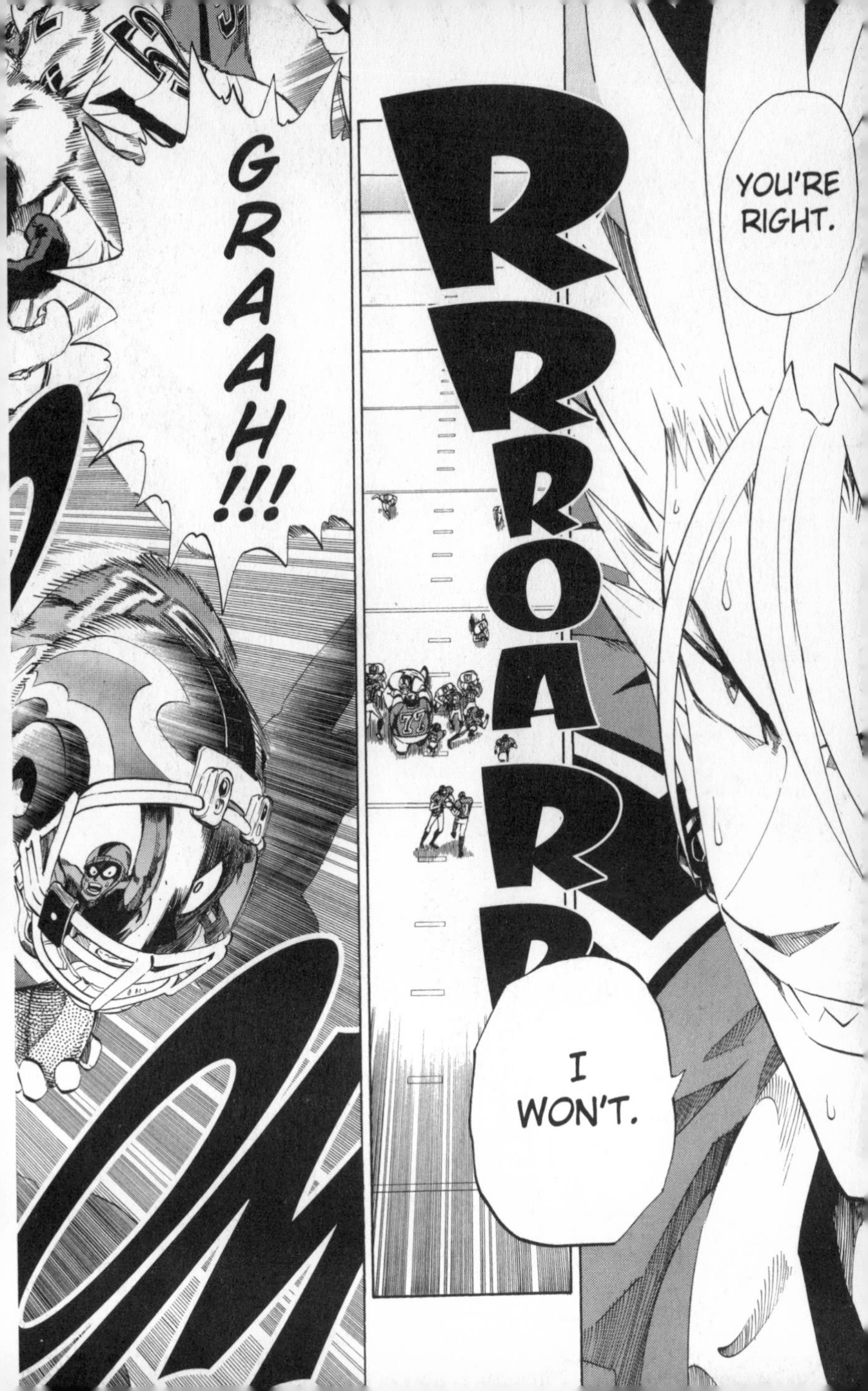
YOU'RE RIGHT.
RRROARR
I WON'T.
GRAAH!!!

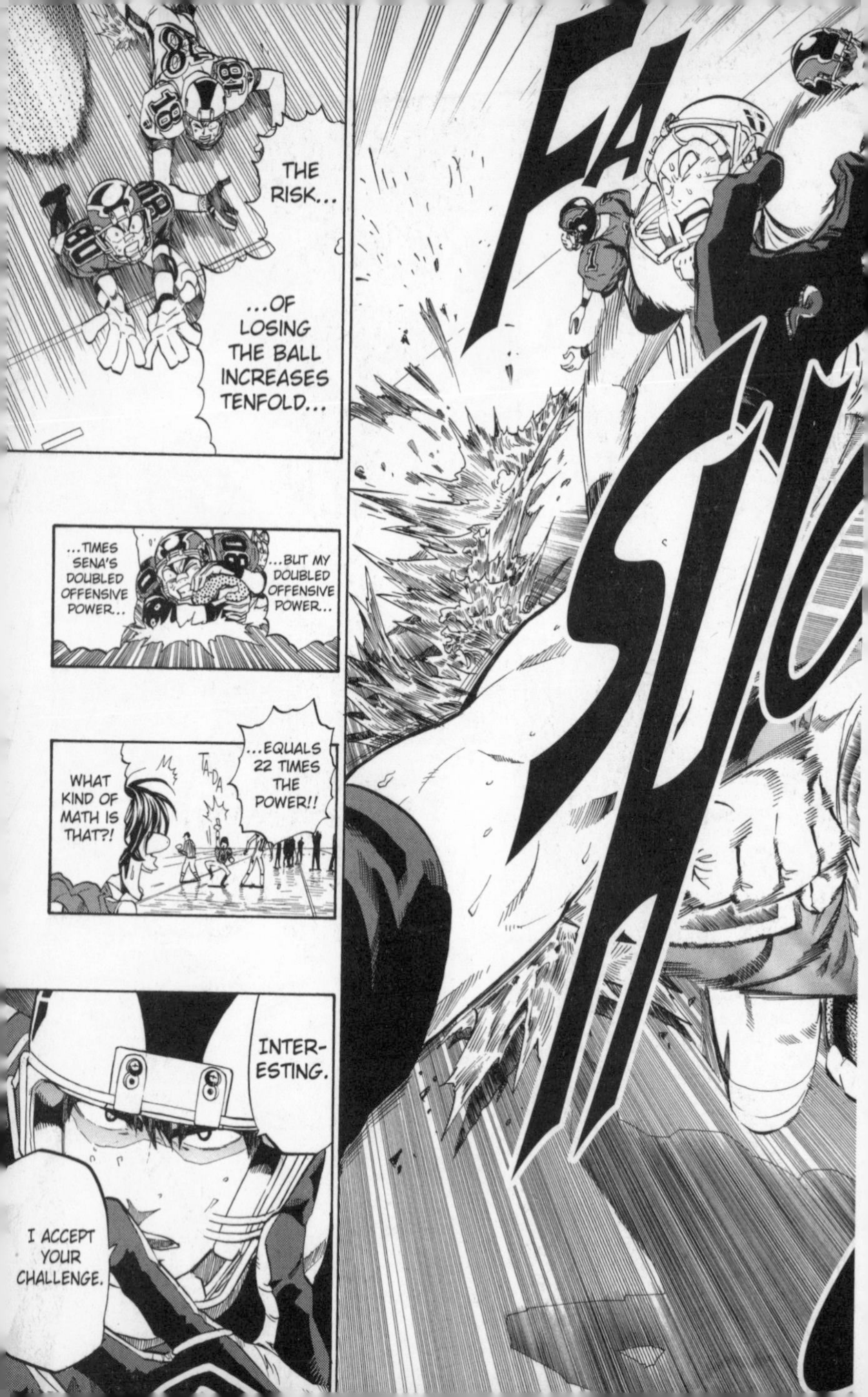
FA
THE RISK...
...OF LOSING THE BALL INCREASES TENFOLD...
...BUT MY DOUBLED OFFENSIVE POWER...
...TIMES SENA'S DOUBLED OFFENSIVE POWER...
...EQUALS 22 TIMES THE POWER!!
TA-DA
WHAT KIND OF MATH IS THAT?!
INTER-ESTING.
I ACCEPT YOUR CHALLENGE.

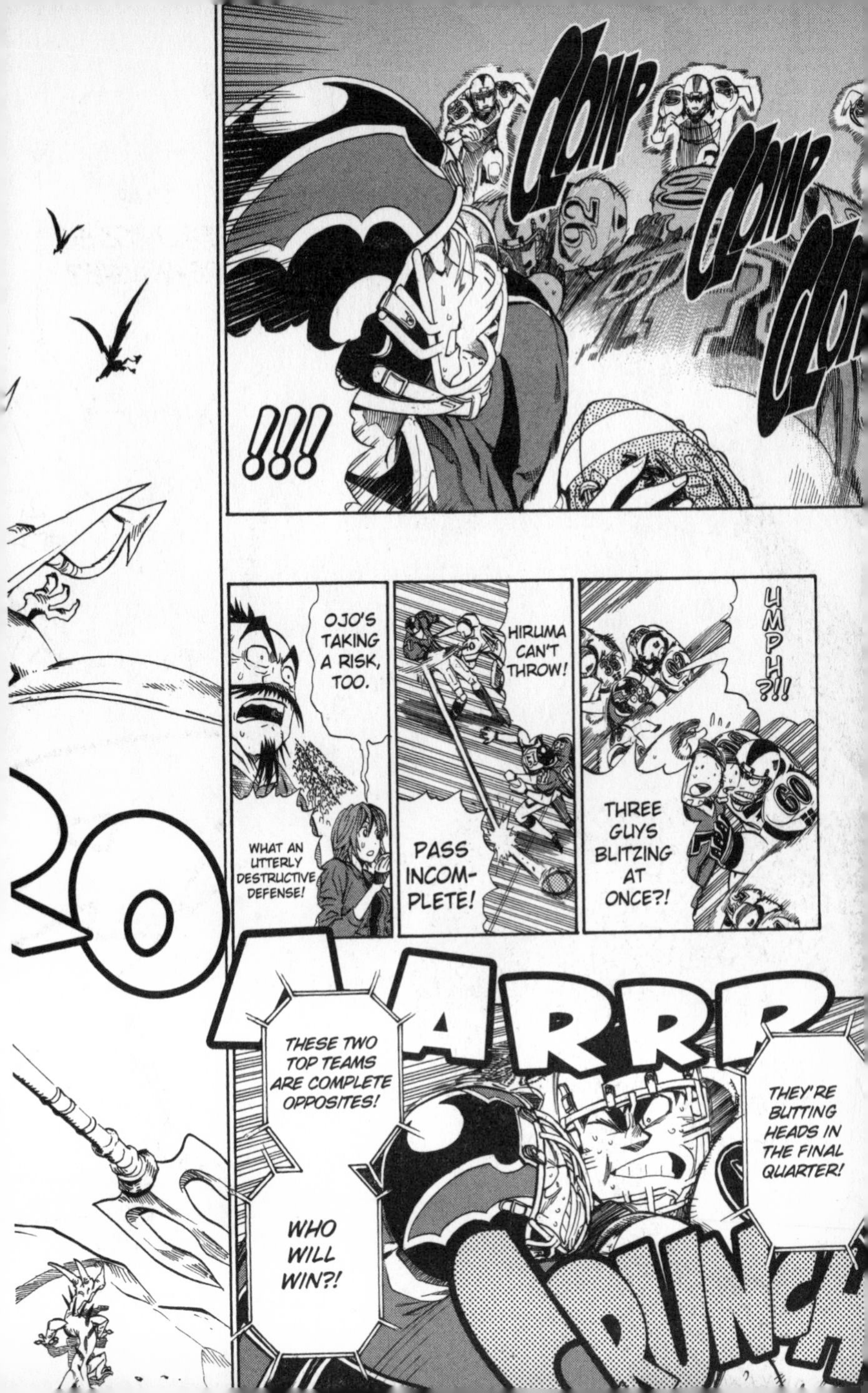
CLOMP
CLOMP
CLOMP
!!!!
UMPH?!!
THREE GUYS BLITZING AT ONCE?!
HIRUMA CAN'T THROW!
PASS INCOMPLETE!
OJO'S TAKING A RISK, TOO.
WHAT AN UTTERLY DESTRUCTIVE DEFENSE!
ROAARRR
THEY'RE BUTTING HEADS IN THE FINAL QUARTER!
THESE TWO TOP TEAMS ARE COMPLETE OPPOSITES!
WHO WILL WIN?!
CRUNCH

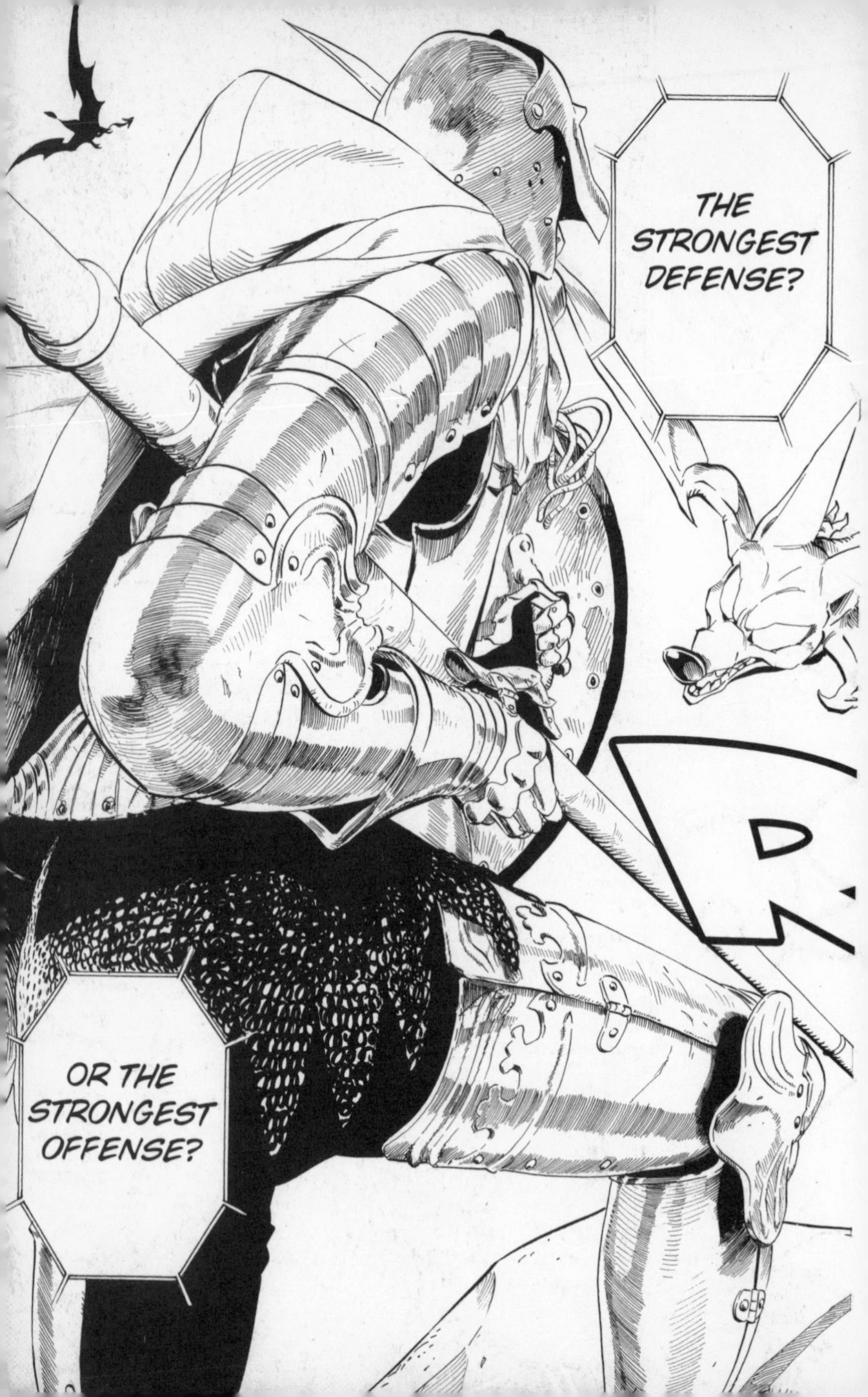
THE STRONGEST DEFENSE?
OR THE STRONGEST OFFENSE?

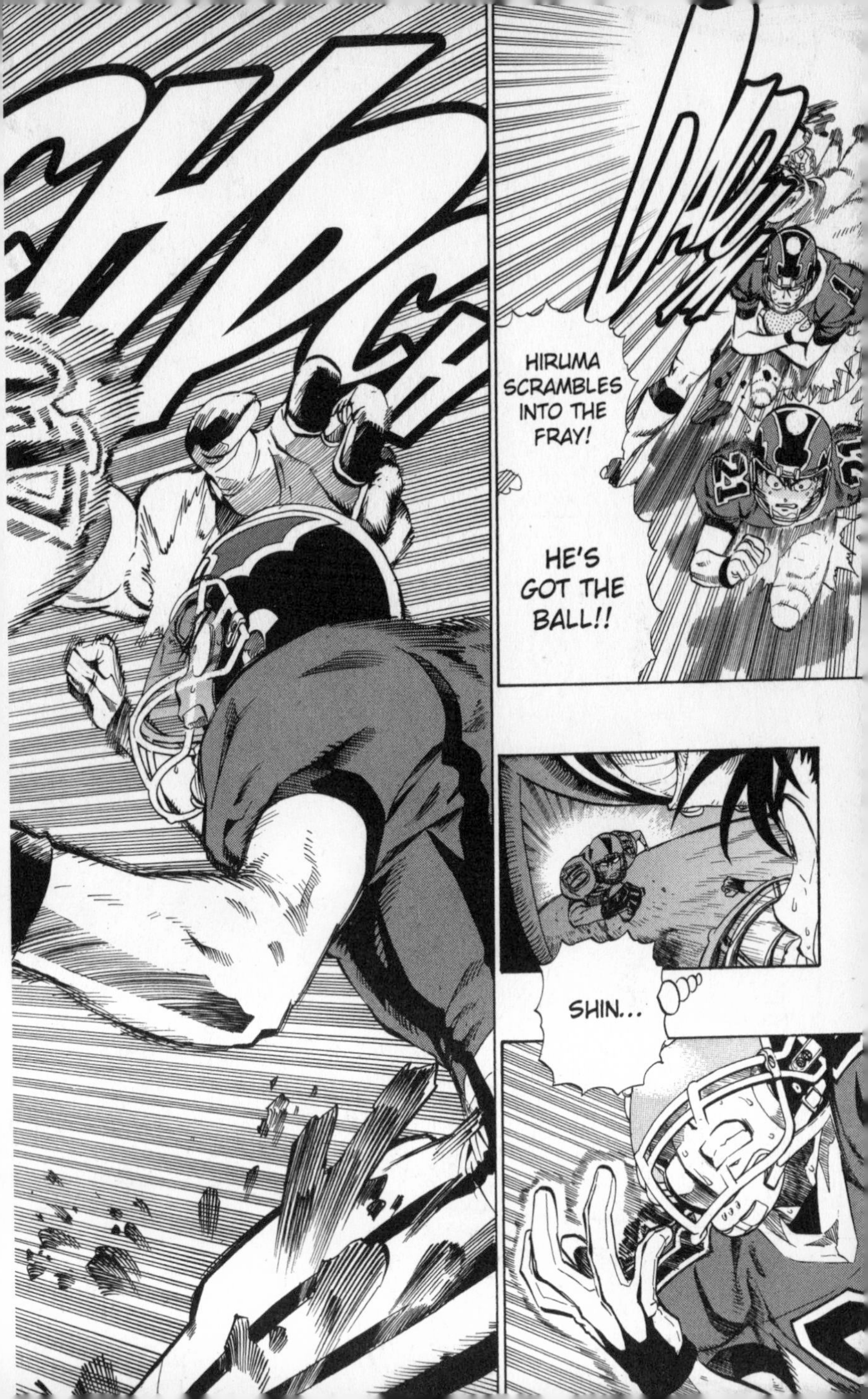
HIRUMA SCRAMBLES INTO THE FRAY!
HE'S GOT THE BALL!!
SHIN...

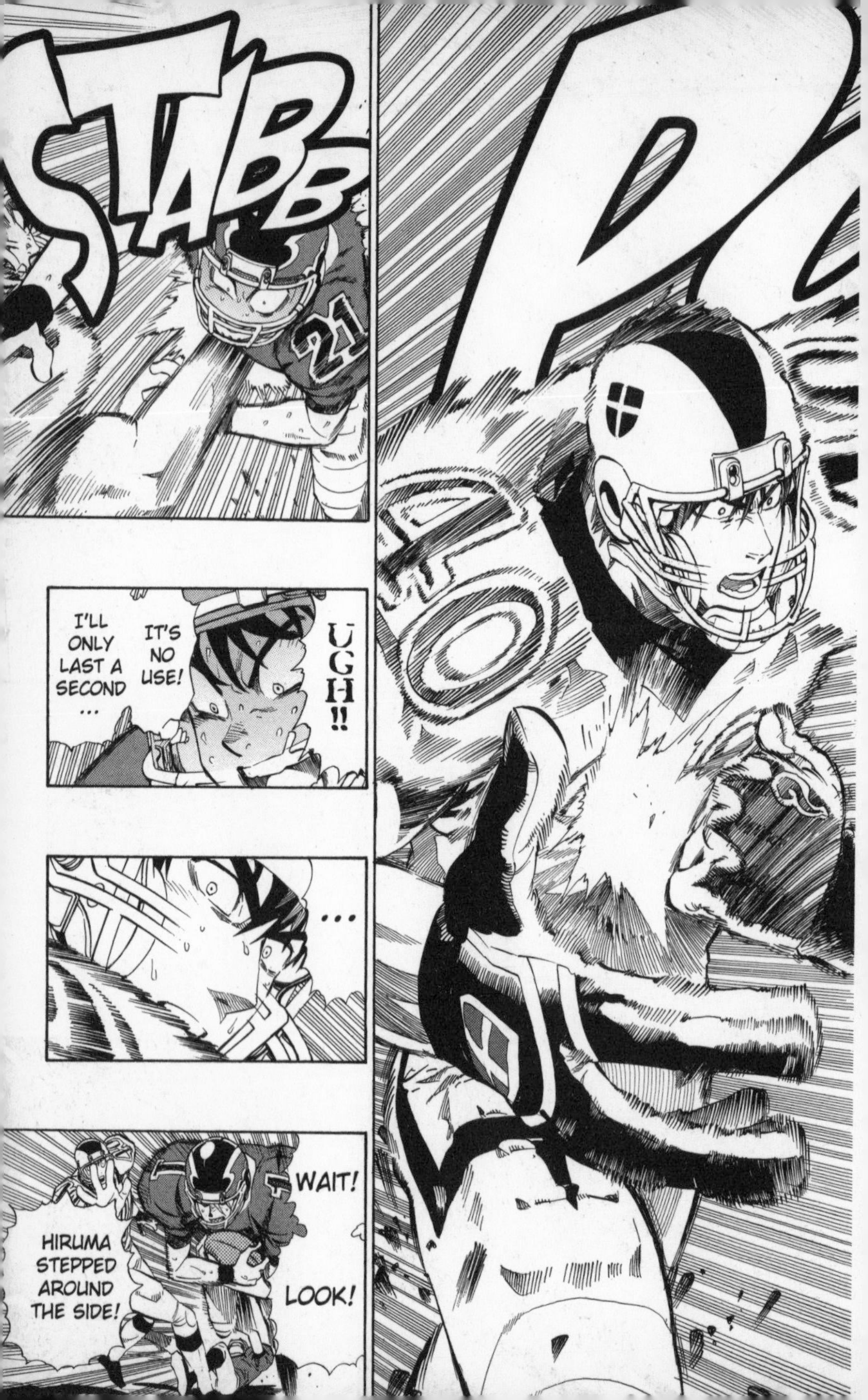
STABB
UGH!!
IT'S NO USE!
I'LL ONLY LAST A SECOND...
...
WAIT!
LOOK!
HIRUMA STEPPED AROUND THE SIDE!

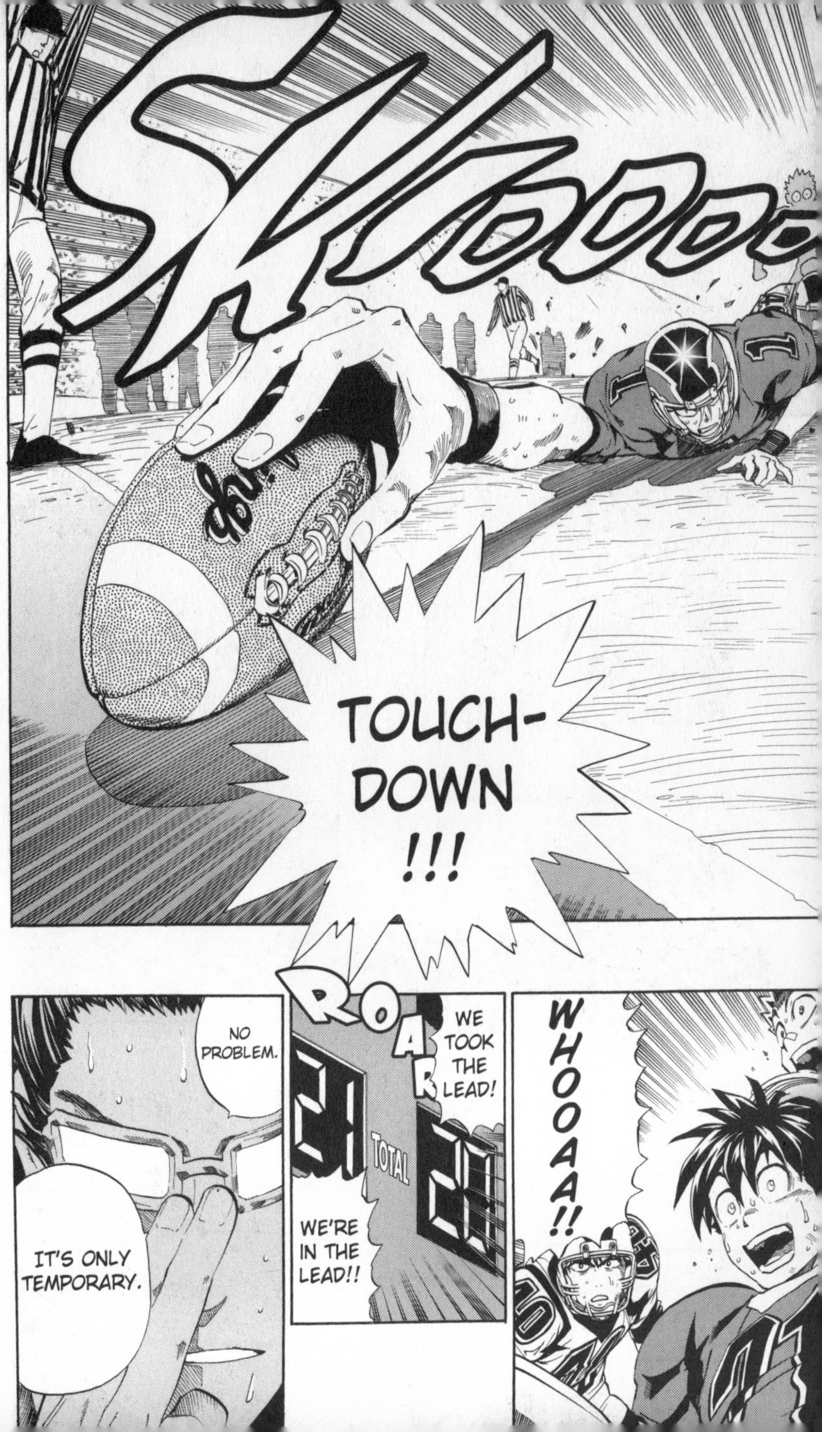
TOUCH-DOWN!!!
WHOOOAAA!!
ROAR
WE TOOK THE LEAD!
TOTAL
WE'RE IN THE LEAD!!
NO PROBLEM.
IT'S ONLY TEMPORARY.

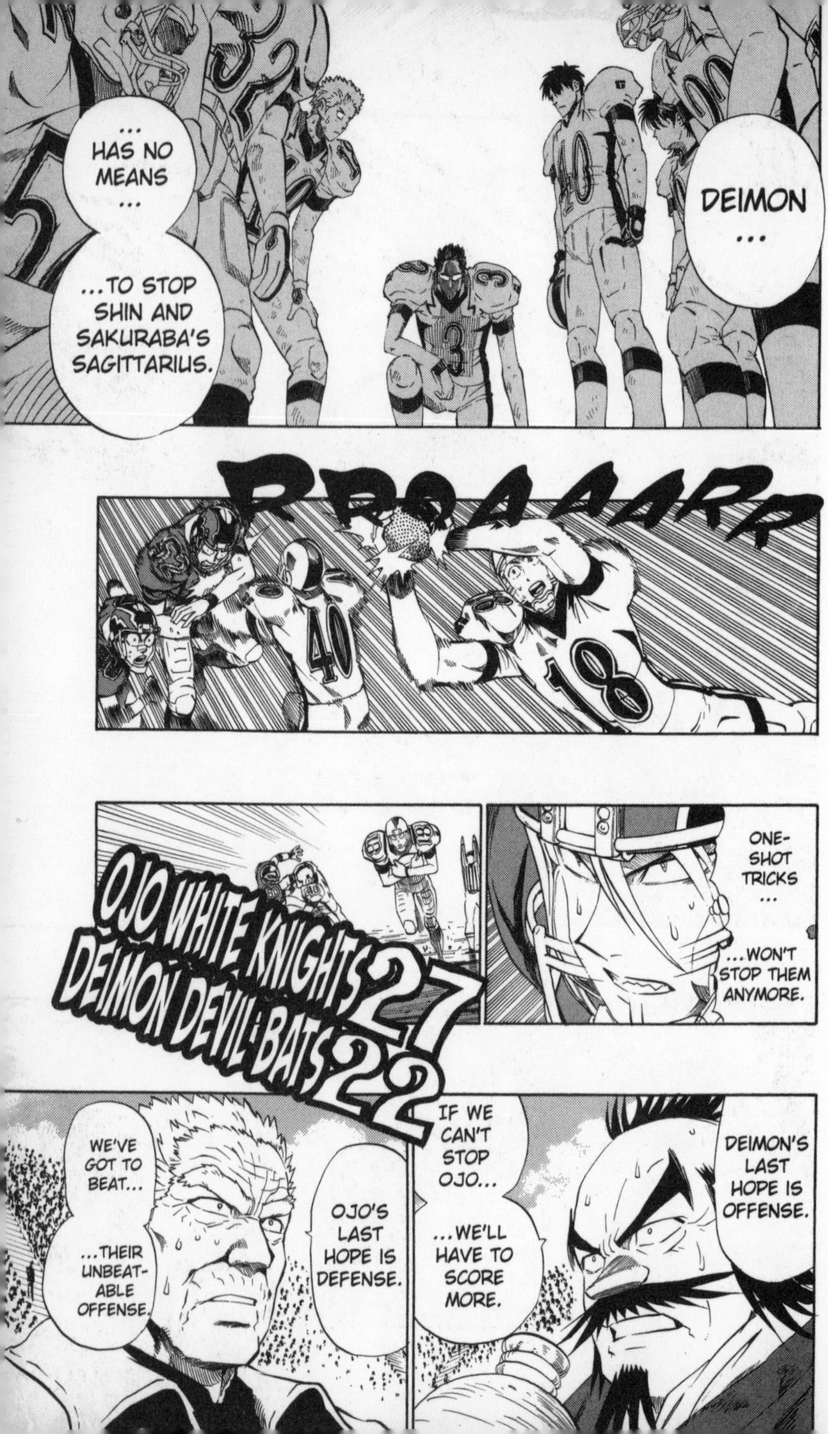
DEIMON ...
... HAS NO MEANS ...
...TO STOP SHIN AND SAKURABA'S SAGITTARIUS.
RROAAARR
ONE-SHOT TRICKS ...
...WON'T STOP THEM ANYMORE.
OJO WHITE KNIGHTS 27
DEIMON DEVIL BATS 22
DEIMON'S LAST HOPE IS OFFENSE.
IF WE CAN'T STOP OJO...
...WE'LL HAVE TO SCORE MORE.
OJO'S LAST HOPE IS DEFENSE.
WE'VE GOT TO BEAT...
...THEIR UNBEATABLE OFFENSE.

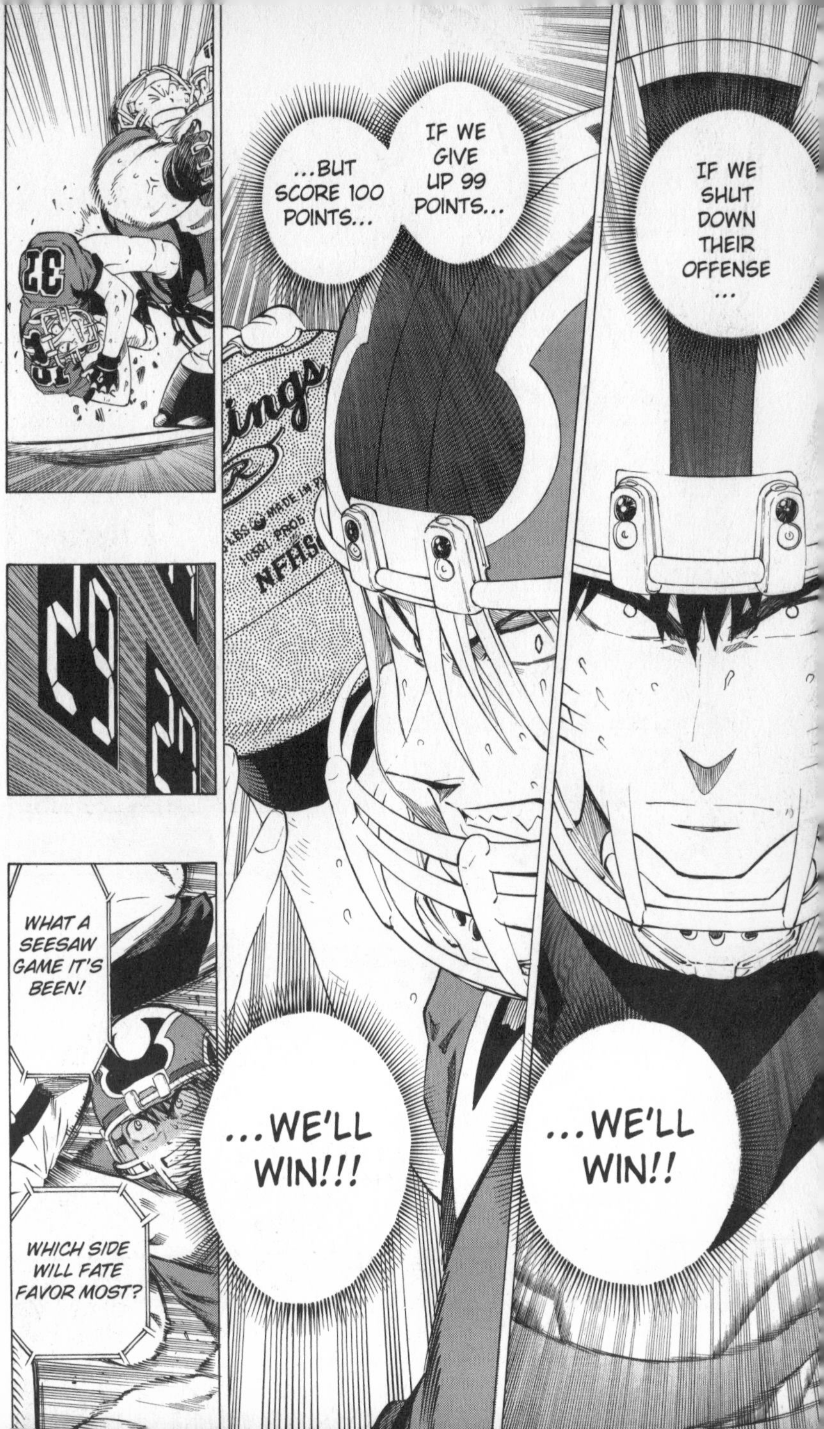
IF WE SHUT DOWN THEIR OFFENSE...
...WE'LL WIN!!
IF WE GIVE UP 99 POINTS...
...BUT SCORE 100 POINTS...
...WE'LL WIN!!!
WHAT A SEESAW GAME IT'S BEEN!
WHICH SIDE WILL FATE FAVOR MOST?

...CONCLUDES!

完全決着

Story by: Riichiro Inagaki
Art by: Yusuke Murata
Chief: Akira Tanaka
STAFF: Takahiro Hiraishi   Kentaro Kurimoto
       Akira Nishikawa   Yukinori Kawaguchi
       Masayuki Shiomura   Lee Sangmi
Kome studio
STAFF: Yusuke Kuji

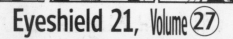

Eyeshield 21, Volume ㉗

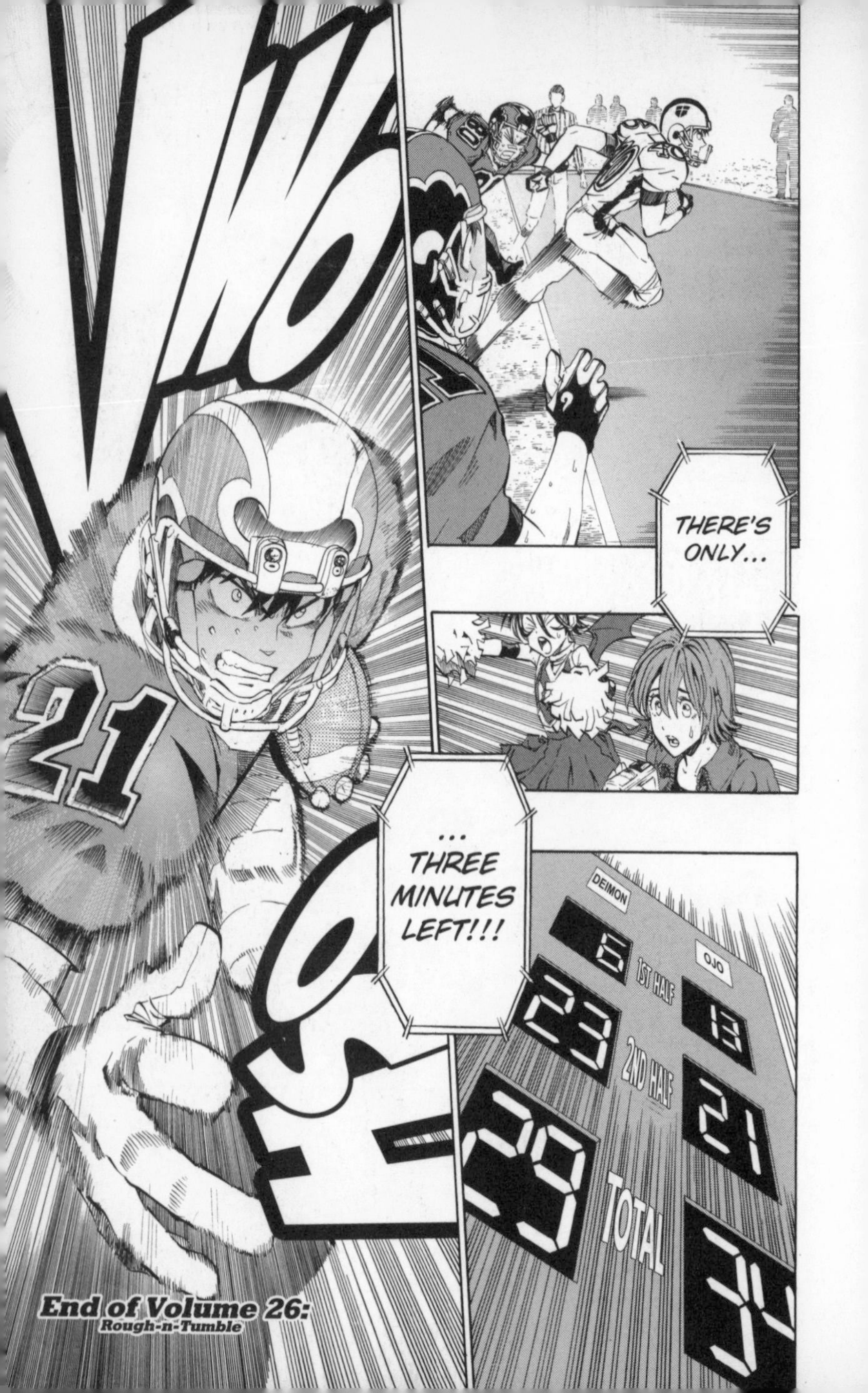
THERE'S ONLY...
... THREE MINUTES LEFT!!!
DEIMON
OJO
1ST HALF
6
13
2ND HALF
23
21
TOTAL
29
34

End of Volume 26:
Rough-n-Tumble

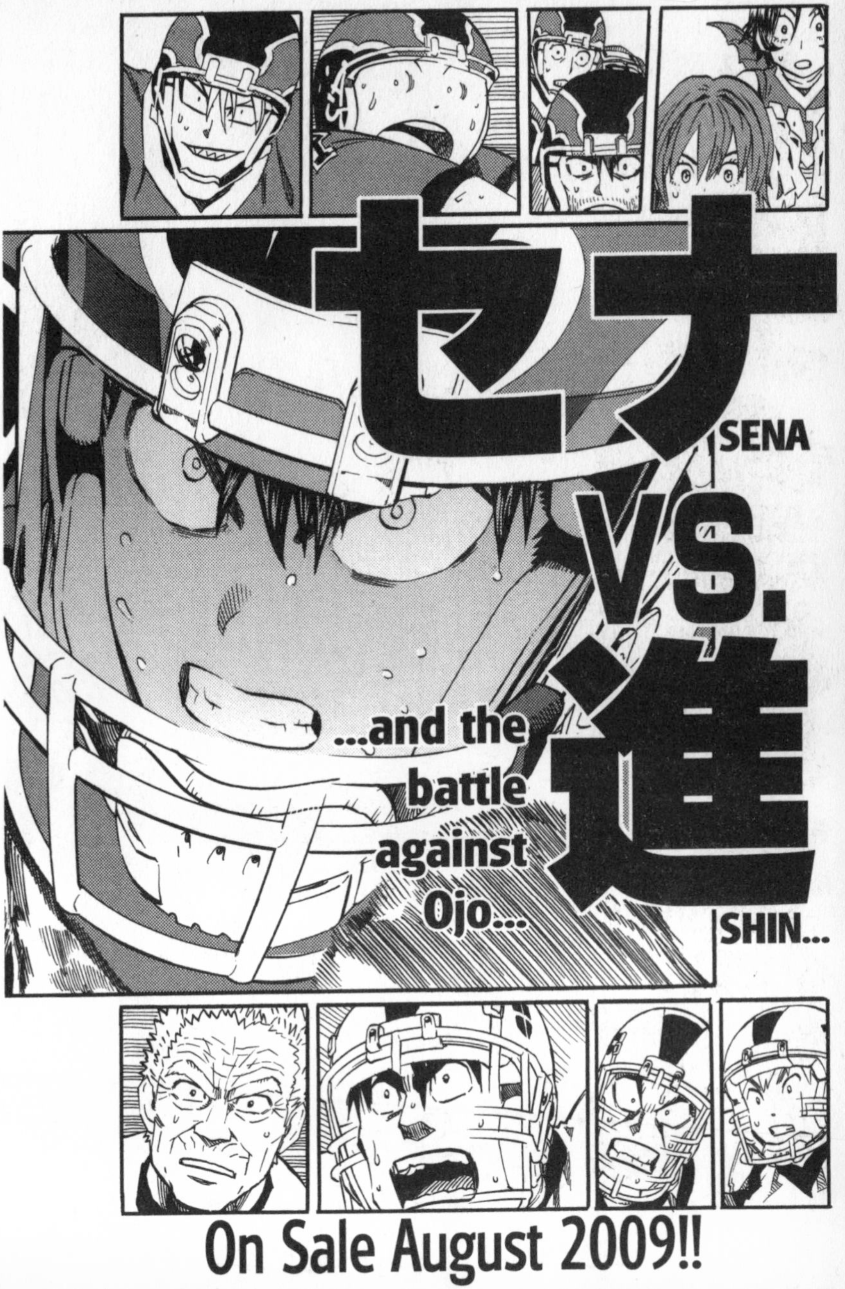
セナ SENA
VS.
進 SHIN...
...and the battle against Ojo...

On Sale August 2009!!